"Prohibition Is Here to Stay"

SONOMA COUNTY

WINE LIBRARY

"Prohibition Is Here to Stay"

The Reverend Edward S. Shumaker and the Dry Crusade in America

JASON S. LANTZER

University of Notre Dame Press
Notre Dame, Indiana

Library of Congress Cataloging-in-Publication Data

Lantzer, Jason S.
   "Prohibition is here to stay" : the Reverend Edward S. Shumaker
and the dry crusade in America / Jason S. Lantzer.
        p. cm.
   Includes bibliographical references and index.
   ISBN-13: 978-0-268-03383-5 (pbk. : alk. paper)
   ISBN-10: 0-268-03383-8 (pbk. : alk. paper)
   1. Shumaker, Edward Seitz, 1867–1929. 2. Prohibitionists—
Indiana—Biography. 3. Methodist Church—Indiana—Clergy—
Biography. 4. Prohibition—Indiana—History. 5. Prohibition—
United States—History. 6. Indiana Anti-Saloon League—History.
7. Temperance and religion—Indiana—History. 8. Religion and
politics—Indiana—History. 9. Religion and politics—United States—
History. 10. Indiana—Biography. I. Title.
   HV5090.I6L366 2009
   363.4'1092—dc22
   [B]   2009002552

∞ *The paper in this book meets the guidelines for permanence and
durability of the Committee on Production Guidelines for Book Longevity
of the Council on Library Resources.*

Contents

Acknowledgments

Writing a book is a massive undertaking that leaves the author with a long list of people to thank. Let me start with my parents, Jack and Juanita Lantzer, who instilled in me as a child a love of learning and the importance of faith. Without either of these two things this book would not have been completed. I owe thanks to all my family and friends, including the ones whom this project consumed, for their generosity of spirit and their guidance as well as for many welcome distractions along the way. When it comes to the latter, perhaps the most important have been the annual guys' weekends shared with Dave Botset and Jeremy Martin, and the fun times I have had with my godson, Jack Sciaudone. And without the love and support of my in-laws, the Honorable James and Kathy Heuer, and Bill and Susan Hebert, it is a safe bet that this book would never have advanced beyond the dissertation phase.

Indeed, the book started life as the culmination of a doctoral degree at Indiana University. I am indebted to my alma mater in many ways, but none more so than in allowing me to work with James Madison, Claude Clegg, Michael Grossberg, and Stephen Stein on this project. And while they may not recognize it, Irving Katz, Nick Cullather, Larry Friedman, and David Thelen also influenced this effort. The History Department's grants and awards helped to make the research and writing possible as well as to give me a cohort of friends and critics in Chad Parker, Matt Stanard, and Fred Witzig.

That kind of institutional support, in terms of finances as well as colleagues, has followed me wherever I have gone since this project began nearly a decade ago. My thanks for the former go to the Cushwa Center at the University of Notre Dame, the Southern Baptist Library and Archives, the Congregational Library and Archives, and the Herbert Hoover Presidential Library and Museum. For the latter, I thank the history departments of IUPUI (especially Bob Barrows), Butler University, and Franklin College together with those students of mine who suffered through lectures on Prohibition. I would be remiss if I did not also thank the staffs of the various churches, archives, and libraries (listed in the bibliography in full) for their help.

At the University of Notre Dame Press, Barbara Hanrahan took an early interest in the project and guided it (and me) through the process of submission, outside reading, and acceptance with a good deal of grace and patience. I am also indebted to other members of the Press who took the finished manuscript and transformed it into the book you now hold in your hands.

This project would not have gone forward, however, without the support of the Shumaker family. Arthur and Julia Shumaker, Edward's son and daughter-in-law, from the moment I met them in the spring of 2000, have answered letters, submitted to interviews, showed me Greencastle, and opened Edward Shumaker's papers to me prior to their being deposited at DePauw University in Greencastle, Indiana. They did so without a single restriction on my research or any demands on the writing of what eventually unfolded. It has been an honor and a privilege to tell Edward Shumaker's story, and I regret deeply that Art did not live to see its publication.

As important as the Shumakers were to telling the story of Prohibition, there is one person who deserves even more credit and praise than they, my wife Erin. She not only suffered through the research, writing, and rewriting but also served as proofreader, research assistant, and legal analyst. Moreover, during the course of my preoccupation with Shumaker, she gave birth to our two children, Kate and Nick, who will never know their father to be anything but a professional historian and who bring both their mother and father nothing but joy. It is to Erin that this book, with all the love that a husband can muster, is dedicated.

Introduction

In February 1929 the Reverend Edward S. Shumaker, the leader of Indiana's "drys"—those who opposed the drinking of alcohol and supported its prohibition—left his Indianapolis home for Putnam County. The route was one he had traveled many times before in his lifelong struggle against the forces of Demon Rum. Indeed, he had gone to college in the county, at DePauw University in Greencastle, and had begun his ministry in its outlying communities. But this trip was different. It came at the end of a protracted legal struggle, and Shumaker was going not to deliver a temperance address in defense of Prohibition but rather to surrender to authorities and to begin serving a prison sentence for contempt of the Indiana Supreme Court. With his devoted wife of nearly thirty years at his side, the sixty-one-year-old minister-reformer headed toward martyrdom for the dry cause.[1]

There are no monuments to Shumaker in the Hoosier State. But if one looks closely, traces of his reform and the culture that produced it are visible, despite the common assumption that Prohibition was an utter failure and properly done away with when the Twenty-first Amendment repealed the Eighteenth in 1933. In the Indiana statehouse rotunda, a place where Shumaker held sway from 1907

1

until his death, there are plaques commemorating Frances Willard's elevation to the presidency of the Woman's Christian Temperance Union (WCTU), another touting the first organized religious meeting in the capital city (a Methodist gathering, which happened to be Shumaker's denomination), and another displaying the motto of the American Legion (whose national headquarters is a few blocks north of the statehouse), "For God and Country." The main floor of the rotunda, with its public displays of religious faith and political activism, is just one story below the Supreme Court chamber where Shumaker was found guilty of contempt. They are visible reminders that the "wall of separation" between church and state in America is hardly as solid or as historic as has often been suggested.

Had Shumaker lived in another time, he almost assuredly would have been counted among the "moral values voters" of the 2004 election, who placed social issues, as shaped by their religious faith, ahead of economic and foreign policy issues. If this at times confuses observers, it should not.[2] American culture has always had an exceedingly moral cast because of the influence and importance of evangelical Protestantism in the nation's history. Understanding the relationship between that faith and politics is fundamental to understanding both America as it is now and how many people think it should be.

In the early twentieth century, the defining moral issue for many Americans was Shumaker's reform, prohibition. A Methodist minister, Shumaker served for nearly a quarter of a century as the head of the Indiana Anti Saloon League, the state arm of one of the most successful Progressive Era reform groups. Historians have identified him as "a great person, violent in his hate for liquor . . . for many years the most powerful man in the prohibition movement in the Midwest," and as a "potent force in Indiana politics" among "the half dozen most politically powerful men in Indiana" during the first third of the twentieth century.[3] His life and work offer us an opportunity to understand better and appreciate both the dry worldview and the larger interplay of religion and politics in wider American culture.

Shumaker's story is that of an America in the midst of a dramatic transformation in its search for the proper path to follow. Born into an agrarian world where the frontier remained a reality, Shumaker witnessed unprecedented immigration, industrialization, and urbanization along with all their associated problems. Reformers in his mold believed they needed to craft an orderly society to deal with this state of cultural flux, which both venerated the past as well as embraced the modern world. They acknowledged that their vision was only one possible path for the country to take; and if it were to be followed, it needed to be contested in the public square. Following his conversion to Methodism as a youth, which came at the same time as his conviction that alcohol was a sin that needed to be eradicated, Shumaker accepted the call to the ministry. Though at first he seemed destined for a life within the pulpit, his faith and the dry cause continually pulled him out into the wider reform world. By the time he was forty years old, Shumaker was the leader of the Indiana Anti Saloon League and on his way to becoming a first-rate political tactician whose reform was consistently part of the landscape of both the state and nation. Shumaker's life is a shining example of the dry crusade, and it illustrates the evolution of prohibition over time, its attraction to people, and how it sustained itself. Furthermore, his life is a window into how drys themselves wrestled with the consequences, both personally and professionally, of their crusade.

The "noble experiment" to which Shumaker devoted his life was not an "aberration," as historians have discovered, but rather one of the "central currents in American culture" during the late nineteenth and early twentieth centuries. This reform movement spawned a massive political mobilization that ultimately amended the Constitution to achieve its goal. Rather than an unpopular reform forced upon the country, the Eighteenth Amendment was the result of nearly a century of local and state activity by drys such as Shumaker, a reform that, as historian Norman Clark reminded readers, succeeded. During national prohibition, most Americans never saw the inside of a speakeasy, alcohol consumption fell off dramatically, and crime stayed remarkably in check, despite constant and eventually successful calls for repeal.[4]

Constitutional Prohibition was the capstone event of the dry movement within evangelical Protestantism that saw alcohol as the central vice affecting the United States. It was achieved during a time of immense struggle between competing visions of American culture. Drys such as Shumaker argued for a homogeneous national culture built upon reforms such as Prohibition, while their opponents sought a more heterogeneous America that avoided any hint of cultural imperialism. Both sides saw this clash as real, with one's cultural worldview being paramount to economic or political considerations.[5] The United States of the twenty-first century is a product, in part, of this struggle.

Not surprisingly, this cultural confrontation and its flashpoint reform have generated considerable scholarly attention. Prohibition has been used as a critique of drug policy, a demonstration of pressure group politics, an example of how interest groups utilize the law, and a sign of an old America searching for a symbolic victory over the new one.[6] Often these accounts have failed to engage one another, and while a good deal is known about what happened during the dry years, the cultural impetus for the reform is often submerged beneath interpretive and narrative frameworks. Furthermore, the beliefs of drys have often been slighted even when their reform and organizations have not. The reasons for this vary, but they are often rooted in the perception of the reform as a failure and in a reluctance to investigate the evangelical Protestant portion of mainstream American culture.[7] This study seeks to rectify that situation.

The Prohibition story cannot be told without taking seriously the role played by religious faith in its rise and fall. Without evangelical Protestantism, there would not have been Prohibition in America. Studies such as Mark Thornton's libertarian economic critique of Prohibition fail to take seriously the moral component that those drys such as Shumaker believed crucial to the reform.[8] Religion was central to why drys became involved in the movement. As one Tennessee Baptist said of alcohol in 1903, "it is the arch destroyer of all that is dear to man and the chief opponent to the work of the Church." If religious people took drinking that seriously, then historians must take them seriously as well.[9] Paying lip service to ministerial credentials and church-based organizations is not enough to fully understand the dry crusade.

Listening carefully to religious voices is imperative. According to Samuel P. Huntington, "in the modern world, religion is a central, perhaps *the* central, force that motivates and mobilizes people." Historian Jon Butler has urged his colleagues to consider religion as a real force in people's lives. And James G. Moseley has argued that historians should treat religion "with a great deal more intellectual respect" than they often do because for many believers, their faith is not confined to their houses of worship; it compels them to act in the world.[10] Drys such as Shumaker were living their faith and changing their world as a result.

Taking religious conviction seriously, however, challenges the prevailing definition of religious experience and how it should be understood. Scholars must be willing to move beyond William James and his insistence upon "original expressions" of "personal religion" since he left no room for "institutional," "ecclesiastical organization," or "systematic theology" in his *Varieties of Religious Experience*. To him, the former was all that mattered. Lives such as Shumaker's, however, do not readily submit themselves to such neat categories. Shumaker's faith was not just personal; it was also institutional. He did not work alone, but was part of something much larger than himself. In order to understand Prohibition, we must investigate Shumaker's entire culture—how he shaped it and how it shaped him.[11]

Shumaker and his fellow drys did not live in a historical vacuum. Evangelical Protestantism emphasized one's being active in society and government, and it traces its roots back to the very beginning of the American experience.[12] In the colonial period, Jonathan Edwards, among others, believed that religion and politics were intrinsically linked to one another on the spiritual battleground that was the world.[13] As Barry Alan Shain has argued, evangelical Protestant ideas expressed by pastor politicians such as John Witherspoon, rather than classical thought, influenced the vast majority of those who launched the American Revolution. Many of the founding generation believed that community standards were equal in importance to personal morality, with everyone having a stake in eradicating sin if all were to receive God's blessing. Founders such as Alexander Hamilton argued that the national government, in representing the will of the majority, had to prod the minority forward toward the greater good.[14]

Such religious and ideological notions continued to influence American politics throughout the antebellum period. Evangelical Protestantism, in the wake of the market revolution and Jacksonian politics, sought to establish an orderly society both on the frontier and in the growing urban areas of the country. In government, as Daniel Walker Howe and others have pointed out, "the sanctified of God" blended "pragmatic innovations with long-standing tradition and its explicit programs with implicit values." These Whigs believed in civil order because they feared what men would do if left to their own devices. Individual liberty was not a license to do wrong; rather, it was to be used by individuals to promote the common good.[15]

In the Midwest during the late nineteenth and early twentieth centuries, evangelical Protestantism merged with Yankee capitalism and Republican politics into a middle class that believed it was not only the sole arbiter of social progress but also in the best position to define what America was. Its causes and institutions, which had once been revolutionary, were now the mainstays of an American culture that had to be preserved in the face of massive immigration, large-scale industrialization, and rapid urbanization.[16] Shumaker and others like him saw themselves as a force for progress and order. Drys were not out to overtly control, but rather to create, a system that harnessed individual passions and decisions in order to avoid the chaos of the mob. They believed that the causes of societal disorder reeked of alcohol; and, if drinking were ended, that everyone would benefit. As a result, the dry ideal, while in competition with other visions, became a contributing force to the creation of modern America.[17]

This Midwest consensus is essential to understanding the dry crusade for Prohibition. While many observers believe the region to be a place more often shaped by "the coasts" than a crafter of American culture, as Lewis Atherton and Robert F. Martin both argue, one cannot understand the United States and its values without looking at the Midwest.[18] Shumaker is a prime example. He was born in Ohio, raised in Illinois, and made his home in Indiana. He lived in the midst of the Hoosier Golden Age, when Indiana laid claim to dominating both national politics and culture.[19] The state, perhaps better than any other in the region, represents the American heartland. Therefore, we may consider Indiana the perfect place, and Shumaker the perfect example, to investigate the dry cause.

What follows is an attempt to recapture the era and synthesize the vast literature on Prohibition within a cultural biographical framework. My study considers the multifaceted nature of the dry crusade and how it marked the intersection for religion and politics during a crucial period in American history. Among the questions considered in the pages that follow are: How did dry culture transform itself from a reformist cause to a national crusade? How did its most successful organization, the Anti Saloon League, function at the local and state levels? How did its message evolve over time? How did white evangelical Protestant reformers reach out to other groups, such as African Americans and Catholics, and why did this rhetoric of inclusion come to be superseded by a more reactionary vision of America put forward by the Ku Klux Klan? And, perhaps most interesting, how did the dominant reform of the largest religious segment of American culture come to be repealed and considered a failure? To attempt to answer these questions, we must begin not on the road to Putnam County but rather in Ohio, in the years immediately following the Civil War.

1 | Origins of a Dry Leader

Before Edward Shumaker could become the Midwestern embodiment of the dry crusade, he first had to become initiated in the ways of the Progressive Era and the Social Gospel. His upbringing and religious faith, coupled with these twin engines of reform, made him a minister with a mission. These forces also compelled him to seek a stage larger than a single pulpit from which to fight for the establishment of God's dry kingdom.

Shumaker's story begins in post–Civil War Ohio. His father, David, from Fairfield County, had served in Company A of the Seventeenth Ohio Volunteer Infantry during the Civil War.[1] After mustering out of the service, he resumed his life as a farmer and in 1866 married Sarah Ann Seitz, sister to two of his former comrades-in-arms.[2] David and Sarah's first child, Edward, was born 30 July 1867 in Greenville, Darke County, near Sarah's family. When Eddie was two, his father bought a 50-acre, swampy farm ten miles outside of town. There, more children followed Eddie into the world.[3]

While family and farming were now David's chief concerns, the war remained the central event of his life. He instilled in his children not only a deep love for the Union, but also a sense that God had a special mission for the country. For Eddie, the eldest son, these convictions never wavered.[4] Such patriotic idealism was important to many veterans and their hopes for their families. Having survived the war, Americans of the late nineteenth century welcomed the new world they saw being created around them and its possibilities.[5]

For the Shumaker family, achieving the American dream meant leaving Ohio. Eddie's uncle, George Seitz, encouraged his brother-in-law to follow him to Illinois, where David purchased a homestead with an already built house and barn in 1873. The farm sat on 100 acres in Effingham County's West Township, with an additional 40 acres in neighboring Mason Township. The county was "mostly level prairie" and almost entirely devoted to commercial agriculture, an undertaking that was aided by the Springfield and Ohio Railroad.[6]

After holding a sale and bidding goodbye to family and friends, David loaded his family and remaining possessions onto a train bound for Illinois. It was here in Effingham County that David thrived, becoming "widely known and universally respected for his many excellent traits of character." Eddie enjoyed the move and seems to have spent a good deal of time in those first few Illinois days playing and exploring the new farm.[7] The Shumakers' Effingham County neighbors were a cross-section of Midwestern America. Most were primarily farmers, like the newly arrived Ohio transplants. In politics, the county was heavily Democratic, with a smattering of Republicans and even some members of the agricultural/populist-based Grange movement. In religion, though many of the newcomers were German Catholics (settling near the town of Teutopolis), most of the county's residents were, in the words of one visitor, "Methodists, Baptists, Unitarians, Presbyterians, etc. and some do not know what religion they profess."[8] This variety was to have important consequences for Shumaker's future.

Eli Shumaker, David's brother, who had helped the family make the move from Ohio, now decided to stay in Illinois as well. An ordained minister in the United Brethren Church, Uncle Eli started a congregation in Effingham County. Meeting at the local schoolhouse, he and his flock soon had the community caught up in a revival. At one meeting, Eddie went forward after the altar call but, as he later remembered, was considered too young to become a church member. He was, however, encouraged by the leaders of the meeting, including his mother, who kissed him when it was her turn to extend the hand of welcome. It was a memory that Shumaker cherished for the rest of his life.[9]

Sarah Shumaker was determined, however, that her son would receive more than just a religious education. When Eddie returned to the schoolhouse, it was for instruction in reading, writing, and arithmetic, not the Christian faith. He proved to be a quick learner, but usually attended school only in the winter months for the next eleven years, as he was needed first and foremost on the farm. Though the quality of his teachers varied, Eddie discovered that he loved learning, and his report card from Mason Public High School in 1886 depicts a bright student who earned a 97 percent average in his classes.[10]

As they had been before the move, the Shumakers were a relatively poor farming family, raising just enough crops and livestock to get by. This meant that Eddie often could not afford to buy his schoolbooks, including the history textbook that was both a requirement and a joy for him to read. He borrowed copies from classmates and worked hard at memorizing every word. David especially enjoyed the times when Eddie "told" him about the Civil War.[11] One can almost picture the father suppressing a smile as the son rattled off facts about Sherman's march through the South.

School was not all about lessons learned in the classroom; sometimes the outside world intruded. The Shumaker family was Republican in a county that was heavily Democratic. Indeed, Eddie was coming of age at a time when politics and religion mattered to Americans in an almost visceral way. At school only Shumaker and the Sisson brothers represented the Grand Old Party in the requisite partisan snowball fights. Words, however, could hurt worse than a well-made snowball. Eddie was taunted with the label of "black Republican," which on at least one occasion sent him home in tears.[12] As he was growing up, he witnessed the rise of the Populists, who were on a "quest for a just social order" that was heavily influenced by evangelical Protestantism.[13] Their notions of broad-based, grassroots political activism influenced Shumaker's later career, perhaps as much as his father's devotion to the party of Abraham Lincoln.

Another reality of Eddie's life during this period was death. In 1876–1877 it visited his world with a vengeance. Since the move, Shumaker had lost two siblings and never forgot his mother's crying after the funerals. Sarah became pregnant again, and Eddie later described her as an "invalid" during those months, coping with both grief and a difficult confinement. In late February 1877 she gave birth to another son. A week later, Shumaker recalled, "The death angel came and took the spirit of the best mother any child ever had to be with Jesus and his holy angels." The reality of death, especially that of his beloved mother, left its mark. The memory of her faith and love, he later wrote, "sustained me in many a trial."[14]

The loss visited upon the Shumaker household brought change to Eddie's world. Though both his uncles moved their families back to Ohio, David Shumaker refused to abandon his Illinois homestead. Realizing that his surviving children needed a mother (perhaps as much as he needed a wife), David found a suitable mate in Maria Smith, a twenty-nine-year-old German immigrant. Maria and David were married in December 1877, spent the next thirty-three years together, and added three more children to the Shumaker household. Maria treated her stepchildren as her own from the moment she entered the family, which made for a happy home.[15]

Looking back on his boyhood, Shumaker described it as "eventful" but also "average." Times were hard, especially for farmers. The Illinois prairie that so captivated David produced as many insects as crops, or so his son later remembered. Still, there was fun to be had if you were a child. Eddie learned to hunt and swim in the nearby woods and streams. Like most farm kids, he was raised to be independent.[16] It was in this rural world that his values were shaped.[17]

Religion was increasingly becoming the most important aspect of Shumaker's life, though it was hardly a rigid denominationalism. Nor was such a blended faith uncommon in the Midwest. The Woman's Christian Temperance Union's Frances Willard went from being a Baptist to a Congregationalist to finally a Methodist while growing up in Wisconsin and Illinois. Carry Nation, the famous axe-wielding saloon smasher, also had had a similar upbringing in her native Kentucky. In nearby Canada, Aimee Semple McPherson, who became both a celebrity as well as an electrifying dry evangelist, grew up in an environment that made her a Protestant without any strong denominational affiliation.[18]

Eddie was exposed to religion at an early age. His parents belonged to an Evangelical Association congregation while living in Ohio, their house was a place for shout-filled "prayer and class meetings." His father was a class leader and saw to it that the family took part in private devotions. In Illinois, they were members of Eli Shumaker's United Brethren congregation, yet a Baptist minister presided at Sarah's funeral, and a Methodist officiated at David and Maria's wedding. Since moving to Illinois, Eddie had worshiped in his uncle's church and had also gone to a German Evangelical Association Sunday school, a Baptist church, and to an interdenominational Sunday school. These experiences exposed Shumaker to the varieties of Protestantism and helped prepare him for future work across denominational lines.[19]

All of this church-hopping ended for him when, in his sixteenth year, the Methodists officially arrived in Effingham County. The Reverend Benjamin A. Hoar launched a revival in the community that led to the construction of Asbury Chapel. While David and Maria joined the congregation immediately, Eddie did not; he still had spiritual issues to deal with. During the revival meeting, he went forward three nights in a row to the altar. On the third night a transplanted Southern Methodist, joined by David and other members of the community, said a "powerful" prayer over him. As Shumaker wrote, "by faith, I at length found Jesus in mighty saving power, my Savior. My father shouted when my conversion took place." His sister and several classmates were also saved during the revival, but for Edward Seitz Shumaker the date 16 January 1884 would always be his day—the day he was saved.[20]

Shumaker's conversion is a classic example of what William James described in his *Varieties of Religious Experience*. There was the process, or the wrestling, the buildup to the moment of surrender on the part of the sinner, which only ended when the person felt the power of God's grace. According to James, conversion brought religion to the center of a person's life, allowing for the "direct religious experience" that came as a result, which was different from the enthusiastic displays that often attended the conversion.[21]

James's theories, however, are different from real-life experience. In the Methodist Church, Shumaker found the fulfillment of his life to that point. The denomination, though it had roots back to the late colonial period, grew immensely during the early nineteenth century along the western frontier. The Northern Methodist Church was devoted to the cause of the Union during the Civil War. Indeed, in the postwar world the denomination saw itself as being called and directed by God on a mission to overcome the moral issues, including the problem of alcohol, that faced the reunited nation. The evangelical Protestantism of which Methodism was a part was on the march and confident in its purpose.[22]

It is significant that Shumaker's conversion to Methodism took place at a revival, for this tool of evangelical America was coming under increasing internal scrutiny. Once, evangelicals such as Charles Finney had seen revivals as the usual way for the Protestant faith to function. However, after the Civil War, leading theologians such as Horace Bushnell argued that Christians could be nurtured or raised, and that there was no need to "save" people via dramatic conversion experiences. This thinking within evangelical denominations corresponded to a wider cultural trend to tone down popular religion. In later years, revivals became scheduled events, not spontaneous occurrences, in the lives of congregations. But Shumaker's experience with revivals as well as his outlook on faith tended to merge these views. According to his son, Shumaker's conversion to Methodism was total, in that Edward believed that once you were saved and became a member of a denomination, you were bound to follow its teachings. As one historian has put it, such acceptance helped the converted know where they stood with God and man, and it gave them "a perspective on life that unbelievers did not have."[23]

Nor was he alone in this experience. Shumaker's future associate in the Anti Saloon League, James Cannon, had followed a similar path to his denomination, occupation, and cause. Born into a devout and loving Southern Methodist home, Cannon showed an initial reluctance to go forward at revival meetings because he sensed that if he did, he would be called to the pastorate. Once he became a minister, he used his pulpit to attack "rum, Romanism, and Bourbonism," and later became one of the leading advocates for national Prohibition.[24] And then there was Billy Sunday. The former baseball player turned saver of souls was one of the leading drys of the late nineteenth and early twentieth centuries and the greatest revivalist of his generation.[25]

Like Cannon and Sunday, Eddie Shumaker's conversion brought him to the pulpit. In January 1885 the Reverend Mr. Hoar asked his congregation to send forth an exhorter. The class leader nominated Shumaker, who expressed "surprise," even though he had talked at least twice with Hoar about the possibility of entering the ministry. Shumaker and another man soon were speaking at prayer meetings. Though he did not think he was very effective, Shumaker was encouraged to keep at it by leaders within the congregation. After a revival broke out on Asbury's circuit, Shumaker found himself addressing packed meetinghouses in order to keep it going. By 1886 he was a licensed local preacher, despite not yet being nineteen years of age.[26]

His choice of vocation caused an argument in the Shumaker home. David discouraged his son from seeking to become a full-time minister. A dutiful son, Edward initially declined the offer to go to the district conference and take the ministerial exams. However, after a sleepless night, he changed his mind and went to be tested on his knowledge of Scripture, the Methodist Discipline, and general education. Shumaker passed the exams and became a licensed Methodist minister.[27] What David's reaction to this disobedience was, his son opted not to record.

Shumaker's story could have been that of countless numbers of young men who entered the ministry if it were not for the dry cause. Between 1884 and 1996, at the same time when he was saved and called to the ministry, he was also called to temperance as a reform. During the nineteenth century, Americans became convinced (rightly, as historians now point out) that the nation had a problem with alcohol. Evangelical Protestants, dating back to at least Lyman Beecher in the 1820s, had been advocates of fighting intemperance, and, now, in the postwar world, the reform returned. This was especially true within the Methodist Church.[28] These two events, happening concurrently, united in the same church, no doubt influenced the decisions made by Shumaker. And just as Hoar played an important role in converting him to Christ, so too did another person convert him into a temperance advocate. Her name was Susan Murphy.

Murphy's influence on the young man is unsurprising. Shumaker grew up at a time when America's churches were often dominated by their female members, who tended to be more interested in practical reforms than in doctrine. Mothers, according to Ann Douglas, heavily influenced boys who went on to become ministers. In Shumaker's case he had both his own mother's faith as a guide, and now Susan Murphy's example, to move him along this path. The Murphy family, originally from Switzerland County, Indiana, were active members of Asbury, and Susan often loaned or sold Edward books about Christian history and evangelism. She was also interested in temperance. Women were the main leaders of the dry movement in the late nineteenth century, from holding prayer meetings in saloons to the formation of the WCTU, and the Midwest was at the heart of their crusade. Soon after the 1884 revival, Susan launched a temperance society at the church and Shumaker was named its president. As he later put it, the meetings in which he took part "settled forever in my purpose the determination to live for the destruction of the beverage liquor traffic."[29]

With Susan's urging, he took his first steps into the wider dry world. Edward not only attended "a patriotic temperance celebration" on 4 July 1884, where he heard speakers from the WCTU give polished addresses, but also was part of the program. The idea of sharing a platform with the WCTU's speakers left Shumaker so "frightened" that he "trembled" while speaking, but was encouraged by the other participants. Soon he was giving addresses all over Effingham County as part of the Young Men's Temperance League, another organization of which he was named president. The group held a dry parade in the heavily German Catholic town of Teutopolis, where they were "hooted" at by "plain saloon bums."[30] All this was solid training for the future Anti Saloon League leader, whose organization eventually surpassed the groups to which Murphy was now introducing him.[31]

In the midst of both conversions, Shumaker decided in the winter of 1885–1886 to become a teacher. One wonders if David Shumaker had a hand in this; he wanted his son, who still lived at home, to have some guaranteed income. After two attempts, Edward received his license and began to teach for $26 per month. During his third year in the classroom, Shumaker also started to moonlight as a minister at a nearby Methodist church. He may well have continued on this dual track of teaching and preaching if it were not for the conviction that he needed a college education.[32]

And so he sought advice. Many older ministers encouraged him to go to college, especially if he wanted to occupy the pulpit full-time, though one cautioned him to "think of the souls you might win for Jesus during the time you are in college!" This conflicting advice worried Shumaker, until a friend assured him that he could both save souls and get an education at the same time. The friend, F. M. Treese, a presiding elder, told Shumaker that college would make him a better man for the denomination. Treese's arguments all but settled the issue of going to school, since Methodism was beginning to demand that its clergy be better educated.[33]

Shumaker had two options. The first was McKendree College, in Lebanon, Illinois, which was his conference school, and he was encouraged to choose McKendree for that reason. The other possibility was DePauw University, in Greencastle, Indiana. DePauw had a reputation for turning out well-educated professionals of "influence and character" who were also devout in matters of faith. Alumni did, or soon would, include such notables as Hoosier politicians Albert J. Beveridge and James E. Watson, Methodist minister and leading Social Gospel advocate Worth M. Tippy, Progressive historians Charles and Mary Beard, and Hoosier newspaper publisher Eugene Pulliam. Furthermore, one of the school's previous presidents had been Methodist Bishop Matthew Simpson (a friend of Abraham Lincoln), so it had a strong reputation and growing student body of around 900. With no regrets, Shumaker packed his bags and headed to Greencastle.[34]

Putnam County, where the college was located, was rural and full of white, native-born Protestants much like himself. For a Hoosier county, it was fairly typical, blending Republican politics (Democrats were still referred to as "copperheads" by one local newspaper), the Methodist religion, and temperance agitation. The *Greencastle Banner* routinely denounced those who looked at the saloons as only a business and called for laws to curb alcohol's influence on both society and politics.[35]

Perhaps as important as the dry rhetoric to Shumaker was that the *Banner* ran the sermons of Thomas DeWitt Talmage. From his Brooklyn Tabernacle Church, Talmage "preached to 5,000 people each Sunday . . . and was syndicated and read by over two million more," according to a biographer, thus influencing a whole generation of American Protestants. One of Talmage's chief themes was that Christians needed to mobilize to deal with sin and instruct people in proper living, in order to maintain order in society. Shumaker probably read the sermon reprints in the paper before anything else, and the sermons he heard in Greencastle reinforced Talmage's printed homilies. Shumaker attended services at College Avenue Methodist and Locust Street Methodist churches while going to school, both of which were staunch bastions of the dry cause.[36]

At the train station, Shumaker met some fellow DePauw students and made arrangements to room with two of them. Their accommodations were both plain and sparse, but living in town no doubt was exciting to the young man from rural Effingham County. After meeting with school officials, Shumaker learned that he would need two to three years of preparatory work before officially matriculating at the college. Preliminary testing in a variety of subjects put him into a middle-level classification, where he immediately started work on algebra, rhetoric, and Latin. His senior year revolved around the classic writings of Xenophon, Cicero, and Shakespeare as well as geometry and art. Whatever extra time he had was spent in the library reading. He moved on campus to Taylor House (known as the "preachers' dorm") and eventually to Florence Hall, where he remained until he graduated.[37]

In 1891, Shumaker was one of twenty-six young men who graduated from the preparatory school and became a "real" college student that fall. Since he was a minister-in-training, he majored in

Greek and minored in philosophy. His classes and assignments ran the gamut of the liberal arts and theology requirements. He wrote an analysis of Longfellow's *Evangeline*, studied the works of Livy, Homer, and Ovid, and read and reread the Bible. On Sundays after church, he attended lectures given by DePauw's professors.[38]

Life was not all academics at DePauw, though Shumaker chose not to continue his precollege roles as leader and public speaker. He seems to have kept something of a low profile on campus. "Generally known as a prohibitionist" (despite trying whisky once in the hope that it would cure a cold), he joined the Students International Prohibition Association. But he did not join the school's debating team (while he was a student, DePauw again won the prestigious Interstate Oratorical Contest), though he did take part in a public debate about prohibition. His time away from studying included playing football and a year of military drill. In many ways he was a typical college student.[39]

The most revealing item that remains from his DePauw years is an essay, "True Greatness," that shows he had not abandoned his career path. Shumaker posed the question, What makes for a great person? His answer was that "all persons truly great are those who have noble aims in life, and who toil diligently to reach these ends." They are "anchored by faith, cherished by hope, and tempered by love" in a life that "is spotless, and above reproach." Furthermore, "a man who is truly great has a love for the distressed and seeks to help them. Although such persons are often hated by the proud, yet they are great in the eyes of a loving Heavenly Father, and shall have their reward." In the end, "true greatness as God sees it" was his goal.[40]

Shumaker paid for his education by preaching part-time in small towns near Greencastle, where he could put his dry ideas to the test. He had no illusions about his early sermons, later writing that "not one of us could really preach a sermon after the standards of today, but we could tell our experiences and could exhort the unsaved to turn to Christ." In 1890 he was appointed as student pastor to the Bainbridge and Mount Pleasant churches, beating out twenty applicants for the job. He launched revivals almost immediately.[41]

His time on the Bainbridge circuit was not without controversy. Shumaker was outraged at the tradition of Fourth of July horse-racing, though he was wise enough to realize his appointment could be jeopardized if he openly condemned it. So he had a friend preach on the dangers of amusements, which angered some members of the congregation. Shumaker confronted them, saying that, as Methodists, they were free to leave the church if they wished, but, having joined the congregation, they knew that the church believed that "dancing, horse racing, card playing, and attending theatres" were in the service of "the devil."[42] It was a bold, calculated move for the young minister to make.

In 1892, Shumaker joined the Northwest Indiana Methodist Conference on trial and asked for a new charge. He was sent to Knightsville, in the middle of the states's coal region, where the congregation was made up chiefly of English, Scottish, and Welsh miners who liked to drink. Though Shumaker worried about fitting in, he ended up staying for three years. "This pastorate," he later wrote, "proved under Divine Providence the most fruitful and delightful one of my ministry," full of good singing, strong revivals, and at least one conversion per week. His time at Knightsville showed him the reality of alcohol problems in human terms, in ways that temperance sermons could not. "The ravages of the liquor traffic in the town were awful," Shumaker wrote. He witnessed the aftereffects of drunken husbands beating and sexually assaulting their wives; one member of his congregation was even killed in a bar fight. As their minister, he had to comfort the injured and conduct the funerals.[43]

These events may have contributed to the sharpness of tone taken by his sermons. His bluntness (Shumaker sometimes named names) won him both praise and enemies over the course of his career.[44] But he also could show tact. After hearing one of Shumaker's temperance sermons in Knightsville, one man stopped coming to church, and another family said that until he promised to stop preaching on temperance, they would not contribute to the offering. Shumaker called on them and showed them a passage in the Bible that condemned drunkenness and taught that alcohol was a stumbling block to salvation. "If preaching against the works of the devil is not the Gospel," he told them, "then pray tell me what the Gospel is." As he later remembered, the family became his biggest supporters.[45] He also garnered some of his first press attention when the editor of the *Clay County Enterprise* paid a visit:

> In the morning we all attended services in the new M.E. church and listened to a well-prepared and well-delivered sermon by Rev. Shoemaker, pastor in charge. The minister is a young man who shows evidence of a studious and well-balanced mind, and who is gifted with a pleasing and eloquent delivery. He is earnest in his work and we believe the church will increase and prosper during his ministration.[46]

Time passed swiftly, and before he knew it, graduation was upon him. At the ceremony on 12 June 1895, Shumaker heard outgoing college President P. D. John urge the DePauw graduates to never rest on their laurels but to "have convictions; not merely adjustable opinions that depend on which way the wind blows; but convictions that you will stand by." He also heard Methodist Bishop W. X. Ninde of Detroit tell the School of Theology's graduating ministers "to show Jesus Christ as the true Savior of the world." These addresses stayed with Shumaker for the rest of his life. Both his immediate and extended family attended the ceremonies. David Shumaker in particular was very proud of Edward. As the younger Shumaker well knew, it was an accomplishment to go to college, let alone graduate. Money had often been tight, and the temptation to return home and teach and preach was constant. But he had persevered, when nearly half of his entering class had not, and a diploma was the result.[47]

Shumaker now had to decide if he would extend his stay in Knightsville. He loved his congregation but felt that he should move on, if for no other reason than to extend his message to other communities. At the conference in 1895 he was appointed to the Plainfield circuit in Hendricks County. His father gave him a horse and, using his savings, Shumaker purchased a buggy. He quickly found to his delight that the Plainfield congregations were more in tune with him theologically than either his Bainbridge or Knightsville charges had been.[48]

The conservative climate he found was in large part due to the strength of the Society of Friends, who became "an inspiration" to him, in the area just west of Indianapolis. As a circuit pastor, Shu-maker had congregations in Plainfield, Bridgeport, Ben Davis, and Mount Olive. He made two hundred visitations during each quarter of his first year, officiated at five funerals, and preached on topics ranging from the "Transfiguration" to "Temperance" to "Dancing" to "Fishing." He found that his congregations did not get "wrought up" or were very "emotional," yet they were "real substantial people."[49]

On the Plainfield circuit, there were no saloons for him to rail against, thanks in large part to the Friends. In 1891 the Society's Indiana Yearly Meeting had called on "Christians and especially Friends" to set a "high standard" and refuse to "compromise with sin." Saloons, they were told, were "a system of organized aggres-sive wickedness" that needed to be attacked. Dry rhetoric, however, thanks to the proximity of Indianapolis, was not enough to keep the problems associated with alcohol from intruding into the lives of Shumaker's parishioners.[50]

In 1898, in all likelihood at his own request, the conference transferred Shumaker to Maple Avenue Methodist Church in Terre Haute. It was a very different place for the young minister. His dry, rural values were about to be tested by real drinking in a way found only in urban America. Upon his appointment, Shumaker met with other Terre Haute pastors to get some insight into his new home. The church was neighborhood-oriented, with 350 members who met in an old building, but it was a congregation deeply divided over the removal of their last pastor and in need of leadership. Both the congregation and the city were bigger and more diverse than the small towns that Shumaker was used to. Vigo County in 1900 was home to over 62,000 people, with large immigrant communities that were heavily involved in manufacturing. Among the city's indus-tries was the brewing of beer, a part of the local economy since the 1830s, which resulted in political influence for Terre Haute's brewers. Shumaker's time in the city also corresponded to the rise of social-ist Eugene V. Debs, who was tapping into the anger of the working classes at their position and lack of power in industrial America.[51]

Thus, the city and the church were vibrant and potentially un-stable places for him to take his ministry. Shumaker discovered in

Terre Haute that evangelical Protestantism needed a way to deal with urban America. Nationally, the result was the Social Gospel movement, which sought to actively apply Christian principles to society as a whole. Saving individual souls was no longer believed to be enough; sin did not just affect the sinner but everyone around him. This idea was especially important in urban America, where an individual's sins became worse due to the closeness of the living and working environments.[52] Methodists, with their notions of holiness and perfectibility, were early adherents to this doctrine. One Hoosier Methodist minister claimed that by applying the Social Gospel, a "Christian state" would see "the cessation of wars, diminution of poverty, better clothing, better shelter, better food for the people, enlarged securities for health, more efficient schools, wiser preaching, more social morality and more respect for character." The Methodist Church would thus not only "win men to Christ" but also "create a force that combats every evil militating against the Kingdom of Christ."[53]

Though a complex and diverse movement, Social Gospel Christianity was a great initiator of reforms during the late nineteenth and early twentieth centuries. One of which—indeed, the one that nearly all Protestants could agree on, as renowned historian Martin E. Marty has pointed out—was prohibition. In 1908 these forces for reform coalesced in the formation of the Federal Council of the Churches of Christ in America. At that meeting, Bishop Luther B. Wilson of the Methodist Church, serving as the chairman of the Committee on Temperance, noted, "In no other movement had the solidarity of the Christian Church yielded more significant results." Indeed, within a few years, the Federal Council's Board of Temperance would be calling on the Methodist Church to make "public sentiment" right on the issue.[54]

To be fully implemented, the Social Gospel needed advocates not only in the pews and pulpits but also in politics. Charles Sheldon, famed author of *In His Steps*, believed that moral suasion had to go hand in hand with the "coercive powers of government to bring about some social reforms."[55] Thus, the Social Gospel became paired with the Progressive movement. According to historian Robert Crunden,

Progressives sought to remoralize society through their occupations in a myriad of professions. In addition, like most advocates of the Social Gospel, a significant number of Progressives came to embrace prohibition as a needed reform.[56] The nucleus of their crusade was now intact.

Shumaker's own writings and activities reflect Social Gospel and Progressive influences. He allied the Maple Avenue church with the local Young Men's Christian Association (YMCA) and Centenary and First Methodist churches in promoting union programming aimed at the "laboring man" to address social problems, relations with industry, and the relevancy of the Gospel. But he was not a friend of what he called "Christian Socialists," or those Social Gospel adherents who increasingly were moving away from orthodox doctrine in their quest to remake society. While Shumaker saw much good in their concerns with the working class, he believed that their goal of saving "humanity" came at the cost of saving individuals. Focusing on the group, he thought, only led to secularization that was harmful to Christianity. For Shumaker, faith in Christ was the only way to save both people and society.[57]

Shumaker's early sermons to his Terre Haute congregation were aimed at bringing its members together under his leadership and included such topics as "Our Strength in Christ" and "Witnessing for Christ" as well as a series on missions. Once the congregation was unified, however, Shumaker began to focus more attention on organizing a dry crusade. He founded a WCTU chapter for the women of the church and put children into temperance debating contests. Shumaker himself became part of a citywide struggle to force the saloons to abide by state laws.[58]

Seeing it as their Christian duty to improve the city where they lived, Terre Haute's evangelical ministers made temperance their chief issue. While Shumaker was part of the movement, he was not senior enough to warrant a leadership position. Speaking at the county WCTU convention in this being, he talked about the responsibility of men to reject the saloon. Indeed, he hoped that one day Americans would realize that all they had to do to end the influence of the saloon was to vote it out of existence. In November 1899, following more temperance speeches, Terra Haute's drys pushed for enforcement of Sunday closing laws. Due to political corruption in the city, the ministers called on Governor James A. Mount to help them. The governor was ultimately obliged to order Terre Haute's police department to enforce the law. But even with this action by the state's chief executive, the local bosses slowly but surely reverted to the status quo. The first trial that resulted from this crackdown was stymied when two saloonkeepers "accidentally" ended up on the jury, which deadlocked 10 to 2. To add insult to injury, one of the dry attorneys was then beaten nearly to death by a wet, who was punished with only a small fine and short jail sentence.[59]

Because he was part of this dry crusade, "wets"—those in favor of alcohol and opposed to prohibition—accused Shumaker of "persecuting" saloon owners, so he fired back. In January 1900 he argued in a strong temperance sermon that the Bible was not just for individuals but also for society; that is, it was essential for Christians to take it with them into politics. The saloon, he told his congregation (who listened "with marked attention"), was a drain on society and must be opposed until it was no more. He trusted that the nation, through Jesus, would see its responsibility to God and mankind and put an end to the misery caused by Demon Rum.[60]

Shumaker believed that he was defending the right that most evangelical Protestants, and especially those advocating the dry cause, took for granted—that they had a duty to speak out on public matters. The *Western Christian Advocate* argued that "the Christian man must recognize that there can be no divorcement between private and public morality and vote his conviction. The commonness of the cry 'no politics in the pulpit,' is equaled only by its silliness." To those who did not think it proper for a denomination to tell its members how to vote, the *Advocate* reminded them that church membership had certain inherent obligations and in America was voluntary.[61]

The more Shumaker became involved in reform work, the sharper his sermons became. In June 1900 he addressed the Terre Haute Ministerial Union on "Dangerous Tendencies in American Life." The speech was heavily influenced by what he saw happening in the city, which he believed was representative of the struggle occurring nationwide between the forces of civil order and their opponents. Shumaker, while trusting that "America has a great future before her," saw many problems for his country in the near term. The wealthy were consolidating the nation's riches. Political bosses ran the cities, where immigrants flocked, each group with its own "colony." From within these foreign enclaves, the liquor interest drew both its customers and its political influence. The "rum power" then caused labor unrest by exacerbating the real problems of workers. Giving men more wages would just give more money to the saloons. In Shumaker's opinion, the cities needed to be purified by eliminating alcohol.[62]

His message blended the revivalism of his youth with the realities he saw in urban America. Being involved in reform did not cause him to be a radical in his theology. If his sermons are any indication, Shumaker spent more time building up his flock's faith than anything else. As a pastor, he was orthodox in his beliefs about the divinity of Jesus Christ, the authenticity and authority of the Bible, and the need for Christians to be saved from sin and to lead Christ-centered lives. About the only innovation in his sermons is a reference to the need for men to become more active in the life of the church by following the example of Jesus.[63]

Shumaker's notion of worldly traps, which was another theme in his sermons, was shaped by his belief in flawed human nature as well as in the reality of twentieth-century temptations. In 1902 he twice delivered a sermon entitled "The Value of God's House, or Advantages in Being a Christian." Therein he told his congregation that the list of worldly snares included food, drugs, alcohol, "lusts of the flesh," fancy and "shameless" clothes, "society, putting a job before family and spiritual commitments, money, play, the ball room" (which he characterized in good Methodist fashion as a place where was found "the undue familiarity of couples in dancing, awakening unholy passions, and leading many women to the brothel"), and cards.[64]

To dry evangelical Protestants such as Shumaker, the problems facing America were moral in nature. His denomination believed that morality in the nation dropped off from 1870 through 1900 because of the growth of Sunday amusements and events that had nothing to do with worshiping God. The Indiana Conference of the Methodist Church said in 1895: "we deprecate the keeping open of saloons, as upon other days, so especially upon the Sabbath. Baseball and other games, driving out for amusement and recreation, with bicycle, carriage, car or other vehicle, Sunday theaters and other entertainments; secular Sunday papers and other publications, which preoccupy the thoughts and distract the attention from sacred themes and associations." This "continental Sabbath" greatly worried American-born Protestants, for they were convinced that many of the sins they now faced were brought into the country and fostered by foreign-born immigrants. As the bulletins of Meridian Street Methodist Church in Indianapolis eventually summarized it, the European institution meant "loose morals and low ideals, and is adapted to a beer-garden civilization."[65]

The two cultures were headed for a showdown. While Shumaker and other dry proponents were concerned with several reforms, they could not be distracted from confronting alcohol. Indeed, the dilution of Protestant reform energy among a myriad of causes, such as public health, prostitution, Sunday baseball games, gossip, cardplaying, dancing, theatergoing, and smoking, was one of the chief obstacles in achieving any moral progress in the years after the Civil War. Drys believed that American Protestants were so concerned about everything that they were unable to effectively organize against anything. Shumaker and others like him did not want to repeat that mistake, and they believed that alcohol was the linchpin in solving all of society's ills.[66]

The Terre Haute congregation embraced Shumaker's more single-minded crusade. They voted overwhelmingly to push for law enforcement. With growing public pressure, the saloon owners promised to close on Sundays if other businesses did so as well. Shumaker was put in charge of brokering a deal between the reformers and the grocery and meat merchants. With the help of the Merchant Retail Dealers Association, he was able to secure a promise from nearly all businesses to close on Sundays. He took away from the experience the conviction that the law could only be broken if a permissive societal attitude allowed it.[67]

Still, Shumaker could not spend all of his time on reform work, important as it was, while ministering to a congregation. Maple Avenue needed a new building to keep up with both congregational and neighborhood growth. Despite poor economic times, he found that members were willing to give, sometimes surprisingly large amounts, to the project. Having gotten them under way on the construction effort, however, Shumaker startled his congregation by deciding to leave. He felt that his work was done in Terre Haute: he had given Maple Avenue both a mission and a new church. After three years, he was ready to move on. His next destination was Williamsport, a town of 1,500.[68]

Perhaps, too, he thought that in Terre Haute he could never lead the reform crusade from the pulpit of his little church. In this regard, his new charge offered more possibilities. Williamsport was the county seat, with the railroad and a stone quarry as its main businesses. It was Shumaker's home for the next two years. The congregation had a history of good pastors and of being the church home of some of the community's leaders. Shumaker's first sermon revolved around the theme of giving the people of Williamsport "over to the work of the Kingdom," and he continued to make the newspapers with inventive sermons. A publicized near lynching in Illinois brought a sermon on the Crucifixion in a non-Easter setting. He floated the title of another, "The Biggest Sin in Williamsport," in the papers to drum up attendance for the topic of "Unbelief." He delivered a sermon on "Hell" in 1902, promising that evil will be punished by God, and that damnation will be eternal for all sinners, including saloonkeepers, unless they repent. Such topics managed to annoy some people in both the congregation and town, but mostly he found Williamsport to be a good fit for him.[69]

As he had in Terre Haute, Shumaker took on the wets. His organizational skills to keep the prohibition issue alive won him the admiration of many in the town. The dry forces of Williamsport sought to vote out of existence, via a remonstrance, the town's five saloons. The attempt had both successes and frustrations. Following a town-wide temperance revival, Shumaker came face-to-face with several of the saloon owners. They asked him, Why was he trying to destroy them financially? The minister replied that it was nothing personal, but he could not abide their business. The saloon owners, for their part, respected Shumaker enough to halt a planned egging of the Methodist pastor and were surprised that the drys did not quit after suffering setbacks.[70]

By the time he took the pastorate in Williamsport, Shumaker had found new reasons to combat Demon Rum. On 12 September 1900 he had married Flora May Holliger of Terre Haute. Together they had five children over the next thirteen years. Shumaker's family became an inspiration in his war on liquor, one that he was increasingly focused on winning.[71] Thus, by the early 1900s, Shumaker had made temperance his favorite sermon topic.[72] In September 1903 at his denominational conference, which was held in South Bend, he was asked if he wanted to take over the pastorate at Wingate or be designated for work with the Indiana Anti Saloon League (IASL). He picked the League. When asked later about this decision, Shumaker replied that "I prayed for light, and at once I saw the way open for my active participation in the prohibition fight."[73] It was a decision that would change not only his life but also the future of the state he called home.

Shumaker, the product of a Midwestern dry culture, had found his calling in prohibition. As a pastor, he had honed his public speaking and organizational skills as well as lived in various rural and urban communities around Indiana. He took these experiences and attributes to his work in the IASL. After a brief respite in Indianapolis, where he met with the League leadership, Shumaker was given his assignment. He packed up his family and headed north. Their destination was South Bend.[74]

2 | South Bend and Beyond

The Reverend Edward Shumaker arrived in South Bend to take part in an evangelical Protestant, Progressive group whose goal was to solve the problem of drinking in America.[1] Reform was now his career, not just a part of his ministry. Though the Anti Saloon League was not the first organization that sought to focus dry sentiment on the creation of an orderly society, it was the eventual means by which drys managed to penetrate the realms of law and politics to fashion their version of God's kingdom on Earth. Indeed, the partisan battles that occupied Shumaker for the rest of his life were fueled by the religious convictions that he and his supporters held. They demanded not only reform but also a crusade.

The League was part of a widespread Protestant belief that the church had to be proactive in the world to halt moral decay. As one historian described the times, "Protestantism knew in its heart that God meant America to be Protestant, Christian, morally upright and just." These Christians believed in a war "to destroy the work of the devil" and expected their pastors to lead the charge. And as one of Shumaker's League colleagues in Tennessee put it, "it is my business as a minister of the gospel to fight the devil. The devil is in the saloon."[2]

Even though drinking was increasingly viewed as disreputable, not everyone thought that the solution was prohibition or that the Anti Saloon League was the best way to achieve a dry America.[3] Since the Civil War, the drys had created a myriad of organizations. Individuals had flocked to the faddish Murphy temperance pledge and its call for personal responsibility in the late 1870s. By the 1880s, Indiana was home to the State Christian Temperance Union (SCTU), the Woman's Christian Temperance Union (WCTU), and the Prohibition Party.[4] However, each of these groups had serious handicaps. In its various incarnations, the SCTU, founded in 1870, attempted to unify drys but found it difficult to build grassroots support.[5] The WCTU, on the other hand, was strong locally among Hoosier women, but it saw reform as multifaceted and attempted to right all wrongs at once, ultimately diminishing its focus as a result. Its chapters also had a tendency to compromise when offenders promised to reform on their own. Moreover, since its members lacked the vote, the women had only a peripheral effect on politics.[6] The Prohibition Party, which took a harder line than the other two groups, was crucial in creating grassroots dry sentiment. It made a strong argument about the need for morality in American politics and the duty of Christians to vote for dry candidates. However, the party could not overcome the majority of voters' attachments to the two mainstream political parties, in part, because of the importance that both Democrats and Republicans placed on Hoosier voters.[7]

Thus, the dry movement was divided and still in search of a winning approach. But all drys believed that since "there will be drunkards as long as there is liquor," the best solution was to take away alcohol. As the pastor of Trinity Methodist Church in Evansville observed, prohibition was "an evolution of the times, and was keeping pace with the advance of thought in every direction."[8]

Part of this evolution was that the Anti Saloon League surpassed the other dry organizations by harnessing evangelical Protestantism from within. Founded in Ohio by ministers who were steeped in the Republican-oriented business ethos of the time, the League sought to weave the various dry strands together by promoting a radical agenda of gradual prohibition. Its founders believed that Christians had to be involved in the wider culture and that the saloon and the continental Sabbath posed the gravest threats imaginable to Christian America.[9] The League put a great deal of faith in the rule of law and worked to pass and enforce dry legislation. As political agitators its members also supported centralized, state-level, law-enforcement agencies to overcome local prejudices.[10] As one leader described it,

> There is no regular membership of the Anti Saloon League. In other words a man does not have to sign a pledge of membership, nor pay any regular dues, or anything of that sort. We extend the right hand of fellowship, so to speak, to all persons who believe that the saloon is a bad thing and ought to be run out of the country. We do not ask whether a man is a Democrat or a Republican or a Progressive or a Socialist, or whether he is a Methodist, a Presbyterian or belongs to any church. If he is willing to work along these non-partisan and inter-denominational lines, and stand with us for the election of men who stand for prohibition, and the legislation in that direction for which we stand, then we are glad to have him consider himself as a member of our organization.[11]

Many Methodists did feel a special attachment to the ASL, however. They believed in its bipartisan activism and were especially well suited for the rigors of League work. The men of Shumaker's generation, after all, were not that far removed from the circuit-rider days of Methodism's past.[12] It is not surprising, then, when given the option, that Shumaker chose the Indiana Anti Saloon League (IASL) over another conventional pastorate.

The ASL arrived in Indiana in 1898 when Howard H. Russell brought the concept to Indianapolis. The new IASL started out small but grew quickly. In 1899 it agitated across the state, organized town and local groups, assisted communities with remonstrances, took aim at illegal saloons, participated in over 400 addresses, published over one million pages of literature, helped law enforcement, and persuaded judges to uphold power of attorney in remonstrance contests. By 1901 the IASL was making an impact in places as diverse as Terre

Haute and Noblesville, and it was at home in congregations across the Protestant spectrum. The League had its headquarters in Indianapolis with regional offices in South Bend, Terre Haute, Evansville, and (after 1907) Fort Wayne. In January 1906 the IASL launched its own newspaper, the *Indiana Issue*. Presbyterian minister W. C. Helt was the first state superintendent, but he was soon replaced by Dr. R. V. Hunter (who served only briefly), Dr. Edwin G. Saunderson (who went on to head the Michigan ASL), and the Reverend Ulysses G. Humphrey, who took charge in December 1903.[13]

Humphrey proved to be a major influence on how Shumaker ran the South Bend office and, later, the state organization itself. He was a thirty-five-year-old Methodist minister from Middletown, Ohio, was married with two children, and stood over six feet tall. Humphrey believed that the League should target wet politicians and saw the saloon as "a menace to public welfare." He streamlined the IASL, set high standards for his field men, and popularized the practice of holding union services in smaller communities to cut down on costs. Humphrey was also the ultimate allocator of funds and decided on how best to budget the League's often meager financial resources.[14]

Fighting the saloon could be dangerous for dry field workers. Humphrey reported that in one Indiana town, "the liquor element . . . have threatened the preachers with dynamite" and smeared pine tar on the houses of drys. Other Hoosier drys faced assault, intimidation, or worse from wets—a minister in Shelburn was shot for leading a remonstrance battle, the home of a local IASL leader was dynamited in Keystone. After a "blind tiger" (another name for an illegal saloon) was raided near Terre Haute, the owner dynamited the Sandford Methodist church and two general stores in retaliation.[15] The home of Fred Rohrer, the founder, editor, manager, and publisher of the *Berne Witness* in Adams County, was dynamited by wets during a heated 1903 remonstrance battle while he and his family slept inside; moreover, he was twice assaulted by wet mobs in his office.[16] Shumaker himself was once struck by a beer bottle thrown by a zealous wet while he was waiting for a train.[17]

This hostile environment greeted Shumaker when he arrived in South Bend to oversee the IASL's work in the northern part of the state. In many ways the city was similar to Terre Haute. South Bend, a growing, thriving industrial community of nearly 60,000 people, was home to the University of Notre Dame, the Studebaker Company (which manufactured wagons and automobiles), and an increasingly influential newspaper, the *South Bend Tribune*, which boasted a circulation of over 6,000. Alcohol consumption and production were also part of the community, thanks to German and Polish ethnic enclaves. The city's Protestant ministers believed that there was a great deal of "evil" in South Bend, in the guise of gambling, liquor, socialism, and "Sabbath desecration." Moreover, mayoral and police corruption were linked to the saloons.[18]

Having grown up in rural America, Shumaker enjoyed the prospect of city living. The family rented a house and joined the congregation of the First Methodist Church, which met in a beautiful downtown sanctuary and had a strong attachment to the dry cause. Shumaker set up his office and soon was ready to do battle with Demon Rum.[19] What he found in South Bend was that urbanization and modern conveniences made it easier to get the dry message out. The IASL utilized the latest technology to advance their agenda, including stereopticon machines. Shumaker thus showed, to great effect, lantern slides depicting how prohibition would help children grow up healthy, aid commerce, promote automobile ownership, create new businesses, and make America a world leader. The presentation was so successful that people begged Shumaker to bring his lantern to their meetings.[20]

The League's regional offices stayed connected via regular correspondence. With multiple mail deliveries each day and with the dispatch of telegrams, the field workers were well informed of each other's activities as well as of directions from Humphrey. The organization's letters provide considerable insight into the day-to-day operations of the League. The Humphrey-Shumaker correspondence, for example, discusses where Shumaker had been, how his addresses had been received, where he was going, and what his needs were. Both men shared a concern about the success of the League and its financial security.[21]

Despite the correspondence, the League's branches did not always function well together. One example in particular involves the man in charge of the Terre Haute district for the League, the Reverend P. H. Faulk. For some reason, Shumaker became a mediator and confidant to Faulk during the latter's tempestuous time as Humphrey's subordinate. Part of Faulk's problem stemmed from a deadly illness that struck his family and sent him into a deep depression, and he was afraid that his subsequent poor performance would cause Humphrey to close down the Terre Haute office. Much of the problem, as best can be reconstructed, stemmed from miscommunication between Faulk and Humphrey because they talked too much through Shumaker and not enough to each other. The Faulk episode prompted Humphrey to make his workers sign contracts with the League in order to avoid "men, who like Faulk, come in for a short period" and then leave.[22]

Terre Haute was a problem for the IASL. Without leadership, the dry organization's work in the city faltered. In January 1906, Humphrey wrote Shumaker about the possibility of returning to Terre Haute. Faulk chimed in, urging Shumaker to take over: "You're the man for this field." Shumaker, however, had other ideas. Writing a fellow dry minister, he said that if he had to move anywhere, it would be to Fort Wayne. In the end, Humphrey decided that it was better for Shumaker to stay where he was. Fort Wayne was a city where drinking was supported by German Lutherans and Catholics, and Shumaker would be fighting an uphill battle there. Shumaker agreed.[23]

Shumaker then worked hard to integrate his district into the statewide strategy crafted by Humphrey. He availed himself of League legal advice, which included both case citation and courtroom strategy. He also dealt with filling subscriptions to the *American Issue*, but his main concern was raising money. Most ASL donations were between 25 cents and $2 per month in pledges. It took hard work to make that money materialize, and Shumaker was tenacious in sending out reminder notices. As Humphrey noted in April 1907, Central Indiana and South Bend were the only districts generating money for the dry cause.[24]

Shumaker succeeded because he used local events to the League's benefit. Chiefly this meant tapping into the cyclical nature of revivals in towns and communities. When a community's morals reached a certain low point, area churches began to advocate for reforms. The public outcry over gambling, drinking, prostitution, or other vices would then prompt local politicians, ever mindful of voters' anger, to crack down by enacting and/or enforcing laws. Over time, police vigilance would slacken, vice problems would again multiply, and the cycle would repeat itself. Shumaker brought the IASL into this grass-roots cycle to the benefit of both himself and the organization.[25]

The ministers with whom Shumaker corresponded about his speaking engagements were sources of information on their local community, making his job easier. When the IASL wanted to come into Winamac in 1905, for example, it was the Methodist minister who proposed a union service with the Presbyterians and urged Shumaker to consider also nearby Star City, "for I feel there is a field that would yield more easily than ours as ours is so strongly Catholic." In December 1905, Shumaker was trying to line up a speaking engagement in Pleasant Lake when he was advised that the town was under quarantine because of a diphtheria outbreak.[26] In turn, he was also a source of information as well as a public speaker. Ministers promoting the dry cause contacted him, and Shumaker answered their questions in minute detail.[27]

The strongest legal tool in the IASL arsenal was the Nicholson remonstrance law, which allowed communities to file an objection to the issuance of liquor licenses. Its author was S. E. Nicholson, a Quaker minister who had served in the state legislature and was a leader in the national ASL. The IASL had held a statewide meeting at Meridian Street Methodist Church in Indianapolis to organize for the law in 1903, and 1,700 ministers promised to devote a Sunday during the General Assembly session to temperance. The law was part of a long line of partially successful liquor legislation in the state, dating from 1873, when Indiana had first licensed saloons. The Nicholson law was considered a needed update to these earlier attempts.[28]

Nicholson remonstrance battles divided communities. Business-men feared boycotts if they supported remonstrances, and saloon owners attempted to intimidate those who did sign by threatening to make remonstrators pay if drys lost. Pressure was exerted by both sides when it came to signing petitions. There was even a "pitched battle" with guns and clubs in one Hoosier town between wets and drys when authorities attempted to enforce saloon closings following a dry victory.[29]

Even with the power of remonstrance, Shumaker's job had its frustrations. Among them were his fellow clergymen, who were key to the League's access to local congregations. Not all ministers liked the fact that the IASL asked for donations during their presentations, and Shumaker had to remind them that this was the chief way in which the IASL raised funds. Nor were ministers always receptive to the idea of the IASL coming to their church and speaking. Shumaker, it seems, picked first a location and a date that suited him and then found a church that would have him. This meant that he often was told, "I do not think this is the best time for you to come," because his plans conflicted with those of the pastor.[30]

As Shumaker became secure in his abilities and position, he used his grassroots organization to work for him in communities.[31] The longer Shumaker was at his job, the more his reputation grew. Success in one town opened doors in others and brought invitations to organize drys from out of state. Increasingly, Shumaker got the lion's share of the credit for dry victories. When the town of Milford went dry in 1905, he was told that he was a "powerful ally . . . I think we should have made a poor showing without you." Humphrey himself paid Shumaker the compliment in December 1905 of saying, "things are certainly booming in your end of the state and you are to be congratulated upon your success." Shumaker's reputation became such that he was courted by Episcopal churches and contacted by leaders of the educational Chautauqua Institute in New York. Even the Prohibition Party asked to borrow a wet/dry map of Indiana created by Shumaker that charted IASL successes.[32]

Shumaker cultivated both his and the League's image as being above the political fray, even as he became increasingly involved in politics. The idea of nonpartisanship was important for Shumaker because of the strength of the Prohibition Party in some parts of Northern Indiana and its animosity toward the Republican Party, to which most Hoosier evangelical Protestants still belonged. When the editor of the *Middlebury Independent* wrote that Shumaker voted the straight

Prohibitionist ticket, Shumaker replied that people should vote for principle, not party, on Election Day. Still, some of the ministers with whom Shumaker worked wanted the League to put more pressure on candidates to state publicly where they stood on issues.[33]

As the IASL grew in strength, the Republican Party began to court it as a means to counter the Prohibitionists. In December 1905, Humphrey wrote to Shumaker that he had been busy in Indianapolis entertaining Republican dignitaries who had come by his office during a recent "love fest" held by the party in the Circle City. James P. Goodrich, the chairman of the Indiana Republican Party, was among those who paid their respects. Shumaker received a letter from Goodrich in January 1906: "I sincerely hope and believe that the Republican Party in this campaign will stand 'four square' on the great questions that interest the people at this time. If they do, they will win. If they don't, they don't deserve to win." Perhaps more telling was the letter to Shumaker a few days later from Carl Riddick of the Republican State Committee, who wote: "at any time you are at Indianapolis I shall be glad to have you call at the headquarters and if there is any way I can serve you at any time, I shall be pleased to do so."[34]

Even as the IASL became more active politically, Shumaker's belief in its mission never wavered: "The League is the sanest, most practical, and effective temperance movement." In an address to IASL county organizations, he not only extolled the League as the proper place for the "religious and moral forces of the state and nation" to converge on the subject of temperance, but he argued forcefully that alcohol was at the root of all other social problems. "The saloon," Shumaker said, "has too long endured. The saloon must die."[35]

Drys viewed saloons as one-stop centers of vice whether they were in urban or rural America. They were, to them, "the devil's headquarters on earth"—bases for prostitutes, venues for gambling and smoking. Saloonkeepers served free, heavily salted lunches to attract customers and boost drink sales. It was a good business tactic, but drys wondered how often this bribe ended up being vomited in the gutter. Though wets argued that it was up to the drinker to take responsibility for his actions, drys countered that saloons were selling alcohol that caused men to lose their reason and so should bear the brunt of the burden. As one historian has posited about the Midwest, people saw the liquor industry as a trust—a big business, like the railroads, that took advantage of its customers.[36]

The evils of saloons and drinking were evident to anyone who picked up a newspaper. A father and son were killed near Greencastle when they attempted to beat a train across the tracks in their horse and buggy after leaving a saloon. Anderson police arrested a Muncie youth in the company of a vagrant who had "induced the boy to get drunk." An Evansville man was arrested with seven teenagers after buying them a three-gallon bucket of beer. A drunken Anderson man killed his mother with a hammer after she asked saloons to stop selling him alcohol. Miami Indian chief John Godfroy was killed by his son after a quarrel in a saloon near Fort Wayne. And a disorderly Indianapolis man who was literally thrown out of a saloon died from a head fracture.[37] Moreover, alcohol had consequences for nondrinkers. When President Theodore Roosevelt persuaded a waiter to serve him a cocktail at Vice President Charles Fairbanks's 1907 Memorial Day party in Indianapolis, the scandal kept the dry Fairbanks from being named as a lay delegate to the Methodist Church's quadrennial conference, and it possibly injured his campaign for the Republican presidential nomination in 1908.[38]

The dry crusade was not about rural America seeing the saloon as an urban problem, for the saloon knew no such boundary. Drinking did not emerge as an issue with urbanization. In rural towns and villages, saloons were places both of escape and of violence, regardless of their locale. In a small town, even one drinking establishment could have an impact. The problems associated with saloons were magnified in urban areas because of larger populations, crowded living conditions, and the sheer number of drinking places.[39]

A business model designed to maximize profits, the saloon had a mystique about it. As Perry Duis has demonstrated, the local saloon was a multifaceted, functioning small business with ties to big business. (Crawford Fairbanks's Terre Haute Brewery, for example, employed 300 men yearround, paid federal taxes in the amount of $312,000, and was the single largest industrial-property taxpayer in the city.) Largely, the saloons were places of recreation and amusement for men. There was intense competition from legitimate and illegal rivals, because the business was so lucrative and because customer demands (for more free lunches, more cigars, more slot machines, more pool tables) had to be met. Furthermore, reformers such as Shumaker pointed to infractions and held up the least reputable saloonkeepers as representative of the entire industry.[40]

Brewers sought ways to improve their image in the face of growing dry propaganda. Considering that they owned 3,500 of the estimated 5,000 saloons in Indiana, we can see why they had such a stake in public relations. The head of the Indianapolis Brewing Company, Albert Lieber, believed that attempts to ban alcohol were doomed to failure because people wanted a "stimulant." He acknowledged problems with the industry, however, and thought that agitation could lead to its "betterment." The Indiana Brewers Association (IBA) in 1903 promised to close those saloons that did not obey the law. The pledge became more earnest as the years went on and the IASL grew in power. Many of the members of the IBA, including Lieber, thought that the state was overly saturated with saloons. Not opening new ones and closing "objectionable" ones, the group believed, would save everyone money as well as help to put an end to dry agitation. This plan included supporting rezoning efforts in urban areas (both in Indiana and nationally) to move saloons and other vice businesses out of residential neighborhoods and into one central location.[41]

The brewers were worried about the dry drift toward prohibition and hoped to ward it off. Nationally, they pushed a $1 billion model license plan with the goal of ending alcohol as a political issue. License advocates said that while they wanted to focus on repeat law violators, dry policy would put out of business law-abiding saloons. Some commentators hailed the proposed Model License League as an organization long overdue.[42] But, according to others, such an idea was too late. Since saloonkeepers and brewers had refused to adhere to the laws for so long, they had turned moderates into radicals. The Indianapolis Ministerial Association blasted the brewers' plan, and Oregon dry leader Clarence True Wilson called the wet proposal "lame in logic and a failure in practice."[43]

Such reform efforts, moreover, rarely lasted long within the industry. Wets decided as early as the 1880s that any temperance movement would "rob" them of their lucrative livelihood, and so there was incentive to frustrate both internal and external reform efforts. Interiors of saloons were designed to obstruct the view of police to the inside, and screens were placed over windows to prevent people from looking in. Wets openly flouted laws, such as those that barred them from opening on Sundays, while officials dodged responsibility in order not to have to investigate complaints. Brewers also published books that blasted opponents of the license system as bad and even un-Christian.[44]

Still, drys kept up the pressure. In Goshen, after protests against lax enforcement were heard in September 1907 from the city's ministers, the mayor ordered the police to make sure that saloons observed the Sunday closing law. This was the beginning of what the *Goshen Democrat* later labeled a "big reform wave" that swept over the northcentral part of the state. By November, both Elkhart and South Bend had also tightened their enforcement of the laws, and drys were talking of carrying the campaign into Warsaw, Mishawaka, and Fort Wayne as well. Making the crusade regional made sense. Clamping the lid down in one community often led to problems in others.[45]

Increasingly cyclical enforcement crackdowns were not enough for drys, who were now interested in electing lawmakers. In 1903 the North Indiana Conference of the Methodist Church said that only religious men should be in government. J. Frank Hanly seemed to fill this requirement. Born in Illinois and a lifelong Republican, he had moved to Williamsport, Indiana, as a young man and became a lawyer. A devout Methodist, who often gave addresses to his church on the topics of "temperance, patriotism, and religion," Hanly hated gambling, liquor, and corruption, and made the fight against them the cornerstone of his political career. After a term in Congress and an attempt to be nominated for the Senate, in 1904 he ran for governor. Hanly's election proved to some observers that Hoosiers would no longer tolerate interference on the part of saloons in politics.[46] Though Shumaker and Hanly did not always see eye to eye, the dry leader had a great deal of respect for the governor.[47]

With Hanly's endorsement, drys worked to strengthen the Nicholson law. According to one report, despite the remonstrance, "Indianapolis had one saloon to every 520 persons. East Chicago showed one saloon to every 55 persons and Anderson one to every 270 persons. There were ten times as many saloons in Indianapolis . . . as school houses." The IASL was at the forefront of this new dry campaign. Shumaker told the *South Bend Tribune* that, in seeking a broader remonstrance power, the League "is only asking for complete local self-government upon the saloon question." This goal dominated the League's field day in South Bend and Mishawaka in January 1905.[48]

There seemed to be a need for a new law besides the wishes of drys. In the Evansville riot of 1903, a mixture of racism and free-flowing liquor largely provoked the massive mob disturbance that was only subdued after Governor Winfield T. Durbin declared martial law and deployed the state militia. Durbin's actions were a benchmark for the man who replaced him, and in his outgoing address Durbin further set the tone for the Hanly administration, telling the General Assembly that the saloon contributed to "the poorhouse, the insane hospital, the jail, and the penitentiary." It was up to the state to use its power to regulate this "evil." Durbin called on the legislature to revise the Nicholson remonstrance law to force people who wanted to open a saloon to petition for a license, not force drys to stop them. Hanly echoed these sentiments in his opening address a few days later, when he called on the legislature to allow a blanket remonstrance that would cover all attempts at getting a liquor license for a given area.[49]

Having both men advocate strengthening the law generated momentum for dry reformers. The IASL launched an aggressive lobbying effort for the bill. Proponents were careful to assert that the proposed Moore amendment would not replace the Nicholson law; it would only enhance it by allowing a remonstrance to be in effect for all saloons in an area, not just one. The liquor interest was unable to stop either a "large and enthusiastic" dry lobby headed by the IASL or the determination of Hanly to see it passed. The IASL's Humphrey believed that the new law would make the state 75 percent dry.[50]

The Prohibition Party saw the Nicholson law as a half measure that warranted neither support nor amending. The party blasted the

IASL for its duplication of effort and what the Prohibitionists considered its close relationship with the Republicans.[51] But when it came to wets and drys in general, the debate over the law centered on the perception of alcohol. Did people have an inherent right to drink, or did the government have a fundamental duty to protect them from an industry that cared only about profit?[52] The Moore amendment was an important shift in this debate in Indiana, because it placed the onus of responsibility on wets to prove that Hoosiers truly wanted saloons in a given area. New saloons, if unwanted, could now endanger the entire trade in a community.[53] This was a significant victory for the dry crusade.

The governor made it a priority of his administration to help communities clamp down on the saloon industry with the new law, despite dissent from some politicians. Shortly after the passage of the Moore amendment, Hanly sent state aid to Elkhart, LaPorte, and Michigan City, vowing that dry laws would be enforced. All three cities were in Shumaker's district. In an editorial cartoon, entitled "Shutting out the Devil," the *South Bend Tribune* depicted a forlorn Satan gathering his minions and leaving the now-closed Muncie, Anderson, Elkhart, and Mishawaka markets because of dry efforts.[54]

South Bend was part of this struggle as well. Though the *South Bend Tribune* depicted Governor Hanly in one editorial cartoon as clamping down the lids on boiling pots labeled Muncie, Kokomo, Anderson, and Elkhart, with the pot labeled South Bend "not quite within his reach," the governor and Shumaker were interested in cleaning up the city. The dry leader was the source for most of the protemperance information that found its way into the *Tribune*. As part of the IASL's statewide strategy of pushing for remonstrance battles, Shumaker organized one in the city's Seventh Ward and defended the Moore amendment against charges by a South Bend police judge that it was unconstitutional. The dry leader, in the words of the *Tribune*, "shot full of holes" the judge's reasoning.[55]

The governor did not neglect other areas of the state in his crusade. When the *Western Christian Advocate* condemned the French Lick and West Baden area, known for its medicinal sulfur springs and casinos, Hanly took on the Orange County resorts. The IASL fully supported the governor's opposition. Attorney General James Bingham called for the creation of a state police force because local law enforcement often tipped off hotel owners (including state Democratic boss Thomas Taggart) ahead of raids. Moreover, the state won a Court of Appeals decision that allowed Hanly to personally revoke Taggart's liquor licenses.[56]

Increased dry agitation also came from many of the state's newspapers. The *Hamilton County Ledger* pointed out that saloons did not pay enough in fees to claim that their closing would hurt the economy. The paper also blasted the notion that saloons were "honorable," considering the violence associated with them. In 1906 the *Indianapolis News* linked Sunday closing laws to decreasing criminal activity. The paper grew increasingly hostile to the liquor trust as 1907 went on, stating that, like the railroads before them, the brewers were on the verge of severe regulation. Its editorials attacked saloon-linked political corruption and called for sending Sunday-closing violators to the workhouse.[57]

Thanks to the Nicholson and Moore laws, there were more and more League-initiated court battles. Hoosier drys had scored a major victory in 1904 when the Indiana Supreme Court ruled that "alley saloons" were illegal, since state law required saloons to face a street. That same year, the Indiana Court of Appeals ruled that a person granted a liquor license could not transfer it to someone else: "the purpose of such statutes is not to encourage the traffic, but rather to narrow its dangers, the extent of which are largely dependent upon the qualifications of the particular persons to whom the control of the business is entrusted."[58]

Greater victory came via the pens of two circuit judges in 1907. Samuel R. Artman of Lebanon ruled that saloons could not be licensed under Indiana law because of the nature of their business, and Ira W. Christian of Noblesville amplified that decision by declaring saloons a public nuisance and thus illegal. The *Indianapolis News* said of the decisions that "liquor people are so stupid, arrogant and greedy" that they had failed to realize that if they did not follow easy laws, they would face outright prohibition. Both judges' rulings were hailed by drys, though the Prohibition Party protested what it perceived to be IASL attempts to take credit for the victory.[59]

These legal victories did not stand for long, however. In 1907 the Indiana Supreme Court decided a remonstrance battle that had originated in St. Joseph County in favor of the saloonkeeper. That same year, in *Sopher v. State*, the court overturned Judge Christian's ruling that saloons constituted a public nuisance. The state high court said, "A nuisance always arises from unlawful acts." Though activities in saloons might be a nuisance, the saloon itself could not be declared as such because "that which is lawful cannot be regarded in a legal sense as a public nuisance." The state had conferred legality on the saloon via the license. However, the court did not stop there, labeling those who sought prohibition as "peculiar," and it endorsed the license system as the only way by which differences of opinion on such a controversial issue could be balanced.[60]

As his final year in office approached, Governor Hanly decided to spend it fighting the influence of the brewers.[61] His crusade garnered him the label of a "great reformer." A vocal supporter of both the ASL and IASL, he was revered by the state's Methodists for his attacks on the liquor trust. In 1906, delegates to the Indiana Conference of the Methodist Church cheered as Hanly called for moral reform and increased law enforcement. Both the governor and Shumaker presided over the temperance meeting at the Northwest Indiana Methodist conference in 1907.[62] Neither man ever expressed doubts that calling on churches, especially their own Methodist denomination, to push for prohibition was encouraging an establishment of religion. The battle against alcohol shaped their worldview. Evangelical Protestants thought that the Methodist Church should be as active in saving America as it was dedicated to overseas missionary work.[63] Religion was part of the public sphere, and such participation was expected and largely accepted by the vast majority of Americans.

The governor believed that religiously influenced laws would also help the Republican Party. Hanly's speeches became grand declarations of a "bitter and relentless war on the liquor traffic." In 1907 he asked the General Assembly for a local option bill because "the right of a free people to exclude from their communities a traffic whose every element is an unmixed evil is fundamental." However, not every Hoosier Republican agreed with this approach. Some feared that Hanly's moral agitation would alienate voters as 1908 approached, while others knew it was hurting the party's fundraising since some Republicans depended on donations from Indianapolis-area brewers.[64]

It was in this politically charged environment that Shumaker was named state superintendent. When Humphrey left to run the League's branch in Wisconsin, Shumaker accepted the call to take over Indiana. The *Berne Witness* declared him "one of the rising orators of the day, of very pleasing and winsome personality"; he "impresses his hearers with his earnestness and sincerity."[65] He was now the man in charge, but he still had much to learn.

3 | A Political Education

Edward Shumaker's perspective of the dry crusade changed when he became state superintendent of the Indiana Anti Saloon League. A telegram sent from Indianapolis at 3 A.M. on 22 July 1907 from U. G. Humphrey announced his unanimous election to the position. It was followed by a letter from the IASL Headquarters Committee, saying, "Our experience of your labors gives good hope that your endeavors in this office will redound to the advantage of this great reform." Humphrey replied, "I have the feeling that the hand of the Lord is in this whole matter." Shumaker's written response to the news (which Humphrey termed "splendid") struck the proper chord. Regretting that Humphrey was not going to remain in Indiana, the superintendent-elect said, "The distinguished honor which the Headquarters Committee confers upon me comes very unexpectedly." He was, he went on, "profoundly grateful, I am humbled with the sense of tremendous responsibility which this position places upon me."[1]

His pro forma modesty aside, Shumaker was the obvious choice. From his post in South Bend, he had created a network across Northern Indiana that included churches, businesses, and newspapers. His close contact with Humphrey gave him insight into the inner workings of the IASL. Having been a pastor in Central Indiana as well as in

Terre Haute, he was familiar with those areas of the state. Supporters from around Indiana were pleased that the committee had picked a Hoosier and assured him that he was the right man for the job.[2]

After a farewell reception in his honor at First Methodist Church in South Bend, Shumaker left for Indianapolis. Once his family settled in, he threw himself into the job of state superintendent. He began a program of centralization, which included the decision to phase out the district offices and run the organization from the capital, in order to exert more political pressure on the statehouse to counter the influence of wet activists.[3] In short, Shumaker was transforming the IASL from an organization that lobbied churches to one that lobbied politicians on behalf of the dry cause. It was the next obvious step in the crusade for reform.

The IASL was ready for another legislative initiative. Thanks to the Nicholson and Moore laws, dry territory in Indiana was expanding, and Shumaker wanted to add more. Though the League's ultimate goal of "abolishing the saloons" never changed, drys saw it as a means to grow into full prohibition. They were not, however, interested in passing a statewide law that was unenforceable (as had happened in Alabama).[4] Drys concluded that county option—a form of local option that allowed entire counties to vote out the saloon, thus negating wet urban enclaves—was the next step. League branches in Illinois, Oregon, and Kentucky were agitating for it with a good deal of success. Not surprisingly, the IASL under Shumaker also began calling for it.[5]

To build public support for county option, Shumaker launched a series of field days around Indiana. He brought the IASL for the first time into Wayne County, where, advocating "straight out local option," he labeled the saloon a "trap" that, if destroyed, would bring salvation to "prodigal sons" and "fallen daughters." Shortly after Shumaker and the IASL visited Noblesville, the city's ministers began to speak out in favor of county option, even those who usually voted for the Prohibition Party.[6]

The shift toward more active participation in politics necessitated a change in rhetoric. Shumaker's argument during these field days was increasingly an economic one, superseding his use of moral suasion. Making a city dry was deemed a boon for businesses because it gave people more disposable income. The League also hammered home its support from business owners, many of whom believed that saloons were bad for both workers' productivity and their companies' bottom line. In Columbus, for example, Shumaker told his audience that if the city stayed wet, neighboring dry towns would surpass it in prosperity because businessmen preferred to invest in dry communities. Brewers were concerned about the force of this economic argument.[7]

Not all Hoosier businesses supported the dry effort. The Indiana Manufacturing and Merchants' Club, a consortium of glass and bottle companies allied to the brewers, vowed to attack any prohibition legislation and to "educate" Hoosiers on the "hysteria" caused by the IASL. According to the organization, if the state ever went dry, Indiana would be ruined economically because nearly $1 billion was invested in the liquor trade. Nor did everyone want to live in a dry community. In Marion County's Washington Township, for example, wets in Broad Ripple attempted to merge their village with Indianapolis in order to drink freely.[8]

Despite wet opposition, drys had shaped public opinion by the dawn of 1908. The *Indianapolis News* now predicted that both the Republicans and Democrats would include some form of local option in their state party platforms. Indiana Republicans were already expected to support county option. Governor J. Frank Hanly was for it, and his rhetoric intensified in his "I Hate It" speech at the party convention, where he blasted alcohol as an "unholy traffic" that should "find no safe habitation anywhere beneath Old Glory's stainless stars." The newspapers believed that the governor's political record "as a moral crusader" had created a "New Republicanism" in Indiana that could launch him into the national sphere of politics. Hanly's endorsement was something of a double-edged sword, however, as there were those who resented his "highhanded tactics" in pushing a moral agenda.[9]

Indiana Republican chairman James P. Goodrich had to reconcile these factions as his party headed into the campaign season. Like his opposite in the Democratic Party, Thomas Taggart, Goodrich took Indiana's politics and its place in the nation seriously. He had no problem with mixing politics and religion. Known as a "partisan Presbyterian," he often surprised politicians by working on Sunday school lessons during breaks in political meetings and rarely missing church services at home in Winchester. But he was also a political strategist who worried about the proper mix of sacred reform in elections, especially the volatile energy of the dry cause.[10]

Goodrich led a seriously divided party. The factions around Vice President Charles Fairbanks and Senator Albert Beveridge supported different candidates for the party's nomination for governor. Fairbanks endorsed Congressman James E. Watson, while Beveridge backed former state attorney general Charles Miller. Hanly, who was nominally a Fairbanks supporter, also backed Miller and urged Goodrich to keep Watson out of the race. Though refusing to block Watson, the Republican chairman did tell him that he could not win the general election because he was not consistent on temperance. Goodrich would later say of Watson that "he has no moral foundation on which to build." Shumaker was supporting a third candidate and was convinced that Beveridge had cut a deal with the brewers. For his part, the senator believed that the IASL was being "hoodwinked" by saloon people into accepting Watson.[11]

Goodrich's qualms about Watson were important, especially if county option was going to be the defining issue of the campaign. The congressman's position on liquor laws varied with his audience. While telling his fellow Methodists, and even the party regulars at the convention, that he endorsed county option with vigor and devoting most of his acceptance speech to this "paramount issue," Watson had enjoyed a good laugh with President Roosevelt over the cocktail fiasco at Vice President Fairbanks's home. Nor could Watson work with Hanly, in private telling all who would listen that the county option plank was a mistake. Though the dry faithful never rallied around him, Watson's opponents refused to unite against him at the convention, and he won the nomination after four ballots.[12]

The Democrats also had their share of convention drama in 1908 thanks to local option. One plank in their party platform endorsed a township and ward provision, which would allow wet areas the chance to exist in dry counties. The Democratic plan walked a fine line between advocating temperance and pacifying the fears of some of the party's chief financial supporters, the brewers. The candidates for the Democratic nomination were Thomas Marshall, a well-liked lawyer (and recovering alcoholic who was now dry) from Columbia City who pledged to uphold the party platform; State Senator L. Ert Slack, a noted temperance supporter from Franklin; Samuel Ralston, party boss Thomas Taggart's candidate from Lebanon; and C. G. Conn, a wealthy musical-instrument maker from Elkhart. Through five rounds of balloting, Slack, whom many saw as the anti-Taggart candidate, gained delegates and was firmly in second place. In the third round, he pulled ahead of Ralston and seemed on his way to victory. But in between the fourth and fifth rounds, Taggart put nearly all of Ralston's support into Marshall's camp, thus cutting a deal to stop Slack and preserve the party's brewer support.[13]

With both parties putting temperance in their platforms, newspapers around the state called it "the paramount issue in Indiana." Discussion of limiting the power of the saloons touched a nerve with Hoosier voters. The *Peru Evening Journal* argued that the people of Indiana were not for prohibition so much as they were against the saloon and wanted alcohol-related corruption out of politics. Tellingly, there was dissent within both parties. Dry Democrats did not like Taggart's alliance with the brewers (despite the money it ensured), while wet Republicans preferred township/ward option to county option.[14]

Where some observers saw an election issue, Hanly saw an opportunity. The governor contemplated calling a special session of the General Assembly to enact county option before the November election. This thought became a conviction after the Indiana Methodist Conference, where he declared liquor forces evil and labeled Marshall the "brewers' candidate." He believed that the law would be the capstone of his administration. Other factors influenced his decision as well. Politically, there was growing concern among dry Republicans that Watson could not be trusted to push the issue on his own, and there were even reports that the Republican state ticket was in trouble and needed to be revitalized. There was also a belief, thanks in part to the Chautauqua movement, that now was the time to act. The IASL thought that county option was so popular at the grassroots that the law would make the state dry in as little as two years.[15]

Therefore, on 4 September 1908, Hanly called for a special session. In his opening address, the governor pleaded with the reassembled legislature to give the people of Indiana county option. He argued that "the traffic in intoxicating liquors is owned and controlled today by a few men. The independent retail dealer, owner of his place of business and responsible to the community where he does business and in which he lives, is fast becoming a memory." According to the governor, "if it is right to enact it [county option] next January, it is right to enact it in September."[16]

Reaction to the governor's plea was not enthusiastic in Democratic quarters. The *Indianapolis Sun* wrote that Hanly had destroyed Republican hopes of victory by reconvening the legislature. Even some Republican newspapers had misgivings. The *South Bend Tribune* said that the governor apparently believed that he was a "law unto himself." The *Indianapolis Star*, like papers on both sides of the aisle, worried about attempting to solve an "election issue" by special session, no matter how Hanly felt.[17] Most of the Republican press, however, supported the governor. This group included Watson's hometown newspaper, the *Rushville Daily Republican*, and the *Starke County Republican* called Hanly's decision to reconvene the legislature "wise and courageous." Many observers saw it as an opportunity for the party to prove its temperance convictions. According to the *Knightstown Banner*, passing the county option bill was the only way Republicans could win in the fall.[18]

Still, many Republican leaders were angry with the governor for forcing them to go on record about reform legislation before the election. Some hoped that the legislature would convene and then adjourn in a single day without voting. Others feared the ramifications of breaking deals they had made with local brewers. However, they put on a united front in public. Watson, who admitted his concern privately to newspapermen, came out in favor of passing county option. Senator Beveridge told state Republicans to stand by the platform. Attorney General James Bingham, a staunch supporter of Hanly's crusade against liquor, now supported the session because the bill would take the issue out of politics.[19]

Goodrich worked hard to deliver this show of unity, despite his own misgivings about the special session. He hoped it would provide the party with some impetus to campaign as actively as the Democrats had. According to his diaries, Goodrich did not "believe the people will sustain us—the saloon and brewers vote as they believe. Temperance people don't." However, this had nothing to do with his faith in the morality of temperance, which he called a "righteous cause."[20]

All eyes now turned to the statehouse. While the Democratic leadership hoped to make county option a party measure, state and national brewers organized to stop it. Taggart ordered them to spend money but to keep a low profile in Indianapolis. Rumors circulated of large-scale bribes of money and beer to sway lawmakers to vote wet. However, Republicans united behind the bill that the IASL had drafted, taking care to ensure that it would not interfere with Nicholson-Moore. Hanly not only supported the League's effort but also made sure that there were no competing pieces of legislation.[21]

The proceedings were not what many observers had come to expect in a gathering of lawmakers, largely due to Shumaker's bringing the full weight of the IASL to bear upon the special session. He and the governor rallied the state's Methodists to the special session cause, urging the denomination's conferences to send people to Indianapolis to fight for county option.[22] Eventually, over 2,000 Methodist ministers set up a prayer and song vigil on the statehouse steps, which one reporter deemed the "greatest demonstration ever given an Indiana legislature." The state's Presbyterian ministers and dry delegations from over a dozen cities joined the Methodists in Indianapolis. In all, some 10,000 drys took part in the rally "with banners and cheers for local option." Cass County's delegation bore signs, which took over twenty people to hold, that stretched nearly the length of the stairs leading into the statehouse. The weight of petition "rolls" required legislative pages to shoulder them in order to bring them before representatives and senators. Drys were everywhere, singing "America" and praying. Governor Hanly even joined the throng.[23]

The rally enabled drys to exert incredible political pressure by using what the *Crawford County Democrat* called the "amen corner" tactic. Working in groups, drys surrounded legislators as they walked around the statehouse and then peppered them with requests to vote for county option. The pressure worked, even causing one representative to weep as he voted for the bill but against his brewer financial support.[24] In this supercharged atmosphere, tensions mounted. Police were called in to clear the House gallery when county option supporters "threatened" several wet state representatives. Over one hundred men and women were forced into the hallways to return order to the proceedings. After the near mêlée, drys temporarily moved their meeting out of the statehouse.[25]

During the session, Shumaker ran into Crawford Fairbanks, the owner of the Terre Haute Brewery. Fairbanks was one of the state's leading manufacturers, co-owner of Taggart's hotel in French Lick, and a major contributor to both the state and national Democratic parties.[26] The *Terre Haute Tribune* reported their meeting as follows:

"I have heard of you before," said Fairbanks. "Yes, and I have heard of you," said Superintendent Shumaker. "You don't look like a bad man," said Shumaker. "No," dryly observed Mr. Fairbanks, "and I haven't got any horns. And, by the way," he added, "you don't look like a very ferocious person." "I'm not," said Shumaker. "I'm the very mildest kind of a man, but I'm against the brewing business." "Sure, you have a right to be if you want to," said Mr. Fairbanks. For 15 minutes the two men discussed the temperance question. Thomas Taggart came along and slapped Fairbanks on the back. "Fight it out," he said, "you're both good fellows." "I guess we have got to fight this thing out," said the brewer to his new acquaintance. "If you beat us we will have no complaint to make." Fairbanks sought to explain to the temperance advocate that beer as compared with whisky is not harmful. "Come down to Terre Haute some day and go through our plant," said Fairbanks. "We'll show you something that will surprise you." "I'll do it," said Shumaker, "for I am always open to argument." "I rather like that man," said Shumaker later. "He talks straight out from the shoulder." "He's not such a bad sort of fellow after all" said the brewer to his friends at dinner. "I like a man who shows you where he stands."[27]

Despite the congenial meeting, tensions between wets and drys were mounting. This was especially clear within the Democratic caucus. Taggart threatened any Democrat voting for county option with no monetary support for the election, this prompting drys, including Hanly, to rally to those on Taggart's blacklist. Senator Slack promised not to tie Marshall's hands by voting for county option, but he publicly endorsed the measure all the same. For his part, Marshall said that members of the state legislature should vote their conscience.[28]

Then came the actual vote. Though Republicans controlled both chambers, drys took nothing for granted. In the House, the Republican floor leader was replaced because he did not adequately support county option. When the lower chamber refused to kill the bill, cheers erupted from dry supporters in the gallery. The final vote was 55 to 45 in favor of county option. When news of the vote reached the *Seymour Daily Republican*, the paper commented, "The greatest victory for good morals in the recent history of Indiana was won this morning." When the bill passed the Senate, the *Rochester Republican* commented that "men and women weep for joy and the voices of the strong tremble with emotion, and temperance people go wild with enthusiasm at the passage of the measure."[29]

Republicans were ecstatic. Goodrich said that the party was pleased with the passage of county option. The people would keep faith with the party at the polls, because the party had kept faith with the people. Republican press reaction was nearly unanimous in its support. The *Winchester Journal* noted that by passing county option, the Republican Party was as "superior" as it claimed. The *Delphi Journal* called the passage "a great triumph." The *Brookville American* said that the party was now in a "commanding position" for the rest of the campaign. The *Rushville Daily Republican* believed that the bill marked "the end of the greatest political battle ever fought in Indiana." And the *Indianapolis Star* ran an editorial cartoon depicting Marshall walking away from the crashed ruins of his campaign, blown down by the strength of the winds of "public opinion for county option."[30]

The reaction was not as joyful in other quarters. Democratic-leaning papers such as the *Crawfordsville Journal* called county option a "drastic" measure. The *Daviess County Democrat* labeled it "a great humbug" and feared that the Republican plan would turn every home in the state into a saloon. The *New Albany Daily Ledger* said it was nothing more than a Republican election-year ploy. And the *Terre Haute Tribune* believed that the people should have decided the issue at the polls, not have it dictated to them.[31] Nor was the Prohibition Party satisfied. The *Patriot Phalanx* believed that existing dry laws were doomed if either Marshall or Watson was elected and called on the legislature to pass a prohibition bill. When the House heeded their call, the Senate quickly killed the measure. The *Vincennes Commercial* reported that ministers and the IASL were on hand for the vote but did nothing to save the bill.[32]

Hanly wasted no time in signing the county option bill into law. Shumaker escorted the legislative delegation to the governor's office, where Goodrich and many IASL luminaries were awaiting the ceremony. The governor used four pens to sign the legislation and gave one to Shumaker. The dry leader promptly "pressed it to his lips" and placed it in his pocket, telling the gathered press that his "father had carried this pen through the civil war." A moment of silence after the governor finished was broken by Shumaker, who leaned down to Hanly and said, "this is the crowning success of your administration."[33]

Shumaker told reporters that the IASL planned a spring push for county option elections in all of Indiana's ninety-two counties. He called the new law "the greatest victory ever won for the moral and religious forces in this state and no small share of credit is due to the united action of the ministers of the state, who stood loyally by the Anti-Saloon League in this fight." Methodist bishops, meeting in Indianapolis, echoed that sentiment. The League predicted that with county option in place, coupled with the Nicholson-Moore remonstrance, the only counties still with saloons by 1910 would be Lake, LaPorte, St. Joseph, Allen, Vigo, Marion, Clark, Floyd, Dubois, Vanderburgh, and Posey. Shumaker told an IASL meeting in Williamsport that Indianapolis brewer Albert Lieber believed that eighty-four counties would be dry under the new law, and Shumaker himself thought that the entire state would be dry by 1912.[34]

A spirit of cautious optimism pervaded Hoosier drys. The *Warren Review* commented that both sides had had thousands of lobbyists at the statehouse, but that the Republicans had triumphed because they were correct. The brewers, the paper warned, were out to control the state and must be stopped. Drys were urged to reach out to wets and work out how the law could be enforced. Newspapers also requested pledges from both parties to uphold Nicholson-Moore no matter what the outcome was in November.[35]

Taggart had lost the battle in the legislature to Shumaker and Goodrich, despite putting intense pressure on Democrats to toe the party line. Both his desire to get party line votes and his nominee had undermined his efforts. But he had powerful friends. Many brewers, including Lieber, felt betrayed by Hanly and the special session because of their past support of Republican candidates. Lieber vowed to Goodrich that he and his fellows would "get even with the damn lying Son of a B[itch]." The Democrats were prepared to help angry brewers do just that.[36]

While Taggart solidified brewer support, Marshall hit the campaign trail. He reiterated his belief that the Democratic plan of township and ward option was the best form of temperance for the state and should replace county option. Marshall vowed as governor to keep the Nicholson and Moore laws. He promised never to pressure the legislature to pass bills not in the best interests of Indiana, thus implying that Hanly and Watson had done so during the special session. And, to counter Republican queries of what he would have done had a county option bill come to his desk as governor, Marshall quipped that he never signed anything he had not read.[37]

Marshall, more than Taggart, it seems, set the tone for the Democratic counterattack. The candidate and the party made Hanly the issue. The *Pike County Democrat* charged that the governor obviously did not trust Hoosiers to choose for themselves which version of local option they wanted for Indiana. The *Corydon Democrat* said that Hanly had used the office of governor to perpetuate his own "greed." Such opinions were common in the state, even among Republicans. Many people believed that Hanly's ultimate goal was political advancement to either the U.S. Senate or the White House.[38]

The brewers attempted to link the IASL with the Prohibition Party as a way to associate in voters' minds county option and prohibition. For their part, the Prohibitionists took the opportunity to attack the League, by asking ministers not to endorse any form of local option.[39] Shumaker and the IASL were forced to step up their rhetoric in response. The dry leader called the present situation a "crisis," saying that wets did not want to debate local option by degree but rather hoped to destroy both it and the remonstrance. Drys were urged to safeguard their cause at the polls.[40]

Not everyone thought it wise for the IASL to align itself so closely with the Republican Party's platform. The *Sullivan Democrat*, which professed support for the League, warned that by backing county option the IASL was interjecting partisanship into its work. When the Terre Haute Ministerial Association met with the League to discuss the election, some members complained that they were being told whom to vote for. Dissent was even more overt in the Indianapolis Ministerial Association, which publicly split over supporting county option after a fight broke out over whether Watson was a drinker and thus deserving of their endorsement. Not all such meetings were so contentious. The Indiana Conference of the Methodist Church endorsed local option in 1908, not statewide prohibition, and the IASL persuaded Columbus Civic League to back county option legislation as well.[41]

Marshall attempted to turn this dissension to his advantage. A staunch Presbyterian who did not trust the IASL, the Democratic nominee attacked the political organizing of ministers by the Republicans; according to him, pastors should stay out of politics. Democratic papers rallied to the sentiment that politicians should not use churches to further partisan goals. Some even made Marshall into a defender of ministers against those unprincipled politicians in the Republican "machine" who were manipulating the state's pastors for their own political ends. The IASL was charged with being "hypocritical" because of its close alliance with the Republican Party, and perhaps it may have even been under its direct control.[42]

The League and its allies condemned Marshall's statements. The Democratic nominee was denounced from Hoosier pulpits for saying that ministers had no place in the political process. Pastors argued that "nine-tenths of all reformers throughout history have been preachers"; that churches had a right to talk about "concrete" sins, not just sin in the "abstract"; that pastors served the Church of Christ, not the brewers of the state, and so on. Others exhorted their congregations and denominations to support only county option candidates. The Republican press joined in, endorsing the "civic right" of pastors to speak out on political issues and doubting if brewers would find it very easy "to put the preachers out of business." The *Columbus Evening Republican* depicted Marshall in a cartoon as being repeatedly stung by a hornet's nest of ministers.[43]

In the wake of this debate, the Republican strategy became one of linking Marshall and the Democratic Party to the saloons. Both Attorney General Bingham and Watson talked of "the saloon-Democracy bond." Indeed, the candidate hit new levels of rhetoric with the issue. In Fort Wayne, Watson blasted the Democrats by saying that a Marshall victory would be a victory for the brewers. He also attacked the Democratic township and ward plan as an attempt by the wets to gerrymander support for their cause. In a speech in Seymour, he said that the plan advocated by Marshall would only serve to undermine the Nicholson remonstrance law, which, he pointed out, had been passed by Republicans.[44]

Despite these Republican efforts, Marshall remained evasive on the liquor issue. The *Crawfordsville Journal*, for example, pressed the Democratic nominee, who was a trustee of Wabash College, on how he could support a plan that would allow "saloon influence" to continue on campus when his opponent's plan would eliminate it. Marshall, sticking to his post–special election strategy, shifted the discussion by blasting the paper for what he called a smear on the reputation of the college. Despite the *Journal*'s demand that he answer the question, the Democrat opted to ignore it.[45]

Having decided that it was easier to beat Watson than to stop county option at the statehouse, the brewers launched a "systematic" campaign in support of Marshall and worked to convince wet Republicans to back him. They ordered his picture to be displayed in their saloons. Their allies in the Indiana Federation of Labor attacked Watson's record on unions. Crawford Fairbanks paid to have posters and billboards depicting ghost towns in Kansas erected throughout the state with the implication that this was the fate of Indiana communities under county option. Handbills saying that county option equaled prohibition were also distributed. Brewer campaign literature declared George Washington a saloon man and called temperance people "anarchists." Wets also spread rumors (some true) about Watson and his tendency to talk temperance in public while courting brewer support in private.[46]

As Republicans pinned their hopes on county option, the question became whether Watson's blatant straddling of the issue could compete with Marshall's honesty.[47] Drys were worried. Shumaker admitted publicly that because the Democrat had the brewers' support, the IASL was actively backing Watson for governor. That partisanship had entered the League was difficult for him to admit. In a Williamsport meeting shortly after passage of the county option law, he had claimed that the IASL was not part of the political process and should remain outside it. But the scale of the brewers' onslaught as well as his own partisan leanings compelled him to take the field for Watson.[48]

Shumaker had to contend not only with the brewers but also with attempts by wets to use race and ethnicity as wedge issues. The continental Sabbath, after all, had its defenders. Among Shumaker's staunchest critics was Phillip Rappaport, a prominent Indianapolis attorney and secretary of both the Indiana German Alliance and the Indiana Manufacturing and Merchants' Club, who claimed that the IASL and the Methodist Church had used "coercion" on the state legislature to deny people their "personal liberty." Rappaport said that county option was prohibition and had nothing to do with true temperance. He urged the state's German population to vote Democratic in order to preserve personal liberty against state intrusion and the "yoke" of "religious fanatics," not to mention the high crime and even higher taxes that would result if Marshall was not elected. The IASL was called a political organization that sought to "dominate and dictate" to the German people.[49]

For Shumaker, the personal liberty argument rang hollow. Drys saw the term as a code for the wet immigrant continental Sabbath. Nor could they understand how their wet opponents could justify "the right to sell death-dealing drugs." To drys, it was not a matter of the "right" to do business or to drink, but rather a cause-and-effect relationship between the selling of alcohol and the damage that drinking did to the individual, the family, and to wider society. It was impossible to deal with those associated problems without eliminating their source.[50] Wets, on the other hand, saw these problems as loosely related at best, with individual responsibility as the proper way to alleviate them.

According to some observers, the brewers' actions and the IASL's response revived Watson's stalling campaign. After Republicans charged that the brewers were attempting to "vilify" Watson, his supporters rushed to his defense. The wet attacks seemed to clarify the stakes of the election for drys and Republicans: it was county option or "the breweries and the brothels." The *Rochester Republican* blasted the "Democratic Liquor Alliance Confederation" for "prostituting" the Indiana Labor Federation. The *Bloomfield News* argued that since all temperance legislation in Indiana's history had been passed by Republicans, then every dry, regardless of party, owed Watson his vote.[51]

The race was extremely close as Election Day neared. Though some observers advised caution, the *Rushville Daily Republican* reported that the campaign rally held by Watson for his hometown had a distinct "air of victory" about it. The paper did not think that Marshall was a bad person, but that his friends were. It was pleased when in the last week of the campaign the brewers finally admitted that they were supporting the Democratic nominee.[52] However, the hopes of both Republicans and many drys were soon quashed. Despite Indiana going for William Howard Taft, the state voted in its first Democratic governor of the twentieth century. Taft's margin over William Jennings Bryan was 16,745 votes. Marshall defeated Watson by nearly the same margin, but many citizens who cast their ballot for Taft did not vote for Indiana's Republican gubernatorial nominee.[53]

In a postelection interview in November 1908, Watson blamed his defeat on county option. He said that it divided the Republican

Party, allowed temperance Democrats and Prohibitionists to not vote for him, and helped turn labor against him. He held this conviction for the rest of his life. No matter how fast they closed ranks following the special session, after the Republican defeat many newspaper editors, abetted by Watson, unleashed their fury at Hanly for pushing county option before the election. The *Starke County Republican*, which in April had called the decision to hold the special session "wise and courageous," now said that the Republicans had lost because they had gotten ahead of the people on temperance. The *South Bend Tribune* also blamed Watson's defeat on Hanly. Further, the *Vincennes Commercial* called the governor a "howling political hypocrite" and an "ingrate" who had destroyed the Republican Party in Indiana.[54]

The reasons for Watson's defeat were more complex than his supporters were willing to admit. Obviously, with county option off the table, dry Democrats had little reason to break party lines and vote for the Republican candidate. However, they almost certainly did not support the Prohibition Party, despite Taggart's efforts to bolster its members' attractiveness to drys of both parties. The party's vote was too small to affect the outcome, as the Prohibitionists themselves were divided. Eli Ritter and other party leaders had endorsed Watson before the election because county option was acceptable to them in the short term. Besides, Watson had plenty of problems beyond county option. During the campaign, Democrats tied the Republican to unpopular labor laws and successfully raised ethical and moral questions about Watson's close relationship with embattled Congressman Joseph "Uncle Joe" Cannon of Illinois. Not even his pandering to drys could overcome these liabilities.[55]

Further analysis undermines Watson's assertions even more. The *Indianapolis News* believed that the people of the state had rejected the Republican nominee because they were ready for a change. It discounted the idea that the brewers and saloonkeepers had won a victory, and it praised the lobbying efforts of the IASL during the special session while chastising drys for being partisan in the fall campaign. The more the *News* looked at the results, the less it seemed that county option played a significant role in the outcome. Labor leaders had told Republican bosses that Watson was an unacceptable candidate prior to the convention. The *Indianapolis Star* doubted if the brewers' endorsement of Marshall had even helped him. In the end, Hoosiers had voted for a man of character and paid little attention to who supported him. The *Greencastle Herald* chided the IASL for not doing its own investigation of Marshall's record and instead for relying on Republican Party operatives to give a slanted view of the Democratic standard bearer.[56]

The election defeat forced Shumaker and the IASL to move up their county option timetable. They decided to organize county option elections wherever they could as soon as possible. Drys sought "psychological victories," since repeal of the law would not affect valid results. Though the state WCTU also called for county option elections, the dry cause remained fractured, as the Prohibition Party refused to join the fight. The three dry organizations could agree only on a joint declaration of opposition to high-fee licenses. The Republican Party was skittish, and some leaders openly discussed dropping their support for county option.[57] Reports from around the state cast doubt on how well current dry laws were being enforced and if county option would be any different. Additionally, wets such as Rappaport were out on the stump calling for an end to the law before it was even passed.[58]

The IASL was undaunted, and, as 1909 dawned, it was hard at work fighting for county option. Petitions were circulated, rallies held, Republican egos massaged, and early victories celebrated. However, the League ran into problems with communities divided over the idea, with opponents arguing "personal liberty," and police and saloonkeepers working together to curb problems ahead of local elections. By June, all ninety-two Indiana counties had voted on county option, and, as Shumaker had predicted, the vast majority (seventy) went dry. The Prohibition Party refused to see this as a success, since not every county went dry.[59]

Drys faced the prospect of what Indiana's new governor was going to do even as elections were being held. Thomas Marshall wanted to control, not eliminate, the traffic in alcohol; and once he was able to gain a Democratic majority in Indianapolis, he pushed for repeal of county option. In 1910, Marshall made a direct appeal to Hoosier voters to give him a Democratic-controlled statehouse in order to enact reforms. That fall, his party captured a 21-seat majority in the House and a 12-seat majority in the formerly Republican-controlled Senate. During the campaign, most Republican candidates decided not even to discuss county option out of fear that the issue would burn them again.[60]

Democrats were now positioned to enact their version of reform, though they were not united on what form it should take. The *Indianapolis Sun*, which supported Marshall, asked Democrats to keep Nicholson-Moore intact even though county option had to go. The paper wanted a new law with severe penalties for violators and the ability for local officials to revoke saloon licenses. Independent saloon owners wanted the brewers expelled from the business. For their part, brewers continued to stress the importance of individual responsibility in dealing with alcohol-related problems.[61]

Most observers expected a bitter fight as the 1911 session of the Indiana legislature commenced. The IASL begged Democrats not to repeal county option. At a public hearing, Shumaker brought newspaperman Fred Rohrer from Berne, industrialist Frank Ball from Muncie, and members of the Indianapolis Ministerial Association to press the IASL's case before the legislature. Nevertheless, Democrats did not believe that the majority of Hoosiers supported county option and went ahead with plans to repeal the law. The Indiana Brewers Association sent the Democratic senators cork insoles for their shoes to help prevent "cold feet" when it came time to vote on the measure.[62]

The governor's point man for change was Senator Robert E. Proctor of Elkhart County. Like Marshall, Proctor believed that prohibition would fail because it would be impossible to enforce and that saloons were better than blind tigers. He fashioned legislation that placed restrictions on who could hold a license (barring noncitizens, recent residents, and those who had been convicted of a liquor-law violation in the past four years), stipulated that each applicant could hold a single license, and required the posting of a bond in case of violations. Proctor also tied the number of licenses that could be issued to size of population and gave local communities the power to screen applicants, set their own license costs, and revoke the licenses of those who violated the law. Repealing county option and replacing it with Proctor's bill was not a problem, but securing all its provisions was. Proctor wanted to set the license fee high enough to restrict the liquor trade, warning of "chaos" if it was too low. He also had to deal with competing legislation offered by Democratic senator Stephen B. Flemming from Fort Wayne, the president of the Indiana Association of Brewers, who wanted to replace county option with a bill asking brewers to be on their best behavior. In the end, Proctor largely triumphed, and his bill was hailed as driving the saloon out of politics.[63]

The ideas behind Proctor's bill were based on a perception of saloons that Shumaker did not accept. Its proponents believed, founded on the prohibition experiences of Georgia and Kansas, that legal saloons were better than blind tigers. While agreeing with drys that laws already on the books needed to be enforced, they also thought that the liquor traffic was legitimate. As historian Jack Blocker has shown, many drys were against high-fee licenses for this very reason. Former judge Samuel R. Artman, in *The Legalized Outlaw* (1908), had argued that only the revenues made by the different levels of the government from licenses and taxes were keeping saloons in business.[64] Shumaker and the IASL stood against Proctor's legislation because it did not actually prohibit the sale of alcohol. The dry leader called license-generated revenue "a direct bribe to induce citizens to tolerate and sustain the most destructive of all evils when otherwise they would prohibit it." Higher-fee licenses did keep some bad men out of the business, but the IASL believed that they also allowed the brewers to consolidate their control over the industry.[65]

In March 1911, Marshall signed both the Proctor local option and high-fee license bills into law, thus ending county option. His action proved to dry newspapers "that the Democratic Party is the Liquor Party." Yet, the governor forbade a "gala" celebration for the signing, even turning down the offer of a gold pen. Marshall told Democratic editors that "I am not allied to the liquor interest and I formed no alliance with them when I signed the bill." A reformed drinker himself, Marshall's words carried extra weight beyond the authority of his office. Senator Proctor warned saloonkeepers to abide by the law, or "something worse" might happen to them.[66]

The coming of the Proctor law brought condemnation from Indiana's Methodists. At a denominational gathering in Kokomo, Shumaker lambasted the brewers for being the source of all drunkenness
in the state. Before the meeting adjourned, a resolution condemning
Governor Marshall was passed. Hoosier Methodists were astounded
that Marshall would later seek the vice presidency after what they
believed to be his assault on their progressive reform in Indiana.[67]

With the new law, wets quickly filed petitions for elections in cities and townships. A week after the repeal of county option, fourteen
such elections were organized. Supporters believed that the Proctor law would generate revenue for municipalities that brought back
saloons. Brewers ordered their saloons to avoid violations, but not
everyone was ready to follow the fine points of the law after years
of open resistance. Saloon owners contested the right of county com-
missioners to deny them licenses and of city councils to raise license
fees. When the South Bend city council refused to raise the fees as
many drys had hoped, it was pointed out that three of the council's
five members owned saloons. In practice, then, Proctor's restrictions
were weak and its temperance achievement spotty. This realization
prompted the *South Bend Tribune* to declare that the "brewers reign
supreme."[68]

Overall, the Proctor law elections divided urban and rural areas
within counties. They also caused drys to see their cause with increasing moral clarity. When Johnson County stayed dry, the victory
was attributed to the "civic righteousness" and "moral conviction" of
its residents. When a Proctor election was planned for Bloomington,
the *Indiana Daily Student* called on students to protect the honor of
Indiana University by turning out and voting against the wets. The
paper pointed out that "West Lafayette, Crawfordsville, and Greencastle the homes of the three most prominent rivals of Indiana are
all dry towns. Since the elimination of the saloons several years ago
both the town and the University have made unusual progress. The
present welfare and the future prosperity of Indiana University de-
pends, in a large measure, on the outcome of the local election."[69]

With the passage of the law, the Prohibition Party set out to
seize control of the dry cause from the IASL. The party believed that

Shumaker's attempt to sway Democrats in the state legislature with petitions to maintain county option had only succeeded in keeping drys busy. Nor did the *Patriot Phalanx* see much reason for Shumaker to boast about forcing a "better" Proctor law out of the Democrats. The Prohibitionists demanded to know why the League refused to support prohibition legislation, what the finances of the IASL were, and why it took credit for the work of others. It was time, the *Phalanx* said, for the state's drys to rally around the Prohibition Party.[70]

Shumaker was forced to fight off this attack while also combatting wets. He set out to raise much-needed funds, brought in speakers from Illinois and Ohio to bolster the spirits of dry reformers, and even agreed to debate the Prohibition Party on why the League's methods were better at advancing the dry agenda. He pointed out that it was difficult to work politically with the Prohibition Party since it had no elected officials in the state. He fired back at accusations made by the *Patriot Phalanx* that money received from IASL field days was used for "fat salaries." To the Prohibitionists' charge that the League's headquarters committee was all Republican, Shumaker countered that its members were also some of the most respected ministers in Indianapolis.[71]

The Prohibition Party and Shumaker could agree, however, that the Reverend W. C. Helt was now a danger to the dry cause. Ever since Watson's defeat, Helt had been estranged from the IASL. His desire to find a "rational" way to advance reform caused Shumaker to fire him. Shortly thereafter, Helt became "converted" to the idea that saloons should be strictly regulated by the state, a notion very similar to the interests of the liquor forces he had once attacked. Both Shumaker and the party believed that the brewers had purchased Helt, who now formed the Rational Reform League to combat the IASL and enlisted likeminded ministers to speak across the state on the themes of increased vice in dry areas, the money hunger of the ASL, and the unprofessionalism of the WCTU.[72] It is difficult to know why Helt left the IASL. Perhaps he felt slighted over not being named state superintendent in 1907 or he had actually changed his views. However, he found little support, and the new organization quickly faded from the scene.

The Helt defection caused Shumaker to consider a change in tactics. He wrote to the head of the ASL, the Reverend P. A. Baker, to find out the League's position on a prohibition constitutional amendment. Shumaker wanted to push for county option, but there was a growing sentiment within the IASL to back a constitutional amendment. Baker replied that "the people" should find candidates who would pledge to support an amendment while the League worked within the state legislatures toward the same goal. Baker went on to say that Shumaker either must do what his state committee instructed, change their minds, or resign. It was the ASL leader's way of not so subtly reminding Shumaker that state superintendents could be replaced.[73]

Shumaker was increasingly coming under attack. Newspapers said that he was "making an ass of himself" by constantly seeking headlines and that his posturing had to do more with his own employment than with the dry crusade. A pamphlet written by Charles G. Sefrit, entitled "Concerning Mr. Shumaker," claimed that Shumaker used "emotional agitation" to keep himself employed. Sefrit termed the professionalization of the dry cause under Shumaker a "disgusting commercialism" that needed to stop.[74]

There is no doubt that Shumaker had overplayed his hand in the 1908 election. While he had a solid statewide network in place, he had used it before establishing his own reputation beyond Northern Indiana. Unlike James Goodrich, who was able to view the legislative process in a detached manner, Shumaker approached politics naively. By openly backing Watson, he retarded rather than advanced the cause he had committed his life to. Furthermore, Shumaker had underestimated the influence that brewers had as a big business while shifting his rhetoric from morality to economics.[75] He had learned some hard lessons since becoming superintendent and would not repeat these mistakes again.

4 | Shumaker Victorious

The Hoosier dry crusade faltered in 1908, but in the decade that followed, Edward Shumaker revamped the Indiana Anti Saloon League and led it to unprecedented successes. By 1917, the forces of dry order were victorious in both Indiana and the nation. Yet, drys soon discovered that the kingdom of God had to be built in the face of persistent opposition; it did not emerge fully formed with the mere passing of legislation. The resulting struggle tested the veracity, scope, and depth of the cause as well as Shumaker's abilities as a leader.

Shumaker's decision to remain in Indiana, rather than move to another state as other ASL leaders did, was key to the eventual dry victory there. Staying allowed him to consolidate and strengthen his power base and ensured that the IASL had both continuity in its leadership and an established relationship with the national office. He became "an exceptionally good organizer and a good politician" during the years following the 1908 debacle, which earned him respect and allowed him to make the IASL into the premier dry organization in the state.[1]

Long-term victory meant abandoning county option, however. With the advent of the automobile, drys discovered the flaws in their local option plan. Improved transportation made it possible for liquor dealers to locate on county lines as well as for brewers to sell alcohol by mail to wets residing in dry counties. Drys believed that in this increasingly mobile world, people needed to be sober. No one wanted "to ride a railroad train run by an engineer whose brain is beclouded with alcohol." Even Henry Ford chimed in, saying, "I wouldn't be interested in putting automobiles in the hands of a generation soggy with drink." Horses could be trusted to find their way home with a drunkard in control. Cars could not. As county option fell out of favor, drys looked at the dispensary system, but direct state control of alcohol, in places such as South Carolina, only tied state revenues directly to alcohol sales. Nor did high license fees hold much attraction for drys since governments would not want to deny themselves the revenues from saloons. Drys also doubted if fees would ever be high enough to cover the societal costs associated with saloons. Thus, prohibition became the only viable option for the dry cause.[2]

Shumaker was now ready to embrace prohibition ideology. The change in message rekindled dry optimism in Indiana and helped "weld together the religious and moral forces of the state into one great fighting army." With the cooperation of Indiana's churches, Shumaker created a stronger grassroots organization, built upon temperance Sundays, county conventions, and "enthusiastic" local organizations that sought out potential political candidates and promoted local law enforcement. The local groups were intensely loyal to the League, and, when Shumaker called them into action, they responded. For example, in 1915 the WCTU and IASL urged drys to send petitions and come to Indianapolis to observe the House Committee on Public Morals debate statewide prohibition. Despite the hisses of wets, Shumaker made the case that with 70,000 petitions in hand from around the state, the House had a duty to pass the bill. Though the effort failed, it proved the mobilization capability of the dry cause.[3]

Nevertheless, the reinvigorated IASL still had to deal with the Proctor law, which, supporters claimed, generated tax revenues and regulated the liquor industry. There was some benefit in the law for the IASL, since it fostered resentment in drys that Shumaker could refocus toward the concept of statewide prohibition. Proctor elections also forced the League to work at the community level and connect with a new generation of voters via news coverage and public rallies.[4]

To take on the law, Shumaker skillfully blended old tactics with new ones. He attacked the Proctor law's provisions as weak and unfulfilling, especially in regard to cutting the number of saloons. The League also kept pressure on local officials to enforce the law, by employing private detectives to gather information that could be made public. Drys printed the names of wets who signed petitions in support of Proctor elections and urged women to influence their husbands and sons to vote dry. Shumaker stressed the pain and suffering that drinking caused families, while arguing that personal liberty had to be sacrificed in order to save people from the temptations found in saloons.[5]

Shumaker utilized economic arguments as he talked about the need for better dry laws. He turned the fact that both saloons and breweries were businesses against the wets. In stronger terms than they had used in the 1908 election, drys argued that the real motivation of wets was not "personal liberty" but "profit," since an estimated one-half of all revenues generated by liquor sales ended up in the pockets of brewers. Shumaker pointed out the relationship between sobriety under dry laws and better business, an argument that bore fruit for the League as business owners such as C. G. Conn of Elkhart and Frank C. Ball of Muncie became vocal supporters of the League. By the turn of the century there were 35,000 workplace deaths in addition to the nearly 2 million injuries per year in the United States. A dry workforce, it was thought by owners, would not only be more productive but also safer. Industrialization required curbing alcohol consumption.[6]

Furthermore, Shumaker reminded Hoosiers of the graft and corruption tied to saloons. Perhaps the best example came from Terre Haute, where one observer quipped that the only difference between the city and Hell was that Hell did not have any railroads. According to Federal Court proceedings, the political machine of Mayor Don M. Roberts was built upon massive voter fraud and kickbacks to his supporters. In return for lax enforcement of liquor and gambling laws, saloon owners created a slush fund with which the mayor paid citizens (in beer vouchers) to vote multiple times (one man testified to voting twenty times in a single election) for designated candidates. The city's policemen raided bars that did not participate in Roberts's plan. The court concluded that the only way to break up the Roberts ring was by eliminating the saloons.[7]

Shumaker's revitalization of the League coincided with the emergence of movements that sought to reenergize his evangelical Protestant base. In 1912 the Men and Religion Forward movement, which aimed to involve men in the nation's churches, held a convention in Indianapolis that addressed the problem of vice in Indiana. The following year, 2,500 Methodist bishops, clergy, and laity who wanted to position their denomination to deal with "the living problems now confronting the Church" (including alcohol) met in the city. By the time the convention ended with a prayer service at Monument Circle, the delegates had "given unanimous approval" to seeking national prohibition.[8]

The state's church federations and ministerial associations further aided Shumaker's cause in this regard. Created as part of the Social Gospel movement that produced the Federal Council of Churches, these organizations saw themselves as the official voice of Christianity in America. Moreover, they believed that Protestant America was on the verge of establishing God's kingdom on Earth. They had played an important role during the 1908 election and now helped Shumaker and the League during the years of revitalization.[9]

Both the IASL and these associations saw the saloon as the center of vice. The Indianapolis Church Federation worked in the early and mid-1910s with the city's mayors to curb "wine rooms, saloons, hotels of prostitution, houses of prostitution, dance halls, and picture shows" as well as to promote "child welfare, Sunday observance, and public health." The Federation's advertisements in the *Indianapolis News* argued that "the Church stands for everything that is good and practical and wholesome in our community life," and they urged lawmakers to use their power to destroy "evil influences." The group had no qualms about telling members of its congregations how to vote and whom to vote for. When it met with mayoral resistance, the

Federation took on the city's leaders, whether Republican or Democratic, by calling for impeachment proceedings if there was no crackdown on vice.[10] Ministers were encouraged to condemn the saloon from their pulpits. Pastors cast doubt on the ability of brewers to regulate their businesses and called on their congregations to mobilize against the evil of drink. Some even urged wets to withdraw from church membership.[11]

Arguments in support of the dry cause came from sources outside of the churches as well. Sociologists writing in the *American Journal of Sociology* said that "whatever morbid craving may operate here [wanting to drink], it is not a normal demand of the body, but the mere tyranny of habit." Even moderate use of alcohol was "conducive to disease," according to "medical science," and "intoxication is not increase of life, but putting the reins into the hands of the animal within us." Experts argued that there was a direct link between alcohol and crime, saying that "the results of the most cautious research show that it [alcohol] is a producer of criminals and of crime on an enormous scale." The benefits of the saloon as a social club could not outweigh "the evil" caused by the alcohol sold there.[12]

Brewers were concerned about the dry resurgence and attempted to counter it. They distanced themselves from the problems of the saloon, while at the same time they attacked the drys' assertion that alcohol was evil. In wet advertisements, readers were told that prohibition would lead to "governmental tyranny." Brewers claimed that drinking beer promoted "the cause of true temperance," since bottling and transportation allowed for home consumption, the alcohol content in beer was lower than in liquor, and beer had health benefits as a "mild food beverage." According to Schlitz Beer, "the barley is food—the hops are a tonic." The Indiana Brewers Association reminded farmers that brewers were among their largest customers, and in a series of articles they attacked prohibition in Kansas, the growth of "professional drys" and their use of political "intimidation," the inability of prohibition to promote morality, and the polarization created by the dry cause. The Pabst brewery ran an advertisement featuring a young woman holding a glass and saying, "and I thought I didn't like beer." More controversial was an Anheuser-Busch campaign that depicted historical figures, including the Founding Fathers, as drinkers. Included in the group, to the anger of drys, was John Wesley, the founder of Methodism.[13]

Drys reacted to the wet blitz with outrage. The Reverend Joshua Stansfield of Meridian Street Methodist Church in Indianapolis, for example, called special attention to Budweiser's Wesley advertisement, which he said was "a slander on the fair name of that Godly man and on the ten millions of his followers on this continent."[14] Moral pressure caused several newspapers in the state to no longer run beer advertisements. Additionally, more newspapers became proactive in their support of the dry cause. The *Noblesville Daily Ledger*, for example, ran ASL-generated editorial cartoons—"The Poor Man's Club and the Way It Works," which showed a "saloon club" smashing a home while a woman and children ran for their lives; "The Saloon is Reaching for the Child," a beastly hand seeking to grab an innocent little girl; "One Effect of the Well Regulated Saloon," a man slumped over his desk and weeping because he had been served with divorce papers; and "The Spender," a man who had plenty of money to buy drinks but none to give his daughter.[15]

All of these efforts eventually paid off for drys. As one early historian of the movement in Indiana asserted, "the public was not satisfied with the new act [Proctor]. After having experienced something better they were not willing to return to a law that seemed to them less efficient and less democratic than the one of 1908." While this is a biased view, there is little doubt that thanks in large part to Shumaker's agitation, disillusionment with the Proctor law opened the door for prohibition.[16]

None of the new dry tactics would matter, however, if they did not result in political victories. Despite the Proctor setback, politics remained the most important area of dry work. Shumaker was now more cautious with his endorsements and more vigilant in projecting the League's official bipartisanship. During the election of 1912, with the Progressive insurgency raging, he (though not the League officially) supported the Republicans and failed to endorse the eventual victor in the gubernatorial race, Democrat Samuel Ralston, despite Ralston's one-time advocacy of county option. As governor, Ralston attempted to stay clear of the alcohol issue, though this was not always possible. His lieutenant governor, William B. O'Neill, caused an uproar by halting the opening prayer of a Senate session after a Baptist minister prayed that Indiana would break free of the liquor trust. Gaveling down the invocation, O'Neill said that he would not allow politics to substitute for prayer. Drys were outraged, but many expected nothing less from the party that had made Thomas Marshall vice president.[17]

The League may have been distracted from helping the Republicans deal with the Progressives by its own need to deal with the Prohibition Party. The party still hoped to absorb the League and claimed that the IASL used "coercion" on churches to raise money and on politicians to get votes. The Prohibitionists even blamed the League for the proliferation of saloons in the state.[18] For its part, the IASL refused to invite the Prohibition Party to dry unity meetings. At one such convention, speakers such as businessman Frank Ball and clergyman Joshua Stansfield argued that prohibition was the paramount issue facing the country and that Christians needed to banish the saloon from America. Former governor J. Frank Hanly also spoke, though his words eventually drew condemnation from the League. He called nonpartisan action "weak" and said that some decisive action on behalf of the cause was needed.[19]

Hanly used the 1916 election to make the dramatic move that the dry cause needed. Since leaving office, he had worked within the Methodist Church at both the state and national levels to promote temperance and encourage the denomination to strengthen its ties to the ASL. He had also launched a nationwide lecture tour on the theme of prohibition. Dubbing it "The Flying Squadron," Hanly recruited such prominent drys as Charles Sheldon and Clarence True Wilson to join him during 1914 and 1915. The group visited all forty-eight states and the District of Columbia and spoke to at least one million people. The experience convinced Hanly to accept the nomination of the Prohibition Party for president in 1916, even though he knew he could not win. The *Patriot Phalanx* hailed Hanly's decision to leave the Republican Party and called on the IASL, who had long promoted Hanly, to support him.[20]

The IASL, however, did not follow Hanly into the Prohibitionist camp. Instead, it remained unofficially aligned with the Republicans. Shumaker's decision had much to do with his relationship with James Goodrich, the Republican gubernatorial nominee and former state party chairman. A devout Presbyterian with strong ties to the church-based dry cause, though he saw the issue as a wild card politically, Goodrich made it clear during his campaign that he favored temperance, but he did not speak directly about the issues of prohibition and women's suffrage. Goodrich also talked to voters anywhere he could find them, including in saloons. Shumaker did not have a problem with this approach because he knew that Goodrich was a strong dry.[21]

Goodrich's decision to blur his own preference on the wet/dry issue divided Hoosier Democrats. Brewer Crawford Fairbanks openly supported the Republican, which prompted some Democrats to discuss enacting another dry law to target brewers in retaliation. Wets in the legislature were fearful and called on the saloons and other brewers to come to their aid. But they lacked organization. National politics distracted Democratic leader Thomas Taggart, and there would be no repetition of the antidry campaign of a decade before.[22]

During the election, both sides remained oddly silent on prohibition. The IASL and its supporters continued to argue that prohibition should not be a partisan issue. After Goodrich's victory, however, calls came from across the state for the governor to make his true stance known. However, the Republican's silence continued, which made some Hoosiers doubt whether he was indeed dry. Goodrich did not mention prohibition in his opening address to the legislature, and the Republican caucus did not discuss the possibility of any dry legislation coming out of the General Assembly.[23]

There was growing sentiment among many Hoosiers to put Indiana firmly in the dry column. The *Warren Review Republican* said that the sooner prohibition came to both Indiana and the nation, "the better it will be for every member of the human race." The *Pike County Democrat* suggested that a prohibition amendment be made part of a new state constitution. The *Evansville Journal* called for the legislature to destroy the "whisky traffic but permit the sale of light wines and beer." Not everyone was on the dry bandwagon, however. The *Terre Haute Tribune* was solidly against prohibition for economic reasons and doubted if drys had "reached the estate for which the Creator intended them."[24]

In December 1916 dry groups from across the state formed the Indiana Dry Federation to push for prohibition. Historian Charles Canup argued in 1920 that the organization of the Federation at last put drys "on equal footing with the saloon element." The IASL was not among the group's founders, which delighted the Prohibition Party. The League resisted joining the Federation because Shumaker saw it as a duplication (and perhaps even threat) to its own lobbying efforts as well as reigniting the debate over the League's partisanship. The latter point was a lasting legacy of the 1908 debacle. The IASL was not alone in its reluctance. The Indianapolis Church Federation, for example, endorsed the statewide prohibition movement but opted not to take an active part in the Dry Federation.[25]

The League did not stay out of the Dry Federation for long, however, and, once it joined, it was clear that Shumaker was in charge. He believed that the dry lobbying effort needed to be on a larger scale than that of nine years earlier. He called on drys to write their legislators and to come to Indianapolis when there were key votes on prohibition. Shumaker lined up drys behind statutory prohibition to avoid debating a state constitutional amendment. He used Huntington County's organization as a template to create a dry direct-action network that reached from its headquarters in Indianapolis back to local organizations in counties across the state. For Shumaker, drys were ready for victory.[26]

Shumaker took the lessons that the IASL had learned since 1908 and applied them to the 1917 situation. His strategy pitted dissatisfied Democrats, who were angry that some brewers had supported Goodrich, against the wets, while he also packed the statehouse daily with hundreds of drys. The IASL, in conjunction with the Dry Federation, called upon Hoosier churches to hold a Prohibition Sunday on 7 January 1917. Petitions were circulated in congregations to be sent to the legislature.[27] The dry machine that Shumaker had crafted was beginning to operate.

Once again, dry voices echoed in the vastness of the statehouse, and people choked its stairways. Shumaker issued a challenge to county organizations to see who could send the most people. Local meetings were held across Indiana, and soon delegations and petitions were arriving in Indianapolis from every corner of the state. Cass County's delegation decorated their cars with signs and streamers and had their photograph taken on the statehouse stairs. Dressed in their Sunday best, the group of men and women held two large banners, "A Dry Bunch: Logansport, Cass County" and "Good Bye John." The Howard County contingent, including its band, also posed outside the statehouse for photographers. The *Indianapolis News* showed five young men who were members of the "Fort Wayne Dry Delegation," with small signs calling for a dry Indiana tucked into their hatbands and "dry" handkerchiefs strategically placed in their vest pockets. A special train car brought Montgomery County drys to the statehouse, and Huntington County had a team of twenty-five men ready to come at a moment's notice, with or without their band.[28]

Hoosier drys also received help from William Jennings Bryan, who was visiting Indianapolis. Though a Democrat, Bryan was "a total abstainer" whose interest in the dry cause helped elevate it as a national political issue. He championed the idea that liquor interests were too powerful for local measures to combat and believed that wets, including those in Indiana, had cost him the presidency. Before addressing the state Senate in January 1917, Bryan met with Governor Goodrich, and the two Presbyterians discussed why Indiana should go dry. To the senators, the Old Commoner talked about the need for prohibition, the right of women to vote, and a new state constitution.[29]

Drys wanted the House to pass prohibition before the Senate did, to put additional pressure on the upper chamber, as the Seventieth General Assembly was made up of 64 Republicans and 34 Democrats in the House, with a 25 to 25 split in the Senate. Randolph County's representative, Frank Wright, drafted the prohibition bill. In calling for his colleagues to vote for it, he said "that welfare can be promoted no better than by the protection of public morals. We owe it to the populace to make it easy for the weakest member to do right and hard for him to do wrong." "Immoral men," Wright continued, needed to be "managed" by the government. The House, inundated with 400,000 petitions in support of prohibition, passed the bill 70 to 28 after "two hours of orating," which was interrupted by wets being "hissed" down by the dry gallery. The victory was met with "wild enthusiasm" by the estimated 25,000 drys in the city for the vote.[30]

A "titanic" struggle was expected in the Senate, however. Drys believed that the upper house was too evenly divided to count on an easy victory. Reporters noted that though they had a full legislative agenda presented to them by the governor, the members inevitably turned their conversations to prohibition. Shumaker brought intense pressure to bear on reluctant senators. The IASL called for 300,000 drys to watch over the Senate proceedings. According to the *Wabash Plain Dealer*, "Scores of towns and cities throughout the state sent hundreds of representatives to Indianapolis to participate. The local organizations prepared further mobilization plans and circulated more and more petitions. Temperance workers with badges and banners parade through the chamber singing religious songs." The Senate had to delay its vote in order to accept over 175,000 dry petitions, which was enough to sway some reluctant members. Each day that dry pressure increased, there were fewer wet legislators to be found.[31]

Indeed, each senator was on trial for his political life. The bill was delivered to the dry-friendly Rights and Franchise Committee, chaired by Arthur Robinson, who guided it, largely unaltered, to the Senate floor.[32] During the debate, Republican Warren T. McCray opened the dry assault by saying that the day of the liquor interests was over in Indiana. His speech was interrupted by applause from the galleries, which Lt. Gov. Edgar D. Bush gaveled down, warning, "this is a senate chamber, not a bowling alley." Senators whose districts were divided on the issue were confronted by dry delegations from home. The strategy forced most senators to recognize that public sentiment was dry. Supposed wets jumped on the dry bandwagon, some citing saloon corruption, others wanting to eliminate a threat to future generations of Hoosiers. All agreed that if the saloon ever did come back, it would have to be "radically different."[33]

The dry victory came in an "unexpected landslide" as party lines collapsed in a 38-to-11 vote. Once drys learned of the vote, the initial applause of the crowds gave way to the singing of "Onward, Christian Soldiers" and other hymns, which echoed throughout the capitol. In the words of one observer, the victory celebration by thousands of drys at the statehouse was one of "the most stirring scenes ever witnessed." "Wild jubilation and enthusiasm" soon spread around the state. Drys believed that a new era was dawning.[34]

Wets had done their best during the session but were blunted at every turn by the IASL. Their petitions were engulfed by the tidal wave of dry ones. Though Senate Democrats amended the bill to give those involved in the liquor trade four extra months—until April 1918 instead of the following January—to put their affairs in order, Shumaker vowed to block any commission that would ease the transition of the wets out of business, believing that it would be a ruse to keep saloons open despite the law. The wet press blamed the "bandwagon" effect for dry success and quickly labeled the new law "drastic."[35]

Some wets held out hope that Goodrich might refuse to sign the bill. The governor had spent little time among the drys in Indianapolis; and when he finally met with them, he merely commented that he was glad to see "the people" outnumbering special-interest lobbyists.[36] But he was more than ready to make prohibition the law of the state. His silence had been the move of a master politician. The signing ceremony was an event worthy of the spectacle that had greeted the bill's passage. It was "lost" for a while, keeping the assembled throng waiting (drys saw it as a spiteful swipe at their law by wets), but eventually it was placed on the governor's desk. All of the state's top drys were on hand to witness Goodrich affixing his signature, and a motion picture camera captured the event. The governor used seven pens to sign the law, including David Shumaker's Civil War pen. A chorus sang "Glory, glory, hallelujah" as the event concluded. One dry later told Shumaker that "Governor Goodrich did a greater and more lasting good thing for Indiana than did Morton—the greatest governor Indiana ever had until Goodrich."[37]

The state's newspapers weighed in on the new dry reality. The *Indianapolis Star* commented, "There was a day when men and women of brains and character might divide on prohibition as an interesting study in philosophic history or individual rights. That day has gone. There remains only a sharply drawn line on one side or the other of which we must all stand, as the friends of progress or the apologists for wrong." Other papers said that the legislature had done the will of the people by passing prohibition because "John Barleycorn" had "taxed the hospitality of the state beyond endurance," since wets had been unwilling to follow the less stringent laws enacted in Indiana over the last twenty years. The new law seemed to be the first step in a very "progressive" legislative session that would allow society to eliminate "whatever is injurious to humanity."[38]

Not all commentators were as optimistic. Several newspapers said that while the coming of prohibition was going to solve a major societal problem in Indiana, it was also going to create new issues, such as reductions in tax revenue and loss of jobs when saloons and breweries closed their doors, which had to be addressed.[39] There was merit to this position. The Indiana Brewers Association estimated that a dry state would lower tax revenues and leave over 13,600 people unemployed. The *Evansville Journal* feared that the state would also lose population. Several brewers told the *Journal* that they planned on returning to Germany when the World War was over, while some saloonkeepers were seeking employment in Kentucky. When prohibition came, brewers helped their employees by launching new ventures, such as porcelain, malted milk products, "soft drinks, ice cream, baker's yeast, refrigerated cabinets and auto and truck bodies" to keep them at work. Owners converted their saloons to soft drink parlors and prayed for a legal victory, or they slashed prices, got rid of their inventory, and sold their buildings.[40]

Wets did not meekly submit to their change in fortune; rather, they pursued legal challenges based on the idea that the manufacture and sale of alcohol were two different things. Shumaker countered that allowing brewers to produce alcohol in a dry state would violate the spirit of Indiana's prohibition law. Depending on which side controlled the local judiciary, this type of lawsuit met with mixed success, which meant that the issue ended up before the Indiana Supreme Court. Both the IASL and the national ASL's Wayne Wheeler helped the state with its case. In June 1918 a divided court ruled the prohibition law constitutional, thus crushing the hopes of wets. The court's majority placed the decision firmly within the rights of the state's police powers, arguing, "There is no difference in constitutional principle between the prohibition of the sale of intoxicating liquor as a beverage and the prohibition of the manufacture in order to stop the sale."[41]

Many commentators blasted wets for attempting to have the state's courts overturn the new law. The *Gary Evening Post*, for example, argued that if the measure was as popular as the statehouse vote indicated, then the courts were not going to void the law. The liquor dealers were wasting everyone's time rather than preparing for a dry future. When attempted again nationally over the enactment of the Eighteenth Amendment and the Volstead Act, the wet legal offensive also met defeat.[42]

Though the Indiana WCTU had said that no single temperance organization could take credit for the victory, the people of the state felt otherwise, if the volume of letters that poured into Shumaker's office is any indication. The IASL's leader himself was hailed, not the Prohibition Party or the Dry Federation. Though some observers were worried that the new law would meet the same fate as county option, most were overjoyed with what had been accomplished. One letter writer went so far as to say, "generations will raise up and call you blessed." Others, not content with the verdict of history, called on Shumaker to run for the U.S. Senate.[43]

Shumaker's campaign was a source of inspiration to his fellow ASL state superintendents. The dry leader in Washington thought that getting the legislature to pass the prohibition law was a brilliant move. The Ohio ASL said the pressure was now really on them to make the Buckeye State dry. And James K. Shields, superintendent of the New Jersey ASL, wrote, "Whatever has got into the folks in the old Hoosier State? Every breeze that comes from the West is one of those 'dry' winds we hear so much about." Transplanted Hoosiers in Oregon also sent Shumaker hearty congratulations. The victory made him a power on the national level, on a par with such figures as the leader of the New York ASL, William H. Anderson.[44] For his part, Shumaker made sure to thank his network of supporters, which included D. S. Ritter, son of the late Prohibition Party stalwart Eli Ritter, as well as the governor of Indiana.[45]

Indiana going dry was just the beginning, for by the spring of 1917 the nation was on the verge of prohibition as well. Many commentators assume that anti-German sentiment sparked by the World War helped bring about the Prohibition amendment. After all, 1917 brought the United States at last into the Great War and, with it, restrictions on all things German—incuding many American brewers—in national life. Longtime Indiana newspaper man, and later spokesman for the beer industry, Harold C. Feightner wrote that "with Hoosier boys falling in France, with the draft coming closer and closer, with meatless days and lightless nights, nobody paid much attention to the social and economic changes" that passing Prohibition was sure to bring.

There is a problem with this argument, however. Indiana went dry before any of the events that Feightner described had occurred. Furthermore, it supposes that the American Expeditionary Force serving in France did not reflect the wet/dry divide of the nation as a whole, but there is evidence that the boys "over there" worried about such issues, just as they had at home. While the war helped propel prohibition from a state issue to a national one, American entry into the war actually pushed it off the front pages of the state's newspapers, not the other way around. National wartime prohibition came about because of fear of shortages in the nation's grain supply and because drys saw an opportunity to push their agenda forward while so many men—that is, voters—were out of the country. Shumaker urged Goodrich to pressure the state's congressional delegation to support wartime prohibition on such grounds, which the governor assured the dry leader he had already done.[46]

This is not to say that drys did not have problems with German Americans, nor that their hatred of the continental Sabbath did not play a role in Prohibition's arrival. In Indiana the North American Gymnastics Union (an athletic club better known as the Turners), whose members included German Americans, was a thorn in the side of Shumaker. Theodor Stempful, its head, argued that prohibition should not be a litmus test for how American a person was and complained that the law had been "railroaded through Congress." According to the Turners, prohibition led only to corruption and to the proliferation of "busybodies" who had nothing better to do than to spy on their neighbors.[47]

With or without the war, however, national prohibition was coming. As a member of the Virginia ASL said in 1917, "we are fighting *immediately* for prohibition for the duration of the war, bur our *aim* is CONSTITUTIONAL prohibition. If we can get the first, the latter will be easier." As early as 1913, with the passing of the Webb-Kenyon bill, which banned the transportation of alcohol into dry areas, some drys believed that the time was ripe for national prohibition. When Indiana went dry, the national debate intensified. The ASL's legislative superintendent said that the Hoosier victory put pressure on the U.S. Congress to act, and the League began to predict a dry nation by 1918. The political decision to push for a constitutional amendment was based on the belief that the public was more apt to support prohibition as part of the Constitution in the long term than they were by any of the other options open to drys.[48]

Shumaker went to Washington, DC, in December 1917 to witness the Senate passing the proposed Eighteenth Amendment. With twenty-seven states already dry, the League was confident that victory was within its grasp. When the House passed the amendment, 282 to 128, the *Indianapolis News* commented that the margin of victory reflected "the opinion of the country, and there is not a doubt that the vote of Indiana congressmen reflects the sentiment of Indiana." The state legislature voted to ratify the amendment on 14 January 1919, and three days later Nebraska became the thirty-sixth state to do so. Thus, a mere thirteen months after it was submitted, the Eighteenth Amendment became part of the U.S. Constitution. Church and courthouse bells rang across the country. The passage was seen as a victory for the nation's "moral forces."[49]

With the coming of national prohibition, newspapers around Indiana grew reflective. The *Connersville News Examiner* commented that the country was "passing into the trial of a very great experiment." Some editors hailed prohibition as the "greatest reform in the United States since the Civil War," believing that "federal prohibition means that the nation is going to be sober. . . . Resistance to the new order is resistance to the government itself." Though others thought there might be eventual modification, all wanted the present amendment obeyed.[50] Summing up the feelings of many drys, the Reverend Philip L. Frick of Meridian Street Methodist Church in Indianapolis said in a sermon:

> How utterly perverted the cry for "personal liberty" when we take into consideration the stupendous social benefits that would accrue from a willing acceptance of this far-reaching Constitutional Amendment. In this crisis of enforcement, let every unselfish, social-minded patriot remember what it will mean to mankind to have America lead the world into that new epoch in which sobriety shall rule in every life and in every nation. The United States needs the touch of God's spirit! Ours, the glorious challenge of becoming "first" in spiritual ideals, in far-reaching sympathies, in unremitting helpfulness, in pioneering with God into new spiritual empires. This is our national destiny! This may be our national glory![51]

Drys had every confidence that if they could make prohibition succeed in the United States, the reform would sweep the globe. It was "intrinsically a national issue with international significance."[52]

Like most Americans, drys believed that the postwar world should emulate the example of the United States. President Woodrow Wilson sought to build a world system that could control as well as export the forces of "progress" around what one historian has labeled a "Presbyterian foreign policy that asserted the virtue of American motives and the superiority of American ideals and insisted on the right to export those ideals to any unstable area in the world." Talk of international prohibition occurred at the same time that the League of Nations and the Interchurch World Movement, which were both considered pillars of the Wilsonian system, were being proposed.[53] Drys created their own international organization patterned after their experiences in working with denominational and transdenominational missionary movements. The ASL's World League against

Alcoholism quickly superseded the older International Prohibition Federation and promoted a dry peace and reconciliation among nations.[54] The United States, Finland, Norway, Iceland, and Turkey all enacted some form of prohibition, while variations of local option prevailed in Sweden, Denmark, Canada, New Zealand, Australia, and Scotland.[55]

Shumaker believed in the international dry cause and promoted the "progress of civilization" for the rest of his life.[56] Like most American drys, he believed that reform needed to be taken to the very birthplace of the continental Sabbath. The effort was complicated by the fact that in the United States, prohibition had become the lingua franca of the dry cause, largely because of the major influence of evangelical Protestants, while in Europe, dry work focused on the Catholic notion of personal abstinence. There were no viable alternatives. The Russian experiment with a state-run license system, which was similar to South Carolina's dispensary model, had been largely discredited on both continents.[57]

Drys were on guard against a wet counterattack at home even as they discussed exporting Prohibition. The IASL warned in 1919 that wets were in the process of buying up newspapers, which would become propaganda rags in the years ahead (drys had long worried about the power of the press in wet hands). Drys also thought that the war had moved up national prohibition by between five to ten years, so they were going to have to guard against any efforts at repeal. They had little use for wet claims that Prohibition would fail because it could not guarantee total prohibition of alcohol. For drys, the issue was the moral principle rather than compliance, since no law was ever followed entirely.[58]

Enactment of Prohibition did require enforcement, however, which fundamentally changed the nature of the dry crusade. In 1919, Congress gave the country the Volstead Act, which outlawed the manufacture, distribution, and sale (but not consumption) of alcohol. The Wilson administration complicated matters, in the midst of the president's stroke, by vetoing it. Supporters of the Volstead Act called the veto "a big mistake and indefensible," and it was overridden by Congress by substantial margins. But Woodrow Wilson became convinced that Americans had not planned on Volstead when they worked for the Eighteenth Amendment, and he sought to revise rather than enforce the law during his remaining time in office.[59]

The Harding administration tried to make sense of the Wilsonian enforcement regulations, but it ran into the political morass that had made national prohibition possible. As Richard Hamm and Ann-Marie Szymanski have pointed out, in order to receive Southern support in Congress, drys had agreed to a "concurrent powers enforcement" clause, which gave the federal government limited ability to safeguard the nation's dryness. Thanks to this states' rights proviso, some states felt free to relax their own enforcement, while the federal government found it had little ability (and perhaps just as little desire) to pick up the slack. When Washington did enforce the law, it created resentment and sparked fears of an out-of-control government. These fears were manifest in Indiana, where judges preferred to suspend and fine violators rather than imprison them, and local, state, and federal officials bickered over who was supposed to enforce the law.[60]

As haphazard and convoluted as enforcement was, it seemed to work. The *South Bend Tribune* reported that in 1917 some 1,304 cases for intoxication had appeared before the city court. By 1919, that number had dropped to 139. In 1922 the WCTU found that conditions at home had improved for women and children, and the *Evansville Journal* reported a year later that crime was down because of Prohibition.[61] But raids uncovered the craftiness and determination of wets to break the law. In Lake County, police found an elaborate series of stills built under sand dunes, and in downtown Indianapolis, a 500-gallon still was discovered. In 1923 a nationwide rum-running syndicate was busted that had as its terminus the Circle City.[62]

Clearly, the enactment of the Eighteenth Amendment and the Volstead Act did not mean that the prohibitionists struggle was over. Those laws had to be followed and enforced. Shumaker vowed that the IASL would seek better, tougher laws by working with its allies in the churches and with state politicians to combat wets.[63] Indeed, drys understood that it was going to take time and effort, perhaps as long as a generation, to achieve complete victory.[64]

Shumaker's endeavor to keep the IASL actively engaged differs from many other dry organizations, which stopped being proactive in shaping American society. The WCTU cut back its support of temperance oratorical contests and educational initiatives in order to focus on other reforms. Many Protestants stopped talking about the moral rationale for Prohibition. The Indiana Prohibition Party announced that it was going to support dry politicians regardless of their party. Drys also tended—and this included Shumaker—to tie Prohibition's ultimate success to the strength of the American economy. The money spent in saloons, drys believed, was going to unleash a wave of economic prosperity that would guarantee the law's future. These economic arguments were to be fatal errors in judgment, though in the early 1920s they seemed perfectly reasonable.[65]

Nationally, proponents of the dry cause seemed securely in control. In a series of articles on Prohibition written by David Lawrence in 1923 that appeared in the *Indianapolis Star*, most observers in the federal government believed that it was just getting started. President Warren G. Harding proclaimed, "Prohibition is here to stay," and vowed that enforcement would continue until wets gave up the fight. Though wets whom Lawrence interviewed wanted modification of the laws, they agreed that the saloon had been a bad institution. He also doubted if demand for poor-quality bootleg whisky would remain very high, considering that the price for illegal alcohol was skyrocketing, thus putting a drink out of the reach of most Americans. By March 1923 the government reported that alcohol consumption had been cut by 90 percent.[66]

After years of strenuous effort, Shumaker allowed himself to expand beyond dry work. He took opportunities to fill pulpits and deliver nonprohibition-related sermons. He served as state commander of the Sons of Union Veterans in 1920 and again in 1921. Victory also gave him time to reflect. Consulting his notes, Shumaker figured that in the fourteen years he had been a part of the IASL, he had made 2,116 addresses (roughly three per week) to 293,478 people, traveled 191,706 miles, had expenses of $5,790.88, and raised subscriptions and collections totaling $80,723.32.[67]

By the mid-1920s, Shumaker and the dry cause had triumphed. National prohibition was popularly enacted and supported by a diverse coalition of people who saw it as "the greatest moral, educational, and economical triumph ever won by any nation in all time."[68] However, though drys did not realize it, the country's mood was already starting to shift. The new decade would prove to be very different from either the 1900s or the 1910s.[69]

5 | The Faulty Alliances of Rhetoric

The dry crusade had triumphed in both Indiana and the nation by 1920 for several reasons. After years of hard work by people such as Edward Shumaker, America's evangelical Protestant churches, business owners, and politicians had rallied to the banner of reform. However, the dry cause's victorious coalition was larger than those three constituencies. Drys believed that Prohibition was going to be a force for social uplift in the United States and around the world. Their rhetoric claimed that Prohibition would help families, benefit all Americans regardless of race, and draw support and agreement from all Christians. Thus, their message attempted to rally families, African Americans, and Catholics to the cause. How the rhetoric stood the test of reality had important consequences for the future of both the dry cause and Prohibition as a reform.

At the time when Shumaker became active in the IASL, the major focus of dry rhetoric was on the family. Drys believed that with Prohibition, the home lives and personal relationships of millions of Americans would improve. As one Hoosier minister put it, "we are what our homes make us and also our homes are what we make them." Drys viewed the saloon as the destroyer of families and counted on the nation's churches to protect "men, women, and children from the devastating social consequences of the liquor traffic"—alcohol-induced poverty and domestic violence. Prohibition promised "a victory for the church, the school, and the home . . . for sad-eyed women and half-clad children." It would end "the liquor curse" and make "America safe for motherhood and childhood."[1]

Drys found ample evidence to support their claims about what drinking did to families. They blamed public and domestic violence on alcohol and argued that drinking was a drain on the pocketbooks of millions of American households. According to the *Western Christian Advocate,* typical working-class men in the early twentieth century earned "a dollar and quarter a day, [of which] thirty-five cents will be spent for beer, leaving ninety cents for the support of a family of five children."[2]

Dry rhetoric about families centered on the role of men in the home. Evangelical Protestants believed that men needed to reclaim their proper place as head of the familial unit. This message was also central to the Social Gospel's "muscular Christianity" and the Men and Religion Forward movement. Drinking kept men from realizing their full potential, while at the same time it forced women to take on responsibilities that were not appropriate for the fairer sex. Since the saloon and fraternal lodges were a means of escaping the home—a place where a man did not have to worry about his wife or child—getting rid of alcohol in these places would encourage husbands and fathers to take part in activities that included their families.[3]

Women, of course, played an important part in the dry cause, both figuratively and literally. Defending womanhood was an important aspect of dry rhetoric: "the chief evils of the traffic in ardent spirits have fallen on women," and they were its "greatest sufferers." However, women were not mere damsels in distress waiting to be saved. They had been at the forefront of the antisaloon movement since the Women's Crusades of the 1870s, which had created the WCTU, and the 1880s. Though empowering to women, the cause was viewed by female drys as a partnership with men "to rid society of corruption." Any other benefits, such as the right to vote, were largely secondary in their outlook.[4]

The goal of dry rhetoric aimed at both men and women was to produce happy, secure, and functioning families. Future Indiana state senator C. Wendell Martin recalled growing up in such an environment: "My parents and their friends were very 'dry,' and we never even thought of having any 'booze' around. Loving the Lord Jesus was a top priority in our home, and the guests in our home had no interest in such drinks as beer, whiskey, etc." Looking back on his experience, Martin believed that it was a "sheltered" way to grow up, but by no means a bad one.[5]

While Martin's testimonial is what drys were hoping to achieve on a national scale, dry rhetoric was not a success in the Shumaker home. Shumaker had been married to Flora May Holliger, a Terre Haute schoolteacher three and one-half years his junior, since September 1900. Together they had five children. Daughter Lois Willard was born in 1901 and was joined by Albert Edmund three years later. They were followed by Paul Russell in 1907, Charles Wayne in 1910, and Arthur Wesley in 1913. Shumaker gave Flora credit in his unpublished autobiography as a great "helpmate," a "self-sacrificing . . . model mother," to whom he owed his success as a pastor and as an official of the IASL.[6]

His accolades are not far off the mark. Shumaker's decision to join the League had important consequences for his wife and children. In 1903, Flora was forced to move from Winchester to Indianapolis and then on to South Bend, while pregnant with Albert and dealing with two-year-old Lois. She accepted this upheaval, believing that Shumaker's work for the dry cause would "remove the temptations and pitfalls" that destroyed families. She was her husband's staunchest advocate and was willing to do her part for the cause. Once, while they were living in South Bend, bottles of beer were left at their house for evidence in a blind tiger case. Flora hid the bottles in the cellar, but when the family was preparing to relocate back to Indianapolis, she wanted to get rid of the beer. To her "dismay," the first bottle she opened to pour down the sink splattered all over the kitchen. After cleaning up the mess, Flora smashed the remaining bottles with a hammer, washed the beer down the sink, and put the glass in the trash.[7]

Once she was married, Flora sought no life outside of her home. She was a devoted, caring mother, and her social life consisted only of her children's activities and church organizations. While it may, in the words of daughter-in-law Julia Shumaker, seem to have been "a rather dull, church-related life," "the children grew up to be successful, considerate adults," and Flora herself never regretted giving up her teaching career for marriage. She played a large role in shaping her children's futures. She guided Paul toward a career in medicine and encouraged Wayne and Arthur to pursue teaching at the college level. She also cared for Albert, who had mental health problems. There may have been a bit of Sinclair Lewis's Carol Kenicott in Flora Shumaker. One wonders if she realized what it actually meant to marry both a minister and a reform leader and, as this reality became apparent, if she ever contemplated leaving him.[8]

The Shumaker family was solidly middle class. Their home in Indianapolis was a twelve-room house in the 2000 block of Broadway. According to various tax forms, Shumaker made $4,000 per year in salary from the IASL (equivalent to an average salary in 2004 of over $43,000). As other drys well knew, having a salary and being paid the full amount were two very different things, but the Shumakers lived comfortably. The family gave money to Broadway Methodist and St. Paul's Methodist churches, the Huddle Church, the [Wheeler] Rescue Mission, the ASL, the Red Cross, and the Church Federation. In 1924 the Shumakers listed in their property assessment two bicycles, thirteen chickens, a lawnmower, five watches, and two typewriters. They also had a phonograph, gold and silver plated ware, an electric washing machine, an electric sweeper, a sewing machine, and a library estimated at $100. For a time, their home was also the residence of Glen Shumaker, Edward's nephew, to whom Edward gave moral guidance. As a boarder, Glen acted as the "man of the house" when Shumaker was absent and helped to pay the bills. Shumaker often put his immediate family aside in order to assist extended kin. He spoke at family reunions and researched and wrote family histories of both his Seitz and Keller relatives, which he published himself. As Flora noted, he did this after working for the IASL all day, sometimes staying up until 2 or 3 A.M. in the process.[9]

As a father, Shumaker had little to do with the day-to-day raising of his children. Generally, he had two Sundays off per year, Easter and Christmas, and every other weekend was devoted to either participating in dry meetings around the state or traveling to and from those meetings, in keeping with the itinerant roots of Methodism. He helped around the house on occasion, sometimes doing the dishes after dinner, but, in the main, Flora raised their children virtually as a single parent, and he only got involved when issues where brought directly to his attention. For example, when Lois was a student at Indianapolis's Shortridge High School and was told to wear bloomers in her physical education class, Shumaker "had a fit and said his daughter would NEVER dress so immodestly." Lois was removed from school and finished her education by correspondence. He was more lenient when it came to his sons, however. When Paul told his father that he was learning how to dance at DePauw, Shumaker was irate but did not pull his son out of college.[10]

Despite his schedule, the family did spend time together. Every year they went to Illinois to visit relatives and sometimes ventured to the Methodist campground at Battle Ground, though the latter may have been more of a working vacation for Shumaker. He enjoyed swimming and fishing and taught his children those sports. Shumaker loved baseball, and he took the boys to games on occasion and played catch with them in the backyard. Arthur remembered how excited he was on the days when his father left work early and took him to see the Indianapolis Indians play. Shumaker and Flora also made sure the children were active in church groups.[11]

In many ways it was for the family that Shumaker fought so hard, yet the consequences on his own family of his calling threatened its very fabric. The dry crusade was a strain on his marriage. He was rarely home. Flora had to step beyond her place, and their children missed time with their father. The dry cause may have changed some roles and decreased drinking, but it was unable to make society, much less the institution of marriage, perfect. Dry reality for the Shumakers hardly matched the rhetoric.

An even clearer example of the mismatch between dry rhetoric and reality can be seen in the case of African Americans, whom drys courted as the cause matured. If we consider that the vast majority of blacks were members of evangelical Protestant denominations, it would seem natural for them to be a part of the dry crusade. As Anne Firor Scott has noted, "the church was so central an institution in the emerging black communities that there was never a clear line between church-related and secular associations." Support of the civil order brought by Prohibition was seen by many African Americans as a way to achieve respectability and equality with whites. That this ended up not being the case was a disappointment to all involved.[12]

Granted, blacks and whites had different goals for the dry cause. African Americans counted on using the dry agenda to further racial equality on their own terms. By openly supporting the Eighteenth Amendment, they hoped to have the Fourteenth and Fifteenth Amendments enforced as well.[13] The quest for black respectability often clashed with white paternalism, racism, notions of "the other," and awkward steps toward equality that transcended the wet/dry divide. Northern Methodism, like most other white evangelical Protestant denominations, thought that whites needed to uplift the nation's blacks by giving them the gift of prohibition. But notions of uplift were also tinged with racism. The *Patriot Phalanx*, the organ of the Prohibition Party in Indiana, stated that "the strongest argument in favor of prohibition is the imperative necessity of keeping whisky out of the reckless, colored, element." Hoosier wets, on the other hand, argued that prohibition in the South had led to increased racial tensions because African Americans were unable to control themselves when alcohol was illegal, since they tended to over "celebrate" whenever they were able to get their hands on it. Shumaker's thoughts on race were molded by this mentality and were similar to those of most white Hoosiers, who had had little or no direct contact with African Americans.[14]

To be fair, dry culture's stance on blacks and Prohibition was ultimately created in the South, not the North, because that is where the majority of African Americans still resided in the early twentieth century. White Southerners had long worried about blacks and alcohol. In the antebellum period, temperance had been a virtue for

whites and a requirement for slaves. After the Civil War and Reconstruction, that virtue became a "moral crusade" heavily influenced
by the emerging Jim Crow social order. Prohibition sentiment advanced in the South due to the racial fears of white Southerners.
Blacks, it was argued in the wake of such events as the 1906 Atlanta
riot, turned violent when they drank, and so both alcohol and African Americans needed to be tightly controlled.[15]

Many African Americans responded by claiming the promise of
respectability that came with the dry cause while paying lip service
to the accusations of racist whites as to why Prohibition was needed.
Adherents to this dual approach argued that doing so was the only
way in which they could work with "the best element of the educated
and church-going white people" in a common cause. Blacks in the
South were told by their ministers and leaders "that in the death of
the liquor traffic the day is at hand when the Negro shall find an exalted plane socially, morally and politically" in the United States.[16]

The idea of accommodating a degree of white prejudice in order
to achieve respectability was advanced by Booker T. Washington.
The Wizard of Tuskegee was quick to make the connection between
alcohol as a means of keeping blacks in a degraded state (as well as in
a state of danger) and prohibition as a means to uplift the entire race,
thus seeing the dry cause as "essentially a moral movement." For
him, the "miraculous sweep of temperance sentiment throughout
the South" was "a long forward step in the working out of our racial
problem," because "when you mix ignorance and bad whiskey, you
will be sure to have a difficulty, whether the individuals are black or
white." Washington, a vocal advocate for the dry cause, argued the
benefits that blacks could reap in places where prohibition laws were
passed and enforced. He believed that temperance was the best thing
to happen to blacks since Emancipation and linked dry laws in the
South to a decrease in the lynchings of blacks.[17]

In their quest for respectability, African Americans developed a
complicated relationship with the ASL. In many respects, the League
was a product of the same Midwestern evangelical Protestantism that
a generation or two earlier had supported the antislavery crusade and
the efforts of Radical Republicans during Reconstruction. However,

as the ASL moved into the South, where it found new fields for its message and both white and black supporters, its Northern leadership was forced to consider race and reform. In order to draw the support of most Southern whites, the ASL accepted the emergence of "separate but equal" temperance societies and accommodationist thought rather than challenge it. As the Reverend B.F. Riley, a white Southern Baptist who served as the general superintendent of the Southern Negro Anti-Saloon Federation, told Ernest H. Cherrington of the national ASL in 1909, his group was a needed "supplemental force" that could do things "in the South which could not be so easily done" by the ASL.[18]

Some black drys attempted to challenge this arrangement. The National Baptist Convention begged the ASL in 1925 to take up the cause of African Americans. Dr. L.G. Jordan, the denomination's historian, wrote to F. Scott McBride before the League's national convention:

> I truly hope that the League will not adjourn without planning for work among Negroes in a greater or less degree, for I am anxious as to the future of my people, especially in the large centers, who are left with no moral suasion or temperance agitation, absolutely at the mercy of the moonshiners and bootleggers. Communists are untiring in their efforts to spread "Red" propaganda among us and law-breakers, sad to say, are finding apt pupils. In my judgment, a department of your work should be organized to offset these growing evils. I do not know to whom to apply, or whom to address, but I believe that with the backing of the League I could organize and educate the Negro so that he will be a helpful asset to you, where he is now a most dangerous menace to our cause.[19]

In a later letter, calling work with African Americans a "neglected field," Jordan made the case that "the Negro should not be conceded to the liquor people without a vigorous protest." The Reverend A.J. Barton, chairman of the League's National Executive Committee, supported Jordan and wrote to Cherrington in January 1926:

"I think it highly important that the Anti-Saloon League secure a strong, capable, reliable Negro leader and put him afield to represent the League among the Negroes. I do not believe there is any more constructive piece of work that we could do." Cherrington told Barton to go ahead and start work on getting an African-American program together; however, he warned him that there would be little financial support from the national office.[20]

Many white Northerners viewed the nation's race issues as a "southern problem." While there was a realization among Hoosier whites that conditions for blacks were not good in the South, black migration to the state was a touchy subject throughout the nineteenth and early twentieth centuries. Readers of Indiana's Republican newspapers were confronted with stories about lynching and African American disenfranchisement. But while these stories condemned what was happening in the South, they also described African Americans accused of crimes as "fiendish" and "brutal," and blacks were said to be "superstitious," of "an inferior race" with "a savage element" in their nature. The *Patriot Phalanx* even ran a column entitled "Uncle Zimri." The drawing of the supposed author was of an elderly African American man, whose "unlearned" English pushed a pro-prohibition message.[21] It is unclear if the column was intended to reach out to blacks in a misguided attempt to talk down to them, or to show readers that even an ignorant black knew that the Prohibition Party was the only route to temperance.

For Hoosiers in communities with long-standing ties to African Americans, relationships could be different. There was pride in the Civil War and in what the North had stood for, and sometimes it still found expression. When Prohibition Party member Albert Carter, "a colored farmer living near Westfield," was denied entry to an elevator at the Claypool Hotel in Indianapolis during a party meeting, white members sneaked him in and the meeting passed a resolution condemning the hotel.[22] This type of reaction was more the exception than the rule, however.

As blacks began to leave the South in large numbers in search of opportunity in the North, white attitudes were further tested. "The Great Migration," according to historian James Grossman, "turned the attention of thousands of black southerners toward a northern industrial world previously marginal to their consciousness." They saw the North as a place where they could enjoy a better life. While Indiana did not receive as many African Americans as did neighboring states during the migration, the black population still doubled between 1910 and 1930, with most of the new arrivals settling in cities such as Indianapolis and Gary. Though there was segregation, it was not as oppressive as it had been in the South.[23]

African-American urbanization, and the crime that many observers associated with it, was a concern for both white and black Americans. Black Hoosiers whose families had migrated to Indiana before the Civil War hoped to see African Americans in the South benefit by coming North, where these "Jim Crow Negroes" would be transformed into productive members of society and thus show whites that "race prejudice is the most foolish thing in the world." To those ends, black ministers railed against saloons and vice from their pulpits as strongly as did their white counterparts.[24] Indeed, the National Baptist Convention, the home denomination for the vast majority of African-American Baptists, had supported dry work since the 1890s, with Hoosiers often sitting on its temperance committee. Its members condemned the liquor traffic in the same terms as their white brethren and equated the sale and consumption of alcohol with sin. Black Baptists were also called on to vote dry and rejoiced with other drys over the coming of national prohibition, believing that it would create better social conditions for all Americans.[25]

Despite the fact that drinking was a problem for some African Americans, the saloon played an important economic role in the black community. As the *Indianapolis Recorder* pointed out, "race prejudice [was] a valuable commercial asset" for African Americans who wanted to operate a business. Advertisements for saloons often appeared in the newspapers. With pool tables, tobacco, and food they were just as active in seeking customers as their white counterparts. But black-owned clubs were also the venues where whites liked to demonstrate their zeal for law enforcement. In 1907, Evansville police raided a "stylish Negro club" because they alleged it was a blind tiger. In 1908, under the same false pretenses, a black-owned hotel in West Baden was dynamited. White-owned clubs rarely faced such official or unofficial harassment.[26]

Indiana—a blend of North and South—held promise for the dry cause as a place where the two races might accomplish something together. The state's WCTU had a long history of outreach to blacks, dating from the 1880s, with African-American associations in Indianapolis, Seymour, Franklin, New Albany, Richmond, Greenfield, and Plainfield. The state's white Baptists believed that blacks could carry the South for prohibition as well as aid in making the North dry. As for the IASL, State Superintendent U. G. Humphrey had made it a point to speak at African-American churches. African Methodist Episcopal (AME) churches were the scene of dry rally events as part of the Proctor Law battles. During the push for statewide prohibition, African-American drys heard speakers claim that saloons were a bigger problem for blacks in 1916 than slavery had ever been, and in the 1920s the League could count on help from the state's black Baptists.[27]

As for Shumaker's stance on race, he left scant record of his personal opinions about African Americans, with the exception of a single page of his unfinished autobiography. During his time as a student at DePauw, he wrote, he was "frequently in tears" while he read *Uncle Tom's Cabin*. "Since then I never could look with anything else than a spirit of Christlikeness toward the Negro."[28] Indeed, he did take one dramatic step during his tenure as leader of the IASL that is worth noting.

Shumaker's overture to African Americans came about because of the 1908 election and the debate over county option. The *Indianapolis Recorder*, the city's chief African-American newspaper, had strong ties to the state Republican Party and was open to IASL propaganda. The paper reprinted the League's survey of candidates for the 1908 election in which the majority of Democrats refused to answer where they stood on temperance, while all the Republicans voiced support for the party's county option plan. The *Recorder* said that "Indiana's temperance hosts know that those not with them are against them," and it took special aim at Thomas Taggart and the Democratic machine. African Americans were warned that no progress on the liquor problem could be expected if the Democrats and their brewer allies won.[29]

Having set the stage, Shumaker now made a bold move. In August 1908 the *Recorder* ran a notice from the National Colored Temperance League stating that "the churches and church auxiliaries of the state" had been encouraged to send delegates to a temperance convention to be held at Indianapolis's Jones Tabernacle in September. The city's Interdenominational Meeting of Ministers endorsed the convention, which ultimately produced the Colored Indiana Anti Saloon League (CIASL). While Shumaker and the Reverend D. F. White addressed the meeting, it was Attorney General James Bingham who gave the keynote speech on the subject of "temperance and good citizenship." He urged the passing of county option and noted, "Drink unfits the poor and the rich, the white man and the colored man. The organization of a colored league in Indiana to oppose the traffic is a source of congratulation to all citizens who have the good of the colored race at heart."[30]

As quickly as it appeared, the CIASL vanished from the historical record, perhaps a victim of Watson's defeat, yet its very existence raises important questions. Could Shumaker have worked more with African Americans? Had he missed an opportunity to permanently broaden the dry coalition? The answer seems to be, yes. Cooperating with the CIASL would have given him a chance to demonstrate, within the racial confines of the time, real leadership. He could have counted on at least some support from the Republican Party as well as from the Methodist Church. Unfortunately, that did not happen. Perhaps he thought that this small group, less than 10 percent of the population of Indiana (even with the Great Migration), was simply not as important as other groups. Or perhaps, because of their strong association with the Republican Party, Shumaker took blacks' support for granted. More unsettling is the possibility that white evangelical Protestants shared the racial bigotry of the wider white society and were unwilling to cross the color line.[31] Like so many other issues in American society, racism eventually kept the dry movement from coming to its fullest, and dry rhetoric about uplift largely contributed to the segregated status quo.

While the attempt to reach out to African Americans was a disappointment, the dry cause's largest failure came in its rhetoric toward Roman Catholics. Many drys, including Shumaker, hoped that Protestants, despite their misgivings about the continental Sabbath, and wet-leaning immigrants could make common cause with the nation's Catholics about the importance of the dry effort. However, achieving this goal of Christian cooperation required American Catholicism to undergo its own internal debate about the intermixing of religion, ethnicity, and nationalism as well as to decide if temperance did indeed equal prohibition.[32]

The two branches of Christianity were not ignorant of one another. Thanks to newspapers, Protestant Hoosiers could hardly escape knowing something about the Catholic Church, even if it was only the name of the pope. There was a good deal of interaction between the two groups on every day of the week except Sunday, and a tradition of Catholics and Protestants working together for philanthropic ends at the local level.[33] Many Catholics were eager to unite with Protestants against the problems facing America and the wider Christian culture, though it is important to note that the two branches often took different approaches toward societal problems. When it came to Hollywood and motion pictures, for example, Protestants sought Sunday closings of movie theaters while Catholics argued for censorship. They compromised with the creation of a "movie czar" to keep the studios in their place.[34] This tendency to seek different means toward the same end would have important consequences for the dry cause.

The Catholic Church in the United States was an immigrant institution made up chiefly of Irish and Italians who had migrated during the late nineteenth and early twentieth centuries, and this influx posed a problem for American Protestants. The Church's American hierarchy sought to forge "unity amid diversity" by having bishops exert more control over ethnic groups so that they could retain both their ethnicity and Catholicism amid Protestant Americans. This dual approach led to the rise of the Catholic ghetto in urban areas, particularly after attempts at compromise with Protestant institutions were turned aside. Immigrant Catholics found it both necessary (in order to cope with Protestant anti-Catholicism) and beneficial (in order to maintain their ethnic heritage) to devote themselves and their resources to their neighborhood parish church, often sacrificing a beautiful home so that they might have a beautiful church. Therefore, while there were external forces that helped form the ghetto and kept Catholics from being fully part of the wider American society, there were also internal Catholic forces that kept out the larger (Protestant) culture. Certain community and religious circles on both sides of the divide had a vested interest in keeping the two groups apart.[35]

The ghetto mentality exacerbated tensions between Protestants and Catholics by fostering anti-Protestantism. Editorials in the *Indiana Catholic* called for Protestants to return to the Catholic Church if they sought true reverence in religious life, labeled Lutherans as bigots, and argued that Protestant Sunday schools were geared toward anti-Catholic indoctrination. In 1917 the *Indiana Catholic* argued that Protestantism at its best was a "weak" faith when compared to Catholicism, and that at its worst, promoted paganism. Protestant revivals were reviled, and the paper blamed Protestants for crime because they did not have true religion. It was also believed that Protestant "preacher reformers" were driving people out of their churches and contributing to Protestantism's "dwindling" status in the state.[36]

Perhaps the best example of the anti-Protestantism that sprang from the ghetto was in the area of education. Catholics wanted their own schools in order to protect their children from Protestant influences as well as to preserve immigrant culture. The *Indiana Catholic and Record* reported in 1912, "Catholics do not want the public schools abolished or abandoned. They serve a most useful purpose for those who do not put religion before material things—the agnostic, the atheist, the socialist." Catholics also opposed Bible reading in public schools because "every one of the English Protestant versions [of the Bible]," drafted as they were by "apostate priests," has been "proven to be downright perversions of God's word."[37]

Some Catholics, however, hoped to achieve a rapprochement by bringing immigrants into the mainstream of American life. Irish

Catholics largely spearheaded the push for Americanization, since they had long dominated the Catholic Church in the United States and had advantages that later arrivals to America lacked—they spoke English, had a shared history as part of the British Empire, and had experience with voluntary church attendance. Additionally, many Irish Catholics, to the delight of Protestant drys, were supporters of temperance.[38]

Thus, the dry cause was seen as a way for Catholics to attain the Americanization of their faith and halt its ghettoization. The University of Notre Dame near South Bend was a bastion of this kind of thinking, and bishops such as John Ireland, John Keane, and John Lancaster Spalding supported legislation to help curb drinking. Ireland was also a supporter of the ASL. Many Protestants hailed the Americanizers because they were fighting to make the Catholic Church adhere to the nation's civil religion of "obedience to law, tolerance of opinion, and loyalty to country."[39]

The Americanizers' great dry hero was the Irish missionary priest Father Mathew, who sought to convert his native Ireland as well as overseas Irish communities in the United States to temperance. Indeed, though the Irish have a solid claim to having alcohol as a central part of their culture, they also, thanks to Father Mathew, as John F. Quinn rightly points out, have a strong claim to teetotalism. Father Mathew, by the end of his life, while still taking abstinence pledges, came to embrace prohibition because he believed that ordinary people could not stand up to the temptations of drink.[40]

As the twentieth century dawned, this was not an easy stand to make within American Catholicism. Though the Church sent representatives to help organize the Indiana Christian Temperance Alliance, Catholics tended to pursue personal abstinence rather than prohibition, as the former was Church supported and sanctioned. Likewise, the very nature of the Church ensured that dry Catholicism would be different from the Protestant variety. A friendly bishop was helpful but a supportive priest was imperative, as only the latter could guarantee the formation of a parish society. Thus, immigrant priests first had to be converted to the dry cause. But the most striking difference between dry Protestants and Catholics was that within the Catholic Church, dry work was almost entirely a male-dominated reform; women were not part of the movement.[41]

Nevertheless, Catholic drys were organized. At Baltimore in 1872 the Catholic Total Abstinence Union (CTAU) was founded. An Indiana chapter was formed the following year, and the Hoosier state hosted the national organization's meetings in 1878, 1886, 1892, and 1912. The CTAU had strong ties to the University of Notre Dame, which was a bastion of Catholic "total abstainer" thought. The organization acted in parallel to the IASL. Its support was largely within Indiana's Irish Catholic community, though drys also found support among Polish Catholics, who, like their Irish coreligionists, condemned excessive drinking because it perpetuated immigrant stereotypes. The CTAU had a difficult time combating the Catholic ghetto's neighborhood saloon, and its influence waned as German Catholics, with cultural ties to drinking and community ties to brewers, rose in power within the Church and became the voice for many new immigrant groups.[42]

The debate over joining the dry cause divided American Catholics. Many were supporters of temperance but were unsure if they should or could support Prohibition because of its Protestant adherents. Some backed county option while fearing that national prohibition would bring lawbreaking and "fanaticism." Others saw intemperance as a "curse" that had to be destroyed. There were doubts if legislation could make men moral, even as most Catholics recognized that the saloon needed to change. The *Indiana Catholic and Record* argued that temperance was a worthy cause for Catholics to address, but that prohibition led only to "fanatical" notions about the use of government. It supported the formation of the National Abstainers Union in 1915, a Protestant organization that followed in the early footsteps of Father Mathew. At the same time, wets such as James C. Kelly, the manager of the Indiana Brewers Association, wrote articles for the paper attacking Prohibition. As the reform became a reality in the state and nation, the antidry rhetoric heated up among Catholics. The *Indiana Catholic and Record* labeled those who supported the Eighteenth Amendment "extremists" and called Prohibition "chimerical" and doomed to failure.[43]

Protestant drys had a difficult time understanding the divisions within Catholicism. Their unease with Catholics tended to be centered on immigrant culture and the Church hierarchy that sustained it rather than on religious faith. Protestants believed that the continental Sabbath posed a direct threat to their vision of what America should be.[44] However, that did not stop drys from trying to reach out to Catholics. The ASL thought that it could bring both branches of Christianity together. In Indiana, there was a long tradition of dry priests working with Protestants such as Shumaker. The Reverend Christopher Peter Baron, a priest who had served congregations in Indianapolis, Edinburgh, Franklin, and Columbus, was vice president of the IASL. In 1915 he was the first to speak to the House Public Morals Committee in support of statewide prohibition and openly backed former governor Hanly's bid for the presidency the following year. For a time, the IASL also found a staunch ally in Father John Kubacki, a priest serving the predominantly Polish congregation of St. Adalbert's Church on South Bend's Westside.[45]

Shumaker had grown up around Catholics in Illinois and had worked among them in South Bend (where Notre Dame's president, the Reverend Andrew J. Morrissey, fought to keep his campus dry). He thought that the League was something that both Catholics and Protestants could unite behind. Shumaker was ready to help Catholics adjust to dry America, as an incident from 1925 demonstrates. There was a fear among Catholics that priests would be unable to obtain sacramental wine because of Prohibition. When "a strong Catholic friend of the dry cause" came to see Shumaker about this concern, the leader of the IASL took immediate action. He recognized that this law could seriously impair relationships between Protestants and Catholics by playing into the hands of those "wet priests" who "have for years been telling them [Catholics] that the prohibitionists would eventually take away Catholic privileges." Accordingly, Shumaker wrote to F. Scott McBride, begging for an authoritative statement from League headquarters decrying such legislation that he could pass along to the state's Catholics. McBride quickly complied.[46]

Though Catholic visitors to the United States described "frightful American banquets" at which there was nothing to drink but ice water, national prohibition did have some Catholic support. Archbishop Patrick H. Hayes told the New York ASL that America's Catholics would obey the dry laws, and the bishops of Pittsburgh and Helena (Montana) were noted proponents of the reform. Prohibition even had the backing of several prominent Catholic politicians, including Senator Thomas J. Walsh of Montana. A Midwesterner by birth, Walsh was an Irish Catholic who "felt a kinship with reformers of the Protestant churches." However, most Church officials, in their support for the ghetto, opted not to discuss Prohibition in a positive light.[47]

Nationally, the chief lay Catholic supporter of Prohibition came from Kentucky. Patrick Henry Callahan of Louisville was a leader in the Knights of Columbus and an outspoken advocate of a wider dry culture. As a young man, Callahan had been a friend and baseball teammate of Billy Sunday, who had convinced him of the importance of prohibition. Working with the ASL, Callahan argued that Catholics individually vote for dry candidates rather than in a religious bloc. Liquor forces, he thought, had misled Catholics into believing that Prohibition was a "Protestant" undertaking. His dry work earned him the moniker of "the Catholic with a Methodist liver" from H. L. Mencken.[48]

Callahan's position on Prohibition made him a lightning rod of controversy within Catholic circles. He believed that by refusing to join Protestants in the dry crusade, which, as he liked to point out, was once championed by Catholics such as Father Mathew, his coreligionists were aiding anti-Catholicism. His opponents saw him as the personification of Americanization and a sellout to the European culture that immigrants deemed part of their Catholic faith. It was difficult for Callahan to find outlets in official Catholic organs for his ideas, and many of them, including the *Indiana Catholic and Record*, were openly hostile.[49]

Perhaps his most famous detractor was Father Charles Coughlin of Detroit. When Callahan visited the Motor City in 1931, the "radio priest" attacked both the man and his cause in a sermon. Coughlin argued that Callahan's followers were small in number and not part of the Catholic mainstream because Prohibition was an idea based upon heretical (Protestant) notions and Islam. Coughlin said that

Catholics should adhere to the virtue of temperance and called drys "fanatics," "scoundrels," "lying voices," "modern Pharisees," and "intolerant bigots" and their reform an "ignoble experiment." He blamed drys for a rise in crime and problems between Catholics and Protestants. For his part, Callahan saw Coughlin as a purveyor of hate and discord, anti-American and anti-Christian in his ideas and actions, who expected to hide from criticism behind his clerical collar.[50]

Without institutional support, the Catholic share of the dry cause eventually withered and died. The differences between Catholics and Protestants were not so much about whether reforms should take place but rather in the details of reform. By the 1920s, the attempt to use Prohibition to promote Americanization had failed. The Catholic hierarchy would not, or could not, support it. Overall, most Catholics saw Prohibition as a Protestant value being imposed on them, and thus such a reform was, in the words of Father John Ryan, not "morally valid." Catholics also believed that growing governmental power, in the guise of "social reform," was linked to nativism. Working within the Democratic Party and with likeminded Protestants to overturn Prohibition, they helped to form the Association Against the Prohibition Amendment.[51] Thus, the pan-Christian dry coalition was shattered.

The dry cause was supposed to unite the country under the banner of reform. However, Prohibition's rhetorical dreams failed to make a new reality for families, or engender better relations between whites and blacks, or bridge the Protestant-Catholic divide. Drys were unable to permanently expand their coalition. Without these added members, the future of both the reform and the cause was in jeopardy if any problems developed. The defects of the alliance system became readily apparent when a new organization emerged that seemed to be its salvation. Instead, it turned out to be the devil incarnate.

6 | Dangerous Friends

As the mid-1920s began, supporters of the dry cause found themselves needing to mount a more vigorous defense of Prohibition than they had originally expected. Even as drys prepared for battle, an organization arose that pledged to come to their aid. With Protestant churches providing ideas and issues and the ASL serving as a model, the Ku Klux Klan wove together a message of defending God, country, and the nation's laws from those who might oppose them.[1] The Klan offered drys a means of escalating the conflict from the arena of abstract laws and rhetoric to a direct strike at their enemies. For many drys the Klan appeared to be an answer to their prayers, an organization that could preserve both their lifestyle and the orderly society that Prohibition was creating. However, this new ally ultimately both disappointed and betrayed the dry cause.

The mainstream nature of the Klan has been difficult for some to fathom. Early studies, such as John Moffatt Mecklin's, assured readers that the Klan was a Fundamentalist institution fueled by rural anger and ignorance. Klansmen, according to John Higham, had "experienced especially intense frustrations. To relieve their own feelings of inadequacy, humiliation and anxiety, they develop resentments against someone else. By suspecting and attacking an unpopular minority, they can bolster their psychic defenses." Frank Bohn echoed these sentiments by describing the Klan as "an expression of pain, sorrow," and its founder, William Simmons, as "an excellent representative of our well-known type of rural, Protestant clergyman." H.L. Mencken, the widely read newspaper columnist, lumped Protestants, the Anti Saloon League, and the Klan together, while *The Nation*'s Louis Francis Budenz blamed the rise of the Klan in Indiana on the "largely crude and ingrown" Hoosier populace who were too devoted to reforms such as Prohibition for their own good.[2]

As later historians discovered, far from being a rural reaction to modernity, the Klan was a copy of moral-reform organizations with an activist orientation that was key to its attraction to urban and rural members from both middle- and working-class America. This approach helped the secretive group to overcome Northerners' memory of the Reconstruction Klan, which the region's churches and press had attacked. The new Klan thrived in areas where evangelical Protestants were strong and where there was a perceived laxity in the enforcement of Prohibition and vice laws. Its hooded members became the "civilian arm of law enforcement," and Protestant ministers found the group a potent ally in their attempt to achieve full compliance with the Volstead Act.[3]

The Klan, reborn in an age of ultrapatriotism, was able to capitalize on the "considerable confusion between religion and patriotism" that took place as a result of the World War. As one historian of Indiana Methodism noted, "in many places . . . the American flag . . . threatened to take the place of the cross of Christ." Churches stressed the idea of loyalty to country coming after only devotion to God and cast doubt on anyone who could muster only "fifty-fifty loyalty" to either. Patriotic Hoosiers were called upon to "stamp out treason, discover disloyalty, and aid in time of common disaster." These sentiments were fundamental to the Klan's success.[4]

The Klan, moreover, represented the hopes (and fears) of white Protestant Americans. It offered the majority of citizens an opportunity to visibly demonstrate against the forces of wet immigrant culture. It is not surprising that such a message was popular among Hoosiers. The Klan was open to any white, native-born Protestant, which meant it was perfect for Indiana, whose population in 1920 was 95 percent native born (only nine out of ninety-two counties had any significant foreign-born residents), 97 percent white (prior to the Great Migration), and 75 percent Protestant. Historian Leonard Moore has argued that the Klan thrived in Indiana because it was seen as defending institutions and ideas that Hoosiers cared deeply about. Chief among them was Prohibition.[5]

The ambitious man who led the Klan in the state tailored this message to Hoosier audiences. D. C. Stephenson, according to his biographer, M. William Lutholtz, combined political skill and a salesman's tactics with the ability to condemn in public those things he enjoyed in private. Stephenson's pitch to Protestants was genius. Opting for Prohibition and Americanism, not hate, to sell the Klan to Hoosiers, he took evangelical Protestant rhetoric and made its goals and enemies the Klan's goals and enemies. Stephenson patterned the Indiana Klan after the ASL, because he saw the state's churches as a means to recruit members and because "Indiana was the most militantly anti-liquor state in the union." By duplicating and taking over existing organizations, he gave frustrated drys an opportunity to strike at wets in familiar ways. He pitched the Klan as a middle-class status symbol to a wide variety of Hoosiers and eventually to other Northerners as well.[6]

Stephenson argued that the Klan was at the forefront of a cultural war between Protestant Americans and Catholic immigrants. His warning was little more than an amplification of existing Protestant fears of Catholicism and their belief that immigrants needed to be "Americanized" if they were to remain in the United States. To many Protestants, the country was "threatened" by "an invasion of millions of immigrants," whose "commercialized" continental Sabbath demeaned the Lord's Day and were both a bastion of wet support and the source of "social and industrial unrest." These all threatened the moral foundation of the nation.[7] One "nationally recognized champion of red blooded Americanism" summed up this sentiment: "The intricate problem of Americanizing the foreigner is before us for solution. To be Americanized means to understand our language; to have ability to use it; to understand our social, political and industrial ideas and ideals; to accept our ideas and our country as a home, and to be willing to sacrifice for America's ideals. The religion of Jesus Christ is one of the most essential things in Americanizing the foreigner."[8]

Like Stephenson and the Klan, Edward Shumaker firmly believed that Prohibition and the civic order it created were under attack because of immigration. He argued that great numbers of immigrants diluted the population homogeneity needed for respect of the law, and they undermined American culture by settling in ethnic "colonies" in the cities. As proof, he sent a report in May 1925 to the national League, which examined Indiana's prison population and the excess of foreign-born violators of the state's dry laws.[9] Indeed, there was a sense that the problems that Indiana and the nation were having with enforcing Prohibition were a result of "outsiders." The *Noblesville Daily Ledger* published on its front page in 1926 a cartoon entitled "Sailing Back Home." Uncle Sam's boot is shown "deporting" the "alien gun man, alien Red, alien bootlegger, alien beer runner, and alien undesirable."[10]

As for Catholicism, most Protestants still thought in Reformation terms, at least when it came to the Vatican hierarchy. There were concerns in some Hoosier churches that Catholics, under orders from the papacy, sought to control education, destroy American Protestantism, and enable immigrants to take over the United States.[11] They read Bertrand M. Tipple's book, *Alien Rome*, which detailed the sins of the Vatican, the schemes of the Roman hierarchy for America, and the need for Protestants to be on guard.[12] Such notions were hardly on the Protestant fringe. Indiana Methodist bishop Edgar Blake stated that "Roman Catholicism in Europe is the same narrow and intolerant ecclesiasticism it always has been. It does not and apparently cannot change. During the past year Protestant Bibles have been burned publicly in the streets of Rome by the authorities of the Church."[13]

The Klan argued that Catholics could not be trusted citizens because their "first and last allegiance is to the pope of Rome," and "only he who owes all his trust and allegiance to the United States is worthy to be called a 100 per cent American."[14] Since the Catho-

lic Church in the United States had rejected internal Americanization attempts and was taking a harsh line toward Protestantism, this
message struck a chord with many Protestants. And where Protestants were most ignorant of Catholics, the Klan could make outland-
ish claims seem probable. Rumors of papal intrigue and of Catholic
armies ran rampant throughout Protestant America, often growing
as the story passed from person to person.[15]

Indeed, Hoosier Catholics and their institutions were the main
targets of Klan intimidation in Indiana. This should come as no surprise since anti-Catholicism was so intertwined with Prohibition
sentiment that it was only natural for the Klan to take on the dry
cause's largest institutional enemy. Catholic churches around the
state were targeted by the Klan for cross burnings. The University of
Notre Dame near South Bend was "in a virtual state of siege" during
the Klan years and was the site of a 1924 Klan parade that turned
into a riot between the hooded marchers and Notre Dame students
and the city police.[16]

As for African Americans, as Emma Lou Thornbrough has shown,
segregation and racism in Indiana did not arise because of the Klan
but, like other issues, were exacerbated by its actions. Even then,
blacks were not the primary targets of the Klan in the Hoosier state.[17]
However, the situation was different in other areas of the country,
and, as we will see, race and regionalism played an important role in
the Klan's future.

The Klan's success came in co-opting not only the messages but
also the messenger in Protestant churches. Through revivals and the
cycle of reform the Klan emerged on the local scene and won converts
such as Daisy Douglas Barr, a well-known Quaker and dry advocate,
as a way to draw members. Perhaps their greatest accomplishment
in central Indiana was winning over the Reverend A.H. Moore of
Noblesville's Christian Church, a prolific and gifted speaker. Klansmen came to one of Moore's revivals to present his congregation
with a $40 gift (a common Klan tactic). This "interruption" allowed
Moore to address the community on the virtues of the organization
and to praise it as the defender of Protestant American values. Moore
further cemented the ties between the Klan and drys by arguing that

preserving Prohibition, which he described as "a social blessing," required the Klan's help.[18]

With such backing, the Klan became very popular in Indiana's
evangelical Protestant churches, a fact often downplayed by later
denominational historians. The Klan accomplished this by playing
"upon traditional Protestant prejudices" and fears and by promising
to help enforce dry laws.[19] But to do so, it had to not only co-opt the
dry message but also overcome Protestant tendencies to condemn
clubs and lodges. Some church leaders believed that voluntary organizations diverted church members' time and treasure away from
the work of God. Yet, despite these admonishments, fraternal organizations such as the Masons, Elks, and Knights of Pythias were
extremely popular among Protestants, and the Klan used the allure
of a fraternal secret society to attract members.[20]

The Klan was also successful because it embraced the conveniences of the modern world and merged them with older tactics,
again building on the ASL model. Like the League, the Klan expertly
used local newspapers to announce their meetings. But it was more
than just a willingness of newspapers to run paid advertisements. In
central Indiana the Klan was so popular that the naming of members in the paper hardly raised an eyebrow.[21] Additionally, the Klan
started its own paper, the *Fiery Cross*, which, like the League's *American Issue*, was a means of communicating with members.

Another modern means employed to attract members was the
use of motion pictures. Historians have long documented the role
that *The Birth of a Nation* played in helping to found the Klan, but
they have not often considered the Klan's own films and the lengths
to which movie theaters would go to cater to their hooded clientele.
The Klan found that crowds would flock to see movies about the
group. In Noblesville, the Opera House showed the Klan-friendly
picture *One Clear Call*, which presented nightriders as heroes. The
American Theatre, which billed itself as "100 percent" with a "cool,
cozy, and clean" building, showed both *The Traitor Within*, "a modern drama full of life and action," and *The Toll of Justice*, a Klan
picture that dealt with Prohibition, which "every red blooded American should see." Advertisements promised viewers "20,000 robed

Klansmen in action," complete with an airplane duel and deadly car chase, all in an effort to defeat "the underworld" and "protect clean womanhood."[22] This pattern was repeated across the state and was a far cry from the League's modest use of stereoptics. The modern Klan was consigning the groups from whom it had borrowed ideology to the dustbin of history.

The Klan also boosted membership and demonstrated its strength through public events. Descriptions of Klan rallies and marches took advantage of the cloak of mystery that enveloped the organization. Often portrayed as spontaneous, the processions were minutely organized—from the explosives and shotgun discharges that signaled the start, to the band and color guard that led the way, to the large cross that was set ablaze, to the choice of the speaker for the postparade address. Such events attracted large crowds. In July 1923, building on previous rallies in the city, the Klan drew over 12,000 people and 2,000 cars to a parade in Noblesville. Large American flags were everywhere. There were riders on horseback, a Klan band, and Klansmen and women carrying signs that proved their civic-mindedness, with slogans such as "100 per cent American," "Join a Church," "Jesus is our leader," "We are pure Americans," "There will be no illiteracy in this county in 1930," "We favor a limitation on immigration," "White supremacy," "We are a charitable organization," and "We stand for a Christian religion." The parades left onlookers with a sense of awe, or perhaps fear (if they were Catholic or African American), and children with a new game: attempting to guess who was under the passing robes by looking at the exposed shoes.[23]

The organization found its greatest success in casting itself as the protector of American morality. As churches concluded that they could not do everything alone, the Klan offered direct action, not just talk, when it came to enforcing the laws. This was a departure from the ASL's thinking and in the 1920s, an attractive one. While the League argued for better legislation, "preventive societies" such as the Klan sought to work outside of the law. Since drys had long accepted a certain level of vigilantism, the Klan had precedent on its side. During the late nineteenth and early twentieth centuries, Hoosier newspapers ran stories of the dynamiting of saloons by zealous drys, citizens participating in raids on blind tigers, and, a year before Carry Nation made the practice popular, a Tipton woman taking a hatchet to a saloon where her husband was drinking. "The pious end" for these reformers, according to Nancy MacLean, "fully justified the illegal means."[24]

While Hoosiers had a tradition of taking the law into their own hands, they also had a legal way to do it. The Horse Thief Detective Association (HTDA), with a state charter, had existed in Indiana since the nineteenth century and continued in some communities into the twentieth. The Klan saw it as a means to provide members with an outlet for direct action while at the same time conferring legitimacy on the Klan's activities.[25] Under the Klan's guidance, the HTDA came to specialize in Prohibition enforcement, often launching raids in the wake of dry agitation. In South Bend, it claimed to have conducted more liquor raids than the city's police force. Klansmen described themselves as "willing and anxious to give their loyal support in the apprehension of offenders, and the collection of evidence." All they asked for in return was quick trials, to turn the innocent free and to send the guilty to jail.[26]

Klan-backed HTDA raids were sometimes fiascos. The best example, as well as proof that the Klan used both the organization and the issue for its own ends, comes from a raid on the Franklin County home of Green Gabbard. The HTDA obtained a search warrant from local officials in February 1923 on suspicion that Gabbard "had in his possession intoxicating liquor and stills, equipment, and devices for the purpose of manufacturing intoxicating liquor." The resulting raid caused such a commotion that Gabbard's wife died. The house was found to be quite dry, and the charges against Gabbard were quickly dropped. In all probability, the raid was conducted because he was a supporter of the anti-Klan Unity League, not because he had anything to do with bootlegging.[27]

By 1923, Stephenson was at the pinnacle of his power. Protestants were flocking to the Klan because of its message and activism. A Klan gathering in Kokomo that July brought over 50,000 cars into the Howard County seat. Stephenson descended into town in an airplane to address a "throng" who had gathered from across the

Midwest. In October the Hoosier Klan claimed 500,000 members, with plans to increase that figure to one million by May 1924. With members came not only power and influence but also money. In a six-month span in 1923, the Indiana Klan sent over $641,000 to the national offices. The Hoosier Klan's sheer size meant that it played an important role in national Klan affairs, which increasingly worried some observers at the Atlanta, Georgia, headquarters.[28]

The Indiana Klan was now ready to enter politics. It was officially bipartisan in its approach (just like the ASL) and courted and endorsed both Republicans and Democrats, including, among the latter, Senator Samuel Ralston, whom the Klan helped put forward as a "dark horse" candidate for the 1924 Democratic presidential nomination.[29] Overall, however, Stephenson attached the Klan to the Republican Party. Though different from what the Klan in the South was doing, this strategy was hardly a daring one considering Hoosier politics. With few interruptions the GOP had dominated (though not always by landslide margins) the state since the Civil War. As future New Dealer Claude Wickard, himself a third-generation Carroll County Democrat, was to recall, "A Democrat in much of the corn belt was as suspect as the village atheist."[30]

The Klan's association with the state's political parties caused divisions and added fuel to old rivalries. Within the Democratic camp, it created a rift between Catholics and Protestants, which was heightened when former vice president Thomas Marshall commented that the Klan was aiding in law enforcement.[31] In the Republican Party, Stephenson tended to back up-and-coming politicians, such as Ed Jackson and Arthur Robinson, against the established leadership (though Senator James Watson was a significant exception). This support only exacerbated tensions between Watson and James Goodrich, as the former governor was increasingly worried about the deals and "double-crossing" that Watson seemed to revel in. The Klan became an issue in the struggle of who would lead the state party, after state chairman Lawrence Lyons faced calls for his resignation when his brief membership in the Klan became public, and when the new chairman, Clyde Walb, was deemed too close to Watson (and Stephenson) for Goodrich's liking.[32]

In practical terms, this meant that by 1923 the Klan was power-ful enough to unseat Indiana's governor. Warren T. McCray, who had been elected in 1920, was arrested and convicted by the federal government in early 1924 for "borrowing" $150,000 from the state board of agriculture to pay personal debts. Though he did not pretend to be innocent of the charges, McCray believed that something more than his illegal use of state funds was behind the case, saying, "There are many angles to this fight. Some of it comes from those who have been disappointed because I could not do what they wanted me to do." One of those people was Secretary of State Ed Jackson, who authorized the Klan's state charter, which McCray opposed. When charges were first considered, the Marion County prosecutor, Wil-liam P. Evans, who was the governor's son-in-law, resigned rather than prosecute McCray. According to Evans, the Klan approached McCray and offered to have the charges against him dropped if he would appoint their man to Evans's post. He refused, and was soon on his way to federal prison.[33]

These tensions, divisions, and accusations burst onto the state political scene during the election of 1924. The Klan debate pushed discussion of Prohibition out of the headlines. Some observers opined that Klan endorsements in the primary (as well as the general) elec-tion could be a major factor in deciding who won and lost, while others did not think membership in a fraternal organization should be a political issue at all.[34]

Both parties had primary battles shaped by the candidates' posi-tion on the Klan. On the Democratic side, Lafayette mayor George R. Durgan based his candidacy upon his anti-Klan position. He char-acterized the Klan as un-Christian, un-American, and dedicated to spreading "hate." Durgan's chief rival was Dr. Carleton B. Mc-Culloch, who opted to use the internal Republican power struggle to his advantage. He told supporters that the Republican Party had been taken over by the Klan and called on those who opposed the organization to flock to the Democratic banner. He also eventually endorsed an anti-Klan plank in the state party platform. Republi-cans had to pick between the popular (and Klan-backed) secretary of state, Jackson, and a vocal critic of the Klan, Indianapolis mayor Lew

Shank. In the end, McCulloch defeated Durgan by nearly 15,000 votes, and Jackson won the Republican primary by over 48,000.[35]

The political parties did not know how to deal with the Klan. Not all Hoosier Republicans embraced Stephenson. Senator Watson claimed to be neutral and did nothing to further the request of African-American Republicans to have the state party platform condemn the Klan. While the organization was strong within the Republican convention, it was nearly equally so, in terms of delegates controlled, at the Democratic gathering. Many Democrats blamed the Republican Party for "politicizing" the Klan, though the Indiana delegation to the national Democratic convention in 1924 refused to support an anti-Klan plank that called the organization by name.[36]

As campaigning came to a close in the fall, both parties made overtures to the center of the Hoosier electorate. As the *Lafayette Journal and Courier* noted, Republicans who had been endorsed by the Klan were talking about civic and religious liberty, while Democrats who had not been so blessed were doing their best to downplay the party's anti-Klan plank. When the balloting was over, 1924 proved to be a Republican year. Though he trailed President Calvin Coolidge in number of votes, Jackson was swept into office. Democrats, whether supported by the Klan or endorsed by the IASL, found it almost impossible to get elected in Indiana. In Madison County, where the Klan was strong, the Republicans won the contests by a 4,500-vote average in an election that saw an 87-percent voter turnout. In Lake County, where fiery crosses signaled the victory of Klan-backed candidates, not a single Democrat was elected. With Democrats more divided than Republicans over the Klan (thanks to the Catholic vote), the Grand Old Party also won in counties that were traditional Democratic strongholds.[37]

Despite the victories, the campaign and election of 1924 raised serious questions about the Klan in the minds of many Hoosiers. For one thing, the margin of victory seemed to cast doubt on how dire a threat to American culture was actually posed by the Klan's opponents. For another, the Klan was dividing Hoosiers against one another. When a debate about the Klan was held at Butler University, its supporters broke it up by brandishing firearms and lighting a fiery cross near the campus. In another incident, when Indianapolis police stopped a planned cross burning, a large crowd jeered at them. HTDA raids only added fuel to the backlash. People began to wonder if membership in the Klan was compatible with civicmindedness. As John Bodnar has pointed out, since Indianapolis's Protestant elites were against the Klan, this meant that Jews, blacks, and Catholics were included in patriotic marches and public events, such as the dedication of the World War Memorial and the annual Saint Patrick's Day parade.[38]

The list of Klan opponents grew as the 1920s progressed. In 1923 the American Legion, American Bar Association, and Methodist Social Service Federation all condemned the organization. The year also saw the Indianapolis Church Federation pass a resolution calling for equitable treatment and improved conditions for the city's African American residents as the "Christian and patriotic" duty of its member congregations.[39] Newspapers spoke out against the Klan. In Indiana the leading anti-Klan paper was the *Indianapolis Times*, which engaged in a newsprint war with the *Fiery Cross* during the 1924 election.[40]

The Klan troubled the backbones of the dry cause, the evangelical Protestant denominations and the ASL. It did receive considerable support from local Protestant churches, in large part because of its activist nature. However, as Robert Moats Miller has shown, the Klan often bore the brunt of criticism from denominational sources. Indiana Methodist Bishop Frederick Leete, for example, was an outspoken critic.[41] This should not be surprising, since from the viewpoint of denominational hierarchies, the Klan was an outside group competing for influence with the Methodist Church.

The Klan posed a greater problem for the ASL. The organization was duplicating the League's ideals, mission, and political tactics. If the League represented the church united, then the Klan seemed poised to be the church in action. Former New York ASL superintendent William H. Anderson wanted to merge the League with the Klan into a new institution called the American Prohibition Protestant Patriotic Protective Alliance in order to combat what he called "political Romanism."[42]

From Shumaker's perspective, the Klan in Indiana clearly built upon the past success of the IASL, especially in the realm of politics, and capitalized on what opponents labeled the "holier than thou" mentality of the IASL. Though the League remained better at influencing the course of legislation, the Klan not only perfected the IASL's tactic of political endorsement but also proved far superior at mobilizing voters behind approved candidates.[43] It was also popular with some of the League's better-known ministerial supporters, and the IASL approved of the Klan's HTDA liquor raids. So, it is appropriate to ask if Shumaker was one of the estimated 70,000 ministers nationwide who joined the Klan.[44]

No one publicly brought up the issue of Shumaker's support until after the Klan was destroyed and wets were seeking to discredit the aging dry leader and his cause. The evidence that later historians used to indict the IASL and the Klan as being part of a "super government" surrounds the reelection campaign of Senator Arthur Robinson. Hugh F. Emmons, a former Klan leader in St. Joseph County, testified that Robinson was a member and that the Klan was ordered to work with the IASL to get him reelected. Emmons even claimed to have met with Shumaker in South Bend to devise a campaign strategy. Some perspective needs to be given to this revelation, however. Attorney General Arthur Gilliom, who was conducting the deposition, was running against Robinson in the Republican primary and was also locked in a legal battle with Shumaker. He was searching for political ammunition while also seeking to rid the state of the Klan.[45]

Shumaker denied the accuracy of Emmons's testimony from the start. In reply to a letter from ASL headquarters in 1924 warning against intermingling state leagues with "other organizations," Shumaker wrote, "I think we are keeping clear of blame in this matter. The Ku Klux Klan, for example, is doing many things which we would have liked to have done, but we are not working with them in either an official or unofficial way. Your warning as to joining with factions in parties is also timely and I heartily agree with you."[46] He had another chance in May 1928, when the *Indianapolis Times* ran a "While you were out slip" from D. C. Stephenson's files. The slip, dated 17 February 1925, noted that a legislator named Johnson had called on the Klan leader while the latter was out of the office. Johnson told the secretary "Mr. Shumaker [had] sent him." Shumaker vehemently denied that the slip referred to him. As he pointed out to the *Times*, there were two Johnsons in the state legislature during 1925, neither of whom he recalled talking to at much length. Furthermore, there was more than one Shumaker in Indianapolis. More important, as Shumaker told the paper, "I have no recollection whatever of having sent any one to see D. C. Stephenson."[47] There is reason to believe Shumaker's denial, primarily because the man in question was addressed as "Mister" in the note, but he was usually referred to as "Reverend" or "Superintendent." It is also noteworthy that the *Times* let the story drop.

Historians such as Kathleen Blee, however, have linked Shumaker to the Klan.[48] However, there is no way to compare Klan membership lists to ASL membership lists because the latter do not exist. The ASL was not something one "joined"; one could be a part of the movement simply by sitting in one's church pew. That temperance activity was a gateway for involvement in the Klan, especially in Indiana, there is no doubt. But it is erroneous to assume, as Blee does, that just because a person was a dry, he automatically joined the Klan. Likewise, without evidence to the contrary, Shumaker must be taken at his word about the IASL's association with the Klan. Either that, or he lied to a man (McBride) whom he deeply respected, and Hugh Emmons was telling the whole truth in his testimony before the attorney general.

There are other reasons to doubt an alliance between Shumaker and the Klan. Take, for example, the dry leader's role in Albert Beveridge's failed 1922 political comeback. Though largely out of touch with current political trends, Beveridge managed to unseat the incumbent Republican senator, Harry New, in the party primary and was prepared to face off against Democrat Samuel Ralston in the fall. However, while the Klan divided the Indiana Republican Party and openly backed Ralston, Beveridge and his anti-Klan position had the full support of Shumaker. From the existing correspondence, it seems that the two men developed a close friendship in the years following the 1908 election debacle, the repeal of county option, and the Progressive insurgency—much more so than previous biographers of the senator have admitted. Their letters, when they are not discussing political strategy, are full of warmth and affection, usually beginning with "Dear Ed" or "Dear Albert" (an anomaly in both men's correspondence) and ending in pledges of loyalty and friendship. Though defeated by Ralston, Shumaker held out the hope that Beveridge would lead dry political forces against the wets.[49]

And then there is the question of power. It was widely believed by men such as newspaperman Irving Leibowitz that Shumaker controlled the legislature and was "the most powerful man in the state" and head of "the most powerful organization" in Indiana. He could crack "the ecclesiastical whip" and get whatever legislation he desired, because of his base within Indiana's evangelical Protestant churches. By the mid-1920s, the Indianapolis area was home to the second largest concentration of Methodists in the country, and some 373,000 statewide.[50] If his influence was real, he simply did not need the Klan, no matter how attractive it might have seemed.

Indeed, it was within the state legislature that the first chinks in the Klan's armor appeared. Following the Republican victory in 1924, all eyes turned to the statehouse to see if it translated into a Klan-dominated legislative agenda. The 1925 legislature saw bills on such topics as effecting stricter Prohibition enforcement, promoting Bible instruction in public schools, and restricting parochial schools. While the Klan played a role in the public discourse that brought these popular issues to debate, it was entirely ineffective in getting laws passed that were solely Klan inspired. Party loyalty remained high, and the state legislature was hardly a rump Klan-dominated body. As Speaker of the House Henry G. Leslie contended in 1928, the Republican leadership worked to stop the Klan within the legislature by killing bills in committee through parliamentary procedure. Furthermore, while the Klan was powerful in Indiana, it was not the only organized lobby in state politics. The IASL, the WCTU, the Farm Bureau, and other groups were also advocating bills.[51]

Even before their legislative agenda ground to a halt, things started to go horribly wrong for the Klan. The organization was in the midst of a power struggle pitting Stephenson against the national

Klan. But, worst of all, Stephenson was charged with the murder of Madge Oberholtzer, the end result of a brutal sexual assault that caused the young statehouse worker to take poison in order to secure her escape from the Klan's Grand Dragon. Stephenson's incarceration and trial in Noblesville turned into a spectacle. People came to the rural community just to see him in handcuffs.[52] The prosecution, thanks to Oberholtzer's deathbed statement, was able to paint Stephenson as a drunken "destroyer of virtue and womanhood." The defense could only try and discredit the victim, arguing that the young woman died from the poison she ingested, not from the wounds that Stephenson had inflicted.[53]

It did not take the jury long (a single ballot) to convict Stephenson in the packed courthouse. Most Hoosiers approved of the jury's verdict, a sentiment that was reflected in the state's newspapers. The *Indianapolis Times* called Stephenson "the man who would be king" and took comfort in the fact that he had been dethroned by his own actions. Hoosiers, the paper said, had let much happen in their name under his watch, but they would not allow the murderer of an innocent woman to go unpunished. The *Kokomo Daily Tribune* called it "madness" that such a man had ever had as much influence in the state as he did.[54]

The backlash was a result of Stephenson's having betrayed some of the key moral principles at the heart of the cause he had hijacked for the Klan. As the *Madison Courier* pointed out, "the life Stephenson was living prior to his arrest was not that of a decent law-abiding citizen." He had violated the very womanhood he had sworn to defend. Though he expected a pardon, there was no way Governor Jackson could grant him one, because the woman was dead. Despite the national Klan's best efforts during the course of the trial, in the minds of many Hoosiers, Stephenson was the Klan incarnate. As a result, when he was exposed, the organization suffered.[55]

Stephenson's moral reform rhetoric and activism had been enough to paper over the deep sectional divisions within the Klan, but in the wake of his conviction this no longer proved possible. The activities of Southern Klansmen stood in stark contrast to many of the values that Northerners, but especially Hoosiers, liked to assume that they stood for. Though not an easy task, Stephenson's extolling of Prohibition and 100-percent Americanism had helped him build up a large membership. When the Klan first appeared in the North, some commentators had labeled it as a group of "Southern bigots and fanatics" who had "invaded the Northern states." Even as the Klan was taking off in Indiana, reports from Louisiana of a "reign of terror" made headlines. Indeed, violence was a mainstay of the Southern Klan and was not stopped even when it was obvious that it was hurting the organization's grab for political power. Hoosier Klansmen tried to differentiate between the Northern and Southern wings to the press with mixed success.[56]

Stephenson claimed that these regional tensions, which pitted him against Imperial Wizard Hiram Evans for control, are what caused him to break from the Klan (or for Evans to kick him out) just before his legal problems began. Evans was worried about Stephenson's success in the North and feared that a sectional rift would dry up Atlanta's money. For his part, Stephenson believed that Evans lacked the necessary political vision to make the Klan a power at the national level. The Hoosier Grand Dragon saw his Imperial Wizard as hamstrung by his Southernness. Stephenson had warned Evans that he and "other honorable men in the Northern states" were worried about the violent actions of their Southern brethren and the negative publicity it created. Stephenson told his Northern followers that this "stigma" would have to be overcome.[57]

In the wake of Stephenson's dismissal and trial, the differences between the Southern national organization and Northern local Klaverns became public. The breaking point came when an effort was made to convince Hoosier members to carry out acts of terrorism more akin to the Southern order. In South Bend, Klansmen were told to tar and feather someone in that "Roman Catholic city," and a proposal was even made to drop dynamite from a hot-air balloon onto the famous golden dome of the University of Notre Dame's Main Building. When the local leaders protested, they were told that some dramatic act was needed to "shake up the Protestant people." And when Southern leaders told members of the Noblesville-Arcadia Klan that they were to kill an African American to assert themselves, members quit in protest. These types of incidents exacerbated tensions between the local and state branches of the Klan. Local members were already wary of the time and money that they saw the state leadership pouring into politics rather than addressing local problems.[58]

Thanks to the Stephenson trial and the attempted Southern takeover, the Klan became an object of ridicule in the state, and its membership plummeted. More people felt free to speak out against the organization. A Lebanon minister called the Klan "absolutely and detrimentally bad, wrong, and iniquitous." Methodists in Noblesville were told to watch for inner sins glossed over by "righteousness on the outside," and the Indiana Conference of the Methodist Church believed that Americanization could be attained without the "surrender" of "the spirit of patience and charity." The Klan was labeled a "menace," and people were urged to live right rather than do a lot of "loud talking." Klansmen attempted to regroup, but the suggestion from the headquarters in Atlanta that members lodge themselves within the Indiana Democratic Party (more evidence of the North-South split) spurred the Indiana Klan to get out of politics all together. By January 1926, membership had dwindled from 178,000 to 50,000 across the state. As the public condemnations increased and the ripple effects of Stephenson's trial and the inter-Klan squabbling continued, that number was soon down to a mere 4,000.[59]

In January 1928, Attorney General Arthur Gilliom began proceedings to revoke the Klan's state charter. He argued that the Klan had been intent upon taking over the state and that Indiana needed to return to "true representative government" rather than rule by "the bigot, the fanatic, and the demagogue." But, by then, the Klan itself was spent as a force. Two years later the new state attorney general, James Ogden, dropped the suit because he saw no reason to "stir things up." The Klan was all but disbanded.[60]

The Klan's demise left serious questions for Hoosiers about why the organization had been so popular. A major reason for its success within Protestant circles was apathy. Drys simply accepted the Klan as part of the mainstream and did not speak out against it. Its disappearance, sped up by the revelations of the Stephenson trial, can also be attributed in part to that same apathy. People joined, but they did not remain active or stopped paying their dues. As the Klan became less able to address the issues of the day, support withered. Nationally, the Klan disappeared as an organization almost as quickly as it had appeared.[61]

There is no doubt that both real and imagined associations between the ASL and the Klan hurt the League. But Shumaker and the IASL still provided, and so, too, did the older institutions of the dry cause. Yet the Klan's hateful legacy helped to shatter any hope for the dry coalition of white evangelical Protestants, African Americans, and Catholics needed to maintain Prohibition as the law of the land.[62] As the late 1920s began, this reality confronted Shumaker.

7 | Trials and Tribulations

The 1920s began on a high note for the dry crusade. Americans voted in Prohibition "hopefully" and wanted to give the reform a chance. Hoosiers in particular seemed to desire the civil order that Prohibition promised.[1] These hopes meant that drys such as Edward Shumaker increasingly focused on law enforcement, which brought them into conflict not only with wets but also with the police, prosecutors, and judges who had to enforce the laws. Drys found that victory was more difficult to maintain than it had been to achieve, and for the first time questions arose about the longevity of their reform.

America's geography and its politics made total enforcement nearly impossible. States such as Florida and Rhode Island had enforcement issues different from those of Indiana, so a uniform policy was not crafted. Thus, enforcement rarely lived up to dry hopes. Fines tended to be little more than old liquor fees with new names, police seemingly targeted only those violators who were not politically connected, and sentences were often suspended. The proliferation of automobiles compounded these problems. By 1926, Indiana had one car for every four people, and the so-called crossroads of America became a bootlegger's paradise, which prompted Shumaker to refer to automobiles as the "old-time saloons on wheels." Furthermore, thanks to the money made in bootlegging, corruption returned to Hoosier politics. In 1923, seventy-five defendants, including the mayor of Gary, were convicted for being part of a ring that resold confiscated liquor in Lake County. Two years later, the mayor of Bicknell in Pike County was put on trial for manufacturing and selling alcohol illegally.[2]

Nevertheless, enforcement was strict enough to inspire those engaged in the illegal trade to be creative. In Hamilton County, for example, bootleggers had customers paint their milk bottles white so that beer or liquor could be concealed inside. Stills were expertly camouflaged; one in Archerville was discovered under a haystack, complete with electric lights and an early-warning alarm bell.[3]

Many drys believed that foreign-born bootleggers were facilitating the flow of alcohol to wealthy Americans. The rich, drys argued, needed to understand that Prohibition applied to them as well. The *Indiana Daily Student*, in an editorial citing Shumaker, said that it was the upper 10 percent of the nation who refused to abide by the law, and it urged a crackdown to remind the wealthy that they were not above it. Drys also grew disgusted with what they saw as the wet bias of many newspapers. Some journalists only covered the complaints of wets who would not accept electoral and constitutional defeat, attacked "professional drys" and their "heavy handed" laws, and sensationalized the activities of bootleggers. Drys even found it difficult to have sympathy for those people who died from drinking poisonous home brews, since wets cited those deaths to call for repeal.[4]

Shumaker knew that not all Hoosiers rejoiced at Prohibition's arrival. Areas of the state, such as the Calumet region and Dubois County, were bastions of the wet cause and places where bootlegging was tolerated, if not encouraged. Speakeasies could be found across the state from corner alleys, to American Legion posts, to the Claypool Hotel in downtown Indianapolis. Illicit drinking undermined respect for the law by making anyone who drank, by definition, a criminal. Shumaker's answer to these problems was to call for new laws and stricter enforcement.[5]

His attention was drawn to the state's judiciary. Shumaker told a Methodist gathering in Evansville that the Indiana Supreme Court was more interested in the nuances of the law than any other legal body in the country and its members dwelt on "too many technicalities" in deciding liquor cases. It was time to challenge lenient judges, he believed, even if they were Republicans.[6] The state Supreme Court was well aware of Shumaker's displeasure, but in the Klan dominated-political environment, the justices were not open to his criticism. In a 1925 ruling the court said that law enforcement by any means necessary could not be "sanctioned by law-abiding citizens. Such expressions are the law of the mob, the 'hijacker,' the bootlegger, the professional law violator, and, in some instances, a conscience balm for the active reformer in his endeavor to mold public opinion and incite public prejudice by misrepresenting the facts or by garbling the law in order to ingratiate himself on an unsuspecting public for his own pecuniary benefit."[7]

With an uncooperative high court, Shumaker sought a stricter dry law for Indiana. In 1925 the IASL drafted a bone-dry bill for the legislature with the help of the Federal Prohibition Office, the U.S. district attorney, and the Marion County prosecutor. The bill closed loopholes in and strengthened the enforcement of the state's existing dry laws, in large part by offering a financial incentive for successful prosecutions. Sponsored by Representative Frank Wright, the bill proved extremely popular, with only one person voting against it in the House and with the Senate passing it 35 to 4. The bill provoked little debate in either chamber, despite opponents charging that drys were "railroading" it through the legislature. With the victory of this "practical" law, the IASL predicted a "long dry spell in Indiana."[8]

The Wright law was part of a national trend of drys working for stricter legislation, since early enforcement plans had been overly optimistic, unorganized, and uncoordinated. The fact that laws drawn up by the ASL at the state level often became harsher through the political process demonstrates, according to Catherine Gilbert Murdock, the strength of dry sentiment at the grassroots. Drys also contemplated dramatic action at the national level. At the 1925 national ASL convention, some delegates advocated the return of wet states to territorial status. Others called for the deportation of convicted aliens and for Prohibition agents to be put under the civil service.[9]

Thanks to the new law and his strong leadership, Shumaker's IASL was a model for the League nationally. The ASL attempted to raid his staff for state superintendents in Washington, Wyoming, and Wisconsin. Shumaker guarded his position carefully, even if it created friction between himself and some officials in the League hierarchy. He was worried that the national League wanted to replenish its own coffers at the expense of his state work. While he was proud to serve on the ASL's Executive Committee, he worked hard to ensure that the ASL was not blurred into the World League against Alcoholism. He was convinced that Ernest H. Cherrington intended to place the World League above the ASL, despite the fact that America was not yet solidly dry.[10]

Shumaker did have a good relationship with F. Scott McBride of the national League, often addressing him in letters as "my Chief." McBride, in turn, expressed admiration for what Shumaker was doing in Indiana. He lauded the Wright law as "probably the most advanced piece of legislation" yet passed by drys, and he hoped to see it duplicated at the federal level. When he witnessed one of Shumaker's carefully planned and executed field days firsthand, McBride was impressed. He asked Shumaker to send him "some sort of summary" of how it was conducted so that he "could use that information in stimulating the field day idea in other states." Shumaker's reply came in the form of a three-page letter that summed up his over two decades of organizing such events.[11]

Shumaker's place in Hoosier politics, however, was coming under attack. Candidates resented his classifying them as wet in the IASL voter guide, as did some members of the press. One of his new enemies was Thomas Adams, the editor of the *Vincennes Commercial*. In a full-page editorial, Adams accused the dry leader of "interfering with local politics" and urged Shumaker to "get the facts or shut up." When Shumaker came to Vincennes to talk to ministers and candidates but not to the *Commercial*, the paper said he was "afraid to admit he is wrong." The rival *Vincennes Sun* accused the *Commercial* of "hypocrisy" and blamed the rise of bootlegging in the area on two officeholders whom Shumaker was attempting to unseat.[12]

In 1924, Shumaker was involved in an election battle over a seat on the Indiana Supreme Court. The incumbent, Benjamin M. Willoughby, was a former Republican state legislator and circuit court judge from Vincennes who had helped craft the court's recent decision that required police officers to obtain a warrant before searching a car for alcohol. Shumaker loathed that decision and threw the full support of the IASL behind Willoughby's Democratic opponent, George Denton. Despite 1924 being a Republican year, no one doubted Shumaker's power and influence to sway voters. The campaign was bitterly fought and the election extremely close. Initially, a single vote gave Willoughby the victory (out of more than 1.2 million ballots cast), while a recount gave the election to Denton by over 400 votes. Secretary of State Ed Jackson, however, declined to accept a second certification of results and ceded the election to his fellow Republican.[13]

State Democrats announced plans to contest the outcome. Denton took his case to the state legislature, a move that was supported by the IASL, church groups, and several state legislators. But the attorney general, Arthur Gilliom, ruled that the legislature lacked the constitutional authority to overturn Jackson's decision. Denton then took his case to the courts. Former vice president Thomas Marshall and Senator Samuel Ralston both joined Denton's legal team, and a special judge was appointed to hear arguments. In March 1925 the judge dismissed Denton's suit, having based his decision on existing legislation. He told the disappointed candidate that the legislature, not the courts, must resolve the problem. Shumaker was angered by the outcome and told drys that, with Willoughby on the bench, it would be difficult for the Supreme Court to "enforce Prohibition." There was no doubt in the mind of Shumaker's son Paul that his father's battle with Justice Willoughby was the beginning of all his subsequent tribulations.[14]

With his intervention in the Denton case, Attorney General Gilliom fully entered the dry leader's life. Shumaker's antagonist was one of thirteen children, born in August 1886 in Missouri, whose family had moved to Adams County, Indiana, in 1891. He briefly attended Goshen College, where he met his wife, before talking his way into the University of Michigan Law School, having convinced the dean to let him prove himself in the classroom. Gilliom excelled at Michigan and, after graduation, returned to Indiana, where he developed a "large practice" in South Bend and Mishawaka. By the early 1920s, Gilliom was politically active. In 1922 he fought the removal of a South Bend school official whom the Klan wanted ousted, and he tried to stop the organization from obtaining a permit to march in the city. In 1924 he ran for attorney general and defeated a Klan-backed candidate at the Republican convention. Despite the Klan's influence within the GOP, Gilliom was warmly welcomed onto the fall ticket and, thanks to the Republican tide that swept the state, was elected attorney general in November.[15]

Prohibition cases engulfed his office. The Wright bone-dry law was raising the number of convictions, but it was also creating a case backlog at both the circuit and appellate levels. One of the law's provisions, and a contributing factor to its success, was that prosecutors received a bonus of $25 for each conviction. Furthermore, extralegal law-enforcement actions by the Horse Thief Detective Association created problems for Gilliom because the HTDA often failed to follow other laws as it sought to enforce Prohibition. Thus, despite plenty of arrests, the finer points of the law lowered the number of convictions. Gilliom urged prosecutors to enforce all statutes equally, not just those that paid them a conviction bonus. Such statements did not endear him to Shumaker.[16]

Both men supported Prohibition, but they were on a collision course on the issue of enforcement. Thinking the attorney general was downplaying the importance of the dry cause, Shumaker responded in his annual report on the League's activities. The 1926 report outlined the "titanic struggle" that the dry cause was entering. Shumaker warned drys that with the reelection of Justice Willoughby, Prohibition had a foe on the state's high court. He also believed that the attorney general's office was not strong enough to prosecute all the offenders of the law. The IASL voted to commend Shumaker in January 1926, and, a few weeks later, the *American Issue: Indiana Edition* ran a copy of the report.[17] Shumaker was well aware that his written words could get him into trouble, but, as he told the national office in 1925, "I have always been exceedingly careful and have never inserted anything without having the authority to back the same up."[18]

The 1926 report, however, tested his theory. Gilliom was outraged by what he read. In a scathing five-page, single-spaced letter addressed to the League's trustees, the attorney general took apart the report as if it were under cross-examination. Gilliom blasted it for its "unjust criticisms . . . of the Supreme Court and its judges," calling many of Shumaker's charges a "misrepresentation of decisions" and arguing that "no one who is competent to judge can justly criticize any of the decisions of the Supreme Court of Indiana in liquor cases, or any of its judges." He also said that because the IASL was active politically, it fell under the Corrupt Practices Act, and he was going to place it under scrutiny.[19] Gilliom ended his letter as follows:

> I am calling these matters to your attention because I assume you are interested in the truth, and that it is your desire that your organization should assist public officers and contribute to a general confidence in government, rather than to obstruct honest efforts under oath of office and to destroy confidence in government. I should be glad to have you make your independent inquiry into the situation, and to that end the office of Attorney General is open to you. But I must say that if further attempt is made to bring the chief law office of the state and the Supreme Court and its decisions into disrepute by means of misrepresentations of facts, I shall, at the proper time, carry the case to the people to the end that good government may flourish under confidence of the people in their institutions and officers. Let no one doubt that I lack the material or determination to do this.[20]

Gilliom's letter also contained an ultimatum to the League: the trustees either had to accept his version of the facts or Shumaker's. If they stood by their superintendent, there would be consequences. To prove that his words were not empty, Gilliom filed contempt charges against Shumaker and two League attorneys. In doing so, he claimed to be protecting Prohibition from professional drys. In his preliminary report to the Indiana Supreme Court, the attorney general painted a picture of Shumaker using his position of trust as a member of the clergy to build up a political machine that influenced the course of elections. In particular, he pointed to the League's voter guides and its rating of candidates as "wet" or "dry." Drys quickly rallied to Shumaker's defense. Though some trustees claimed to have asked him to alter the wording of his report, in the end, they supported their superintendent. The League refused to accept Gilliom's assertion that it was a political organization because it printed voter guides. Both sides would have to be patient, however, as the high court adjourned without taking up the attorney general's petition.[21]

In April 1926, when the state's high court brought the two sides together to discuss Gilliom's charges, Shumaker's attorneys asked the justices to order the attorney general to specify his complaint against the dry leader. Gilliom complied, "going into minute detail."[22] Shumaker wrote McBride in May that his attorneys had determined that "there is no contempt in anything that I said. However, a majority of our Supreme Court is wet, of that I feel no doubt. From what I can learn further they are very sensitive to comments that have been made upon quite a number of their decisions." The real problem, Shumaker believed, was "that the Supreme Court has arbitrary power in the matter" and "means to slap somebody." But he took solace in the fact that "Church people throughout the state are all wrought up over it. The way letters and resolutions expressing confidence have been coming in to this office is to me a revelation."[23]

While he waited, Gilliom continued to press his case. He wrote, as a private citizen, to many of the state's leading attorneys and politicians, arguing that Shumaker and the IASL were constructing a "super government" in Indiana. He received a flood of responses from these influential people, many of whom viewed Shumaker as a threat to their own power and position. Their letters expressed their "contempt" for the IASL and its tactics and approved of curtailing the "political activities" of "certain professional reformers." The correspondents also praised Gilliom's efforts. A lawyer from Indianapolis congratulated him for going after "professional prohibitionists," while both the Allen County and Starke County Republican organizations urged him to continue to fight "fanatics" such as Shumaker. The letters spread rumors about Shumaker for Gilliom's use, including one that claimed that the dry leader was paid large amounts of cash by a Detroit bootlegging syndicate. The writers also encouraged Gilliom to run for governor.[24]

Shumaker was soon fighting back. He blasted the high court for deciding cases on "technicalities" rather than on the law, and he told audiences that he refused to allow "a wet Attorney-General to hold any club over me." Requests to speak and letters of support poured into his office from around the state. Ecumenical dry support was a constant for Shumaker throughout the legal struggle. The League's law-enforcement rallies, often held in the ornate Roberts Park Methodist Church in Indianapolis, became "love feasts" for Shumaker, where listeners could hear such notables as McBride, Clarence True Wilson, and Indiana University's President William Lowe Bryan praise the work of the IASL and its superintendent as well as attack the attorney general. Gilliom countered by threatening Shumaker with more charges if he uttered any other contemptuous comments.[25]

In June 1926, Shumaker was ordered to answer the charges before the court. The dry leader told the justices that he had not meant to be contemptuous and asked for the charges to be dismissed. His qualified apology might have been the end of the matter, except that the attorney general proposed that the Supreme Court assemble a friends-of-the-court committee to see if the case should proceed. Shumaker's attorneys were against the idea, but the justices agreed.[26] This committee was a Who's Who of legal talent in the state. It consisted of two former presidents of the Indiana State Bar Association, a former special assistant to U.S. Attorney General A. Mitchell Palmer, Governor Samuel Ralston's former attorney general, and two past Indiana Supreme Court justices. More important, they were all men connected to the Democratic and Republican power structures in the state.[27]

Not surprisingly, the formation of the committee drew mixed reviews. The *Indianapolis Star* backed the idea and thought that "Dr. Shumaker, in his zeal as a reformer, probably did not stop to consider how some of the statements in his annual report sounded."

The paper supported holding Shumaker in contempt because "when Indiana reaches the point where any one or any organization can expect the courts to decide cases as partisans or a cause, not only the future of justice but the whole fabric of free government will be in danger." Shumaker was angry, telling McBride, "we were not consulted about the appointment of this committee or its personnel. The appointment of such a committee is an unheard of thing, at least in Indiana judicial matters." Moreover, it was "handpicked and the cards are stacked against us."[28]

The outcome was as he had feared. The panel ruled in July that the statements in the report were contemptuous. Five members said that Shumaker should be found guilty, with only one believing that he had purged himself of contempt. All six men held that League attorneys Ethan A. Miles and Jesse E. Martin should go free since Shumaker alone was responsible for writing the report. According to the dry leader, the committee had reached this conclusion by reading Gilliom's brief against him, not by actually looking at the transcripts of the three cases he was accused of misrepresenting. Had they done so, Shumaker was sure, they would have seen that it was the attorney general, and not he, who was in the wrong.[29]

Hope was not yet lost, however. Shumaker told McBride that rumors were circulating that Senators James Watson and Arthur Robinson were going to intervene in the matter, because they thought "that if the Supreme Court does so [convict him] it will mean the defeat of the Republican Party this fall." Shumaker had contacted both senators, telling Watson, who was up for reelection, that delaying the matter looked "very much like a case of politics" and was a "scheme" to protect the Republican Party from angry drys. Shumaker wanted Watson to either bring pressure for a decision before the election, which was his right, or issue a statement that the "Republican organization" was not supporting the attorney general. While Watson said he could do neither, Robinson at least offered his full moral support. Not surprisingly, when he eventually learned of these discussions, Gilliom was angry. The episode only steeled his resolve to convict the dry leader.[30]

Shumaker's case was not occurring in a legal vacuum. There was hope that there would be few consequences even if he were convicted, as the case of Muncie newspaper editor George Dale had seemed to prove. In an effort to battle the political corruption in his city, Dale had minced no words and was charged with contempt by some of the same individuals whom he had attacked in print. Dale's lawyers argued that since his statements took place outside the courtroom, there could be no contempt. The Indiana Supreme Court disagreed, ruling that while it acknowledged the possibility that courts might abuse the power to broadly construe contempt, it did not believe that potential abuse meant the power should not exist. As to whether it mattered if what Dale said was true or not, the Court said:

> It is not a justification for contempt such as will purge one of the charges, even though it be shown that the article published was true, if it in any way hindered the orderly process of the court and brought it into contempt before the people. If the language used, as ordinarily and fairly interpreted, tends to degrade the court and embarrass it in the consideration of a pending case, the only issue is whether the words or article was actually spoken or published. The truth of the article is not a matter of defense, neither is it a defense to show that there was no intent to commit a contempt.

Governor Jackson eventually pardoned Dale. But, drys pondered, would he do the same for Shumaker?[31]

Hoosier drys rallied around their leader as the struggle intensified. The IASL expressed its "unbound confidence" in Shumaker by presenting him with a Chevrolet sedan "as a token of esteem from many friends over the state" at his sixtieth birthday party at Indianapolis's Garfield Park. Contributions came from some of the most prominent businessmen in the state, with at least thirty-five people contributing toward the $700 goal. Frank Ball of Muncie commented, "I trust you will be able to purchase . . . a very good car which will be worthy of the most excellent man who will drive it." One contributor hoped there was money left over for gas so that "Brother Shumaker" could "run the wet bunch off [the] earth." Others pledged their support of Shumaker in his contest with Gilliom, and many said that the people of the state "owe this to Dr. Shumaker."[32]

It was the state's high court, not the people, however, who would decide Shumaker's fate. In addition to Willoughby, the court consisted of Willard B. Gemmill, David Myers, Chief Justice Julius Travis, and Clarence R. Martin. They all had extensive legal experience, most having served as prosecutors and at the circuit court level. One had been in the state legislature, another a member of the Indiana Court of Appeals, and yet another had served as general counsel to the U.S. Senate.[33]

On 5 August 1927 the parties assembled in the packed Supreme Court chambers in the statehouse. Before the verdict was read, Shumaker joked with reporters that his bags were already packed. In a more serious vein, he said that a suspended sentence would be a restraint on his activities. At 10:30 A.M., the justices entered the room and took their seats. The court ruled that Shumaker was guilty of contempt in a 3-to-2 decision. He was fined $250 and ordered to serve sixty days at the state prison farm. Shumaker said that the verdict would not keep him from his Christian duty and Constitutional right to speak out on behalf of Prohibition. The IASL vowed to stand behind him, and his legal team began to look into an appeal.[34]

The majority opinion was crafted by Justice Myers, with the aid of Chief Justice Travis and Justice Willoughby. While admitting that no one was contending "that judges are beyond fair and respectful criticism," the majority believed that Shumaker's report went beyond those bounds. The court said that since he was a member of the clergy and had "admission to the pulpits of various churches of the state," Shumaker had abused his position "to impress the people with the truthfulness and fairness of his statements that this court, by splitting judicial hairs in liquor cases, holds that the guilty 'must be turned free,' and 'substantial justice has been defeated repeatedly.' These statements are false," and "it would be monstrous if any political party or any body or association of people, having the power to elect or defeat judges, could control or dictate decisions of courts." Since Shumaker did not care about "the result of any specific case" but was only "interested in the result of a class of cases," the threat of his influence would never go away. The court found League attorney Jesse Martin guilty as well, but not Ethan Miles.[35]

Justice Martin's dissent, joined by Justice Gemmill, took up Shumaker's cause. Point by point, the minority opinion looked at the IASL report and discussed why its statements made it free speech and not contemptuous, including the statements about past rulings by the court:

> The majority opinion also seems to make the point, although it does not do so clearly, that because there were, at the time of the publication of respondent's criticism, other cases pending in this court in which were involved legal questions similar to the questions decided in the criticized cases, the court could therefore proceed as though the criticism was of pending cases. No case has been cited in support of such a theory, and on principle I do not believe it to be sound.

Martin pointed out the obvious—that no matter how similar cases appear to be, "no two cases are ever exactly alike and rarely have exactly the same questions involved." All three men, the dissent argued, should be given their discharge.[36]

The majority decision was taken to task by a number of law journals and reviews. According to the *Harvard Law Review*, "the danger that judges may be influenced by criticism which tends to prevent their reelection furnishes a stronger basis for the decision. But such danger is outweighed by the consideration that an elective judiciary loses its basic justification if there can be no outspoken criticism of candidates." The *Yale Law Journal* openly questioned if "a contempt had been committed." The *Indiana Law Journal* found "that sounder reason is on the side of the dissenting opinion," and that following the high court's reasoning about not commenting on cases pending because it might influence future cases was self-serving. The *Michigan Law Review* said that just because Shumaker had an important position did not mean that his opinion was any less protected when it came to his right of "free expression of sentiment." The *Texas Law Review* argued that the right to criticize decisions of the court had to be upheld. And the *Cornell Law Quarterly* declared that while the court had to retain the right to find people in contempt, there also had to be in place some sort of remedy, such as a gubernatorial pardon, to "mitigate the punishment."[37]

The majority did have its defenders, however. The *Illinois Law Review* agreed with the high court that Shumaker "went beyond the bounds of fair comment." The *St. John's Law Review* believed that Shumaker's report to the trustees had struck at the "integrity and intelligence" of the court and so could not be considered "fair criticism." The *Notre Dame Lawyer* said that Shumaker could have been pardoned had he been accused and convicted of indirect contempt. And the *University of Pennsylvania Law Review* believed that the Indiana decision had found "a middle ground between the United States and English views [of contempt]."[38]

The state's newspapers were also divided. The *Evansville Journal* said that Shumaker, because of his power and position, should have recognized that there were limits to his speech. The *Jasper Herald* could not believe that Hoosier Methodists still supported Shumaker, since no one should be "exempt" from the law or show disrespect to the courts. The paper warned that the people of the state were tired of professional reformers and that Shumaker needed to heed what had happened to D. C. Stephenson before it was too late for him.[39] On the other hand, the *Kokomo Daily Tribune* supported Shumaker, saying that if he had really wanted to show contempt for the court, he would have used much stronger language. Thus, Shumaker should consider his sentence a well-deserved, state-paid vacation. The *Delphi Citizen* asked how Shumaker could be guilty of contempt if his comments had come after cases had already been decided. And the *Lafayette Journal and Courier* argued that the 3-to-2 verdict was hardly a warning to the "overzealous" and noted that the deciding vote was cast by Justice Willoughby, whom Shumaker had worked to unseat. The paper concluded, therefore, that "executive intervention is perhaps in order."[40]

It did not take Shumaker and his legal team long to appeal the decision. Constitutional issues about free speech were involved, and support for an appeal was found even among Shumaker's detractors. The *Indianapolis Times*, though it believed Shumaker to be "intolerant" of others, thought that he could be a champion of free speech in Indiana. The paper argued that the court was overreaching itself; and while the attorney general had every right to stop the creation of a super government, the way he was going about it was destroying freedom of speech. At their next meeting, Gilliom opposed the appeal motion, saying that the dry leader should deal with the consequences of his actions. He also asked the court to extend Shumaker's sentence, which the justices refused to do. Looking around the packed courtroom, full of WCTU members, Flora Shumaker said it was obvious that the court was afraid of the women.[41]

Shumaker now went on the offensive. In a July address he charged the attorney general with hypocrisy, since Gilliom had recently attacked the Indiana Supreme Court over a ruling on tax refunds.[42] On 18 August 1927, Shumaker gave the welcoming address to the 2,500 dry delegates of the World League assembled at Winona Lake, and was cheered. Many in attendance blasted officials who drank and then passed judgment on those who did not. Elizabeth Stanley of the WCTU told the gathering that if judges did not get out of politics, then the women of the country would turn them out of office. Shumaker was hailed as a victim of "stifled speech," and his address, which focused on the benefits of Prohibition rather than on his case, was widely praised. After leaving Winona Lake, Shumaker spoke at a union revival in Noblesville where he was also warmly received.[43]

The battle between the dry leader and the attorney general soon took another turn. In May 1927, Gilliom announced that he supported the legalization of medicinal alcohol. In a letter to the state's prosecutors, the attorney general assured them that medicinal alcohol only violated the letter of the law, not its spirit. Gilliom did not drink; his only vice was smoking cigars, but he did have very personal reasons—three, to be exact—for not liking the Wright bone-dry law's provision on medicinal alcohol. No one knows to what extent he felt a conflict between his job, the law, and his family, but when his sons were stricken with typhoid fever and their doctor told him that only medicinal alcohol could save them, Gilliom did not rest until he procured some, and the boys recovered. The attorney general again obtained alcohol when his sister was ill, and again when Governor Jackson's wife developed double pneumonia. These secret efforts became public shortly after his statement and even made the New York and Chicago newspapers.[44]

Hoosier drys were incredulous. They saw medicinal alcohol as a form of nullification, since wet doctors were sure to write prescriptions for anyone who asked. Some drys even accused the attorney general of using illness as an excuse to buy alcohol for himself. The WCTU condemned Gilliom for saying that medicinal alcohol had saved his sons' and sister's lives as well as the life of the state's First Lady, and they demanded his resignation. The Adams County WCTU, with Gilliom's sister at the meeting, called for the attorney general's indictment. The Adams County prosecutor resisted these demands but conceded that pressure was mounting. The Cass County prosecutor saw no excuse for the attorney general to break the law. Gilliom defended himself by saying that medicinal alcohol was on a par with sacramental wine. Would not any parent do everything in his power to save his child's life? To his supporters, the law was simply "criminally stupid."[45]

The attorney general was not alone in having to face some consequences over the medicinal alcohol episode. The *Indianapolis Times* chided the governor for obtaining it for his wife. Ed Jackson admitted doing so but also issued a statement against modifying the law. The *American Issue: Indiana Edition* was quick to report that the American Medical Association had come out against medicinal alcohol, and it speculated that Gilliom's stand sprang from the attorney general's aspirations for higher office. The League would dedicate several other issues in the year ahead to discussing and attacking Gilliom and medicinal alcohol.[46]

Meanwhile, Shumaker believed that the case against him was little more than "a political grudge" and that his lawyers had largely failed "to handle the case on its real merits." If he could raise sufficient funds, he might take his case to the United States Supreme Court. There, it would give the High Court the "best opportunity it ever would have to utter a timely warning against state courts that are becoming more and more autocratic and visiting their displeasure upon people who exercise their constitutional rights to employ freedom of speech and of the press," thus protecting Americans from "the exercise of tyranny by persons in a position to abuse their power."[47]

Had he pressed on, Shumaker might very well have seen his case make history. After all, in 1941's *Bridges v. State of California*, a case very similar to Shumaker's, the High Court held that a newspaperman was not guilty of contempt just because, in the words of Justice Hugo Black, he had published "views concerning cases not in all respects finally determined." The decision protected the public's right to freely express its opinion on current events. However, while this ruling sounds promising for Shumaker, the *Bridges* decision came from a Supreme Court very different from the one that would have heard his case. Shumaker would have faced the Taft Court, headed by the former president turned chief justice, William Howard Taft, who rarely overturned state Supreme Court decisions. The 1941 Court was headed by Chief Justice Harlan Fiske Stone, and eight of its members had been appointed by Franklin Roosevelt. Even then, the Stone Court decided *Bridges* 5 to 4. It is very likely that, had Shumaker pressed his case, he would have met defeat.[48]

Instead, Shumaker was back before the Indiana Supreme Court in November 1927, as Gilliom attempted to get his sentence extended because of the dry leader's contact with Watson and Robinson. Once again, supporters such as Frank Wright flocked to the court's chambers. During the hearing, Gilliom called an array of witnesses, including Republican State Chairman Clyde Walb, to bolster his contention that Shumaker sought to dictate and dominate Indiana politically. However, none of the witnesses, including Gilliom himself (who testified about the correspondence between Shumaker and Watson), could convince the court to lengthen Shumaker's sentence.[49]

Many observers wondered how Gilliom had learned of Shumaker's discussion with the senators, let alone gotten copies of their correspondence. The *South Bend Mirror* contended that the culprit was Senator James Watson. According to the paper, Watson was close to Klan leader D. C. Stephenson and was locked in a struggle with Shumaker over control of political patronage and dominance of the Republican Party in Indiana. Therefore, he helped delay the dry leader's trial until after the 1926 election, despite Gilliom's readiness to proceed beforehand (in order to ensure his own reelection), and then leaked his correspondence to the attorney general to eliminate Shumaker as a political rival.[50]

The deals and political alliances that were once the stuff of closed, smoke-filled back rooms came to the public's attention at the same time when the specter of the Klan was so vivid in the minds of Hoosiers. As a result, rumors began to circulate that a super government was running the state. In this atmosphere it was difficult for Gilliom to conclude that the IASL had to be a part of it. By the mid-1920s, charges that the ASL's state branches were seeking to dominate state legislatures were common, and there was even a precedent for going after a state superintendent because of them. The New York ASL leader, William H. Anderson, who had attacked the Episcopal Church hierarchy in New York as being wet and had stood up to the Rockefeller family (who were major contributors to both the New York and national Leagues), was charged with grand larceny and third-degree forgery in 1923. A friendly relationship with the Klan, along with his unwillingness to admit that his bookkeeping practices were unprofessional, if not illegal, had led to his ouster. Perhaps Gilliom was hoping to achieve something similar with Shumaker. However, the ASL rallied around the Hoosier leader in a way that it did not around Anderson, with McBride offering to help Shumaker in any way he could.[51]

The attorney general denied rumors that he was using the case to propel himself to higher office. Yet, as early as the 1926 campaign season, while he was on the stump for other Republicans, he had seen the potential for linking the Klan to the IASL in an effort to attack the Democrats. Gilliom believed that he could reunite the Indiana Republican Party in the wake of the Klan scandals by vowing to end the super government once and for all. He told the Greencastle Rotary Club that "we can be for the Eighteenth Amendment, without being unreasonable and fanatical, and without demanding that the courts nullify the Bill of Rights." At a South Bend Knights of Columbus meeting, Gilliom labeled Shumaker as the "head of this super government" and promised to end his influence entirely.[52]

Gilliom's desire to combat the super government and his political ambitions coalesced around the Senate seat of Arthur Robinson. In

1925, Robinson had been appointed to fill the vacancy caused by the death of Samuel Ralston, getting the nod over the likes of Jackson (who some thought might take it himself), Albert Beveridge (who had previously held the seat and who had been defeated by Ralston in 1922), Warren Fairbanks (son of the former vice president and owner of the *Indianapolis News*), Thomas Adams (editor of the *Vincennes Commercial*), and even Gilliom. With D. C. Stephenson on trial, there were accusations that Jackson had picked the forty-four-year-old Robinson because the two men were both members of the Klan—charges that Robinson repeatedly denied. Actually, Robinson's appointment made solid, if not spectacular, political sense. As a young politician, he had been a favorite of Governor Goodrich's; he was an ardent dry (having helped to usher the state prohibition law through the Senate in 1917), and he was a World War veteran who, upon his return from the service, had been appointed a judge by Governor McCray.[53]

Regardless, the election was an opening for the attorney general. With the Klan and IASL as his issues, Gilliom entered the 1928 Senate primary, arguing that it was time to free the Republican Party from both these organizations. Though the Klan had been in decline since Stephenson's trial in 1925, the attorney general now stressed to Hoosiers the dangers implicit in any Klan control of government. He called Shumaker a "henchman" of the Klan and warned that the Republican Party must purge itself of all Klan ties. Gilliom's campaign advertisements hammered home this theme. One urged voters to "destroy super government!" Gilliom, it continued, "opposes domination of our party and government by influences which are dangerous to the welfare of the Nation." Another said that "either Republicanism will defeat Klanism in May or Klanism will jeopardize Republicanism in November." Gilliom's advertisement in the *South Bend Tribune* summed up his campaign aptly: "He stands for tolerance, decency, honesty and common sense in government. He believes our government should be run by the people through their duly chosen representatives rather than by self-imposed dictators of secret and super-government."[54]

The idea that the Klan dominated Indiana's government was not new. Stephenson's postconviction revelations showed that many

Hoosier politicians had been elected with Klan support.[55] What is unclear then, and remains unclear to the present, is to what degree Stephenson's power was the result of the Klan or the personal relationships he was able to forge with politicians, in large part because he was the head of such a large and popular organization. Was it easier for Hoosiers, including Gilliom, to blame the Klan for things done in their name than to take responsibility for electing certain politicians on their own? Gilliom's answer was to make attacks on the Klan-IASL super government the core of his campaign.

Gilliom made the most of his allegations. He believed that Robinson was the missing link between the Klan and the IASL. The attorney general pointed to an alleged meeting between Shumaker, the senator, and the head of the St. Joseph County Klan in 1926 at the Jefferson Hotel in South Bend as proof of the existence of a super government. However, the charges are problematic since F. Scott McBride, of the national League, was in South Bend at the time to visit Shumaker. Moreover, the attorney general released a copy of a 1924 letter from Richmond's mayor, which claimed that Shumaker had said in a letter that the Democratic Party did not need an anti-Klan plank. For Ralph Kane, Gilliom's campaign manager, this proved that Shumaker was so wrapped up in wet and dry issues that he ignored the Klan as a problem. The attorney general called for a bipartisan condemnation of the IASL's voter guides and for a repudiation of the ASL and the Klan.[56]

His charges had supporters. The *Indiana Catholic and Record* believed that Shumaker had proved by his actions that a super government was operating in Indiana. By asking both U.S. senators to intervene on his behalf, Shumaker, it was alleged, was demonstrating that he could influence the course of politics. The paper claimed that Catholics had been warning about such a union since 1923. It hailed the attorney general's call for education, not stricter Prohibition enforcement, saying, "a few more officials with the courage of Mr. Gilliom will soon bring the death of fanaticism in Indiana." The paper also trumpeted the fact that Gilliom had been against the Klan from the start of his political career.[57]

For the IASL, Gilliom's entry into the 1928 Senate primary race put the last two years in perspective. Whereas Solon J. Carter (a former Gilliom assistant and World War veteran) was running against Prohibition as being "too much" for the government while also attacking Robinson's law firm for defending bootleggers, drys believed that Gilliom was crafting a "damp" middle ground, with his super government rhetoric, in order to wage a populist reformer campaign. The IASL found it interesting that a man who used medicinal alcohol would call himself "dry" and saw Gilliom as "obsessed" with the idea of super government. It noted a direct link between wet newspapers and charges of a Klan-League alliance. The IASL wanted to know, Who was paying Gilliom's campaign expenses? And why was the attorney general attacking Robinson for his supposed ties to the Klan while not accusing Watson, whose links to the Klan were much clearer?[58]

More legal drama was the result. Just before the primary election, the attorney general cited Shumaker under the Corrupt Practices Act for calling him a "wet" in the IASL voter guide, and he ordered the dry leader arrested. Ralph Kane then alleged that Shumaker, a "deceitful" and "resentful" person was using the IASL to further a personal grudge against Gilliom, and once again he insinuated that the Klan and League were working together. Gilliom went further, saying that Shumaker was in "fellowship" with the "wizard." Shumaker countered that the attorney general was engaging in "political prosecution"; "the IASL has nothing to do with the Klan. It is just as free of the Klan as is the Red Cross society. It was never connected with the Klan in any of its work." The dry leader also said that he was not responsible for Gilliom's being labeled a wet of record, as the attorney general had done so himself when he came out in favor of medicinal alcohol.[59]

Many observers across the state were shocked that Gilliom had ordered Shumaker arrested. As the *Indianapolis Star* put it, "such an affront to the dry leader has been unheard of in Indiana politics." The *Indianapolis News* remarked that Gilliom's use of the law in this case hinged on the word "falsely." If Shumaker had lied when he labeled the attorney general a "wet of record," then the superintendent was guilty as charged. But if the attorney general was, in fact, a closet wet, then this spat between the two men was merely politics. The *Indianapolis Times* called for a public trial of the dry chief to settle, once and for all, the allegations that were swirling around the state ahead of the election.[60]

Shumaker surrendered in South Bend before a large crowd that had gathered at the St. Joseph County courthouse. Gilliom asked for an immediate trial, while Shumaker's attorneys argued that there should be a delay until after the primary. The attorney general offered to end his campaign in order to prosecute the dry chief. Shumaker took advantage of the media attention to repeatedly deny that either he or the IASL had any association with the Klan and to blast the attorney general. He warned that "Gilliom hasn't shaken the confidence among the church and dry forces and since his last action against me I have made more friends than ever before, and I believe when this case is through I will have still more." The *Indianapolis Star* weighed in, arguing that the state had bigger issues facing it in the spring of 1928 than this sort of petty bickering. The judge assigned to the case apparently agreed, as he quickly dismissed the charges.[61]

What was occurring was the splintering of dry culture. Hard-line drys, such as Shumaker, were becoming more rigid about enforcement and frustrated at the failure of full compliance and prosecution of the law. Moderate drys, such as Gilliom, were seeking to modify existing laws in order to subvert wet calls for repeal or nullification. This polarization helped to loosen the ties of alliance between the various branches of the broader dry culture, such as relations between Protestants and Catholics, and contributed to a loosening of party (and even denominational) cohesion as well. As the *New York Times* noted, "an outsider finds difficulty in making political predictions about Indiana, owing to the fact that there are at present almost as many political factions as there are voters."[62]

After all the fuss, allegations, court charges, and campaigning, Robinson easily won the primary. Several newspapers noted that Gilliom and one of his Democratic counterparts had run as anti-Klan candidates and that neither had made much headway with the electorate. Nor did voters seem to care about the attorney general's charge that the IASL had too much influence in the state. In the end, Gilliom's campaign had been hurt not only by his message but also because he was not the sole challenger. Solon Carter scored good headlines during the primary battle, winning votes that could have gone to the attorney general. Yet, neither challenger could rouse the strength to upend an incumbent with the full support of Shumaker.[63]

In between 1928's elections, Shumaker's case returned to center stage. In July the court ruled that Jesse Martin had purged himself of contempt, declined to increase Shumaker's penalty, and held that the dry leader should not be granted another hearing. Drys across the state called the decision an "injustice" and wanted Shumaker to appeal to the United States Supreme Court. Senator Watson refused to comment on Shumaker's having to serve time but did say he was glad that the penalty was not increased. The dry leader told reporters in October that he had gotten an unfair trial. When asked if he would seek a pardon, Shumaker replied that he would not, nor would a pardon take away the "stigma" of his trial. He surrendered himself and, accompanied by a long car caravan of supporters, drove to the state farm. Upon his arrival, however, he found a pardon waiting for him. Governor Jackson's intervention now changed the nature of the fight. Gilliom demanded that Shumaker be made to serve his term, declaring Jackson's pardon "void." Another court battle resulted, and, not surprisingly, the 3-to-2 split held, with the majority finding that the governor's power to pardon was not absolute, especially in matters of contempt. The minority, as well as the *Yale Law Journal* and the state's drys, disagreed, but to no avail.[64]

Shumaker's dry network continued to support him. Friends compared him to the Apostle Paul because of his suffering at the hands of government officials. The IASL's attorney, Ethan Miles, published a pamphlet denouncing the state Supreme Court's finding of contempt against Shumaker as well as its overturning of Jackson's pardon. The League's headquarters committee issued a statement that Shumaker's defense of freedom of speech was bigger than the IASL or Prohibition. McBride told the ASL Executive Committee that the League would back Shumaker. However, while his allies were quick to offer their moral support, few gave money to Shumaker's defense fund. This lack became a consideration as the battle approached the start of its third year.[65]

In the midst of the legal wrangling came the 1928 presidential election, which the ASL viewed as "the most important choice between candidates in the history of the prohibition movement." Shumaker agreed and saw it as a referendum on Prohibition nationally as well as on his case. When Indiana not only went Republican but also dry, he believed himself and his cause vindicated. However, the election was also a sideshow for Shumaker. His colleague, the Quaker S. E. Nicholson, took the lead in defending the Hoosier state from Democrat Al Smith in the fall. Of course, Smith was a candidate laden with liabilities in Indiana. A wet Catholic New Yorker, with ties to Tammany Hall, he was running against a seemingly sound economy. Shumaker did not need to concern himself with the outcome, and Republican Herbert Hoover's victory gave a boost to the dry cause everywhere.[66]

After being reelected head of the IASL in January 1929, Shumaker told reporters that the state was in good hands and drier than it had been two years ago. Perhaps to recharge himself, he launched a "whirlwind tour" of Northern Indiana later that month, which took him to many of the places he had first visited over two decades ago, during his early days with the League. He traveled throughout Elkhart County, then to South Bend, and, in early February, to Terre Haute.[67] This trip to old haunts may have helped him come to a momentous decision. On 11 February 1929, Shumaker announced that he was ready to give up his fight and serve his sentence. Though the IASL announced plans to keep on fighting, there was little they could do. With dwindling funds and little hope that the United States Supreme Court or President Hoover (via a pardon) would intervene, all Shumaker could do was surrender.[68]

There were other factors at play in the decision. With Hoover elected, Shumaker believed that the issue of Prohibition was settled nationally. At home, he was content with the Wright bone-dry law. He also realized how the struggle was affecting his family, who were being forced to endure the persecution alongside him. But more important, Gilliom was out of office, and there was some hope that the next attorney general, James Ogden, might drop the whole matter.[69]

Despite the publicity surrounding his case, and the motorcade that had brought him to the state farm the first time, this second journey was done in stealth to avoid the media glare. When Shumaker arrived, he was designated Number 39424 and given a new wardrobe. He was forbidden to preach to his fellow inmates but could attend chapel services. His first breakfast as a convict was milk, rolled oat bread, coffee, and fruit. Like other inmates, Shumaker was allowed two letters per month and visitation from his immediate family every two weeks, when they could give him fruit, candy, gum, and tobacco (though he did not use the latter). Shumaker was assigned to the dairy, which was considered a good job since those prisoners were permitted to receive two shaves per week instead of one.[70]

After his appeal to the federal courts was rejected and he was actually at the state farm, Indiana's newspapers chimed in. The *Indianapolis Times* thought that Shumaker was getting what he deserved for trying to have Watson and Robinson intervene on his behalf. However, the paper also blasted the Indiana Supreme Court and its unbridled power in matters of contempt. Other papers thought Shumaker had been too "aggressive" in defending the Wright law and that his stalling to "evade" his sentence was self-serving. Now, as the *Evansville Journal* put it, he was leaving behind his "high rent" Indianapolis office for the "bleak rooms" of the state farm.[71]

Rather than a champion of free speech, Shumaker became a martyr for the dry cause. Though his clash with Gilliom and the Indiana Supreme Court had much to do with personality conflicts and political agendas, it also represented a rift within the dry cause. The orthodoxy of Prohibition was cracking under the weight of enforcement. In the end, Shumaker's sacrifice was not enough to bridge this divide.

8 | The Death of a Man and His Dream

After a three-year court battle, as we know, Edward Shumaker was sentenced to the state farm, where he and his fellow drys believed him to be a martyr for their cause. Little did they realize that his time in that role would be short and that their chief accomplishment was not only about to come to an end but would also call into question their very future.

Shumaker was an inmate in Indiana's minimum security prison. The state farm's goal was to rehabilitate prisoners by engaging them in both agriculture and manufacturing on its grounds. Despite the fact that many of the wardens and guards supported both Prohibition and Shumaker, he was treated like any other prisoner. Assigned to the dairy, he worked eleven hours per day. As the *Lebanon Reporter* put it, the IASL's leader was now milking cows dry.[1]

Imprisonment allowed Shumaker to meet men convicted under the Wright bone-dry law. He later recounted that on the first night, his cell mates chided him for getting locked up, but when one prisoner started to make derogatory remarks, others told the man to "shut his trap." While prison life took some adjustment, Shumaker soon won the men over by showing that he was suffering as they were. To some, he became a friend and pastor, a role he had not played for nearly a quarter of a century. Many of these same men would rush to the gate to tell him goodbye when he was released.[2]

In all, he served fifty-three days of his sixty-day sentence, gaining his release on 5 April 1929. That morning, Shumaker arose early, in order to take care of the dairy herd one last time. After breakfast, a bath, shave, and "civilian" haircut, he exchanged his prison garb for his own clothes. Flora was brought in to see him and, after introducing her to the foreman of the dairy, they both stepped out into a rainstorm to greet the supporters who had made the trek to Putnam County.[3] At the prison gates, Shumaker gave a brief speech, vowing to continue his work against wets. His incarceration had "brought new angles to my experiences that I had never dreamed of," since befriending those men convicted of breaking dry laws only made him hate alcohol more.[4]

A car caravan of supporters followed him home to Indianapolis, where a celebratory dinner was held in his honor at Broadway Methodist Church. Over 250 people were guests, including delegations from the IASL, WCTU, Indianapolis Church Federation, and local Baptist and Presbyterian congregations as well as Senator Arthur Robinson, the Kentucky and Michigan ASL superintendents, and F. Scott McBride of the national office. They all reaffirmed their confidence in Shumaker as the dry cause's leader in Indiana. Churches from around the state requested that he plan a speaking tour and sent their congratulations on his martyr-like status. Shumaker was presented with a leather-bound copy of his case and told those assembled that he was ready to return to battle. McBride showered praise upon him for making Indiana the "truest" state in the union to the dry cause. Indeed, the *Indianapolis Times* noted that his stay in prison had actually strengthened his power in the state.[5]

Shumaker attempted to go back to work for the IASL. He faced new challenges, such as the proposed ending of primaries in Indiana, which would negate the effectiveness of the IASL's voter guides. However, he was confident he could overcome this obstacle, since few Hoosiers in 1929 had as much experience lobbying the state legislature as he did.[6] Additionally, Shumaker was writing his autobiography, perhaps as a way to cash in on the fame of his case. He had started the project prior to going to the state farm and had been allowed to work on it while in prison. He had drafted chapters up to 1903, when he first joined the League, but had gotten no further. For it was then that he became ill.[7]

Few friends who saw him in the days after his release were surprised. Shumaker had lost thirty-nine pounds while at the farm, something that "astounded" him when he saw himself in a mirror at home. Comparing pictures of the man upon his arrival at the farm in February 1929 to those upon his release in April is like looking at two different people. The Shumaker who entered prison was a slightly overweight, robust man in late middle age. The Shumaker who exited to the cheers of his supporters was an emaciated old man. Some observers noted that he looked "weary and thinner," though they initially attributed his loss of weight to the "rigid dieting at the penal farm" as well as to the stress of his case. Despite Flora's home cooking, he did not regain the lost weight and found it difficult to get back into his old routine. He grew sick and "went to bed."[8]

When his illness became known, the ASL came to his aid in a more concrete way than it had during his legal battle. The League arranged for Shumaker to go to the Kellogg Sanitarium at Battle Creek, Michigan, where the ASL paid for his room and board and the Kellogg treated him for free. One supporter sent him a check for $100 shortly after his arrival to cover any additional expenses. At Battle Creek, Shumaker became Case Number 212699 and was placed under the care of a specialist in internal medicine. He was diagnosed with a wide range of maladies, including a lung infection, hardening of the arteries in his feet, a gallstone, an enlarged liver, problems with his pancreas and colon, a bad tooth, and possible diabetes.[9] Shumaker then wrote to the IASL headquarters committee on 6 July, telling them that he was much sicker than he had originally thought, but that he would be better after his "vacation." He was also sure that once he returned to the stump, the League's monetary situation would improve. Moreover, he was still working on his book and was in negotiations with Bobbs-Merrill to publish it. "The national situation over prohibition is interesting," Shumaker continued in his letter, because it was obvious that President Hoover was not so staunchly dry as had once been thought. However, Shumaker told them, "I still believe that God is in his Heavens, that He is having care for His own and that everything will yet come out right."[10]

Such optimism did not last very long, for wets were waiting to attack. After his return home from Michigan, a story began to circulate that Shumaker was taking medicinal alcohol. He was called a hypocrite by wets. The reality was that while it had been prescribed, he refused to drink it. Still, he had to spend time and energy refuting the story.[11] In the end what killed him were not malicious rumors, but rather a "malignant tumor." Shumaker went to his reward at 4:40 P.M. on 25 October 1929. According to his family, his eyes opened to look at them and "something beyond," before closing one last time, and he died with a smile on his face.[12]

His funeral took place at Broadway Methodist Church under the direction of the Reverend John W. McFall and the superintendents of the Michigan, Kentucky, and Illinois ASLs. Friends and family filled the Shumaker house and the church. The service was long, as his son Arthur later recalled, because of all the eulogists. F. Scott McBride gave the main eulogy, and other speakers included representatives from the Indianapolis Church Federation, IASL, and WCTU. Shumaker was hailed as an "outstanding leader in his generation in the struggle for national Prohibition." He was laid to rest in Crown Hill Cemetery in Indianapolis and his gravestone was paid for by a Who's Who of the dry cause from across the state and nation.[13] Among those sending their condolences were Senators Watson and Robinson, and Congressman Albert H. Hall.[14] As a Mr. and Mrs. Christgau wrote to Flora, "You have our heartfelt sympathy. Brother Shumaker's unfailing kindness, his unselfishness, sincerity, and unfaltering industry made his life a great inspiration to his fellow workers in the cause he loved. May the knowledge that multitudes of friends share your grief help comfort you in your great sorrow."[15]

In death, he was hailed by the state's newspapers. The *Evansville Journal* called Shumaker an "ardent reformer" who "had the courage of his convictions," while the *Oxford Gazette* said he was a "crusader" whose work in making Indiana dry "will live long after the Indiana Supreme Court judges . . . are dead and forgotten." The

Connersville News Examiner wrote that Shumaker's "vigorous crusading" had made him a "national figure." The *Lake County Times* called him "rum's bitter enemy." The *Anderson Herald* thought it "doubtful if Indiana ever will produce as famous a foe of liquor," and the *Kokomo Daily Tribune* called him "a devout and righteous crusader in a great cause." The *Shelbyville Republican* said in its editorial: "So far as his temporal tabernacle is concerned he simply cast it off, his soul passing into eternity. It is a pleasing thought that he still lives. . . . His mission in life was to uplift fallen humanity. He simply went about doing good."[16] And the *Indianapolis Star* eulogized him as follows:

> Dr. Shumaker's death will be a great loss to the cause he served so faithfully. It will be no easy thing for the anti saloon organization to fill the place that has been left vacant. Dr. Shumaker was well acquainted with conditions in this state and was astute and forceful in dealing with the problems that were presented to him for solution. He was an able and fearless crusader who performed yeoman service in the crucial period of the fight for prohibition.[17]

Shumaker's death was very hard on his youngest son, Arthur, who as a boy of sixteen had to contend with the stigma—no matter how noble the label of martyr made it sound—that his father had been a convict.[18] Shumaker's death was also difficult for Flora, who had no job, two children at home, and two more in college. She took in boarders and relied on the money that her brother sent her to get by. The family pitched in and rallied around each other, especially once the Depression hit. Flora worked hard to keep Shumaker's memory alive, never believing that her husband had attempted to build up the IASL for his own gain. She called him "an innocent, patriotic, noble, godly man" who was assailed with "cruel persecutions" by his enemies. Wayne briefly followed in his father's footsteps by working for the IASL.[19]

Shumaker's reform and the cause behind it continued after his death, yet many supporters feared the IASL was in danger of floundering without his leadership and doubted if Shumaker could be replaced. During his illness, the League had been placed in the hands of Disciple of Christ minister Charles H. Winders. Prior to his appointment, Winders had served congregations in his native Missouri and in Indianapolis and had been the executive secretary of the Indianapolis Church Federation. In his new post, he vowed to work with the churches and the WCTU and to avoid supporting "any factions or cliques or political parties." In many respects, he was a good replacement for Shumaker since he had extensive pastoral and organizational leadership experience. However, less than a year after assuming the post, Winders turned over the reins of the IASL to the League's field secretary, L. E. York, a former member of the Illinois legislature and a school superintendent, whose wife was very active in the Indianapolis WCTU. They lived near the Shumakers and were also members of Broadway Methodist Church.[20]

Shumaker's death and York's untried leadership opened the door to more attacks on the IASL's tactics, something that was also happening to the national League. The ASL was labeled a "racket" and an "interest group" that had too much influence on the nation's political process.[21] In 1931, Hoosier wets struck at the Wright bone-dry law. A medicinal alcohol bill was proposed in the House and the IASL found itself powerless to stop it from getting out of committee. During the fight, wets resurrected the old charge that the IASL and Ku Klux Klan were linked. They claimed that D. C. Stephenson had drafted the bone-dry law and that the League, along with bootleggers, were being paid a kickback for each conviction under it. The IASL denied that Stephenson had anything to do with either the League or the law. During the "boisterous" hearings, wets hissed at the WCTU president, and Boyd Gurly, editor of the *Indianapolis Times*, spoke passionately against both the law and organized temperance forces. Though the full House voted down the bill, it was obvious that dry strength was ebbing away.[22]

Accusations of "super government" were once again heard in the state. Though the charges linking the IASL with the Klan may have been more in the realm of partisan politics than in reality, this is not to say that the 1920s were not a time of immense political corruption in Indiana and that this had an effect on the dry cause. The editor of the *Vincennes Commercial*, Thomas Adams, spearheaded a drive to investigate "Stephensonism" and to clean up the state Republican Party. Adams was initially at odds with Arthur Gilliom and other Republican leaders, who saw the investigation as a threat to their power. Senator Watson protested that every politician in the state knew Stephenson because he was a man who could deliver votes. Republican state chairman Clyde Walb saw the probe as a way for "international bankers" to oust Robinson and Watson for their anti–League of Nations stance. However, Adams had the support of former governor James Goodrich and soon everyone else got on board.[23]

The Adams probe, in conjunction with the investigations launched by the *Indianapolis Times* and eventually the state under Gilliom, did purge the Republican Party of Klan influence, but it also destroyed the careers of Governor Ed Jackson and Walb as well as other politicians in the state. With Stephenson's cooperation the extent of Jackson's involvement in Governor Warren McCray's ouster became known, and, though he escaped conviction of attempted bribery because of the statute of limitations, Jackson's reputation was ruined. Walb, who had helped guide Jackson to the state's highest office, was sent to federal prison for violating banking laws.[24] Drys were tainted with guilt by association.

None of these unfolding scandals hurt the Republicans at the polls in 1928, however. Drys believed that Governor Harry Leslie would safeguard the Wright bone-dry law in the face of wavering federal enforcement, and drys feared for the future of both the Volstead Act and the Eighteenth Amendment. To show its strength in April 1932, the IASL hosted a large meeting on Prohibition in Indianapolis, which coordinated forty-five church services throughout the city and boasted national ASL figures as speakers.[25]

Some Hoosier drys still trusted in the man whom they had helped put in the White House. President Hoover had been raised a Quaker and thus was a part of the dry Protestant cause, and most historians now recognize that his religious upbringing had an influence on his actions as president. Furthermore, Hoover believed that presidents swore to uphold the Constitution as they found it and had no right to advocate changes to it.[26] Nevertheless, as some drys had long feared, they were ultimately betrayed by the man whom they had trusted. Hoover felt compelled to modify his support of Prohibition in order to survive politically. Drys became angry as this happened. P .R. Wadsworth, a Washington, Indiana, attorney, wrote to Hoover telling him not to make "a great big mistake" by faltering "in standing for the eighteenth amendment."[27] Others, however, were pleased with the president's change of heart. One Evansville woman promised the president that she would support him no matter what, as those preoccupied with Prohibition really did not care about temperance or "the depression" created by their reform.[28]

The dry cause was falling apart. Shumaker's old Quaker ally, S. E. Nicholson, believed that drys needed a new strategy. He argued that drys had to embrace the concept of a national referendum to prove that they were "not afraid of a rehearing." If they did so, Nicholson was sure that they could then start talking about the benefits of Prohibition, and people would listen. His was a lone voice, however, as many drys were hardening their stance toward wets. Indeed, rather than modification, some drys wanted Hoover to employ the same violent tactics he had used against the Bonus Army in July 1932 to suppress wets once and for all.[29]

What was at stake was the very definition of the dry cause. The Eighteenth Amendment was designed to shut down the liquor industry, not to stop people from drinking. On its own terms, it worked. "Everyone" was not drinking. America's young people are a prime example. Historian Paula Fass has argued that a youth culture emerged in the 1920s that rebelled against the drab, puritanical culture of their parents, with one of the chief battle lines being Prohibition. But Fass's sample of middle class youth is skewed. According to the Intercollegiate Prohibition Association's 1930 survey of colleges and universities across the country, drinking was down dramatically. Indiana University's response was typical of other schools in the state and Midwest. In Bloomington, "conditions . . . are infinitely better than they were during the days of open saloon . . . not more than one per cent [out of 4,000 students] are habitual drinkers. This estimate is . . . high. Moreover, drinking among students is steadily declining. The amount of drinking at present is distinctly less than it was five years ago." Though the youth generation nationally may very well have been more willing to modify Prohibition than their parents, it should also be noted that representative members of that generation, such as F. Scott Fitzgerald, had never supported the reform. Moreover, many young people as late as 1932 wanted to retain Prohibition.[30]

Drys, nevertheless, were anxious about the future of the "great good" they had given to the nation. They saw a concerted effort on the part of wets to weaken and demoralize the ASL and WCTU in order to achieve repeal. The Indiana Annual Conference of the Methodist Church took as a badge of honor "the well known hatred of the old saloon power." But they also realized that obeying the law was a personal decision that people could not be coerced into making. As a moral reform, though, Hoosier Methodists insisted that Prohibition remain in place.[31]

A return to moral rhetoric was necessary because of the worsening economic conditions in the country. Drys had long contended that Prohibition was good for the economy, that it was paying for itself, and that it was allowing individuals to be consumers at rates and of goods never before imagined—in other words, that it was the essence of national prosperity. However, with the onset of the Great Depression, Prohibition's days were numbered. As Edward Behr has argued, the depression exacerbated preexisting problems with Prohibition, such as lax enforcement. Wets now had the opportunity to aim straight at people's pocketbooks. Beer might not be soup, but it could mean jobs; and if it also meant money in the wallets of workers and owners as well as tax revenue for local, state, and national governments, so much the better.[32]

Prohibition's future was one of the key issues in the 1932 election cycle, even more than the growing unemployment figures, according to some commentators. Both the Republican and Democratic parties in Indiana came out for repeal, something drys could hardly believe. For Republicans it was a matter of political survival. James Goodrich agreed with his party's decision to call for repeal, but he did not think that it needed to pledge to end the Wright bone-dry law, since the latter could be taken care of quietly once national repeal was passed. Betrayed at home, many Hoosier drys held out hope for the national Republican Party. Despite their professed "confidence in the Christian character of President Hoover," they watched in dismay as both national parties added planks to their platforms that called for repeal.[33]

The dry cause was in trouble. Before the election, a special session of the Indiana legislature was held in which the House voted to overturn the Wright bone-dry law by a vote of 58 to 38. Supporters of repeal called it a "drastic" measure that allowed the Horse Thief Detective Association to extract "tribute" for the Klan. In the state Senate, however, drys were able to kill the bill. York and the IASL took credit for this victory, not knowing at the time that it would be the final legislative victory in the League's history.[34]

Democratic presidential nominee Franklin Roosevelt made the ending of Prohibition one of the cornerstones of his 1932 campaign, with the promise to balance the legal return of alcohol with its strict enforcement. This theme was picked up in Indiana by the state Democratic standard-bearer, Paul V. McNutt. The dean of Indiana University's law school and past state and national commander of the American Legion, McNutt swore to bring a "new deal" of his own to Indiana if elected. He had been raised a Methodist and knew what it would take to defuse the IASL. November produced a Democratic landslide in both the state and nation, with 73 percent of Americans voting in support of repeal-oriented candidates. Drys waited to see exactly what wets would do with this newfound power.[35]

After Roosevelt's inauguration in March 1933, the pace of events accelerated. Congress authorized the sale of 3.2 percent beer and began to draft a proposed Twenty-first Amendment to repeal the Eighteenth. At the same time, stronger government directives were issued, ordering the states to crack down on speakeasies while federal agents concentrated on the "sources" of illegal alcohol. This was a signal for McNutt, who had been focusing on other issues since his own inauguration in January, to go after the Wright law. While the governor began pardoning some of those convicted under its provisions, he called for the state legislature to end the law. Labeling the legislation passed with so much fanfare in 1925 "obnoxious," the Democratic-dominated General Assembly did just that and authorized the return of beer to Indiana beginning in April as well. Drys were shocked at what was happening on both the state and national levels.[36]

McNutt next moved to control alcohol's reappearance. The governor saw that the return of "states' rights" to the issue of Prohibition gave him an opportunity to broaden his power base within the context of both repeal and the New Deal. McNutt called on former University of Notre Dame president John W. Cavanaugh to design a system that would be acceptable to Hoosier Catholics. He then had Frank McHale, a Catholic lawyer who had guided McNutt to the American Legion national commandership and to the Indiana's governor's office, draft the Alcohol Beverage Act. The genius of the system for McNutt was that only his friends and supporters were granted the privilege of selling alcohol in the state.[37]

The new law was stricter than many wets expected. McNutt viewed the return of beer as a "temperance test" that, if not managed properly, could prompt a dry backlash. The price for giving Hoosiers their beer was more power for the governor. McHale's act, which created "a state controlled, monopolistic wholesale system," divided Indiana into ten districts, allowed no outside importation without a stiff fee, and initially barred restaurants from serving alcohol. Overseeing it was Linton car salesman Paul Fry, who had worked for the governor at the Democratic state convention. Fry set the price of legal beer lower than that of bootleg brew to destroy illegal competition.[38] On 7 April 1933 legal beer returned to Indiana. So "thirsty" were some Hoosiers that when a beer truck overturned near Wabash, its contents were consumed on the spot.[39]

With the Wright law ended, beer once again being legally sold across Indiana, and the United States Congress sending the issue of repeal to the states, McNutt's next task was to construct a ratification process for the proposed Twenty-first Amendment.[40] Drys in many states expressed surprise at the momentum behind repeal and believed that Indiana offered them a real opportunity to slow the wet tide. As such, there was a sense of urgency for Hoosier drys. "Indiana's loss would end dry hopes," according to the *Pike County Democrat*, as nine states had quickly voted for repeal. But a Hoosier dry victory could "halt the steamroller of the liberals"; furthermore, drys had an "even chance" at stopping repeal.[41]

Wets were prepared. Repeal was a partisan issue, just as fighting for dry legislation had once been. The Marion County Bi-Partisan Repeal Committee went on the radio on WKBF in Indianapolis. The governor was blasted by the *Kokomo Daily Tribune* for saying that it was up to the Democratic Party in Indiana to organize wet forces for victory, since in many counties both political parties were working for repeal. Indeed, state and national Democratic leaders warned wets to be neither overconfident nor indifferent about the coming repeal election and to reach out across the aisle to ensure victory.[42]

To combat these tactics, drys returned to the strategy that Shumaker had perfected in their drive to victory: grassroots activism and rallies in the state's evangelical Protestant churches. The Indianapolis Church Federation, Indianapolis Council of Federated Church Women, Northwest Indiana Conference of the Methodist Church, and other groups mobilized to save the Eighteenth Amendment, vowing that if Prohibition "goes down, we go down fighting for it." Even the Flying Squadron was brought back into action. In the state's churches, ministers rallied their congregations. In Garrett, for example, an all-day prayer service was held at the Church of Christ in mid-April on behalf of retaining the Eighteenth Amendment, and Tabernacle Presbyterian Church in Indianapolis, home of the Gilliom family, invited IASL speakers to address the congregation in the weeks leading up to the repeal election. Drys in Steuben County put on Upton Sinclair's play *The Wet Parade*. In Wabash County a fifty-car "young people's caravan" toured the area on behalf of Prohibition. And Howard County drys gathered petitions and held a joint rally with fellow antirepealists from Grant and Tipton counties.[43]

Such dry rallies boasted nationally known speakers. Those filling the oratorical void left by Shumaker's death included Methodist (South) Bishop James Cannon, who crisscrossed the state. Preaching to large dry gatherings, Cannon labeled the push for repeal a "wet rebellion" that needed to be crushed, and he reminded Hoosiers that the "eyes of the nation" were on Indiana. If drys fought, they would win.[44] Other speakers included former Indianapolis Methodist bishop, and now Detroit bishop, Edgar Blake, who attacked the notion that repeal would lower taxes, and Methodist bishop Edwin Holt Hughes, former president of DePauw University, who decried wet attempts to "dignify" beer.[45] Clarence True Wilson of Oregon also contributed articles on behalf of the Eighteenth Amendment to Hoosier newspapers.[46]

Drys could also count on leading Hoosiers to speak out for Prohibition. Prominent among them was the Speaker of the Indiana House, Earl Crawford. Though a loyal McNutt man, the Wayne County Democrat was also the leader of Indiana's dry Democrats. He had voted against repeal in the state legislature and warned drys that, if it came, the cause of temperance would be set back fifty years. To the very eve of the election, Crawford held out hope that drys would be victorious.[47] Drys also had the support of many of the state's college administrators, which gave their cause intellectual respectability. Grant County drys picked the dean of Marion College as one of their delegates, while Johnson County elected the acting president of Franklin College as one of theirs.[48] Manchester College's president, Ortho Winger, who had long been active in promoting Prohibition within the Church of the Brethren, was named a dry delegate from Wabash County. He vowed that the "fight is on with all vigor."[49]

The drys' most vocal supporter on college campuses was William Lowe Bryan, president of Indiana University. The son of a Presbyterian minister, Bryan was convinced of the wisdom of the dry cause, having once characterized the struggle as an "eternal war" between good and evil. He took the lead in organizing Monroe County, which had gone for McNutt in 1932 but had a long dry tradition, to fight repeal.[50] His most famous remarks on prohibition came in a widely distributed speech entitled "Out of the Jungle—Straight On," in which he challenged wets "to name one restrictive liquor law anywhere of any time which the liquor forces have obeyed." He concluded: "My friends, we have fought our way for a hundred years through the liquor jungle against foes whose never-changing policy has been defiance of every law made for their control. We have fought our way up to the hill and now stand entrenched in the impregnable Constitution. We are not going to retreat. We are not going back into the jungles. We are going to march straight on."[51]

There were signs of hope for drys. The defense of Prohibition united Protestants across the state and overcame theological divides. While Northern Indiana tended to endorse repeal, Southern Indiana seemed staunchly in favor of Prohibition. Drys believed that since more men than women were signing repeal petitions, perhaps women would save the reform. In some counties, wets had problems organizing, while in others they squabbled over whom to select as their candidates and to what degree the election should be partisan in nature. The united drys relished such disharmony among their foes. They asked people old enough to remember the saloon if they really wanted it to return, and they pointed out the offenses of both past and present wets, who had "engaged in an orgy of lawlessness." Men and women were urged to vote based on who the friends of each amendment were: the Eighteenth had ministers, while the proposed Twenty-first had lawbreakers. Indeed, the *Baptist Observer* argued that the election was a contest in which voters would have to pick either "Christ or Satan." Indeed, "this is not just an election; it is a battle for righteousness."[52]

Wets were using new tactics in the battle for repeal, however. They successfully tied the dry cause to states' rights. Calling federal efforts a "failure," the *French Lick Springs Valley Herald* said that repeal of the Eighteenth Amendment did not have to mean a dry defeat. Rather, "thinking drys" would see that returning the problem to the states would allow for a real solution. The Twenty-first Amendment would give drys an opportunity to "build block by block, state by state, a structure of such aridity as was impossible to construct on the national scale." Many drys saw this as a wet mirage, if not a massive setback, but it was effective propaganda all the same.[53]

Franklin Roosevelt's New Deal was at the heart of the repeal campaign. Wets argued that repeal would lower taxes and possibly end the Depression. Indeed, the president invested considerable amounts of his early political capital in repeal. He was worried that if he did not move quickly on its behalf, drys might rebound from their 1932 election setbacks. A full-page advertisement in the *Craw-*

fordsville Journal told readers that if the country could not be dry, at least it could be temperate, and voting for repeal of the Eighteenth Amendment would "help line up Indiana for the New Deal." Another advised, "if you want a New Deal—Vote for Repeal." On the eve of the vote, Postmaster General James A. Farley sent a message to Indiana on Roosevelt's behalf calling for a vote for repeal and vowing to control liquor. The administration even went so far as to say that Congress might have to raise taxes if the repeal effort was not successful.[54]

Wet advertising in newspapers was powerful. Prohibition was linked with failure, and repeal with a return of economic prosperity. In rural areas the pitch was made directly to the farmers who were selling grain to breweries. Repeal would be a "business stimulant." A wet advertisement in a Jackson County newspaper said, "A vote for ratification is a vote for real temperance, prosperity, lower taxes, and against crime and racketeering." Another one in the *Kentland Democrat* called Prohibition "an expensive fizzle." A straightforward one stated that "the long sought opportunity to rid our country of the vicious effects of the Eighteenth Amendment" was now at hand. Still other advertisements were more subtle: why, if Prohibition was so successful, did drys need to rally support?[55]

The most effective wet advertisements featured Roosevelt himself. The president highlighted the economic argument in his call for repeal, letting others blame Prohibition for the rise of gangster-backed crime and other problems. In some dry states it was hinted that FDR was going to be happy with just the return of beer. In a full-page notice run in the *Logansport Pharos Tribune*, the president told readers that "it is your patriotic duty to vote for repeal Tuesday." Another suggested that the state heed the "advice" of the president when it came to repeal, since it would "reduce taxes and increase" revenues. In others, Roosevelt vowed that the saloon of old would not return, and he assured readers that a vote for repeal would be a vote for prosperity. Further, "we have elected Franklin D. Roosevelt as our president and charged him with the task of leading us out of the depression. He asks for repeal of the Eighteenth Amendment as part of his program. LET'S BACK HIM UP!"[56]

Drys countered the wet advertising blitz by running ads of their own. Would the economy really improve just because of repeal? And would the legislation of liquor indeed bring prosperity? They warned "voters under 30" to be wary of wet propaganda and half-truths about what drinking was like in the days of the saloon. Dry advertisements also reminded dairy farmers that milk consumption had increased dramatically under Prohibition and could be jeopardized if the Eighteenth Amendment was repealed.[57]

Drys were cautiously optimistic. The *Anderson Herald* commented to its readers that for those old enough to remember, the weeks leading up to the repeal election were reminders of the passionate debates over liquor from earlier in the century. Once again, the state's churches were the battle stations for drys under attack, with the Sunday before the election bringing a flurry of sermons. In Terre Haute the pastor of Centenary Methodist Church had the spotlight sermon of the week in the *Terre Haute Star*; there, the Reverend George E. Francis urged readers to vote their conscience and not allow the return of an evil that "kills our citizens and ruins their families." These sentiments captured the tone of the dry cause across the state as churches held meetings to discuss what was at stake in the election. Evangelical Protestants raged against "the outlaw who would come back" and heard scathing sermons in defense of the Eighteenth Amendment. But the Sunday School lesson in the *Indianapolis News* written by West Morris Street Christian Church summed up the fears of many drys: its title was "Jesus Faces Betrayal, Denial, based on Mark 15:17–31."[58]

On Election Day the dry cause suffered defeat. The *Indianapolis Times* ran the headline, "Anti Saloon Yoke Thrown off by Indiana Voters." Drys must have wondered how it had come to this. In reviewing the ending of Prohibition, the *Goshen Daily Democrat* said that the vote really had nothing to do with drinking, but rather that national Prohibition's enforcement had been a failure. Moreover, with the coming of a poor economy, the American people were no longer willing to continue the Noble Experiment. The *Pulaski County Democrat* argued that the repealists were helped a great deal by the Great Depression, but that most citizens were not "fanatics" either way on the issue of drinking. They just wanted the best form of control.[59]

Drys could not have disagreed more. The *Warren Review Republican* said that individual profit had driven repeal, not the prospect of the return of national economic prosperity. After all, Canada, Germany, and England were all suffering from the Great Depression, and none of them had enacted Prohibition. Furthermore, the paper blasted the idea that "everyone" was drinking under the Eighteenth Amendment and asked why, if that were the case, the nation had bothered going through the repeal process. The *Oxford Gazette* warned that there were still issues relating to alcohol's return—chiefly, drunk drivers and the reappearance of the saloon—which the government would now have to address.[60]

Some drys hoped to turn defeat into victory. For L. E. York, the IASL was ready to start over again. He believed that drys had done very well, considering the pressure that the McNutt and Roosevelt administrations had exerted in order to win repeal. He vowed to seek a local option law immediately.[61] For his part, McNutt was "radiant" at the news of the wet victory, despite the "supreme effort" of the drys. The governor commented, "It was a distinct indication that Indiana has chosen the New Deal."[62]

In the end, the wet victory had followed McNutt's predetermined path. Though a national organization, the Voluntary Committee of Lawyers, drew up a model convention plan that many states adopted, it was up to each state to decide how to hold its vote. The governor assigned one delegate for every 10,000 residents per county, making a total of 328 delegates dispersed over Indiana's 92 counties. McNutt's formula had major implications for the vote in the Hoosier state. By tying delegation size to population rather than to some other unit, such as representation in the General Assembly or even one county, one vote, the governor ensured a wet victory—all that was needed was a simple majority, or 165 delegates. With larger counties accounting for 184 total delegates, McNutt could feel confident before a single ballot was cast. But he left nothing to chance. The ballot was written without mention of the Eighteenth Amendment, and the election was scheduled for early June (in the hope that the rural vote would be low during one of the farmers' busiest seasons). McNutt also publicly said that Prohibition was a system that simply did not work, but he could show, as he did by releasing the first of the beer-tax and license-fee money to the counties shortly before the election, that his system of temperance backed up by state control did.[63]

Using McNutt's script, wets did well all over the state, winning a total of fifty-five counties and 245 delegates to the convention. Both rural and urban counties, as well as those with large and small populations voted wet.[64] The drys had their best showing in Central Indiana, though they were competitive in all three regions of the state. But in the end, too many traditional dry strongholds went wet.[65] Though some of the wet victories were by rather small margins (twenty-nine counties went wet by 1,000 votes or less), and thus drys were extremely close to more than doubling their total of county victories, even then they would not have been able to prevent Indiana from going into the wet column on Election Day.

The actual repeal convention at the statehouse was anticlimactic. There was some squabbling among wet delegates about the degree to which the governor should control the convention and over the issue of draught beer, but in the end everything went as McNutt wanted. As a token of respect, five dry delegates, including President Bryan of Indiana University, were placed on the permanent organizing committee.[66] The dry crusade in Indiana had come to a close.

Many observers had considered the Hoosier State a barometer of dry strength in the nation, yet the wets' strategy was such that not even Shumaker could have stopped them. Drys were left feeling dazed and betrayed, but with no way to vent their frustrations. They were disorganized and left to ponder what might have happened had potential dry bastions in the West and South even held conventions. Drys had nothing with which to counter the economic forces of the Great Depression and New Deal, and politicians such as Franklin Roosevelt and Paul McNutt and, in the end, only one state, South Carolina, voted against the Twenty-first Amendment.[67]

Historian Donald Meyer once labeled Prohibition a "burden" for Protestants,[68] yet they vigorously fought repeal. The failure to keep Prohibition in force was not from either a lack of effort or because the majority of Hoosiers (or the rest of the American people) now rejected the concept of moral order. Rather, Roosevelt and McNutt's genius was in offering a different version of that order to many of those within and outside of the dry cause. Though Shumaker's reform was over, the culture that had produced it was not.

9 | Everything Old Is New Again

By December 1933, Prohibition was finished. Drys never got a delay in the repeal process to regroup.[1] The dry cause had been too successful for its own good. By closing down the saloon and the brewers, drys had destroyed or weakened their enemies without preparing themselves for what came next. Most drys saw their work as done, and the movement neglected to educate the next generation on the dangers of alcohol that had prompted the enactment of Prohibition. Though the reform remained officially a part of evangelical Protestantism, the crusade nature of it began to wither. Furthermore, drys never succeeded in fashioning a coherent enforcement plan that integrated the local, state, and national levels. And thanks to new immigration laws, the fear of a foreign wet culture submerging a dry American one lost its power as an argument. Without these conditions, and because modern America had the technology to negate some of the dangers of the saloon (via home refrigeration of beverages) and because it needed jobs (due to the Great Depression), alcohol returned.[2]

Drys now faced an America that saw their reform as both a failure and wrong, despite the prevalence of their evangelical Protestantism. Still, many drys remained steadfast in their belief that that the crusade had been the right course for the nation to take. They bemoaned the lack of Prohibition as this country entered the Second World War. Howard Hyde Russell of the national Anti Saloon League thought drys could reorganize and make a victorious comeback if they were given enough time. The WCTU vowed to continue the struggle, along with willing denominations, and fought against advertising for alcohol in newspapers, magazines, and on the radio, at times even urging Congressional hearings on the matter. As late as 1947, the Indiana Conference of the Methodist Church declared that "the greatest foe of America today . . . is [the] organized liquor business."[3]

The dry cause's main response was to create a new organization. Alcoholics Anonymous (AA), founded in 1935, inherited many of the ASL's spiritual goals toward solving the problems of drink and stressed a collective approach to sobriety. Indeed, AA's roots stretch back to the 1840s temperance movement and are steeped in evangelical Protestant and Catholic teetotalist ideas. According to Alfred McClung Lee, drys concluded that they could not solve the liquor problem "by outright and immediate suppression" and instead had to save each drinker individually.[4] They were, in other words, going back to the beginning.

New organizations such as AA were needed because the old ones had shriveled up after repeal. The state arms of the League found rebuilding nearly impossible. L. E. York continued to lead the IASL, but as the 1930s gave way to the 1940s, the organization became less and less active until it was a mere shadow of its former self. The IASL limped on, still arguing that the societal costs of alcohol were not covered by the taxes generated from its sale and still trying, as late as 1948, for a local option law for the state. York watched as Edward Shumaker's once-powerful organization was folded into the newly created Indiana Temperance League, which itself eventually disappeared. Other state leagues met similar fates. Both the Georgia and the Kentucky ASLs expanded their list of societal concerns to include other moral issues, such as gambling. While Hoosiers still hear the occasional call for local option, twenty-first-century drys in states that retained such laws are fighting a losing battle to keep them intact.[5]

The national ASL, which had been so brilliant at fighting for Prohibition, largely proved inept at keeping the cherished reform. As K. Austin Kerr has noted, the ASL was not prepared for victory. It had internal divisions, never devised a broad education initiative, could not sustain itself financially, and gave in to the lure of Republican prosperity. Indeed, abandoning the moral track for the economic one was the primary cause of both the ASL's and Prohibition's downfall, for with the coming of the Great Depression the Noble Experiment's monetary benefits vanished.[6] No better example of the breakup of the dry cause can be found than in two Hoosier refugees, Governor Paul McNutt and the eventual 1940 Republican presidential nominee, Wendell Willkie. Neither man, despite their Methodist roots, supported either the League or Prohibition.[7]

The Prohibition Party fared little better than its old antagonist within the dry cause. Nationally, the party found it increasingly difficult to get its name on ballots. In Indiana, while remaining a statewide organization, at least on paper, the Prohibitionists of the mid-twentieth century were confined to a smaller denominational base (the Church of the Brethren rather than the Methodists), due to what they credited as "brainwashing" by "powerful liquor interests." In 1966 the state party had a mere 66 contributors, though the national body found Indiana a receptive place in which to operate, and it held its increasingly faction-ridden national conventions there in the 1940s and 1950s. As the twenty-first century dawned, the party was attempting to reorganize itself at the local, state, and national levels, and it even made overtures to America's Muslim population in an effort to expand its constituency.[8]

Other allies saw their roles change as well. The waning influence of church federations reflected on a local level what had happened to the Federal (later National) Council of Churches at the national one as the century progressed and the growth and diversity of Protestantism diluted its voice. Indianapolis's Church Federation is an example. Today it no longer speaks for its constituent members in the way it did during the time of Shumaker. According to the Reverend John B. Wantz, former senior pastor of Meridian Street United Methodist Church in Indianapolis and past president of the Federation, member churches worry about what may happen if they take a stand on controversial issues.[9]

Drys adapted to the reality of repeal in a variety of ways. Many took their cue from former Pennsylvania governor Gifford Pinchot, who urged them to work against the evils of liquor in society.[10] Former state and national Republican leader Will H. Hays channeled evangelical Protestantism's reform ethos into Hollywood without repeating the mistakes of Prohibition. As the nation's movie czar, Hays brought Hoosier values to the rest of the country, but he thought that the dry cause, in which he was steeped both personally and professionally, had gone too far with the Eighteenth Amendment.[11] Hoosier newspaperman Eugene Pulliam continued to espouse dry principles by adjusting his tone to the times. As a young newspaperman working for the *Franklin Evening Star*, Pulliam had urged statewide prohibition in 1917. In his *Lebanon Reporter* in 1934, while supporting the IASL's efforts on behalf of local option, he argued that prohibition had been a mistake. After purchasing the *Indianapolis Star* in 1945, Pulliam made attacks on liquor-license patronage a cornerstone of his politics.[12] Charles Halleck, who in 1935 entered Congress, where he became a leader in the Republican Party, also represents this trend. As Jasper-Newton County prosecutor in the 1920s, he demanded full enforcement of Prohibition, and his devotion to prosecuting violators under the Wright bone-dry law became legendary. But with the coming of repeal, Halleck stopped his endorsement of the dry cause. His political opponents, including former Lafayette mayor George Durgan, tried to use his dry roots against him, but to little avail. Halleck had moved beyond his dry past without repudiating it, and so had Indiana.[13]

Some drys found entirely new crusades. The Reverend Gerald L. K. Smith, for example, had been a strong advocate of Prohibition within the Indianapolis Church Federation. Smith had replaced the outspoken anti-Klan pastor at Indianapolis's Seventh Christian Church in 1922. Shortly after transferring to University Place Christian Church, he left for Louisiana in 1929. There, Smith found a situation not unlike the one he had left in Indiana. Louisiana had a strong Klan presence, particularly in Shreveport where his new church was located, as well as wet bastions (especially New Orleans) and dry strongholds (the Protestant northern parishes). As prohibition sentiment began·to wane, Smith turned his powers of oratory to the service of Governor Huey Long, eventually quitting his pastorate and working full-time for the Kingfish.[14]

Most drys, however, were exhausted and unable to reignite the fires of a moral crusade to create God's kingdom on Earth. When repeal came, Methodist (South) bishop James Cannon was a broken man, both within his church and in terms of his health.[15] Louisville's Patrick Henry Callahan, the nation's leading lay dry Catholic, believed that the dry cause's leadership was too old to carry on the fight and had largely lost the younger generation. Like other Catholics, he now stressed the need for personal temperance.[16] Some drys thought they had achieved Prohibition too quickly. Harry Emerson Fosdick, the pastor to the Rockefellers, argued that had the drys not been eager for national prohibition during the World War, local option victories could have made the nation dry by 1930.[17] Prominent dry Clarence True Wilson did not believe that Prohibition had been given enough time to take hold nationally, and, with the coming of Repeal, thought drys had missed their chance.[18]

In post-Repeal America, discussions of modification became the great "what ifs" of Prohibition's history. According to William and Arthur Link, the best chance for drys to retain Prohibition would have been to make a deal with wets that allowed beer and light wine while abolishing the saloon. By looking at Shumaker's life, however, we can see why such a compromise never occurred. Prohibition became "entrenched" within the dry culture. And, as Gregory A. Mark and Christopher L. Eisgruber have pointed out, when ideas "bind the culture" that produces them, it is difficult to consider alternatives. During the late 1910s and early 1920s, that is exactly what happened to prohibition and the dry cause. By the 1930s, when drys needed to compromise, they simply were unable to do so.[19]

Shumaker's death spared him the anguish faced by his contemporaries as they contemplated the "what ifs" in the wake of their defeat. But Shumaker himself was hardly forgotten in the years after Repeal. The lives of moral reformers make for great (and not so great) fiction. The ASL and the Klan were the inspiration for Sinclair Lewis's *Elmer Gantry*,[20] while Walter Myers, in his thinly veiled novel about the McNutt years in Indiana, based the leader of his book's Anti-Liquor League on Shumaker. Myers depicted the Reverend Silas Bootear as a toad-like "bigot in his beliefs and a tyrant in the exercise of power," with a nose "big enough to be poked everlastingly in other people's business." In the novel, Bootear is allied with the leader of the Ku Klux Klan, E.C. Steffens, and when the latter is imprisoned, the minister attacks the state Supreme Court and is sent to jail for contempt.[21] Shumaker fared better in denominational histories, where, as late as the 1950s he was remembered as an "able" leader of the dry cause, though his memory outside of evangelical Protestant circles has faded away.[22]

Despite the literal and literary angst, dry ideas did not die out with the passing of the Twenty-first Amendment. Albert and Arthur Shumaker really "stuck" by the beliefs of their father, and their brother Wayne even worked as an IASL speaker for a time.[23] The dry defeat was resounding, however, and continues to shape the way in which Prohibition is remembered. Though both the Great Depression and the Second World War overshadow it, Prohibition still fascinates us, and we find references to it in museums, movies, and pop culture.[24] And while the myth of failure may prevail in the public's memory of Prohibition, alcohol consumption was, in fact, reduced dramatically during that era. As observers at the time noted, Repeal increased drinking nationwide. If "everyone" was drinking during Prohibition, as is so often claimed, this should not be the case.[25] Indeed, there were fewer breweries (only 750 of the pre-Prohibition-period total of 1,568 reopened) and fewer places to buy alcohol. Furthermore, states rigorously pursued and sought convictions of violators of the new laws.[26]

Nevertheless, Hoosiers took part in perpetuating the myth of failure. Virginia Somes Jenckes, a Democratic congresswoman from Indiana during the 1930s, said that Prohibition was the result of "all of our youth [being] in Europe. All of our women didn't have a vote, so the vote for prohibition was a very limited one." Yet even after those two conditions changed, the nation repealed Prohibition only with the onset of the Great Depression. In 1971 the *Indianapolis Star* claimed that Shumaker had pushed through Prohibition "as Indiana boys fought to make the world safe for democracy." In reality, Prohibition had come to Indiana before the United States entered the World War and was the culmination of a decade of work by Shumaker as head of the IASL, with temperance as a reform in Indiana predating the *Star*'s creation. A 2003 story in the Indianapolis weekly *Nuvo* argued that "alley hooch, white mule and bathtub gin" were so common in Indiana that it proved that "God-fearing, law-abiding Hoosiers have always been willing to break laws that interfere with their God-given right to drink." This notion is also refuted by the facts of Shumaker's life and work.[27]

The failure myth's strongest advocate is the alcoholic beverage industry. With the dry cause on the wane, the industry returned to its pre-Prohibition position of big business in search of profit. John Burnham has argued that the liquor industry has worked since Repeal to change the way that Americans think about alcohol. Today the industry still cites individual responsibility when it comes to drinking and contends that alcoholism is a disease, not a moral issue. Yet Burnham believes that the industry, in its quest to make money, exhibits the same level of disrespect for minimal laws governing consumption that prompted Prohibition. To hear or read such an argument is troubling, yet there is a good deal of evidence to support it. Brewers are quick to label any outside attempt at regulation as "neo-prohibitionist." When a 2004 poll revealed that the majority of Americans, including most Hoosiers, believed that alcohol could be taxed at a higher rate, industry lobbyists decried the findings as skewed and claimed that taxes on their output were too high already. Rhetoric aside, the numbers seem to be against the industry. In 2004 the average tax per gallon of beer in the United States was 19 cents. In Indiana, it was 11.5 cents.[28]

Despite industry claims, alcohol remains a source of problems that must be confronted. Drunk driving is a real danger on the nation's roadways, moonshine is a concern in some areas of the country, hard-liquor advertising remains controversial on the nation's airwaves, and underage alcohol abuse is a problem at the nation's colleges and universities. In 2004 both Indiana University and Ball

State students suffered alcohol-related deaths, and in the same year, Indiana University again garnered headlines when the *Chronicle of Higher Education* reported that it was second in the nation in alcohol-related arrests in 2002.[29]

Americans live in a country whose liquor laws were largely written during Repeal. Indiana saw litigation in 2002 over the "exclusive beer distribution territories" for brewers created by McNutt.[30] In the federal court system there was recently a battle over the exporting of alcohol between states. In 1933 this was seen as a sop to drys, as part of the states' rights approach to repeal. However, over the years, states have used the law to protect their citizens not from alcohol but from imports, when the law became a favorite of small, local wineries who were worried about out-of-state competition. In a 2005 decision the United States Supreme Court sided with those seeking to strike down such laws, since "alcohol is viewed as an ordinary article of commerce," unlike the perception during the dry cause's heyday.[31] As for Shumaker's case, it is still cited as a warning that one's published works can present a "clear and present danger" to courts if they "intimidate, influence, impede, embarrass, or obstruct" decisions, no matter the intent, according to one law textbook. Perhaps more important, the Shumaker case still guides the way in which the Indiana Supreme Court considers the issue of contempt.[32]

Prohibition's legacy, therefore, is multifaceted. It does not begin or end with the wet triumph in 1933. The Noble Experiment helped to expand the scope of the federal government (a limited government, or at least one that citizens want to remain limited, does not outlaw entire industries), while showing the limitations of constitutionally based reforms. Prohibition revolutionized American law enforcement by helping to create new state and federal police agencies as well as legal tools such as plea-bargaining and wiretaps.[33] It also affected gender roles. Men and women now drink together and the all-male saloon is no more. Perhaps more important, women became involved politically not only to make America dry but also to make it wet.[34] Additionally, in places such as New York City, Prohibition had made homosexuality more public because the nightlife culture of which it had long been a part was suddenly trendy.[35]

The dry cause, however, was hardly vanquished by repeal. At an Indianapolis substance-abuse group meeting in May 2004, one of the members talked about his success in staying clean and sober from drugs and alcohol while he passed around his six-month medallion from AA. The spirit pervading the meeting—one of accountability for one's actions, of devotion to a power higher than oneself, and of the need to stay away from temptations—certainly would be understood by Shumaker and other drys. It had been their message before the advent of prohibitionist thought. They knew the pitfalls of drink and addiction and the pain it caused to both the user and the user's family and friends, and they tried to stop it once and for all. The dangers they saw in alcohol were, and are, real; the people gathered at the AA meeting can attest to that. Thus, dry culture, still alive, is trying to save America one soul at a time.[36]

The dry cause did not disappear after Repeal. It could not, because it was part of evangelical Protestantism, and that faith is at the heart of the American religious experience. Moreover, the Twenty-first Amendment did not resolve the problems of drink. Rather, it was a bargain between drys and wets that became a full-blown compromise. As long as brewers, bars, and drinkers followed the laws and checked excess, agitation stopped. It is a deal that has largely held to the present. But if the compromise fails in the twenty-first century, we are likely to see new Shumakers arise in America.[37]

Notes

Introduction

1. *Indianapolis Times*, 12 February 1929.
2. *Newsweek*, 15 November 2004.
3. Richard H. Gemmecke, Sesquicentennial Indiana History Conference, Indiana Division, Indiana State Library, Indianapolis, Indiana, 1966, 28; James H. Madison, *Indiana through Tradition and Change: A History of the Hoosier State and Its People, 1920–1945* (Indianapolis: Indiana Historical Society, 1982), 42–43. The author has not added a hyphen to Anti Saloon in accordance with the Indiana League's own usage.
4. William A. Link and Arthur S. Link, *American Epoch: A History of the United States since 1900,* volume 1, *War, Reform, and Society, 1900–1945* (New York: McGraw-Hill, 1993), 211; David E. Kyvig, *Repealing National Prohibition* (Kent, OH: The Kent State University Press, 2000), xi–xii, 12; Norman H. Clark, *Deliver Us from Evil: An Interpretation of American Prohibition* (New York: W. W. Norton and Company, 1976), 9, 144–149; Ballard C. Campbell, "Did Democracy Work? Prohibition in Late Nineteenth-Century Iowa: A Test Case," *Journal of Interdisciplinary History* 8 (Summer 1977): 87–116; Justin E. Walsh, *The Sesquicentennial History of the Indiana General Assembly, 1816–1978* (Indianapolis: Indiana Historical Bureau, 1987), 296; Jack S. Blocker, Jr., "Did Prohibition Really Work? Alcohol Prohibition as a Public Health Innovation," *American Journal of Public Health* 96 (February 2006): 233–243.

5. Paul Kleppner, *The Cross of Culture: A Social Analysis of Midwestern Politics, 1850–1900* (New York: The Free Press, 1970), 167, 371; Paul Kleppner, *Who Voted? The Dynamics of Electoral Turnout, 1870–1980* (New York: Praeger Publishers, 1982), 145–147; George M. Marsden, *Fundamentalism and American Culture: The Shaping of Twentieth Century Evangelicalism, 1870–1925* (New York: Oxford University Press, 1982), v; John D. Buenker, *Urban Liberalism and Progressive Reform* (New York: Charles Scribner's Sons, 1973), 186.

6. Alan Brinkley, *Liberalism and Its Discontents* (Cambridge, MA: Harvard University Press, 1998), 116–118; John Kobler, *Ardent Spirits: The Rise and Fall of Prohibition* (New York: G. P. Putnam's Sons, 1973); Thomas M. Coffey, *The Long Thirst: Prohibition in America, 1920–1933* (New York: Dell Publishing Company, 1976); K. Austin Kerr, *Organized for Prohibition: A New History of the Anti-Saloon League* (New Haven, CT: Yale University Press, 1985), 6–7; Edward Behr, *Prohibition: Thirteen Years that Changed America* (New York: Arcade Publishing, 1996), 3; Joseph R. Gusfield, *Symbolic Crusade: Status Politics and the American Temperance Movement* (Chicago: University of Illinois Press, 1986); Richard F. Hamm, *Shaping the Eighteenth Amendment: Temperance Reform, Legal Culture, and the Polity, 1880–1920* (Chapel Hill: University of North Carolina Press, 1995); Thomas R. Pegram, *Battling Demon Rum: The Struggle for a Dry America, 1800–1933* (Chicago: Ivan R. Dee, 1998), xii; Ann-Marie E. Szymanski, *Pathways to Prohibition: Radicals, Moderates, and Social Movement Outcomes* (Durham, NC: Duke University Press, 2003).

7. Jack S. Blocker, Jr., *American Temperance Movements: Cycles of Reform* (Boston: Twayne Publishers, 1989), xi; Gaines M. Foster, *Moral Reconstruction: Christian Lobbyists and the Federal Legislation of Morality, 1865–1920* (Chapel Hill: University of North Carolina Press, 2002); Nathan O. Hatch, "The Puzzle of American Methodism," *Church History* 63 (June 1994): 175–189. Fundamentalist Christians are another group that has been often ignored or marginalized. See Marsden, *Fundamentalism*, 141, 187–188, 214.

8. Mark Thornton, *The Economics of Prohibition* (Salt Lake City: University of Utah Press, 1991).

9. Daniel T. Rodgers, *Atlantic Crossings: Social Politics in a Progressive Age* (Cambridge, MA: The Belknap Press of Harvard University Press, 1998); Albert W. Wardin, Jr., *Tennessee Baptists: A Comprehensive History, 1779–1999* (Brentwood, TN: Executive Board of the Tennessee Baptist Convention, 1999), 262, 339; Stephen L. Carter, *God's Name in Vain: The Wrongs and Rights of Religion in Politics* (New York: Basic Books, 2000); Jeffrey H. Morrison, *John Witherspoon and the Founding of the American Republic* (Notre Dame, IN: University of Notre Dame Press, 2005). Morrison argues that a desire to ignore the importance of religion in American history, which Rodgers demonstrates in his look at the Progressive Movement, is behind the neglect of Founding Father John Witherspoon.

10. Samuel P. Huntington, *The Clash of Civilizations and the Remaking of World Order* (New York: Simon and Schuster, 2003), 66, emphasis in the original; Jon Butler, "Jack-in-the-Box Faith: The Religion Problem in Modern American History," *Journal of American History* 90 (March 2004): 1357–1378; James G. Moseley, *A Cultural History of Religion in America* (Westport, CT: Greenwood Press, 1981), 161–162; T. S. Eliot, *Christianity and Culture: The Idea of a Christian Society and Notes towards the Definition of Culture* (New York: A Harvest Book, 1976), 6, 69.

11. William James, *The Varieties of Religious Experience: A Study in Human Nature* (New York: A Mentor Book, 1958), 24, 41–42. Fran Grace does this well in her biography of famed dry Carry Nation. See Fran Grace, *Carry A. Nation: Retelling the Life* (Indianapolis: Indiana University Press, 2001).

12. James A. Morone, *Hellfire Nation: The Politics of Sin in American History* (New Haven, CT: Yale University Press, 2003), 1–3.

13. George M. Marsden, *Jonathan Edwards: A Life* (New Haven, CT: Yale University Press, 2003), 196–197, 458.

14. Barry Alan Shain, *The Myth of American Individualism: The Protestant Origins of American Political Thought* (Princeton, NJ: Princeton University Press, 1994); Morrison, *Witherspoon*, 19–43; James H. Read, *Power versus Liberty: Madison, Hamilton, Wilson, and Jefferson* (Charlottesville: University Press of Virginia, 2000), ix, 16, 57, 72, 86–87, 122; Cedric C. Cummins, *Indiana Public Opinion and the World War, 1914–1917* (Indianapolis: Indiana Historical Bureau, 1945), 210–211. Cummins refers to Shumaker's Indiana as being very Hamiltonian in its politics.

15. Clifford S. Griffin, "Religious Benevolence as Social Control, 1815–1860," *Mississippi Valley Historical Review* 44 (December 1957): 423–444; Gordon S. Wood, *The Creation of the American Republic, 1776–1787* (Chapel Hill: University of North Carolina Press, 1998), 20–23; Daniel Walker Howe, *The Political Culture of the American Whigs* (Chicago: University of Chicago Press, 1979), 3, 18, 31–35, 101, 163. It should be pointed out that the Whigs were also temperance advocates.

16. Andrew R. L. Cayton and Peter S. Onuf, *The Midwest and the Nation: Rethinking the History of an American Region* (Indianapolis: Indiana University Press, 1990), 85, 88, 109, 111–115, 118. Similar things were also occurring in places such as Oregon, which had more than its fair share of transplanted Midwesterners. See Robert D. Johnston, *The Radical Middle Class: Populist Democracy and the Question of Capitalism in Progressive-Era Portland, Oregon* (Princeton, NJ: Princeton University Press, 2003).

17. T. J. Jackson Lears, *No Place of Grace: Antimodernism and the Transformation of American Culture, 1880–1920* (Chicago: University of Chicago Press, 1994), xv, 8; Lynn Dumenil, *In the Modern Temper: American Culture and Society in the 1920s* (New York: Hill and Wang, 1995), 6.

18. Lewis Atherton, *Main Street on the Middle Border* (Bloomington: Indiana University Press, 1984), xvi; Robert F. Martin, *Hero of the Heartland: Billy Sunday and the Transformation of American Society, 1862–1935* (Indianapolis: Indiana University Press, 2002), 23; Kurt Vonnegut, "To Be a Native Middle-Westerner," *Nuvo*, May 20–27, 1999, 12–14. For more on the importance of place, and for the possibility that regions such as the Midwest are often ignored in American history, see Belden C. Lane, *Landscapes of the Sacred: Geography and Narrative in American Spirituality* (New York: Paulist Press, 1988); and Laurie F. Maffly-Kipp, *Religion and Society in Frontier California* (New Haven, CT: Yale University Press, 1994).

19. Ralph D. Gray, ed., *Gentlemen from Indiana: National Party Candidates, 1836–1940* (Indianapolis: Indiana Historical Bureau, 1977); James H. Madison, *The Indiana Way: A State History* (Indianapolis: Indiana University Press, 1990), 187–190, 208–229; *Indianapolis News*, 5 June 1918, 27 April 1927; *Indianapolis Times*, 15 February 1934; *Indianapolis Star*, 30 April 1927; Will H. Hays, *The Memoirs of Will H. Hays* (Garden City, NY: Doubleday and Company, 1955), 65.

1 | *Origins of a Dry Leader*

1. Fairfield County Chapter OGS, "Fairfield County in the Civil War," http://www.fairfieldgenealogy.org/research/faircivil.html, 10 February 2003; Ehistory.com, *The War of the Rebellion: A Compilation of the Official Records of the Union and Confederate Armies*, Series 1, Volume 38, Part 1, 774–776; Series 1, Volume 38, Part 3, 358–360; Volume 47, Part 1, 555; C. T. Develling, *History of the 17th Regiment, 1st Brigade, 3rd Division, 14th Corps, Army of the Cumberland, War of the Rebellion* (Zanesville, OH: E. R. Sullivan, 1889), 21, 64, 77–89. David's last name is misspelled as "Shoemaker" in the company history. Fairfield County was also the home county of Union general William Tecumseh Sherman. David Shumaker saw action in Sherman's Atlanta and Carolina campaigns.

2. Newton Bateman, ed., *Effingham County* (Chicago: Munsell Publishers, 1910), 855; "Seitz Branch" notes, courtesy of Cynthia Hendee Henry, in possession of author; Karl Seitz, correspondence with author, 22 February 2004; Rev. Edward S. Shumaker to Belle Mechling, 6 August 1919, courtesy of Cynthia Hendee Henry, in possession of author. Sarah had three brothers who deserve some mention. George and Noah both served in the Seventeenth with David Shumaker. Another brother, Enoch, was a teacher in Ohio and in Missouri, where one of his pupils was future general John Pershing.

3. 1860 Census; Edward S. Shumaker, *The Autobiography of Edward Seitz Shumaker* (Unpublished, 1929), 1–3, 6–10. Much of the information on Shumaker's early life comes from his unpublished autobiography. Though writ-

ten near the end of his life, the work provides insight into how Shumaker remembered events that otherwise would be missed by biographers.

4. Shumaker, *Autobiography*, 57–58; Minutes and Roster of the 43rd Annual Reunion of the 17th OVI, Lancaster, Ohio, 20 September 1923, Box 2; "Honor to Whom Honor Is Due," 30 May 1920, Box 1; 1902–1903 version, 1918–1919 version, 1927–1928 version; "The Flag," N.D., Box 2, Edward S. Shumaker Papers, in possession of author, hereafter cited as ESS Papers.

5. Stephen E. Ambrose, *Crazy Horse and Custer: The Parallel Lives of Two American Warriors* (New York: Anchor Books, 1996), 123; Robert H. Wiebe, *The Search for Order, 1877–1920* (New York: Hill and Wang, 1999), 44–45.

6. Allan G. Bogue, *From Prairie to Corn Belt: Farming on the Illinois and Iowa Prairies in the Nineteenth Century* (Chicago: University of Chicago Press, 1963), 259–287; Bateman, *Effingham County*, 855–856; Effingham County, "History of Effingham County Townships," http://www.effingham.com/kperkins/Townships.htm, 22 August 2002; 1870 Census; 1880 Census.

7. Shumaker, *Autobiography*, 4, 11, 12–15.

8. Ibid., 16–17; West Township, Effingham County, Illinois, 1880 Census; Effingham County, "Early Effingham County," http://www.effingham.com/kperkins/early.htm, 18 February 2002; Travel Account of L.F. Dick, 1868, Conner Prairie Archives, Conner Prairie Living History Museum, Fishers, Indiana.

9. Shumaker, *Autobiography*, 18.

10. Elliot J. Gorn, ed., *The McGuffey Readers: Selections from the 1879 Edition* (New York: Bedford/St. Martin's, 1998); Shumaker, *Autobiography*, 18–23; Mason Public High School Report Card, 7 April 1886, Box 2, ESS Papers.

11. Shumaker, *Autobiography*, 24.

12. Richard Jensen, *The Winning of the Midwest: Social and Political Conflict, 1888–1896* (Chicago: University of Chicago Press, 1971); Shumaker, *Autobiography*, 24.

13. Lawrence Goodwyn, *Democratic Promise: The Populist Moment in America* (New York: Oxford University Press, 1976); Norman Pollack, ed., *The Populist Mind* (Indianapolis: The Bobbs-Merrill Company, 1967), xix; Robert C. McMath, Jr., *American Populism: A Social History, 1877–1898* (New York: Hill and Wang, 1993), 41, 52, 170–171; Walter T.K. Nugent, *The Tolerant Populists: Kansas Populism and Nativism* (Chicago: University of Chicago Press, 1963); Joe Creech, *Righteous Indignation: Religion and the Populist Revolution* (Chicago: University of Illinois Press, 2006).

14. Shumaker, *Autobiography*, 25–27.

15. Ibid., 27–29.

16. Ibid., 30–31; Michael McGerr, *A Fierce Discontent: The Rise and Fall of the Progressive Movement in America, 1870–1920* (New York: The Free Press, 2003), 26.

17. Jack S. Blocker, Jr., *Retreat from Reform: The Prohibition Movement in the United States, 1890–1913* (Westport, CT: Greenwood Press, 1976), 8, 12–14; Atherton, *Main Street on the Middle Border*, xvi; Cayton and Onuf, *The Midwest and the Nation*, 85, 88, 109, 111–115, 118. The contrast between these interpretations, especially in the nature of the dry cause, with that of Richard Hofstadter's is quite stark. See Richard Hofstadter, *The Age of Reform: From Bryan to FDR* (New York: Vintage Books, 1955), 288–293.

18. Ruth Bordin, *Frances Willard: A Biography* (Chapel Hill: University of North Carolina Press, 1986), 27–29; Edith L. Blumhofer, *Aimee Semple McPherson: Everybody's Sister* (Grand Rapids, MI: William B. Eerdmans Publishing Company, 1993), 10–11; Grace, *Carry A. Nation*, 75, 142–145.

19. Shumaker, *Autobiography*, 9, 27–28, 31–32.

20. Ibid., 32–33.

21. James, *The Varieties of Religious Experience*, 67, 98–99, 162, 184; Ann Taves, *Fits, Trances, and Visions: Experiencing Religion and Explaining Experience from Wesley to James* (Princeton, NJ: Princeton University Press, 1999).

22. Robert T. Handy, "The Protestant Quest for a Christian America, 1830–1930," *Church History* 22 (March 1953): 12–14; Marion L. Bell, *Crusade in the City: Revivalism in Nineteenth-Century Philadelphia* (Lewisburg, PA: Bucknell University Press, 1977), 20; Charles I. Foster, *An Errand of Mercy: The Evangelical United Front, 1790–1837* (Chapel Hill: University of North Carolina Press, 1960), viii, 132–135, 167–177, 210–211; Nathan O. Hatch, *The Democratization of American Christianity* (New Haven, CT: Yale University Press, 1989); William Warren Sweet, *The Methodist Episcopal Church and the Civil War* (Cincinnati: Methodist Book Concern Press, 1912); Donald G. Jones, *The Sectional Crisis and Northern Methodism: A Study in Piety, Political Ethics, and Civil Religion* (Metuchen, NJ: The Scarecrow Press, 1979); Kevin J. Corn, "'Forward Be Our Watchword': Indiana Methodism and the Modern Middle Class" (M.A. thesis, Indiana University, 1996); Kleppner, *The Cross of Culture*, 73–74; Timothy L. Smith, *Revivalism and Social Reform: American Protestantism on the Eve of the Civil War* (Baltimore: Johns Hopkins University Press, 1980); Ralph E. Morrow, "Northern Methodism in the South during Reconstruction," *Mississippi Valley Historical Review* 41 (September 1954): 197–218; David Newsome, *The Victorian World Picture: Perceptions and Introspections in an Age of Change* (New Brunswick, NJ: Rutgers University Press, 1997), 134, 192; *Western Christian Advocate*, 8 September, 15 September 1880, 17 May, 14 June 1893; Melinda Lawson, *Patriot Fires: Forging a New American Nationalism in the Civil War North* (Lawrence: University of Kansas Press, 2002); *Noblesville Independent*, 6 November 1880.

23. William G. McLoughlin, Jr., *Modern Revivalism: Charles Gradison Finney to Billy Graham* (New York: The Ronald Press, 1959), 150–151, 166–167, 342;

Leigh Eric Schmidt, *Hearing Things: Religion, Illusion, and the American Enlightenment* (Cambridge, MA: Harvard University Press, 2000); James H. Timberlake, *Prohibition and the Progressive Movement, 1900–1920* (Cambridge, MA: Harvard University Press, 1963), 10, 16; Dickson D. Bruce, *And They All Sang Hallelujah: Plain-Folk Camp-Meeting Religion, 1800–1845* (Knoxville: University of Tennessee Press, 1974); Roger Robins, "Vernacular American Landscape: Methodists, Camp Meetings, and Social Respectability," *Religion and American Culture* 4 (Summer 1994): 169, 172; Lears, *No Place of Grace*, 24; Arthur Shumaker, interview with author, 24 March 2000; Bruce Catton, *Waiting for the Morning Train: An American Boyhood* (Detroit: Wayne State University Press, 1987), 29.

24. James Cannon, Jr., *Bishop Cannon's Own Story: Life as I have seen it* (Durham, NC: Duke University Press, 1955); Robert A. Hohner, *Prohibition and Politics: The Life of Bishop James Cannon, Jr.* (Columbia: University of South Carolina Press, 1999), 2–5.

25. Lyle W. Dorsett, *Billy Sunday and the Redemption of Urban America* (Grand Rapids, MI: William B. Eerdmans Publishing Company, 1991).

26. Shumaker, *Autobiography*, 33–36. The seeming contradiction in how he remembered being called to preach is probably due to a gap of over forty years between the event and the writing.

27. Ibid., 37–39. Shumaker did not relate his father's reaction to his decision.

28. W. J. Rorabaugh, *The Alcoholic Republic: An American Tradition* (New York: Oxford University Press, 1981); Lyman Beecher, *Six Sermons on the Nature, Occasions, Signs, Evils, and Remedy of Intemperance* (New York: American Tract Society, 1827); Clarence E. Flynn, ed., *The Indianapolis Area of the Methodist Episcopal Church, 1924–1928: A Record and History* (Anderson, IN: Herald Publishing Company, 1928), 41.

29. Ann Douglas, *The Feminization of American Culture* (New York: Alfred A. Knopf, 1979), 97–100, 154; Shumaker, *Autobiography*, 40–41; "Edward Seitz Shumaker" in Ernest Hurst Cherrington, ed., *Standard Encyclopedia of the Alcohol Problem*, Volume 5 (Westerville, OH: American Issue Publishing Company, 1929), 2436; Blocker, *American Temperance Movements*, 61–94. In 1880 the *Western Christian Advocate* advertised over 100 books intended for Sunday school libraries from the National Temperance Society. See *Western Christian Advocate*, 7 July 1880.

30. *Indianapolis News*, 26 October 1929; Shumaker, *Autobiography*, 42–46.

31. Blocker, *American Temperance Movements*, 98–99.

32. Shumaker, *Autobiography*, 47–55.

33. Ibid., 61–62; Hohner, *Life of Bishop James Cannon*, 33.

34. McKendree College, "Then and Now," http://www.mckendree.edu/ A_03/Welcome/then_now.htm, 28 August 2003; Shumaker, *Autobiography*,

62–63; James E. Kirby, "Dearest Ellen: Correspondence between Bishop Matthew Simpson and His Wife," *Methodist History* 42 (April 2004): 139, 147; John Braeman, *Albert J. Beveridge: American Nationalist* (Chicago: University of Chicago Press, 1971), 6–13; Russell Pulliam, *Publisher: Gene Pulliam, Last of the Newspaper Titans* (Ottawa, IL: Jameson Books, 1984), 8–21; George B. Manhart, *DePauw through the Years,* Volume 1, *1837–1919* (Greencastle, IN: DePauw University, 1962), 4, 208, 263, 290–293, 297; *Greencastle Banner,* 17 January 1878, 22 January 1880, 6 June 1889; *Greencastle Banner Times,* 17 May 1895.

35. *Greencastle Banner,* 28 January, 11 March, 12 August 1875, 14 June 1877, 27 August 1885, 4 March, 20 May, 22 July, 29 July, 5 August 1886, 22 September 1887; 1890 Census; 1900 Census.

36. Howard Louis Milkman, Jr., "Thomas DeWitt Talmage: An Evangelical Nineteenth Century Voice on Technology, Urbanization, and Labor-Management Conflicts" (Ph.D. diss., New York University, 1979); Shumaker, *Autobiography,* 76; *Greencastle Banner,* 11 October 1883, 7 May, 21 May 1885, 19 May, 28 July 1887, 9 August 1888, 31 July 1890, 16 April 1891.

37. Shumaker, *Autobiography,* 64–68.

38. *Greencastle Banner and Times,* 11 June 1891; Shumaker, *Autobiography,* 69–70; The Keystone Notebook 601; E. S. Shumaker Notebook, Essay Book, E. S. Shumaker Essay Book, Box 1; "German and French History" notebook; "Ancient Greek" notebook, Box 2, ESS Papers.

39. Arthur Shumaker, interview with author, 24 March 2000; Shumaker, *Autobiography,* 69–73, 76; *Indianapolis News,* 26 October 1929.

40. E. S. Shumaker Essay Book, Box 1, ESS Papers.

41. Shumaker, *Autobiography,* 76–81.

42. Ibid., 81–83.

43. Ibid., 84–86, 89; *Clay County Enterprise,* 20 October 1892, 14 January, 14 April 1892, 3 August 1893; 1900 Census.

44. Arthur Shumaker, interview with author, 24 March 2000.

45. Shumaker, *Autobiography,* 87–88.

46. *Clay County Enterprise,* 15 June 1893.

47. Commencement book, courtesy of Cynthia Hendee Henry, in possession of author; Shumaker, *Autobiography,* 73–75; DePauw University Commencement Program, 12 June 1895, Box 2, ESS Papers; *Greencastle Banner Times,* 14 June 1895.

48. Shumaker, *Autobiography,* 90–92; 1900 Census.

49. Plainfield Pastorate Book, Box 2, ESS Papers; Shumaker, *Autobiography,* 93–95.

50. Indiana Yearly Meeting of Friends Pamphlet, "An Appeal to Christians and Especially Friends for More Diligent, Consecrated, and Consistent Effort to Overthrow the Modern 'Abomination of Desolations', the Liquor

Traffic," 1891, Indiana Historical Society, Indianapolis, Indiana; Thomas D. Hamm, *The Transformation of American Quakerism: Orthodox Friends, 1800–1907* (Indianapolis: Indiana University Press, 1992); Shumaker, *Autobiography*, 96.

51. *Terre Haute Express*, 15 July, 14 September 1898, 23 March 1902; 1900 Census; Paul Boyer, *Urban Masses and Moral Order in America, 1820–1920* (Cambridge, MA: Harvard University Press, 1997), viii; Nick Salvatore, *Eugene V. Debs: Citizen and Socialist* (Chicago: University of Illinois Press, 1982).

52. Walter Rauschenbusch, *A Gospel for the Social Awakening* (New York: Association Press, 1950), 31, 81; Winthrop S. Hudson, ed., *Walter Rauschenbusch: Selected Writings* (New York: Paulist Press, 1984), 4, 28, 33–34; Donovan E. Smucker, *The Origins of Walter Rauschenbusch's Social Ethics* (Montreal: McGill-Queen's University Press, 1994), 3–4; *Western Christian Advocate*, 20 August 1890, 14 July 1920; "The Christian Objective" by S.E. Nicholson, Undated, S. Edgar Nicholson Papers, Archives of Earlham College Library, Richmond, Indiana, hereafter cited as EC Archives.

53. Donald W. Dayton, "The Holiness Churches: A Significant Ethical Tradition," http://www.religion-online.org/showarticle.asp?title=1862, 6 March 2005; Philip Williams, *Walls that Human Hands Have Raised: A History of Central Avenue United Methodist Church* (Indianapolis: Central Avenue United Methodist Church, 2000), 7; First Quarterly Conference, 10 December 1917, Minutes and Board Meetings 1864–1918 book, Archives of Meridian Street United Methodist Church, Indianapolis, Indiana, hereafter cited as MSUMC Archives.

54. Charles Howard Hopkins, *The Rise of the Social Gospel in American Protestantism, 1865–1915* (New Haven, CT: Yale University Press, 1967), 12, 280–317; Elias B. Sanford, *Origin and History of the Federal Council of the Churches of Christ in America* (Hartford, CT: S.S. Scranton Company, 1916), 259–260; Elias B. Sanford, ed., *Federal Council of the Churches of Christ in America: Report of the First Meeting of the Federal Council, Philadelphia, 1908* (New York: The Revell Press, 1909), 267–273; Donald K. Gorrell, *The Age of Social Responsibility: The Social Gospel in the Progressive Era, 1900–1920* (Macon, GA: Mercer University Press, 1988), ix; Douglas Jacobson and William Vance Trollinger, Jr., eds., *Re-Forming the Center: American Protestantism, 1900 to the Present* (Grand Rapids, MI: William B. Eerdmans Publishing Company, 1998), 1–14, 317; Martin E. Marty, *Pilgrims in Their Own Land: 500 Years of Religion in America* (Boston: Little, Brown, and Company, 1984), 375–377; Norris Magnuson, *Salvation in the Slums: Evangelical Social Work, 1865–1920* (Metuchen, NJ: The Scarecrow Press, 1977), 132–133, 140–142; Bordin, *Frances Willard*, 6; Lester G. McAllister and William E. Tucker, *Journey in Faith: A History of the Christian Church (Disciples of Christ)* (St. Louis: CBD Press, 1989), 291–293; Paul A. Carter, *The Decline and Revival of the Social Gospel: Social and Political Liberalism in American Protestant Churches, 1920–1940* (Ithaca, NY:

Cornell University Press, 1956), 12–13; Charles S. MacFarland, ed., *Christian Unity at Work: The Federal Council of the Churches of Christ in America in Quadrennial Session at Chicago, Illinois, 1912* (New York: Federal Council of Churches, 1913), 253; Robert H. Wiebe, *Businessmen and Reform: A Study of the Progressive Movement* (Cambridge, MA: Harvard University Press, 1962), 17; Second Quarterly Conference, 5 February 1908, Minutes and Board Meetings 1864–1918 book, MSUMC Archives. For a contemporary example of such unity, which brought together William E. Borah, Harry Emerson Fosdick, Francis J. McConnell, and Wayne B. Wheeler, see Jerome Davis, ed., *Christianity and Social Adventuring* (New York: The Century Company, 1927).

55. Timothy Miller, *Following In His Steps: A Biography of Charles M. Sheldon* (Knoxville: University of Tennessee Press, 1987), 159, 164–172.

56. Robert M. Crunden, *Ministers of Reform: The Progressives' Achievement in American Civilization, 1889–1920* (Chicago: University of Illinois Press, 1984), ix; Eldon J. Eisenach, ed., *The Social and Political Thought of American Progressivism* (Indianapolis: Hackett Publishing Company, 2006); Peter G. Filene, "An Obituary for the 'Progressive Movement,'" *American Quarterly* 22 (Spring 1970): 20–34; Otis L. Graham, Jr., *An Encore for Reform: The Old Progressives and the New Deal* (New York: Oxford University Press, 1967), 9, 15, 92; David Traxel, *Crusader Nation: The United States in Peace and the Great War, 1898–1920* (New York: Alfred A. Knopf, 2006), 10; McGerr, *A Fierce Discontent*, xiv–xvi, 65–80; Dumenil, *In the Modern Temper*, 18; John Marshall Barker, *The Saloon Problem and Social Reform* (Boston: The Everett Press, 1905), v; *Western Christian Advocate*, 11 April 1855, 8 December 1880; *Noblesville Ledger*, 12 August, 12 December 1887; Wiebe, *The Search for Order*, 62–63; Kyvig, *Repealing National Prohibition*, 8–10; Hofstadter, *The Age of Reform*, 204, 289–290; Wiebe, *Businessmen and Reform*, 7; David E. Kyvig, ed., *Law, Alcohol, and Order: Perspectives on National Prohibition* (Westport, CT: Greenwood Press, 1985), 68–69; Lynn Dumenil, "'The Insatiable Maw of Bureaucracy': Antistatism and Education Reform in the 1920s," *Journal of American History* 77 (September 1990): 502–503; Timberlake, *Prohibition and the Progressive Movement*, 1–3; John Whiteclay Chambers II, *The Tyranny of Change: America in the Progressive Era, 1890–1920* (New Brunswick, NJ: Rutgers University Press, 2000), 144, 164; Boyer, *Urban Masses and Moral Order in America*, 195–199; J. Leonard Bates, *Senator Thomas J. Walsh of Montana: Law and Public Affairs from TR to FDR* (Chicago: University of Illinois Press, 1999), 261; Marian C. McKenna, *Borah* (Ann Arbor: University of Michigan Press, 1961); Leroy Ashby, *The Spearless Leader: Senator Borah and the Progressive Movement in the 1920s* (Chicago: University of Illinois Press, 1972); Richard Coke Lower, *A Bloc of One: The Political Career of Hiram W. Johnson* (Stanford, CA: Stanford University Press, 1993), 40–42; David P. Thelen, *Robert M. LaFollette and the Insurgent Spirit* (Boston: Little, Brown and Company, 1976), 139.

57. *Terre Haute Express,* 10 December 1899; "Recent Christian Socialism and the Laboring Classes," N.D., Box 2, ESS Papers; Glenn Spann, "Theological Transition within Methodism: The Rise of Liberalism and the Conservative Response," *Methodist History* 43 (April 2005): 198–212.

58. "History of Maple Avenue Methodist Episcopal Church," N.D., Box 2, ESS Papers; Shumaker, *Autobiography,* 98–103; *Terre Haute Express,* 9 October 1898, 29 January, 26 February, 5 March, 23 April, 4 June, 24 September 1899, 28 April 1901.

59. *Terre Haute Express,* 19 February, 5 March, 21 May, 20 November, 24 November, 25 November, 26 November, 28 November 1899, 15 February, 18 February, 10 April, 12 June 1900, 24 June 1901; Shumaker, *Autobiography,* 104.

60. *Terre Haute Express,* 15 January 1900; Shumaker, *Autobiography,* 104.

61. *Noblesville Independent,* 14 June 1879; *Western Christian Advocate,* 26 July 1893, 4 July 1900.

62. *Terre Haute Express,* 11 June 1900; "Dangerous Tendencies in American Life," 3 versions, N.D., Box 2, ESS Papers.

63. "That Ye Might Believe," N.D.; Easter Missionary Sermon: "The Open Door," 12 April 1903; "Life More Abundant," N.D.; "Salvation," 26 April 1903; "The Heavenly Vision," 10 May 1903; "Making of the New Testament," N.D.; "Paul the Letter Writer," N.D.; "Paul the Prisoner," N.D.; "Facing Jerusalem," N.D.; "Closing Days," N.D.; "The Last Hours," N.D.; "Arrest, Trial and Crucifixion," N.D.; "The Jerusalem Church," N.D.; "Paul and the Church of the Empire," N.D.; "Our Riches," N.D. 1902; "Love," N.D.; "The Life with Men," N.D., Box 2, ESS Papers; John W. Storey, *Texas Baptist Leadership and Social Christianity, 1900–1980* (College Station: Texas A&M University Press, 1986), 4; Spann, "Theological Transition within Methodism," 198–212.

64. "The Value of God's House, or Advantages in Being a Christian," 21 September, 5 December 1902, Box 2, ESS Papers.

65. Jack J. Detzler, *The History of the Northwest Indiana Conference of the Methodist Church, 1852–1951* (Nashville, TN: The Parthenon Press, 1953), 95; Herbert L. Heller, *Indiana Conference of the Methodist Church, 1832–1956* (Indianapolis: History Conference of the Indiana Conference, 1957), 130; Bulletin, 26 December 1920, Bulletins 1871–1922 book, MSUMC Archives.

66. *Indianapolis Star,* 23 January 1905; *Kokomo Daily Tribune,* 28 August 1907; *Fort Wayne Journal Gazette,* 29 February 1908; *Terre Haute Tribune,* 1 March 1908; *Marion Chronicle,* 24 March, 7 April 1911; Cassandra Tate, *Cigarette Wars: The Triumph of "the Little White Slaver"* (New York: Oxford University Press, 1999); Egal Feldman, "Prostitution, the Alien Woman, and the Progressive Imagination, 1910–1915," *American Quarterly* 19 (Summer 1967): 192–206; Robert E. Riegel, "Changing American Attitudes toward Prostitution (1800–1920)," *Journal of the History of Ideas* 29 (July–September 1968):

437–452; Richard H. Shryock, "Sylvester Graham and the Popular Health Movement, 1830–1870," *Mississippi Valley Historical Review* 18 (September 1931): 172–183. Graham, who is perhaps best remembered for the graham cracker, started out as a temperance reformer before expanding his concern beyond alcohol.

67. Shumaker, *Autobiography*, 105–106; *Terre Haute Express*, 27 March 1901.

68. Shumaker, *Autobiography*, 107–111.

69. Ibid., 112–115; Sermon on "Hell," 16 November 1902, Box 2, ESS Papers.

70. Shumaker, *Autobiography*, 115–121.

71. Ibid., 107; Arthur Shumaker, interview with author, 14 March, 24 March 2000. A more in-depth discussion of Shumaker's family will appear in chapter 5.

72. Shumaker, *Autobiography*, 118.

73. *South Bend Tribune*, 1 September, 2 September, 3 September, 4 September, 5 September, 8 September 1903; *Evansville Journal*, 20 January 1929; Shumaker, *Autobiography*, 123B. Shumaker's narrative ends with his mentioning of the 1903 conference. After his death, his wife Flora attempted to finish the story, beginning farther down the page, hence the designation of 123B.

74. Shumaker, *Autobiography*, 123B–124.

2 | *South Bend and Beyond*

1. *The Baptist World*, 16 November 1911, 28 August 1913.

2. Edwin L. Becker, *From Sovereign to Servant: The Church Federation of Greater Indianapolis, 1912–1987* (Indianapolis: The Church Federation of Greater Indianapolis, 1987), 8–10; *Marion Chronicle*, 2 December 1907; "Reply to a Speech by the Honorable Jesse M. Littleton," Folder 2, Box 1, E.E. Folk Papers, Southern Baptist Historical Library and Archives, Nashville, Tennessee, hereafter cited as SBC Archives; William Vance Trollinger, Jr., *God's Empire: William Bell Riley and Midwestern Fundamentalism* (Madison: University of Wisconsin Press, 1990), 16. Riley, who carved a fundamentalist regional empire for himself in Minneapolis, was born in Green County, Indiana, attended Valparaiso and Hanover colleges, and started his pastoral career in Lafayette.

3. Susanna Barrows and Robin Room, eds., *Drinking: Behavior and Belief in Modern History* (Los Angeles: University of California Press, 1991), 125.

4. *Noblesville Independent*, 18 January, 24 May, 31 May 1878; *Indiana Phalanx*, 12 March 1885.

5. *Western Christian Advocate*, 23 March, 14 September 1870, 15 January, 22 January 1890; *Noblesville Republican Ledger*, 4 February, 1 April, 8 April, 15 April 1887. The group was also known as the Indiana Christian Temperance Alliance.

6. *Hamilton County Ledger*, 21 June 1901; *South Bend Tribune*, 12 October 1903; *Jasper Weekly Courier*, 18 March, 26 March, 1 April 1904; *Poseyville News*, 23 October 1908. It was not until 1920 that the Nineteenth Amendment granted suffrage to women.

7. *Noblesville Republican Ledger*, 31 October 1884, 27 November 1885, 24 September 1886, 15 July 1887; *Noblesville Ledger*, 19 August, 26 August, 16 September, 30 December 1887; *Richmond Evening Item*, 11 April 1904; *Indianapolis Star*, 3 November 1904; *Patriot Phalanx*, 7 June 1906; *Sheridan News*, 31 August 1906; *Wakarusa Tribune*, 17 September 1908; *South Bend Tribune*, 29 June 1904, 27 July 1908; *Berne Witness*, 19 October 1906, 15 September 1908; "Felix T. McWhirter, PhD," page 6–7, Biographical and Genealogical Material Folder, F.T. McWhirter Manuscript Collection, Lilly Library, Indiana University, Bloomington, Indiana; *Indianapolis News*, 1 July 1916; *Indiana Phalanx*, 10 September 1885; Thornton, *The Economics of Prohibition*, 49; Kleppner, *The Cross of Culture*, 6, 15; A.B. Leonard to H.L. Peeke, 19 June 1903, Correspondence 1903 Folder, Hewson Lindsley Peeke Papers, Archives of the Congregational Church, Boston, Massachusetts. Indiana Prohibition Party leaders included Eli Ritter and F.T. McWhirter.

8. *Noblesville Independent*, 19 May 1882; *Noblesville Republican Ledger*, 14 August 1885; *Western Christian Advocate*, 9 July 1890; *Evansville Journal*, 23 September 1907.

9. Kerr, *Organized for Prohibition*, 2–3, 8, 25, 90; Hamm, *Shaping the Eighteenth Amendment*, 132–136; Behr, *Prohibition*, 56–57; Jensen, *The Winning of the Midwest*; *Indiana Issue*, January, February, July, November 1906; Szymanski, *Pathways to Prohibition*, 1–5; *Patriot Phalanx*, 22 March, 5 April 1900; Rev. U.G. Humphrey to Rev. Edward S. Shumaker, 3 April 1907, Box 2, ESS Papers.

10. William B. Weeden, *The Morality of Liquor Laws* (Boston: Roberts Brothers, 1875); Robert Bagnell, *Economic and Moral Aspects of the Liquor Business* (New York: Funk and Wagnalls Company, 1912); David P. Thelen, "LaFollette and the Temperance Crusade," *Wisconsin Magazine of History* 47 (Summer 1964): 291–300; Ann-Marie E. Szymanski, "Dry Compulsions: Prohibition and the Creation of State-Level Enforcement Agencies," *Journal of Policy History* 11 (1999): 115–146; *Sheridan News*, 29 June 1906. The League's use of detectives to investigate saloons for violations of the law had its problems. If detectives were unable to testify, cases were dismissed. There was also the fear of violence. In 1907 a prosaloon posse followed IASL detectives

on a train back to Indianapolis after the detectives had gathered evidence near Terre Haute; and in Ohio's Licking County, a dry detective was lynched in 1910 by a wet mob after he was discovered investigating the existence of blind tigers. See *Hamilton County Ledger,* 31 October 1902, 23 January 1903; *Indianapolis Star,* 23 September 1907; and *Advocate,* 17 June 2002.

11. Edward J. Richardson to Frank Allen, 30 March 1917, Reel 3, Anti-Saloon League Papers, Microfilm Edition of the Temperance and Prohibition Papers, Ohio Historical Society, Columbus, Ohio.

12. Francis I. Moats, "The Rise of Methodism in the Middle West," *Mississippi Valley Historical Review* 15 (June 1928): 69–88; Detzler, *The History of the Northwest Indiana Conference of the Methodist Church,* 97; Emory Stevens Bucke, gen. ed., *The History of American Methodism,* Volume 3 (New York: Abingdon Press, 1964), 335; Timberlake, *Prohibition and the Progressive Movement,* 20. Timberlake says that while Presbyterians supported the ASL, Methodists were the ASL. The Disciples of Christ were also very important in the makeup of the IASL. See Henry K. Shaw, *Hoosier Disciples: A Comprehensive History of the Christian Churches (Disciples of Christ) in Indiana* (Indianapolis: Bethany Press, 1966), 284–285; and Robert T. Handy, "The American Religious Depression, 1925–1935," *Church History* 29 (March 1960): 12.

13. *Western Christian Advocate,* 14 March 1900; *Hamilton County Ledger,* 16 February 1900, 8 November, 12 November 1901; *Indiana Issue,* January 1906; Clifton J. Philips, *Indiana in Transition: The Emergence of an Industrial Commonwealth, 1880–1920* (Indianapolis: Indiana Historical Bureau and Indiana Historical Society, 1968), 496; "Indiana" entry in Cherrington, gen. ed., *Standard Encyclopedia of the Alcohol Problem,* Volume 3, 1309.

14. *Berne Witness,* 4 December 1903; *Richmond Evening Item,* 8 March 1904; Humphrey to Shumaker, 6 October, 14 October, 22 December, 23 December 1905, 4 January, 6 January, 11 January 1906, Box 1; Humphrey to Shumaker, 14 February, 6 March, 8 March 1907, Box 2, ESS Papers; *South Bend Tribune,* 19 January 1903.

15. Humphrey to Shumaker, 20 February 1906, Box 2, ESS Papers; *South Bend Tribune,* 3 September, 4 November 1903; *Berne Witness,* 26 February 1907; *Indianapolis Star,* 1 September 1907; *Marion Chronicle,* 13 December 1907; *Sullivan Democrat,* 28 May 1908; *Madison Courier,* 3 June 1908. When drys got angry enough or felt overly frustrated, they too turned to violence. A Wells County saloon was dynamited in 1904 because convictions of saloon-keepers operating in violation of the law had been impossible to obtain in jury trials. See *Berne Witness,* 29 July 1904.

16. *South Bend Tribune,* 20 November 1903; *Berne Witness,* 11 September, 15 September, 18 September, 20 November 1903, 27 March 1906; *Nichols v. Lehman et al.,* 42 Ind. App. 384; 85 N.E. 786 (1908); Fred Rohrer, *Saloon Fight*

at Berne, Indiana: Not a Novel, But Real History: Truth Stranger than Fiction (Berne, IN: The Berne Witness Company, 1913).

17. Shumaker, *Autobiography*, 122–123. As Shumaker recalled, the young man who threw the bottle later got into a drunken fight with the town barber and was killed by a razor slash to the stomach.

18. *South Bend Tribune*, 1 January, 13 January, 17 January, 21 January, 28 February, 14 March, 16 March, 27 March, 10 April, 17 April, 29 October 1903, 9 February, 5 April 1904; 1900 Census; Shumaker, *Autobiography*, 125.

19. William Happ to Shumaker, 27 September 1905, Box 1, ESS Papers; *South Bend Tribune*, 31 December 1903; *Fourteen Decades: A History of First United Methodist Church of South Bend*, 1972, pages 23–24, 33, First United Methodist Church (South Bend) Records, Archives of the University of Notre Dame, Notre Dame, Indiana, hereafter cited as Notre Dame Archives.

20. McIntosh Stereopticon Company to Shumaker, 30 December 1905; Rev. Owen Wright to Shumaker, 9 February 1906; Rev. A.H. Lawrence to Shumaker, 13 March 1907, Box 1, ESS Papers; *Evansville Journal*, 24 March 1904. A set of slides made after the Eighteenth Amendment was passed, and geared for use in spreading the dry message in England, were put up for sale on Ebay in 2001. The author has in his possession a printed version of the Ebay ad, dated 24 July 2001, that shows the slides in detail.

21. Humphrey to Shumaker, 5 October 1905; Rev. W.C. Helt to Shumaker, 22 January 1906, Box 1, ESS Papers.

22. Rev. P. H. Faulk to Shumaker, 5 January, 24 October, 1 December, 23 December 1905, 12 March 1906, Humphrey to Shumaker, 9 November 1905, 19 January 1906, Box 1, ESS Papers; Humphrey to Shumaker, 14 March 1906, Box 2, ESS Papers. H.C. Johnson replaced Faulk in 1906, who in turn was replaced by Roscoe Fertich in 1907.

23. Humphrey to Shumaker, 24 January, 9 February, 14 February, 6 March, 7 March, 8 March 1906; Shumaker to Humphrey, 7 March, 8 March 1906; Faulk to Shumaker, 13 February, 14 February 1906; Shumaker to Rev. Frank Fox, 14 February 1906, Box 2, ESS Papers.

24. *South Bend Tribune*, 7 December 1903; Timberlake, *Prohibition and the Progressive Movement*, 136; Rev. A.H. Lawrence to Shumaker, 25 April 1906; John F. Lewis to Shumaker, 24 February, 15 March 1906; R.C. Minton to Shumaker, 15 April 1907, Box 1, ESS Papers; Humphrey to Shumaker, 17 February, 24 February 1906, 13 April 1907, Box 2, ESS Papers.

25. Noblesville in Hamilton County is a prime example. Between 1901 and 1921 there were no fewer than eight communitywide revivals, some of which lasted for months. See *Hamilton County Ledger*, April, May 1901, October 1903, May, August, September, October, November, December 1906; *Noblesville Daily Ledger*, January 1913, January, February, May 1914, January

1916, January 1918, January, February, September, October, November, December 1921.

26. Rev. A. S. Warriner to Shumaker, 3 January 1905; Shumaker to Seldon Roberts, 20 December 1905, Box 1, ESS Papers.

27. Rev. W. R. Wines to Shumaker, 10 November 1905; Rev. Vernon Stauffer to Shumaker, 22 February 1906; Rev. Preston Polhemas to Shumaker, 5 March 1906, Box 1, ESS Papers.

28. *Indianapolis News*, 19 January 1895; *Western Christian Advocate*, 13 February 1895; *South Bend Tribune*, 30 January, 3 February 1903; *Berne Witness*, 19 December 1902, 3 February, 6 February, 18 August 1903; *Goshen Democrat*, 28 April 1908.

29. *South Bend Tribune*, 29 July 1903, 13 February 1906; *Berne Witness*, 24 July 1903; *Richmond Evening Item*, 18 November 1907; *Rochester Republican*, 5 December 1907; *Vincennes Commercial*, 2 January 1908.

30. Shumaker to Rev. A. E. Sarah, 13 September 1904; Rev. Dunning Idle to Shumaker, 6 November 1905; Rev. Nebin B. Mathers to Shumaker, 5 February 1906, Box 1, ESS Papers; W. W. Wartin to Shumaker, 30 August 1904, Box 2, ESS Papers.

31. Charles R. Jones to Shumaker, 4 January 1906; Shumaker to Frank Spaulding, 10 March 1906; Nels Sorenson to Shumaker, 11 March 1907, Box 1, ESS Papers.

32. *Patriot Phalanx*, 30 June 1904; W. H. Hickman to Shumaker, 7 September 1905; Rev. Howard Wright to Shumaker, 19 September 1904; H. J. Vesey to Shumaker, 2 November 1905; A. A. Turner to Shumaker, 21 November 1905; Humphrey to Shumaker, 8 December 1905; Rev. Jesse D. Hickman to Shumaker, 24 January 1906, Box 1, ESS Papers; Rev. Charles Abbot Smith to Shumaker, 7 February 1906; J. W. DeLong to Shumaker, 26 December 1906, Box 2, ESS Papers.

33. Rev. C. H. Muray to Shumaker, 17 September 1904; Shumaker to *Middlebury Independent*, 19 September 1904, Box 1, ESS Papers.

34. Humphrey to Shumaker, 29 December 1905; James P. Goodrich to Shumaker, 20 January 1906; Carl Riddick to Shumaker, 1 February 1906, Box 1, ESS Papers.

35. Shumaker to Rev. H. L. Kindig, 6 April 1907, Box 1, ESS Papers; "Militant Organization of Temperance Hosts," N.D., Box 2, ESS Papers.

36. Clark, *Deliver Us from Evil*, 58, 63; John C. Burnham, *Bad Habits: Drinking, Smoking, Taking Drugs, Gambling, Sexual Misbehavior, and Swearing in American History* (New York: New York University Press, 1993), 7; *South Bend Tribune*, 9 November 1903; Larry Engelmann, *Intemperance: The Lost War against Liquor* (New York: The Free Press, 1979), 8–10; Elaine Frantz Parsons, *Manhood Lost: Fallen Drunkards and Redeeming Women in the Nineteenth-Century*

United States (Baltimore: Johns Hopkins University Press, 2003), 22–23, 46, 55, 137.

37. *Hamilton County Ledger,* 24 April 1900; *Anderson Morning Herald,* 11 March 1904; *Fort Wayne Journal Gazette,* 12 March 1904; *Evansville Journal,* 17 October 1907; *Marion Chronicle,* 16 November 1907; *Columbus Evening Republican,* 23 March 1908; *Kokomo Daily Tribune,* 8 September 1908.

38. *South Bend Tribune,* 28 September 1907; *Anderson Morning Herald,* 28 September 1907; *Richmond Evening Item,* 1 October 1907; *Columbus Evening Republican,* 1 October, 3 October 1907; Gray, ed., *Gentlemen from Indiana,* 185.

39. Robert A. Orsi, ed., *Gods of the City: Religion and the American Urban Landscape* (Indianapolis: Indiana University Press, 1999), 6, 16, 31–32; Owen Chadwick, *The Secularization of the European Mind in the Nineteenth Century* (New York: Cambridge University Press, 1995), 103–107; Kyvig, ed., *Law, Alcohol, and Order,* 35, 38; John J. Rumbarger, *Profits, Power, and Prohibition: American Alcohol Reform and the Industrializing of America, 1800–1930* (New York: State University of New York Press, 1989); Eric H. Monkkonen, "A Disorderly People? Urban Order in the Nineteenth and Twentieth Centuries," *Journal of American History* 68 (December 1981): 540; *The Baptist World,* 21 October 1915. This is not to say that there were no working-class urban saloons. Historians Roy Rosenzweig, Peter Stearns, and Jon M. Kingsdale have made substantial contributions toward our understanding of saloons as important to immigrant, working-class neighborhoods. See Roy Rosenzweig, *Eight Hours for What We Will: Workers and Leisure in an Industrial City, 1870–1920* (New York: Cambridge University Press, 1986), 11, 47, 51, 54, 89, 93, 97–100; Peter N. Stearns, "The Effort at Continuity in Working-Class Culture," *Journal of Modern History* 52 (December 1980): 626, 639; Jon M. Kingsdale, "The 'Poor Man's Club': Social Functions of the Urban Working-Class Saloon," *American Quarterly* 25 (October 1973): 472; *Noblesville Republican Ledger,* 25 November 1881; Timothy J. Meagher, *Inventing Irish America: Generation, Class, and Ethnic Identity in a New England City, 1880–1928* (Notre Dame, IN: University of Notre Dame Press, 2001), 34–35; and Madelon Powers, *Faces along the Bar: Lore and Order in the Workingman's Saloon, 1870–1920* (Chicago: University of Chicago Press, 1998).

40. Perry R. Duis, *The Saloon: Public Drinking in Chicago and Boston, 1880–1920* (Chicago: University of Illinois Press, 1983); Kingsdale, "The 'Poor Man's Club,'" 474–475, 478; Blocker, *American Temperance Movements,* 66; Clark, *Deliver Us from Evil,* 4; Barrows and Room, eds., *Drinking,* 113; *Evansville Journal,* 31 January, 8 March, 24 April 1904; *Jeffersonville Evening News,* 21 March 1904; *Delphi Journal,* 27 August 1908; *Terre Haute Tribune,* 26 February 1908.

41. *Muncie Evening Press,* 26 December 1907; *Berne Witness,* 31 May 1907; *South Bend Tribune,* 17 July, 4 August 1903, 20 July, 25 July, 26 July, 21 August, 7 December, 9 December 1907, 4 May 1908; *Albion New Era,* 2 September 1908;

Madison Courier, 24 April 1908; *Indianapolis Star*, 6 September 1907, 27 September 1934. The late novelist Kurt Vonnegut, Jr., was Lieber's grandson.

42. *Vincennes Commercial*, 16 February 1908; *Evansville Journal*, 22 January, 23 January 1908; *Fort Wayne Journal Gazette*, 8 March 1908; *Lafayette Journal*, 22 January 1908; *Berne Witness*, 10 July, 28 August 1908; *South Bend Tribune*, 8 June 1908; *The Baptist World*, 18 May 1916.

43. David G. Downey, E. W. Halford, and Ralph Welles Keeler, eds., *Militant Methodism: The Story of the First National Convention of Methodist Men* (Cincinnati: The Methodist Book Concern, 1913), 137; *Terre Haute Tribune*, 7 March 1908; *Patriot Phalanx*, 12 March 1908.

44. *Noblesville Republican Ledger*, 10 June 1881; *Evansville Journal*, 8 March 1904, 4 August, 13 September, 19 September, 22 September 1907, 14 April 1915; *Richmond Evening Item*, 5 April 1904, 15 November 1907; *Fort Wayne Journal Gazette*, 15 November, 6 December 1907; J. A. Homan, *Prohibition: The Enemy of Temperance* (Cincinnati, OH: The Christian Liberty Bureau, 1910); M. Monahan, *A Text-book of True Temperance* (New York: U.S. Brewers Association, 1911); Wiebe, *Businessmen and Reform*, 92, 200; *Anderson Morning Herald*, 22 November, 14 December, 24 December 1907; *Lafayette Journal*, 22 November 1907; *Terre Haute Tribune*, 8 October 1907, 10 February 1908; *Jeffersonville Evening News*, 2 September, 10 September, 25 September, 2 October 1907, 5 February, 10 February, 13 February, 15 February, 17 February, 26 February, 3 March, 4 March 1908; *Hamilton County Ledger*, 29 March 1907. Other businesses, especially the theater, were also targets of Sunday closing by churches.

45. *South Bend Tribune*, 24 April 1905; *Goshen Democrat*, 3 September, 17 September, 1 October, 4 October, 8 November, 15 November 1907; *Fort Wayne Journal Gazette*, 5 September 1907.

46. Philips, *Indiana in Transition*, 97; Gray, *Gentlemen from Indiana*, 240, 250; *Lafayette Journal*, 18 April, 27 April 1904; *Berne Witness*, 4 November 1904; *Hamilton County Ledger*, 14 April 1903, 11 November 1904; *South Bend Tribune*, 25 June 1903, 27 April, 21 May, 3 November 1904; Fourth Quarterly Conference, 16 September 1911; Fourth Quarterly Conference, 14 September 1913; First Quarterly Conference, 10 November 1914, Minutes and Board Meetings 1864–1918 book; Bulletin, 29 December 1918, Bulletins 1871–1922 book, MSUMC Archives. Hanly was an ally of Fairbanks's against Beveridge. See J. Frank Hanly to Charles Warren Fairbanks, 15 December 1900; and Hanly to Fairbanks, 9 November 1904, Charles Warren Fairbanks Papers, Lilly Library, Indiana University, Bloomington.

47. "Death of J. Frank Hanly," N.D., Box 2, ESS Papers.

48. *Indianapolis News*, 2 November, 4 November, 7 November 1904; *South Bend Tribune*, 24 August, 15 December 1904, 7 January 1905.

49. Brian Butler, *An Undergrowth of Folly: Public Order, Race, Anxiety, and the 1903 Evansville, Indiana Riot* (New York: Garland Publishing, 2000); *Evansville Journal News*, 5 July, 6 July 1903; *Indianapolis Star*, 7 January, 10 January 1905; *South Bend Tribune*, 6 January, 9 January 1905. Hanly told S.E. Nicholson, the author of the Nicholson law, that he believed his inaugural comments about liquor went "as far as public sentiment would warrant, and that to go farther would imperil all." See J. Frank Hanly to S.E. Nicholson, 12 January 1905, S. Edgar Nicholson Papers, EC Archives.

50. *Indianapolis Star*, 13 January, 14 January, 17 January, 20 January, 24 January, 31 January, 1 February, 3 February 1905; *South Bend Tribune*, 28 January, 2 February, 4 February, 15 February, 23 May 1905.

51. *Patriot Phalanx*, 9 June 1904, 2 February 1905; *Indianapolis News*, 21 December 1904.

52. *South Bend Tribune*, 6 February 1907.

53. Ibid., 4 October 1905, 22 September 1906.

54. Ibid., 7 April, 10 April, 21 April, 22 April, 27 June 1905, 10 January 1906.

55. Humphrey to Shumaker, 30 December 1905, Box 1, ESS Papers; *South Bend Tribune*, 11 April, 20 April, 6 June, 14 June, 8 December, 27 December 1905; January, February, March, 10 September, November, December 1906; January, 7 August, 6 November, 7 November 1907. During months listed without particular dates, coverage was intense and nearly daily.

56. James Philip Fadely, *Thomas Taggart: Public Servant, Political Boss, 1856–1929* (Indianapolis: Indiana Historical Society, 1997), xi, 59–82, 110–114; *South Bend Tribune*, 8 August, 9 August 1905, 23 June, 27 June, 7 July 1906, 26 November 1907; *Evansville Journal*, 6 May 1908; *Fort Wayne Journal Gazette*, 29 May 1908; *Lafayette Journal*, 29 May 1908. James Bingham was the Fountain County prosecutor before moving to Muncie to open a law practice. In 1906 he was elected attorney general and quickly became an ally of the governor's. See *Indianapolis Star*, 20 August 1940.

57. *Hamilton County Ledger*, 2 March, 13 March 1906; *Indianapolis News*, 28 April 1906, 30 September, 13 November, 19 November, 12 December 1907.

58. *State v. Dudley*, 33 Ind. App. 640; 71 N.E. 975 (1904); *Indianapolis News*, 11 October 1904, 7 February 1905; *Fort Wayne Journal Gazette*, 30 April 1904.

59. *Sheridan News*, 8 February, 10 February, 15 March, 7 June 1907; *Hamilton County Ledger*, 16 April 1907; *South Bend Tribune*, 14 February, 18 April, 6 June 1907; *Patriot Phalanx*, 31 January, 21 February, 7 March 1907; *Indianapolis News*, 15 April 1907.

60. *Sopher v. State*, 169 Ind. 177; 81 N.E. 913 (1907); *Barnes v. Wagener*, 169 Ind. 511; 82 N.E. 1037 (1907).

61. *Indianapolis Star,* 4 September, 5 September 1907; *Kokomo Daily Tribune,* 3 September, 4 September, 5 September, 7 September, 9 September 1907; *Indianapolis Sun,* 6 September 1907; *Richmond Evening Item,* 4 September 1904, 5 October 1907; *Madison Courier,* 24 April, 29 September 1908; *Fort Wayne Journal Gazette,* 4 September 1907, 24 April, 20 May 1908; *South Bend Tribune,* 19 May, 22 May 1908.

62. *South Bend Tribune,* 18 October 1906; *Hamilton County Ledger,* 4 August, 24 November 1905, 9 January, 16 February 1906; Quips Folder, Archives of Roberts Park United Methodist Church, Indianapolis, Indiana; *Indiana Issue,* February 1906; *Indianapolis Star,* 2 October 1906; *Greencastle Herald,* 10 August 1907; *Indianapolis News,* 15 April, 30 September 1907; Detzler, *The History of the Northwest Indiana Conference of the Methodist Church,* 129; Flynn, ed., *The Indianapolis Area of the Methodist Episcopal Church,* 111.

63. E. Glenn Hinson, *A History of Baptists in Arkansas, 1818–1978* (Little Rock: Arkansas Baptist State Convention, 1979), 217–218; Wayne Flynt, *Alabama Baptists: Southern Baptists in the Heart of Dixie* (Tuscaloosa: University of Alabama Press, 1998), 209; *The Baptist World,* 27 July 1911. This was not the case in other parts of the country, however. In Utah, where the Mormon Church was dominant and called on Latter Day Saints to abstain from alcohol, its leaders were reluctant to support prohibition. Utah History Encyclopedia, "Prohibition," http://www.media.utah.edu/UHE/p/PROHIBITION.html, 20 August 2002.

64. J. Frank Hanly to S.E. Nicholson, 27 July 1905, S. Edgar Nicholson Papers, EC Archives; *Journal of the Indiana State Senate during the 65th Session of the General Assembly* (Indianapolis: William B. Burford, 1907), 118; *Fort Wayne Journal Gazette,* 6 September 1907; *Jasper Weekly Courier,* 10 April 1908; *Madison Courier,* 3 April 1908; *Lake County News,* 17 October 1907; *Plymouth Tribune,* 14 May 1908.

65. *Indianapolis Sun,* 4 September 1907; *South Bend Tribune,* 24 July, 8 November 1907; *Berne Witness,* 29 October 1907.

3 | *A Political Education*

1. Rev. U.G. Humphrey to Rev. Edward S. Shumaker, 22 July, 24 July 1907; Rev. Frank O. Ballard to Shumaker, 22 July 1907; Shumaker to Ballard, 24 July 1907, Box 2, ESS Papers.

2. Alfred S. Warriner to Shumaker, 27 July 1907; Charles J. Orbison to Shumaker, 25 July 1907; C. W. Riddick to Shumaker, 25 July 1907; C.W. Crooke to Shumaker, 23 July 1907; C.A. Brooke to Shumaker, 27 July 1907; Paul C. Curnick to Shumaker, 5 August 1907; Rev. P. H. Faulk to Shu-

maker, 4 August 1907; F. A. Miller to Shumaker, 12 August 1907, Box 2, ESS Papers.

3. *South Bend Tribune*, 24 August 1907; "Impressions from the International Epworth League Meeting in Indianapolis," 20–23 July 1899; "Legislature of 1907" Memo Book, Box 2, ESS Papers; Shumaker, *Autobiography*, 126; Rev. E. E. Folk to M. F. Caldwell, 22 July 1904, folder 30, Box 1, E. E. Folk Papers, SBC Archives.

4. *Jasper Weekly Courier*, 4 March 1904; *South Bend Tribune*, 16 January 1907; *Fort Wayne Journal Gazette*, 3 December, 4 December 1907; *Richmond Evening Item*, 23 November, 7 December 1907.

5. Robert Dean McNeil, *Valiant for Truth: Clarence True Wilson and Prohibition* (Portland, OR: Oregonians Concerned about Addiction Problems, 1992), 26; Thomas R. Pegram, "The Dry Machine: The Formation of the Anti-Saloon League of Illinois," *Illinois Historical Journal* 83 (Autumn 1990): 176; *Vanceburg Sun*, 25 July 1907; *Lafayette Journal*, 11 November 1907; *Scottsburg Chronicle*, 29 October 1908.

6. *Richmond Evening Item*, 20 November, 22 November, 25 November, 26 November, 27 November 1907, 15 September, 16 September 1908; *Hamilton County Ledger*, 8 September, 15 September, 22 September 1908.

7. *South Bend Tribune*, 25 January, 27 January, 13 February, 27 February, 28 February 1908; *Columbus Evening Republican*, 7 October, 14 October, 28 October, 25 November, 4 December, 10 December 1907, 6 January, 14 March, 16 March, 18 March, 23 March, 28 March, 30 March, 13 April, 27 April 1908; Thornton, *The Economics of Prohibition*, 52; University of North Carolina at Chapel Hill Libraries Documenting the American South, "Anti-Saloon League of Charlotte, N.C.: It Helps Business and Is a Blessing. What Leading Business Men, Bankers, Farmers, Laborers and Others Say about Prohibition in Charlotte, N.C.," http://docsouth.unc.edu/nc/antisaloon/antisaloon.html, 19 July 2002.

8. *Marion County Mail*, 26 January 1906, 8 October, 15 October 1909; *Fort Wayne Journal Gazette*, 15 April, 5 May 1908; *Lafayette Journal*, 8 May 1908.

9. *Indianapolis News*, 16 March, 2 April 1908; *French Lick Springs Valley Herald*, 28 April 1905; *Goshen Democrat*, 19 November 1907, 13 March 1908; *Richmond Evening Item*, 30 May 1908; *Elkhart Truth*, 26 October 1908; *Marion Chronicle*, 1 April, 2 April 1908; *South Bend Tribune*, 5 September 1907; *Baptist World*, 14 December 1916; Philips, *Indiana in Transition*, 99.

10. *Indianapolis Star*, 25 January 1904.

11. *South Bend Tribune*, 19 November 1907; *Valparaiso Daily Vidette*, 13 October 1908; Albert J. Beveridge to Charles Warren Fairbanks, 30 March 1908, Charles Warren Fairbanks Papers, Lilly Library, Indiana University, Bloomington; Braeman, *Albert J. Beveridge*, 68–81, 144–149; Dane Starbuck,

The Goodriches: An American Family (Indianapolis: Liberty Fund, 2001), 75–76, 206; Albert J. Beveridge to A. M. Glossbrenner, 6 February 1908; A. H. Godard to Beveridge, 19 March 1908, Folder G, Box 161; Lucius B. Swift to Beveridge, 11 July 1908, Folder S, Box 164, Albert J. Beveridge Papers, Library of Congress, Washington, DC. Goodrich was not alone in his appraisal. Beveridge had disliked Watson since they were both students at DePauw. As future governor Warren T. McCray said of Watson, "Jim is a politician, and if he thought the voters of Indiana were especially anxious for any one thing, he would throw his weight in favor of it more readily than for any other cause." William P. Evans, a leading Marion County Republican, commented, "Watson at heart was not a prohibitionist. But he was for the winning side no matter whatever it was." Echoing these sentiments, Harold Feightner, an Indiana newspaperman, believed that Watson "didn't denounce anybody until after the votes were in." See Warren T. McCray to Charles L. Harper, 29 December 1925, November 1923–1925, Folder 1, Warren T. McCray Collection, Indiana Historical Society, Indianapolis, Indiana; William P. Evans, Oral History Project, Indiana Division, Indiana State Library, Indianapolis, Indiana, 1969, 8; Harold Feightner, Oral History Project, Indiana Division, Indiana State Library, Indianapolis, Indiana, 1968, 26.

12. James E. Watson, "Policies of Republicanism in State and Nation: Keynote Speech of the Honorable James E. Watson Republican Candidate for Governor of Indiana, Delivered at Ft. Wayne, August 26 1908" (Indianapolis: William B. Burford, 1908), 24–32; James E. Watson, *As I Knew Them: Memoirs of James E. Watson, Former United States Senator from Indiana* (Indianapolis: Bobbs-Merrill Company, 1936), 84–86; Herbert J. Rissler, "Charles Warren Fairbanks: Conservative Hoosier" (Ph.D. diss., Indiana University, 1962), 217; Philips, *Indiana in Transition,* 101; *Anderson Morning Herald,* 4 April 1908; *Brookville American,* 9 April 1908; *Vincennes Commercial,* 3 April 1908; *Marion Chronicle,* 4 April 1908; *Columbus Evening Republican,* 2 April 1908.

13. *Evansville Journal,* 8 February 1908; *Pulaski County Democrat,* 9 April 1908; *Goshen Democrat,* 3 March 1911; *Lake County News,* 30 July 1908; *Starke County Republican,* 2 April 1908; *Franklin Democrat,* 7 February, 14 February, 21 February, 28 February, 6 March, 13 March, 27 March 1908; *Richmond Evening Item,* 30 May 1908; *Madison Courier,* 26 March 1908; *Greencastle Herald,* 26 March 1908; Suellen M. Hoy, "Samuel M. Ralston: Progressive Governor, 1913–1917" (Ph.D. diss., Indiana University, 1975), 4–5; Philips, *Indiana in Transition,* 101; Fadely, *Thomas Taggart,* 114–115, 165; David J. Bennett, *He Almost Changed the World: The Life and Times of Thomas Riley Marshall* (Bloomington, IN: Author House Press, 2007).

14. *Marion Chronicle,* 24 April, 2 May 1908; *Madison Courier,* 7 September 1908; *Starke County Republican,* 1 October 1908; *Lafayette Journal,* 29 October

1908; *Delphi Journal,* 27 August 1908; *Warren Review,* 27 August 1908; *Hamilton County Ledger,* 11 September, 15 September 1908; *Peru Evening Journal,* 2 September 1908; *Vincennes Commercial,* 8 March 1908; *Plymouth Tribune,* 6 August 1908; *South Bend Tribune,* 29 June, 5 August, 6 August, 11 August, 25 August 1908; Philips, *Indiana in Transition,* 102.

15. *Rushville Daily Republican,* 14 September 1908; *Shelbyville Democrat,* 14 September 1908; *Warsaw Daily Union,* 15 September, 16 September 1908; *Anderson Morning Herald,* 9 September, 19 September 1908; *Lafayette Journal,* 22 October 1908; *Weekly Clintonian,* 4 September 1908; *South Bend Tribune,* 18 July 1908; *Indianapolis News,* 14 September 1908; Jeffrey Simpson, *Chautauqua: An American Utopia* (New York: Harry N. Abrams Publishers, 1999); Harry P. Harrison and Karl Detzer, *Culture under Canvas: The Story of Tent Chautauqua* (New York: Hastings House, 1958), 128–129.

16. *Kokomo Daily Tribune,* 4 September, 18 September 1908; *Fort Wayne Journal Gazette,* 5 September, 19 September 1908; *Jasper Weekly Courier,* 25 September 1908; *Journal of the House of Representatives during the Special Session of the 65th General Assembly* (Indianapolis: William B. Burford, 1908), 17–22.

17. *Pulaski County Democrat,* 10 September 1908; *Jasper Weekly Courier,* 11 September 1908; *Princeton Clarion News,* 19 September 1908; *Indianapolis Sun,* 10 September 1908; *Indianapolis Star,* 5 September, 7 September 1908; *South Bend Tribune,* 5 September 1908.

18. *Hamilton County Ledger,* 8 September, 25 September 1908; *Starke County Republican,* 10 September 1908; *Indianapolis News,* 8 September 1908; *Plainfield Friday Caller,* 11 September 1908; *Warren Review,* 17 September 1908; *Knightstown Banner,* 11 September 1908; *Rushville Daily Republican,* 4 September, 12 September 1908.

19. *Indianapolis Star,* 6 September 1908; *Daviess County Democrat,* 12 September 1908; *Richmond Evening Item,* 5 September, 8 September, 9 September 1908; *Warsaw Daily Union,* 8 September 1908; *Rochester Republican,* 10 September 1908; *Indianapolis Sun,* 5 September, 25 September, 27 September, 9 October 1908; *Anderson Morning Herald,* 11 September 1908.

20. *Winchester Journal,* 9 September, 23 September 1908; 1908 Diary, Diaries 1908–1911 file, Box 3; James P. Goodrich to J. Frank Hanly, 4 September 1908, Indiana Politics: J. Frank Hanly 1908–1920 file, Box 12, James P. Goodrich Papers, Herbert Hoover Presidential Library, West Branch, Iowa.

21. *Peru Evening Journal,* 12 September, 22 September 1908; *Richmond Evening Item,* 10 September 1908; *Kokomo Daily Tribune,* 11 September 1908; *Logansport Pharos,* 21 September 1908; *Warsaw Daily Union,* 10 September, 25 September 1908; *Huntington Herald,* 18 September 1908; *Columbus Evening Republican,* 23 September 1908; *Indianapolis Star,* 20 September 1908; *Terre Haute Tribune,* 18 September 1908. Goodrich had spies within the Democratic

Party who helped him plot Republican strategy. See James P. Goodrich Autobiography (c. 1939), 81, Pages 1–95 file, Box 4; James P. Goodrich Papers,
Herbert Hoover Presidential Library.

22. *Indianapolis News*, 7 September 1908; *South Bend Tribune*, 2 September 1908; *Indianapolis Star*, 20 September 1908.

23. *Indianapolis News*, 21 September 1908; *Indianapolis Star*, 22 Septem-
ber, 24 September 1908; *Elkhart Truth*, 21 September 1908; *Rushville Daily Republican*, 22 September, 23 September 1908; *South Bend Tribune*, 21 September
1908; *Peru Evening Journal*, 21 September, 22 September 1908; *Seymour Daily
Republican*, 26 September 1908; *Princeton Clarion News*, 21 September 1908;
Kokomo Daily Tribune, 21 September 1908; *Madison Courier*, 21 September
1908; *Journal of the House of Representatives during the Special Session of the 65th
General Assembly*, 1908, 36–37, 41–43, 52–55; *Journal of the Indiana State Senate
during the Special Session of the 65th General Assembly* (Indianapolis: William B.
Burford, 1908), 36–40, 46–50, 52–56, 68–71. Shumaker's tactics were a
reflection of the popular politics of the period, which, according to histo-
rian Michael McGerr, were in decline. See Michael E. McGerr, *The Decline of
Popular Politics: The American North, 1865–1928* (New York: Oxford University
Press, 1986).

24. *Terre Haute Tribune*, 26 September 1908; *Crawford County Democrat*,
1 October 1908.

25. *Indianapolis Star*, 23 September 1908; *Warsaw Daily Union*, 23 September 1908; *Logansport Pharos*, 23 September 1908. Others estimated the number at forty to fifty people. See *Richmond Evening Item*, 23 September 1908.

26. *Terre Haute Tribune*, 29 May 1924.

27. Ibid., 18 September 1908.

28. *Peru Evening Journal*, 26 September, 28 September, 29 September,
30 September, 1 October, 4 November 1908; *Columbus Evening Republican*,
29 September 1908; *Princeton Clarion News*, 23 September 1908; *Wabash Daily
Plain Dealer*, 1 October, 2 October, 4 November 1908; *Scottsburg Chronicle*,
8 October 1908.

29. *Peru Evening Journal*, 22 September 1908; *Princeton Clarion News*,
22 September 1908; *South Bend Tribune*, 24 September 1908; *Seymour Daily Republican*, 26 September 1908; *Warsaw Daily Union*, 28 September 1908; *Rochester Republican*, 1 October 1908; *Garrett Weekly Clipper*, 1 October 1908.

30. *Indianapolis Star*, 12 September, 27 September 1908; *Brookville American*, 1 October 1908; *Winchester Journal*, 30 September 1908; *Delphi Journal*,
1 October 1908; *Rushville Daily Republican*, 26 September 1908; *Kokomo Daily
Tribune*, 10 October 1908.

31. *Greencastle Herald*, 28 October, 29 October 1908; *Crawfordsville Journal*, 1 October 1908; *Daviess County Democrat*, 8 August, 29 August 1908; *Terre*

Haute Tribune, 25 September, 27 September 1908; *New Albany Daily Ledger,* 9 October, 10 October 1908. Additionally, both Hanly and Watson were accused (and quickly cleared) of offering bribes for votes on county option at the end of the special session.

32. *Patriot Phalanx,* 11 June, 10 September, 17 September, 1 October, 15 October 1908; *Vincennes Commercial,* 27 September, 29 September 1908; *Terre Haute Tribune,* 12 February 1908.

33. *Rushville Daily Republican,* 28 September 1908; *Anderson Morning Herald,* 27 September 1908; *Indianapolis Star,* 27 September 1908.

34. *Peru Evening Journal,* 25 September 1908; *Attica Ledger,* 22 October 1908; *Princeton Clarion News,* 29 September 1908; *Warren Review,* 8 October 1908; *Knightstown Banner,* 2 October 1908; *Kokomo Daily Tribune,* 2 October 1908; *Indianapolis Star,* 27 September, 30 October 1908. Shumaker's list of wet counties reflected urbanization, immigration, and industrialization realities that tended to support the continental Sabbath.

35. *Indianapolis News,* 18 September 1908; *Greencastle Herald,* 28 September 1908; *Warren Review,* 1 October 1908.

36. *Seymour Daily Republican,* 26 September 1908; *Vevay Reveille,* 29 October 1908; *Madison Courier,* 21 September 1908; James P. Goodrich Autobiography (c. 1939), 62–64, Pages 1–95 file, Box 4; J. Frank Hanly to Goodrich, 8 April 1910, Indiana Politics: J. Frank Hanly 1908–1920 file, Box 12, James P. Goodrich Papers, Herbert Hoover Presidential Library.

37. *Indianapolis Star,* 9 September, 7 October 1908; *Rockport Democrat,* 9 October 1908; *Huntington Herald,* 9 October 1908; *South Bend Tribune,* 3 October 1908; *Indianapolis News,* 15 September 1908.

38. *Pike County Democrat,* 16 October 1908; *Frankfort Daily Crescent,* 19 September 1908; *Corydon Democrat,* 30 September 1908; *Logansport Pharos,* 26 September 1908; *Knightstown Banner,* 19 September 1908; *Terre Haute Tribune,* 18 September 1908; *Plymouth Tribune,* 17 September 1908.

39. *South Bend Tribune,* 13 June, 14 July, 21 July 1908; *Elkhart Truth,* 10 September 1908; *Starke County Republican,* 3 September 1908.

40. *South Bend Tribune,* 12 August 1908; *Rushville Daily Republican,* 3 September 1908.

41. Heller, *Indiana Conference of the Methodist Church,* 136; *Columbus Evening Republican,* 9 September, 14 September 1908; *Sullivan Democrat,* 20 August 1908; *Terre Haute Tribune,* 19 October, 22 October, 28 October, 2 November 1908; *Shelbyville Democrat,* 15 September 1908; *Daviess County Democrat,* 19 September 1908; *Greensburg New Era,* 24 September 1908.

42. *Greensburg New Era,* 30 September 1908; *Warsaw Daily Union,* 17 September, 18 September 1908; *Rockport Democrat,* 28 August 1908; *Jasper Weekly Courier,* 9 October 1908; *Frankfort Daily Crescent,* 18 September 1908; *Booneville*

Weekly Enquirer, 2 October 1908; *Jeffersonville Evening News,* 23 October 1908; *Pulaski County Democrat,* 24 September 1908; *Daviess County Democrat,* 19 September 1908; *Pike County Democrat,* 30 October 1908; *Corydon Democrat,* 28 October 1908; *Fort Wayne Journal Gazette,* 28 October 1908; *Lafayette Journal,* 17 October 1908; Thomas R. Marshall, *Recollections of Thomas R. Marshall, Vice President and Hoosier Philosopher: A Hoosier Salad* (Indianapolis: Bobbs-Merrill Company, 1925), 167–168, 172, 188. This validation did not stop the Presbyterian synod from endorsing county option. Marshall believed that this incident propelled him to victory.

43. *Madison Courier,* 11 September 1908; *Indianapolis Star,* 14 September 1908; *Hamilton County Ledger,* 22 September 1908; *Lafayette Journal,* 7 October 1908; *North Vernon Plain Dealer,* 17 September 1908; *Huntington Herald,* 18 September 1908; *Columbus Evening Republican,* 16 September 1908; *Peru Evening Journal,* 28 October 1908; *Logansport Pharos,* 30 October 1908.

44. *Delphi Journal,* 20 August 1908; *Warren Review,* 6 August, 20 August 1908; *Seymour Daily Republican,* 2 September 1908; *Evansville Journal,* 31 October 1908; *Indianapolis Star,* 5 June 1908; *Rushville Daily Republican,* 27 August 1908; *Bloomfield News,* 28 August 1908; *Rochester Republican,* 10 September 1908.

45. *Crawfordsville Journal,* 13 October, 15 October, 30 October 1908; *Attica Ledger,* 22 October 1908; *Warren Review,* 29 October 1908; *Michigan City Evening News,* 26 October 1908.

46. *Terre Haute Tribune,* 6 March 1908; *Vincennes Commercial,* 2 October, 8 October, 22 October 1908; *Lafayette Journal,* 14 October, 16 October, 30 October 1908; *Marion Chronicle,* 14 October 1908; *Princeton Clarion News,* 7 October, 14 October 1908; *South Bend Tribune,* 15 October, 17 October 1908; *Monticello Herald,* 15 October, 22 October 1908; *Kokomo Daily Tribune,* 13 October 1908; *Valparaiso Daily Vidette,* 20 October 1908; *Delphi Journal,* 22 October 1908; *Crawfordsville Journal,* 21 October 1908; *Warren Review,* 15 October, 22 October 1908; *Huntington Herald,* 16 October, 30 October 1908; *Michigan City Evening News,* 29 October, 31 October 1908; *Anderson Morning Herald,* 28 October, 29 October 1908; *Rockport Democrat,* 18 September 1908; *Logansport Pharos,* 15 September 1908. The governor of Kansas, when sent one of the handbills from Indiana, hotly denied the wet insinuation. The use of billboards by wets and drys was nothing new. In the early 1900s the WCTU and other temperance groups had sponsored signs near Carmel, Indiana, that read, "Saloons heavily increase taxes" and "Is it right to license wrong?" See Frances Hendrickson, *Hoosier Heritage, 1874–1974: Woman's Christian Temperance Union* (Indianapolis: WCTU of Indiana, 1974), 62.

47. James P. Goodrich Autobiography (c. 1939), 79, 82, Pages 1–95 file, Box 4, James P. Goodrich Papers, Herbert Hoover Presidential Library; *Indianapolis News,* 2 November 1908

48. *Valparaiso Daily Vidette,* 17 October 1908; *Warren Review,* 8 October 1908; *Lafayette Journal,* 17 October 1908; *Sheridan News,* 21 February 1908; *Crawfordsville Journal,* 17 October, 19 October 1908.

49. *Valparaiso Daily Vidette,* 27 October 1908; *Greensburg New Era,* 24 September 1908; *Monticello Herald,* 22 October 1908; *Peru Evening Journal,* 14 September 1908; *Crawfordsville Journal,* 10 October 1908; *Jasper Weekly Courier,* 2 October 1908; *Columbus Evening Republican,* 7 October 1908; *Lafayette Journal,* 2 November 1908; *Fort Wayne Journal Gazette,* 20 March 1908. Joseph Keller and Fritz Francke, the latter being Albert Lieber's brother-in-law, were also part of the Alliance.

50. Bulletin, 26 March 1922, Bulletins 1871–1922 book; Bulletin, 14 January 1923, Bulletins 1923–1926 book, MSUMC Archives.

51. *Richmond Evening Item,* 19 October 1908; *Columbus Evening Republican,* 22 October 1908; *North Vernon Plain Dealer,* 1 October 1908; *Versailles Republican,* 29 October 1908; *Rochester Republican,* 29 October 1908; *Kokomo Daily Tribune,* 9 September 1908; *Vevay Reveille,* 8 October 1908; *Bloomfield News,* 2 October, 9 October, 23 October, 30 October 1908.

52. *Warsaw Daily Union,* 22 September, 30 October, 5 November 1908; *Rushville Daily Republican,* 31 October, 2 November 1908.

53. *Indianapolis News,* 4 November, 7 November 1908.

54. *North Vernon Plain Dealer,* 5 November 1908; *Peru Evening Journal,* 4 November 1908; *Lake County News,* 5 November 1908; *Columbus Evening Republican,* 4 November 1908; *Lafayette Journal,* 5 November 1908; *Starke County Republican,* 10 September, 5 November, 12 November 1908; *South Bend Tribune,* 6 November, 7 November 1908; *Vincennes Commercial,* 6 November 1908; *Rushville Daily Republican,* 4 November 1908; Watson, *As I Knew Them,* 208.

55. *Shelbyville Democrat,* 10 September 1908; *Pike County Democrat,* 30 October 1908; *Plymouth Tribune,* 29 October 1908; *New Albany Evening Tribune,* 31 October 1908; *Richmond Evening Item,* 24 November 1908; *Greensburg New Era,* 1 October, 15 October, 22 October, 29 October, 12 November 1908; *South Bend Tribune,* 6 November 1908; *Brookville American,* 5 November 1908; *Sullivan Democrat,* 12 November 1908; *Crawford County Democrat,* 12 November 1908; *Attica Ledger,* 5 November 1908. Of the counties surveyed for election returns, only in Fountain County, where the Prohibition Party's candidate for governor picked up 104 votes, could Watson say that the issue had cost him victory.

56. *Indianapolis News,* 4 November, 5 November, 16 November 1908; *Rochester Republican,* 5 November 1908; *Seymour Daily Republican,* 5 September 1908; *Delphi Journal,* 3 September, 5 November 1908; *Indianapolis Star,* 5 November 1908; *Greencastle Herald,* 5 November 1908.

57. *Berne Witness*, 3 December 1907; *Peru Evening Journal*, 5 November 1908; *Richmond Evening Item*, 25 November, 1 December 1908; *South Bend Tribune*, 5 December 1908.

58. Goodrich to George B. Lockwood, 4 April 1912; Lockwood to Goodrich, 6 April 1912, George B. Lockwood 1912–1932 file, Box 13, James P. Goodrich Papers, Herbert Hoover Presidential Library; *Indianapolis News*, 10 November, 11 November, 12 November, 13 November 1908; H. A. Gobin to Beveridge, 27 February 1909, W. G. Bridges to Beveridge, 27 February 1909, Indiana Politics Folder, Box 167, Albert J. Beveridge Papers, Library of Congress.

59. *Hamilton County Ledger*, 11 December 1908, 8 January, 19 January 1909; *Berne Witness*, 1 December 1908, 22 January 1909; *Richmond Evening Item*, 14 November, 18 November, 19 November, 20 November, 21 November, 24 November, 25 November, 30 November, 15 December 1908; *Rockville Tribune*, 3 February 1909; *Versailles Republican*, 3 March, 17 March, 24 March, 31 March, 7 April, 14 April, 28 April, 5 May, 12 May, 19 May, 2 June 1909; *Indianapolis News*, 19 June 1909; *Patriot Phalanx*, 10 June 1909, 6 January, 24 March 1910.

60. *Warsaw Daily Union*, 5 November 1910; *Indianapolis Star*, 2 February, 6 February 1909, 5 April, 10 November 1910; *Berne Witness*, 5 March 1909; *Goshen Democrat*, 27 January 1911.

61. *Indianapolis News*, 12 November, 14 November 1908; *Indianapolis Sun*, 2 January, 6 January, 27 January 1909; *A Textbook of True Temperance* (New York: United States Brewers Association, 1911).

62. *Berne Witness*, 23 December 1910; *Indianapolis Star*, 7 January, 20 January 1911.

63. *Goshen Democrat*, 28 February, 3 March, 7 March, 24 March 1911; *Berne Witness*, 27 December 1910; *Patriot Phalanx*, 1 July 1909; *Fort Wayne Journal Gazette*, 19 January 1911; *Anderson Morning Herald*, 24 February 1911; *Columbus Evening Republican*, 24 January 1911; *Indianapolis Star*, 12 January, 13 January, 25 January, 27 January, 2 February, 3 February, 22 February 1911; *Terre Haute Tribune*, 1 March, 12 March 1911; *Madison Courier*, 4 March 1911; *Lebanon Pioneer*, 9 February 1911.

64. *Lafayette Journal*, 8 January, 25 January, 24 February 1908; Blocker, *American Temperance Movements*, 53; Samuel R. Artman, *The Legalized Outlaw* (Indianapolis: Levey Brothers and Company, 1908). Artman had authored one of the legal decisions in 1907 that made similar arguments.

65. *South Bend Tribune*, 9 January 1907, 13 March, 17 March 1911.

66. *Columbus Evening Republican*, 4 March 1911; *Liberty Herald*, 9 February 1911; *Berne Witness*, 7 February, 10 October 1911; Bennett, *He Almost Changed the World*.

67. *Richmond Evening Item*, 1 April, 5 April, 10 April 1911; Detzler, *The History of the Northwest Indiana Conference of the Methodist Church*, 129.

68. *Berne Witness*, 14 February 1911; *Lake County News*, 4 May 1911; *Evansville Courier*, 12 March 1911; *Jeffersonville Evening News*, 6 March 1911; *Richmond Evening Item*, 10 February 1911; *Vincennes Commercial*, 18 March 1911; *Madison Courier*, 7 April 1911; *South Bend Tribune*, 6 March, 7 March, 16 March, 28 March 1911.

69. *The Franklin*, 27 April 1910; *Indiana Daily Student*, 25 April 1911; *Lebanon Pioneer*, 30 March 1911.

70. *Patriot Phalanx*, 10 November 1910, 6 January, 13 January, 17 February, 26 May, 7 July 1911.

71. Ibid., 4 August, 11 August, 25 August, 15 September, 29 September, 6 October 1911; Madison Swadener to William Lowe Bryan, 28 February 1912, IASL 1905, 1909, 1912 folder, William Lowe Bryan Papers, Archives of Indiana University, Bloomington, Indiana; *Indianapolis Star*, 27 February, 30 July 1911.

72. *Evansville Journal*, 13 March 1908; *Patriot Phalanx*, 18 August 1910; *Berne Witness*, 23 August 1910.

73. Shumaker to Rev. P. A. Baker, 6 January 1907; Baker to Shumaker, 7 January 1910, Box 2, ESS Papers.

74. *Washington Herald*, 20 December 1909; *Indianapolis Sun*, 14 August, 17 September, 24 September 1912; Charles G. Sefrit, "Concerning Mr. Shumaker," pamphlet, Box 2, ESS Papers.

75. Goodrich to George B. Lockwood, 4 April 1912, George B. Lockwood 1912–1932 file, Box 13, James P. Goodrich Papers, Herbert Hoover Presidential Library; *Anderson Morning Herald*, 22 February, 1 April, 2 April, 14 April, 22 May, 26 May, 12 July 1908.

4 | Shumaker Victorious

1. Harold Feightner, Oral History Project, Indiana Division, Indiana State Library, 1968, 9; Thomas R. Pegram, "Temperance Politics and Regional Political Culture: The Anti-Saloon League in Maryland and the South, 1907–1915," *Journal of Southern History* 63 (February 1997): 57–90; *Berne Witness*, 8 February 1910; "Assessment of the Future of Quakerism in America" by S. E. Nicholson, 20 December 1918, S. Edgar Nicholson Papers, EC Archives; Handbook of Texas Online, "Anti Saloon League of Texas," http://www.tsha.utexas.edu/handbook/online/articles/print/AA/vaa2.html, 9 August 2002.

2. *Baptist World*, 28 October 1915; *Indianapolis Star*, 18 June 1909, 2 January, 5 January, 7 January 1910; *French Lick Springs Valley Herald*, 8 February

1917; Willis F. Dunbar and George S. May, *Michigan: A History of the Wolverine State* (Grand Rapids, MI: William B. Eerdmans Publishing Company, 1995), 469–470; Rev. T. S. Buckingham to Rev. E. E. Folk, 23 January 1909, Folder 37, Box 1, E. E. Folk Papers, SBC Archives; Bulletin, 17 June 1923, Bulletins 1923–1926 book; Bulletin, 6 March 1927, 28 October, 2 December 1928, 6 October 1929, Bulletins 1927–1929 book, MSUMC Archives; Stephen Kantrowitz, *Ben Tillman and the Reconstruction of White Supremacy* (Chapel Hill: University of North Carolina Press, 2000), 181–197; *Baptist Observer*, 14 July, 21 July, 11 August, 18 August 1910, 12 January, 4 May, 14 September 1911, 13 March, 27 March 1913, 19 November 1914, 4 February, 25 March, 29 July, 21 October 1915. This is merely a sampling. Between 1910 and 1920, nearly every issue of the *Baptist Observer* contains some reference to temperance or prohibition work.

    3. *Baptist World*, 26 August 1915; *Lafayette Journal*, 17 February 1913; *Muncie Evening Press*, 6 December, 9 December 1912; *Indianapolis Star*, 2 November 1914; *Noblesville Daily Ledger*, 2 November 1914; *Richmond Evening Item*, 26 March 1915; *Indianapolis News*, 19 February, 24 February 1915.

    4. Charles W. Eagles, "Congressional Voting in the 1920s: A Test of Urban-Rural Conflict," *Journal of American History* 76 (September 1989): 532–533; 1910 Census; *Fort Wayne Journal Gazette*, 1 March 1911; *Lafayette Journal*, 1 April, 5 April, 28 April, 29 April, 1 May 1911; *Noblesville Daily Ledger*, 19 April 1915; *Goshen Democrat*, 3 March, 31 March, 4 April 1911; *Muncie Evening Press*, 3 May 1911; *Marion Chronicle*, 1 March, 2 March, 9 March, 11 March, 27 March, 1 April 1911; *Richmond Evening Item*, 16 April 1915; *Goshen Daily Democrat*, 6 March, 19 March, 23 March, 24 March, 26 March, 28 April 1915; *Terre Haute Tribune*, 29 March 1911; *Rochester Sentinel*, 8 June 1911, 8 March, 16 April, 20 April, 21 April, 22 April, 22 May, 25 May 1915; *Columbus Evening Republican*, 26 March 1915. According to the Census, Indiana was 58 percent rural (the national average was 54 percent) and 42 percent urban (with the national average being 46 percent).

    5. *Warsaw Daily Union*, 5 November 1910; *Indianapolis News*, 10 July 1911; *South Bend Tribune*, 13 March 1915; *Marion Chronicle*, 5 May, 21 May, 22 May 1915; *Noblesville Daily Ledger*, 28 July 1915; *Pekin Advance*, 14 December, 21 December, 27 December 1916, 4 January, 11 January, 18 January, 25 January, 1 February, 8 February, 15 February 1917.

    6. Robert J. Norrell, "Labor at the Ballot Box: Alabama Politics from the New Deal to the Dixiecrat Movement," *Journal of Southern History* 57 (May 1991): 209–210; *Marion Chronicle*, 10 February 1911, 19 May, 24 May 1915; Rumbarger, *Profits, Power, and Prohibition*; Timberlake, *Prohibition and the Progressive Movement*, 71; *Rochester Republican*, 25 May 1911; *Hamilton County Ledger*, 8 January, 15 January 1908; *Vincennes Commercial*, 7 January 1908;

Sheridan News, 24 March 1911; *Goshen Democrat*, 21 March 1911; Frank Clayton Ball, *Memoirs of Frank Clayton Ball* (Muncie, IN: Scott Printing Company, 1937), 80–81, 187, 212.

7. *Indianapolis Star*, 12 March, 13 March, 18 March, 26 March 1915; *Anderson Herald*, 13 April, 21 April 1915; *Richmond Evening Item*, 17 March, 18 March 1915; *Terre Haute Tribune*, 21 March, 22 March, 24 March, 25 March, 28 March, 8 April, 12 April, 15 April, 22 April, 26 April, 28 April 1915; *South Bend Tribune*, 18 March, 23 March, 6 April 1915. Roberts was impeached to prevent him from attempting to run the city from prison.

8. Downey, Halford, and Keeler, eds., *Militant Methodism*; *Indianapolis Star*, 28 January, 31 January, 1 February, 2 February, 5 February 1912, 26 October, 27 October, 28 October, 29 October, 30 October, 31 October, 1 November 1913. It is unclear if Shumaker attended the convention. Though he was not one of the speakers, consultation of his speaking book shows that while he was in Connersville the weekend prior to the convention and in Hamilton County the weekend afterward (both short interurban rides away from Indianapolis), he did not have any public IASL events scheduled for the last week in October. In many ways it is difficult to imagine him not being there.

9. *Peru Evening Journal*, 19 October 1908; *Hamilton County Ledger*, 30 January 1900; *Indianapolis News*, 3 February 1917; *Anderson Herald*, 8 April 1913; *Portland Commercial Review*, 13 August 1909; *South Bend Tribune*, March, April, May 1913; *Evansville Journal*, 28 March 1915.

10. Department of Social Service, 29 October 1913, 29 January, 20 March, 8 October 1914, 1913–1914 Folder 1, Box 1, Indianapolis Church Federation Executive Committee Minutes, Indiana Historical Society, Indianapolis, Indiana; *Indianapolis News*, 30 November, 2 December, 5 December 1914, 23 January, 30 January, 12 June 1915, 20 February, 28 October, 4 November 1916, 2 November 1918; *Indianapolis Star*, 8 January, 24 January, 27 January, 31 January, 8 March 1910, 3 July, 13 July, 14 July, 15 July, 16 July, 20 July, 1 October, 19 October 1912; Letter from Vinson Carter, 9 July 1912, Roberts Park Methodist—Miscellaneous Reports file, Archives of the Polis Center, Indiana University–Purdue University Indianapolis, Indianapolis, Indiana, hereafter cited as IUPUI; Becker, *From Sovereign to Servant*, 9; *Patriot Phalanx*, 9 February, 16 February, 15 March, 3 May, 10 May 1912. The mayors in question were Republican Lew Shank and Democrat Joseph Bell.

11. *Noblesville Daily Ledger*, 20 July, 27 July 1914, 11 March, 23 October 1915.

12. Joseph Henry Crooker, "The Psychology of Drink," *American Journal of Sociology* 18 (July 1912): 25, 28, 32; George Elliott Howard, "Alcohol and Crime: A Study in Social Causation," *American Journal of Sociology* 24 (July 1918): 61, 80.

13. *Goshen Daily Democrat*, 15 April 1915; *Jasper Weekly Courier*, 9 April, 16 April, 30 April, 7 May, 14 May, 21 May, 18 June 1915; *Anderson Morning Herald*, 19 January, 20 January, 21 January, 24 January, 16 April 1915; *Rochester Sentinel*, 4 March 1915; *Terre Haute Tribune*, 24 November 1907, 21 April 1908; *Richmond Evening Item*, 24 April 1913; *Indianapolis Star*, 12 October 1906, 25 September 1908; *South Bend Tribune*, 3 June 1903, 16 May, 5 August 1908, 4 April 1913; *Fort Wayne Journal Gazette*, 2 February, 16 February, 1 March 1908; *Lafayette Journal*, 1 April 1904; *Vincennes Commercial*, 15 April, 29 April 1915; *Evansville Journal*, 17 March, 24 March 1908. Shakespeare was depicted in the series, as was Bismarck, prior to World War I. The Founders in the advertisements were George Washington, John Adams, John Hancock, Thomas Jefferson, James Madison, Alexander Hamilton, and the signers of the Declaration of Independence.

14. *Indianapolis Star*, 14 September 1908; *Lafayette Journal*, 20 March 1915.

15. *Muncie Evening Press*, 21 January 1913; *Noblesville Daily Ledger*, 1 April, 2 April 1913, 1 October, 2 November, 3 November 1915.

16. Charles E. Canup, "The Temperance Movement in Indiana," *Indiana Magazine of History* 16 (June 1920): 147–148; Hendrickson, *Hoosier Heritage*, 8.

17. McGerr, *A Fierce Discontent*, 88; Hoy, "Samuel M. Ralston," 16–17, 31–32, 37–38; *Berne Witness*, 9 July 1912; Charles S. Sefrit to Rev. Edward S. Shumaker, 21 September 1912; Wilson Roose to Shumaker, 21 September 1907; Ralph Kane to Shumaker, 23 September 1907; Owen N. Heaton to Shumaker, 27 September 1907, Box 2, ESS Papers; *Indianapolis Star*, 28 March, 29 March 1914; *Vincennes Commercial*, 21 February 1913; *Kokomo Daily Tribune*, 20 February 1913; *Lafayette Journal*, 22 February 1913; *South Bend Tribune*, 14 March 1913. The ASL endorsed Woodrow Wilson for governor of New Jersey in 1910. See Kleppner, *Who Voted?* 78.

18. *Patriot Phalanx*, 1 December 1911, 26 July 1912, 23 May 1913, 25 September 1914, 23 July 1915; 1900 Census; 1910 Census.

19. *Patriot Phalanx*, 29 October, 19 November 1915; *Indianapolis Star*, 16 November, 17 November, 18 November 1915.

20. Gray, ed., *Gentlemen from Indiana*, 241–242; J. Frank Hanly and Oliver Wayne Stewart, eds., *Speeches of the Flying Squadron* (Indianapolis: Hanly and Stewart, 1915); William P. Evans, Oral History Project, Indiana Division, Indiana State Library, 1969, 3–4; *Marion Chronicle*, 27 April 1915; *Noblesville Daily Ledger*, 14 January 1916; *Remington Press*, 12 January 1917; *Indianapolis Star*, 5 January 1941; Unidentified Newspaper Clippings, James Hanly (and Family) Indiana Biography File, Indiana Division, Indiana State Library; *Indianapolis News*, 7 November 1916; *Patriot Phalanx*, 21 April, 16 June, 21 July, 28 July, 18 August, 1 September, 29 September 1916; *Baptist Observer*, 29 June,

10 August 1916. Hanly was the third Hoosier in the race, with Marshall and Fairbanks as their respective party's vice presidential nominees again.

21. Starbuck, *The Goodriches*, 10, 17, 19, 24–27, 71, 84–85, 91, 97; Benjamin D. Rhodes, *James P. Goodrich, Indiana's "Governor Strangelove": A Republican's Infatuation with Soviet Russia* (Selinsgrove, PA: Susquehanna University Press, 1996), 22–23, 28; James P. Goodrich Autobiography (c. 1939), 103, 113, Pages 96–188 file, Box 4, James P. Goodrich Papers, Herbert Hoover Presidential Library; *Noblesville Daily Ledger*, 3 March 1916; *Patriot Phalanx*, 14 April 1916.

22. *Kentland Democrat*, 3 November 1916; *Indianapolis Star*, 20 November 1916; Fadely, *Thomas Taggart*, 159; *South Bend Tribune*, 5 January 1917; *Brookville American*, 1 February 1917; *Fort Wayne Journal Gazette*, 28 February 1915; *Indianapolis News*, 9 January 1917; *Terre Haute Tribune*, 29 May 1924.

23. *Bluffton Evening News*, 22 January 1917; *Indianapolis News*, 8 January 1917; *Lafayette Journal*, 9 January 1917; *Bloomington Evening World*, 6 January 1917; *North Vernon Sun*, 11 January 1917; *Huntington Herald*, 12 February 1917.

24. *Pike County Democrat*, 5 January 1917; *Warren Review Republican*, 18 January 1917; *Evansville Journal*, 25 January 1917; *Terre Haute Tribune*, 1 February 1917; *Winchester Democrat*, 4 January, 11 January, 18 January, 25 January, 1 February 1917; *Martinsville Democrat*, 2 February 1917.

25. Canup, "The Temperance Movement in Indiana," 149; *Patriot Phalanx*, 1 December, 8 December, 15 December, 29 December 1916, 2 February 1917; "The ASL States Its Relation to the So Called Dry Federation," pamphlet, Box 2, ESS Papers; Executive Committee, 13 December 1916, 9 January 1917, 1916–1917 Folder 2, Box 1, Indianapolis Church Federation Executive Committee Minutes, Indiana Historical Society. The original members of the Indiana Dry Federation were the WCTU, Prohibition Party, state and local chapters of Church Federation, Flying Squadron, Civic Union of Indiana, Legislative Council of Indiana Women, State Sunday School Association, American Temperance Board, Dry Democrats Federation, Intercollegiate Prohibition Association, State Horticultural Society, Catholic Total Abstinence Union, Christian Women's Board of Missions, Presbyterian Temperance Board, National Christian Board of Temperance, and the Legislative Council of Indiana Women.

26. *Huntington Herald*, 2 January, 4 January, 5 January, 10 January, 11 January, 17 January, 27 January, 30 January 1917; *Rushville Daily Republican*, 23 January 1917; *Logansport Reporter*, 26 January 1917.

27. *Daviess County Democrat*, 2 February 1917; *Noblesville Daily Ledger*, 1 January 1917; *Bloomington Evening World*, 2 January, 3 January 1917; *South Bend Tribune*, 3 January 1917.

28. *Indianapolis News*, 8 January, 1 February 1917; *Indianapolis Times*, 31 January 1917; *The Franklin*, 24 January, 2 February 1917; *Franklin Evening Star*, 15 January 1917; *Marion Chronicle*, 1 January 1917; *Greencastle Herald*, 30 January 1917; *Columbus Evening Republican*, 15 January, 18 January, 22 January 1917; *Monticello Evening Journal*, 30 January 1917; *Berne Witness*, 31 January 1917; *Huntington Herald*, 31 January 1917; *Kokomo Daily Tribune*, 31 January 1917; *Crawfordsville Journal*, 31 January, 1 February 1917; *Logansport Reporter*, 1 February 1917.

29. *Indianapolis Star*, 19 November 1916; *Elkhart Truth*, 15 November 1916; *Pulaski County Democrat*, 25 January 1917; *Bluffton Evening News*, 20 September 1917; *Vincennes Commercial*, 20 January 1917; *Starke County Republican*, 11 January 1917; Paul W. Glad, *The Trumpet Soundeth: William Jennings Bryan and His Democracy, 1896–1912* (Lincoln: University of Nebraska Press, 1960), 105–106; Lawrence W. Levine, *Defender of the Faith: William Jennings Bryan: The Last Decade, 1915–1925* (New York: Oxford University Press, 1965). Women's suffrage had not prevailed in Michigan and Wisconsin because of the brewers' fears that it would be another step toward prohibition. Hoosier women believed that until the brewers were defeated, women would never get the right to vote. See David Traxel, *Crusader Nation: The United States in Peace and the Great War, 1898–1920* (New York: Alfred A. Knopf, 2006), 14.

30. *Madison Courier*, 4 January 1917; *Daily Clintonian*, 16 January 1917; *Michigan City News*, 24 January 1917; *Wabash Daily Plain Dealer*, 22 January 1917; *Bloomington Evening World*, 26 January 1917; *Winchester Democrat*, 8 February 1917; *Garrett Weekly Clipper*, 8 February 1917; *Owen Leader*, 31 January 1917; *Vincennes Commercial*, 26 January 1917; *Rushville Daily Republican*, 26 January 1917; *Lafayette Journal*, 26 January 1917; *Connersville Evening News*, 26 January 1917; *Martinsville Democrat*, 2 February 1917; *Huntington Herald*, 31 January 1917. Fifty-two Republicans and eighteen Democrats voted for it, while twelve Republicans and sixteen Democrats voted against it.

31. *Bluffton Evening News*, 25 January, 30 January 1917; *Seymour Daily Republican*, 30 January 1917; *Frankfort Daily Crescent*, 30 January 1917; *Columbia City Commercial Mail*, 2 February 1917; *Sullivan Democrat*, 1 February 1917; *Daily Clintonian*, 26 January 1917; *Wabash Plain Dealer*, 2 February 1917; *Elkhart Truth*, 29 January 1917; *Bloomington Evening World*, 27 January 1917.

32. *Indianapolis News*, 12 January 1917; *Lafayette Journal*, 10 January 1917; *Goshen Daily Democrat*, 10 January 1917; *Madison Courier*, 9 January, 12 January, 29 January 1917; *South Bend Tribune*, 10 January 1917; *Huntington Herald*, 12 January 1917; *Marion Chronicle*, 12 January 1917; *Monticello Evening Journal*, 18 January 1917; *Richmond Evening Item*, 13 January, 31 January 1917; *Fort Wayne Journal Gazette*, 31 January 1917.

33. *Seymour Daily Republican*, 30 January 1917; *Frankfort Daily Crescent*, 2 February 1917; *Bluffton Evening News*, 24 January 1917; *Rushville Daily Re-*

publican, 29 January 1917; *Michigan City News,* 31 January 1917; *Kentland Democrat,* 2 February 1917; *South Bend Tribune,* 31 January 1917; *Starke County Republican,* 1 February 1917; *Wabash Plain Dealer,* 2 February 1917; *Crawfordsville Journal,* 2 February 1917; *Pulaski County Democrat,* 8 February 1917; *Monticello Evening Journal,* 31 January 1917; *White County Democrat,* 2 February 1917; *Rockville Tribune,* 6 February 1917.

34. *Connersville Evening News,* 2 February 1917; *Vincennes Commercial,* 3 February 1917; *Michigan City News,* 7 February 1917; *Monticello Evening Journal,* 2 February 1917; *Martinsville Democrat,* 9 February 1917; *Gary Evening Post,* 2 February 1917; *Columbia City Commercial Mail,* 9 February 1917; *Seymour Daily Republican,* 1 February, 2 February 1917; *Franklin Evening Star,* 26 January 1917; *Lafayette Journal,* 3 February 1917. Twenty Republicans and eighteen Democrats voted for the bill.

35. *Bloomington Evening World,* 3 February 1917; *Gary Evening Post,* 2 February 1917; *Indianapolis Star,* 2 February, 3 February, 23 February 1917; *Columbia City Commercial Mail,* 19 January 1917; *Goshen Daily Democrat,* 3 February 1917; *Fort Wayne Journal Gazette,* 3 February 1917.

36. *Anderson Herald,* 24 January 1917; *Bloomington Evening World,* 2 February 1917; *Bedford Daily Mail,* 9 February 1917; *Greencastle Herald,* 5 February 1917; *Martinsville Democrat,* 23 February 1917.

37. *Indianapolis Star,* 10 February 1917; *Warren Review Republican,* 15 February 1917; *Berne Witness,* 12 February 1917; *Fort Wayne Journal Gazette,* 10 February 1917; *Lafayette Journal,* 10 February 1917; *Huntington Herald,* 12 February 1917; *Patriot Phalanx,* 16 February 1917; *Gary Evening Post,* 9 February 1917; *Lake County News,* 15 February 1917; *Indiana Daily Student,* 10 February 1917; *Muncie Evening Press,* 9 February 1917; C. A. Robinson to Shumaker, 10 February 1917, Box 2, ESS Papers. Governor Oliver P. Morton led Indiana during the Civil War.

38. *Indianapolis Star,* 3 February 1917; *Indianapolis News,* 3 February 1917; *South Bend Tribune,* 5 February 1917; *Wabash Daily Plain Dealer,* 26 January 1917; *Fort Wayne Journal Gazette,* 4 February 1917; *Vevay Reveille,* 15 February 1917; *Brookville American,* 8 February 1917; *Plainfield Messenger,* 8 February 1917; *Baptist Observer,* 8 February 1917.

39. *Peru Evening Journal,* 2 February 1917; *Poseyville News,* 9 February 1917.

40. Duis, *The Saloon,* 302; Russ Banham, *Coors: A Rocky Mountain Legend* (Lyme, CT: Greenwich Publishing Group, 1998), 28–31; Anheuser Busch, "Anheuser Busch Companies at a Glance," pamphlet, 2001; American Breweriana, "Brewing in Fort Wayne, Indiana," http://www.americanbreweriana.org/history/ftwayne.htm, 16 October 2002; *Jasper Weekly Courier,* 16 February 1917; *Vincennes Commercial,* 3 February 1917; *Evansville Journal,* 2 February, 3 February 1917; *Indianapolis Star,* 9 February 1917; *Rochester Sentinel,* 3 April 1918; *Lake County News,* 4 April 1918.

41. *Indianapolis Star*, 22 February, 23 February 1917, 2 April 1918; *Goshen Daily Democrat*, 1 April, 4 April 1918; *Rochester Sentinel*, 2 April 1918; *Anderson Herald*, 2 April 1918; *Indianapolis News*, 2 April 1918; *Schmitt, Superintendent of Police v. F. W. Cook Brewing Company*, 187 Ind. 623; 120 N.E. 19 (1918); *Noblesville Daily Ledger*, 28 June 1918.

42. *Gary Evening Post*, 6 February, 8 February 1917; *Goshen Daily Democrat*, 5 January 1920; *Hawke v. Smith*, 253 U.S. 221 (1920); Gray, *Gentlemen from Indiana*, 268. Hanly was part of the dry legal team that argued *Hawke v. Smith* before the United States Supreme Court over the constitutionality of the Eighteenth Amendment. He died in a car accident in 1920 and thus did not live to see what ultimately became of his life's work.

43. Hendrickson, *Hoosier Heritage*, 71; J.A. Miller to Shumaker, 26 January 1917; Rev. Edward A. Robertson to Shumaker, 5 February 1917; Rev. Ulysses S.A. Bridge to Shumaker, 3 February 1917; A.W. McDaniels to Shumaker, 5 February 1917; S.M. Smith to Shumaker, 9 February 1917; G.F. Taylor to Shumaker, 10 February 1917, Box 2, ESS Papers.

44. George D. Conger to Shumaker, 28 February 1917; James A. White to Shumaker, 3 February 1917; James K. Shields to Shumaker, 3 February 1917; Elisha A. Baker to Shumaker, 7 February 1917; Rev. Joshua Stansfield to Shumaker, 4 February 1917, Box 2, ESS Papers; William H. Anderson to Shumaker, 6 November 1920, Reel 76; Edwin Rawden to Ernest H. Cherrington, 3 May 1918, Reel 7, Ernest H. Cherrington Papers, Microfilm Edition of the Temperance and Prohibition Papers, Ohio Historical Society, Columbus, Ohio; *Patriot Phalanx*, 23 March 1917; Oregon State Archives, "Prohibition in Oregon: The Vision and the Reality," http://arcweb.sos.state.or.us/50th/prohibition1/prohibintro.html, 20 August 2002.

45. D.S. Ritter to Shumaker, 7 March 1917; Governor James P. Goodrich to Shumaker, 13 February 1917, Box 2, ESS Papers.

46. Philips, *Indiana in Transition*, 494–495; Madison, *Indiana through Tradition and Change*, 40; American Breweriana, "Brewing in Fort Wayne, Indiana"; Irving Leibowitz, *My Indiana* (Englewood Cliffs, NJ: Prentice-Hall, 1964), 182, quoting Harold C. Feightner; *Evansville Journal*, 3 February 1917; Szymanski, *Pathways to Prohibition*, 12; Shumaker to Belle Mechling, 6 August 1919, courtesy of Cynthia Hendee Henry, in possession of author; Shumaker to Goodrich, 4 June 1917; Goodrich to Shumaker, 5 June 1917, Correspondence Shreeve-Sims folder, Box 147, Goodrich Papers, Indiana State Archives, Indianapolis, Indiana; Executive Committee, 30 April 1917, 1916–1918 Folder 2, Box 1, Indianapolis Church Federation Executive Committee Minutes, Indiana Historical Society; *Noblesville Daily Ledger*, 3 April, 14 April, 16 April 1917; *Warsaw Daily Union*, 6 April 1918; *Baptist World*, 30 September 1915; *Stars and Stripes*, 15 November 1918, 17 January, 14 February, 18 April 1919.

47. Shumaker to Theodor Stempful, 11 May 1914, and Stempful to Shumaker, 13 May 1914, "National Council Correspondence-Chronological," Folder 19, Box 7; 1919 Convention, Folder 34, 1923 Convention, Folder 36, 1925 Convention, Folder 37, 1927 Convention, Folder 38, 1929 Convention, Folder 39, Box 14, American Turners Records, Archives of Indiana University-Purdue University Indianapolis, Indianapolis, Indiana; *Milwaukee Journal Sentinel*, 15 January 1998.

48. *Baptist World*, 6 March, 29 May 1913; E. J. Richardson to E. W. Winfrey, 23 May 1917, Reel 3, Anti Saloon League of America Papers, Microfilm Edition of the Temperance and Prohibition Papers, Ohio Historical Society, emphasis in the original; *Vincennes Commercial*, 10 January 1917; *Oxford Gazette*, 16 February 1917; *Daviess County Democrat*, 9 February 1917; Edwin Dinwiddie to Shumaker, 2 February 1917, Box 2, ESS Papers; William Jennings Bryan to Woodrow Wilson, 21 November 1918; Joseph Patrick Tumulty to Wilson, 17 December 1918, Woodrow Wilson Papers, Volume 53, 150, 413; From Ray Stannard Baker's Diary, 13 March 1919, Woodrow Wilson Papers, Volume 55, 489; Telegram from Tumulty, 9 May 1919, Woodrow Wilson Papers, Volume 58, 603–604; Telegram from Tumulty, 10 May 1919, Woodrow Wilson Papers, Volume 59, 38–39, in Arthur S. Link, ed., *Woodrow Wilson Papers* (Princeton, NJ: Princeton University Press, 1986).

49. *Indianapolis Times*, 18 December 1917; *Indianapolis News*, 18 December 1917, 29 January 1919; *Noblesville Daily Ledger*, 9 January, 14 January, 17 January 1919, 15 January 1920; *Baptist Observer*, 6 February 1919; *Wabash Daily Plain Dealer*, 2 February 1917; *Indianapolis Star*, 3 April 1918, 3 April 1919; *Evansville Journal*, 10 January 1920; *Terre Haute Tribune*, 16 January 1920; *Hartford City News*, 19 January 1920; Bulletin, 30 March 1919, 3400 Sunday Bulletins-2 1919–1933; Letter from Senator Harry New, 28 May 1919, Letter from Representative Merrill Moores, 28 May 1919, Letter from Senator James Watson, 29 May 1919, Folder 2, Miscellaneous 2300, Archives of First Baptist Church, Indianapolis, Indiana; 1917 Appeal by Anti-Saloon League of Virginia, 15 July 1917, Reel 3, Anti-Saloon League Papers, Microfilm Edition of the Temperance and Prohibition Papers, Ohio Historical Society.

50. *Gary Evening Post*, 16 January 1920; *Connersville News Examiner*, 16 January 1920; *South Bend Tribune*, 17 January 1920; *Indianapolis Star*, 16 January 1920; *Muncie Evening Press*, 16 January 1920; *Terre Haute Tribune*, 16 January 1920.

51. Bulletin, 20 November 1927, Bulletins 1927–1929 book, MSUMC Archives.

52. Bulletins, 6 November 1921, 4 June, 12 November 1922, Bulletins 1871–1922 book; Bulletins, 11 May, 27 July 1924, Bulletins 1923–1926 book, MSUMC Archives; "Glory of Christ's Kingdom," N.D., Box 2, ESS Papers.

53. Frank Ninkovich, *The Wilsonian Century: U.S. Foreign Policy since 1900* (Chicago: University of Chicago Press, 1999); Crunden, *Ministers of Reform*, 226; *Noblesville Daily Ledger*, 4 March 1920; Paul Kramer, "Empires, Exceptions, and Anglo-Saxons: Race and Rule between the British and United States Empires, 1880–1910," *Journal of American History* 88 (March 2002): 1315–1353.

54. *Baptist Observer*, 17 October, 24 October 1918, 19 August 1920; Christian Endeavor, "The History of Christian Endeavor," http://www.christian endeavor.org/history.htm, 22 August 2002; Behr, *Prohibition*, 74–75; Ian Tyrrell, *Woman's World, Woman's Empire: The Woman's Christian Temperance Union in International Perspective, 1880–1930* (Chapel Hill: University of North Carolina Press, 1991); *Marion Chronicle*, 12 January 1920; *Kokomo Daily Tribune*, 19 August 1927; Anti-Saloon League, "Related Organizations: World League against Alcoholism," http://www.wpl.lib.oh.us:80/AntiSaloon/related/World.html, 4 May 2000. "Alcoholism" in the name of the World League probably stemmed from the use of the term in France to cover all the problems associated with alcohol abuse. For an example, see *Baptist World*, 11 July 1912.

55. A. E. Dingle, *The Campaign for Prohibition in Victorian England: The United Kingdom Alliance, 1872–1895* (New Brunswick, NJ: Rutgers University Press, 1980), 7.

56. Shumaker Letter to Pastors, 13 October 1921, Archives and Special Collections, Roy O. West Library, DePauw University, Greencastle, Indiana; *The World League against Alcoholism November 24–29, 1922 Meeting in Toronto* (Westerville, OH: American Issue Press, 1922), 392; *Indianapolis News*, 17 January 1920.

57. *Evansville Journal*, 3 March 1917, 27 December 1919; *Columbus Evening Republican*, 9 January 1920; Andrew Davies, "The Police and the People: Gambling in Salford, 1900–1939," *Historical Journal* 34 (March 1991): 87–115; David M. Fahey 2000 Presidential Address, "The Politics of Drink in Britain: Anglo-American Perspectives," http://www.athg.org/faheypresidential .html, 23 October 2002; Patricia Herlihy, *The Alcoholic Empire: Vodka and Politics in Late Imperial Russia* (New York: Oxford University Press, 2002), 53; *Warsaw Daily Union*, 28 October 1922.

58. *Baptist World*, 26 September 1912; United Temperance Workers to E.Y. Mullins, 23 August 1911, Microfiche 122, 533/2044, E.Y. Mullins Papers, SBC Archives; *Baptist Observer*, 4 December 1919, 30 December 1920.

59. Carter, *The Decline and Revival of the Social Gospel*, 38; News Report, 11 October 1919; News Report, 19 October 1919; News Report, 23 October 1919; A Veto Message, 27 October 1919, Woodrow Wilson Papers, Volume 63, 562, 582, 590, 601; J.P. Tumulty to Edith Bolling Galt Wilson with Enclosure, 26 March 1920, Woodrow Wilson Papers, Volume 65, 128–134; Joseph P.

Tumulty, *Woodrow Wilson As I Know Him* (New York: Doubleday, Page and Company, 1921), 409–421; Homer Stille Cummings to Wilson, 31 May 1920; Homer Stille Cummings to Wilson, 17 June 1920; Memorandum by Carter Glass, 19 June 1920, Woodrow Wilson Papers, Volume 65, 346–347, 424, 435–436; Frank Irving Cobb to Wilson, 27 March 1923; Louis Dembitz Brandies to Wilson with Enclosure, 15 April 1923, Woodrow Wilson Papers, Volume 68, 304–305, 334–335. The veto was overridden 175 to 55 in the House and 65 to 20 in the Senate.

60. Hamm, *Shaping the Eighteenth Amendment*, 255, 266–267; Szymanski, "Dry Compulsions," 138–139; Dumenil, "'The Insatiable Maw of Bureaucracy,'" 522; *Indianapolis Star*, 15 January 1920, 21 May 1921; Robert K. Murray, *The Harding Era: Warren G. Harding and His Administration* (Minneapolis: University of Minnesota Press, 1969), 403–407, 444, 536–537. Will Hays forced the New York GOP to get in line behind Prohibition. See Buenker, *Urban Liberalism and Progressive Reform*, 191.

61. *South Bend Tribune*, 1 January 1920; *Kokomo Daily Tribune*, 14 August 1922; *Evansville Journal*, 11 February 1923.

62. *Lake County Times*, 7 July 1921; *Indianapolis Star*, 8 October, 9 October 1922; *Indianapolis News*, 17 March 1923.

63. *Marion Chronicle*, 22 January 1923; *Lebanon Pioneer*, 9 November 1922; Olive Beldon Lewis, Oral History Project, Indiana Division, Indiana State Library, Indianapolis, Indiana, 1969, 55–56; Fadely, *Thomas Taggart*, 174, 181–182; *Indianapolis Star*, 9 February, 25 October 1922; *Noblesville Daily Ledger*, 18 July 1921; Blocker, *American Temperance Movements*, 54; *Jeffersonville Evening News*, 12 June 1923; Executive Committee, 14 January 1919, 1918–1919 Folder 3, Box 1, Indianapolis Church Federation Executive Committee Minutes, Indiana Historical Society.

64. Bulletin, 24 February 1924, 24 January 1926, Bulletins 1923–1926 book, MSUMC Archives. Commerce Secretary Herbert Hoover wrote to an English friend in 1922 that "it will take ten years to prove whether or not Prohibition can be made a success." See Herbert Hoover to F. A. Govett, 28 June 1922, Prohibition 1922–1924 file, Box 486, Commerce Series, Herbert Hoover Papers, Herbert Hoover Presidential Library.

65. *Baptist World*, 24 October 1912; McGerr, *A Fierce Discontent*, 92–93; William B. Walter 1936 interview by Arline Dickinson, Indiana Federal Writers Project Papers, Microfilm Roll 1; Edmund C. Pinsho to S.E. Nicholson, 17 January 1919, S. Edgar Nicholson Papers, EC Archives; *Indianapolis Star*, 3 April 1918; W. S. Mosher to Herbert Hoover, 15 December 1925, Prohibition 1925 November–December file, Box 486, Commerce Series, Herbert Hoover Papers, Herbert Hoover Presidential Library; *Indianapolis Times*, 16 April 1923.

66. *Indianapolis Star,* 20 February (including the quotation of Warren G. Harding), 21 February, 22 February, 23 February, 24 February, 25 February, 26 February 1923; *Indianapolis Times,* 30 March 1923; *Fort Wayne Journal Gazette,* 27 February 1923; Monkkonen, "A Disorderly People?" 547; *Evansville Journal,* 16 January 1920.

67. ESS Record IASL 15 April 1917–1 April 1920 book, Box 2, ESS Papers. Using constant 1917 dollars, Shumaker's expenses in 2004 would have amounted to $85,508.13, and he would have raised $1,192,093.44 in that same fourteen-year span; "Prayer," 5 September 1921, Box 2, ESS Papers; "Division Commander's Report," 5 December 1920, Box 2, ESS Papers; Sons of Union Veterans of the Civil War, "Department of Indiana Commanders and Encampments," http://suvcw.org/in/indeptcmd.html, 5 February 2003.

68. Blocker, *American Temperance Movements,* 87; Richard W. Leopold, *Elihu Root and the Conservative Tradition* (Boston: Little, Brown and Company, 1954), 170; *Western Christian Advocate,* 7 January, 21 January, 7 July 1920; General Board of Church and Society, "The United Methodist Building," http://www.umc-gbcs.org/75th-book.htm, 20 September 2002; *Ninety-Third Session of the Indiana Annual Conference of the Methodist Episcopal Church,* 1924; Canup, "The Temperance Movement in Indiana," 151.

69. Thomas D. Clark, *Indiana University, Mid-Western Pioneer: In Middle Passage* (Bloomington: Indiana University Press, 1973), 268; McGerr, *A Fierce Discontent,* 315.

5 | *The Faulty Alliances of Rhetoric*

1. *Hamilton County Ledger,* 22 May 1903, 19 March 1907; *Indianapolis Star,* 3 February 1917; *Indiana Issue,* March 1906; Bulletin, 2 October 1921, 26 February 1922, Bulletins 1871–1922 book; Bulletin, 25 November 1923, Bulletins 1923–1926 book; Bulletin, 31 March 1929, Bulletins 1927–1929 book, MSUMC Archives; Meagher, *Inventing Irish America,* 55; *Baptist World,* 18 July 1912.

2. Kingsdale, "The 'Poor Man's Club,'" 481–482; *Evansville Journal,* 26 December 1907; *Western Christian Advocate,* 5 September 1900.

3. Mary Ann Clawson, *Constructing Brotherhood: Class, Gender, and Fraternalism* (Princeton, NJ: Princeton University Press, 1989), 162; Kingsdale, "The 'Poor Man's Club,'" 485–487; Parsons, *Manhood Lost,* 3; Clifford Putney, *Muscular Christianity: Manhood and Sports in Protestant America, 1880–1920* (Cambridge, MA: Harvard University Press, 2003); *Fort Wayne Journal Gazette,* 29 February 1904; *South Bend Tribune,* 23 May 1903; Gail Bederman, "'The Women Have Had Charge of the Church Work Long Enough': The Men and

Religion Forward Movement of 1911–1912 and the Masculinization of Middle-Class Protestantism," *American Quarterly* 41 (September 1989): 432–465.

4. Hendrickson, *Hoosier Heritage*, 19; Kathleen Kerr, "How Did the Reform Agenda of the Minnesota Woman's Christian Temperance Union Change, 1878–1917?" http://womhist.binghamton.edu/wctu/intro.htm, 13 August 2002; Morone, *Hellfire Nation*, 243; J. H. Beadle, *The Women's War on Whisky* (Cincinnati: Wilstach, Baldwin and Company, 1874), 9. Not all women rallied to the dry banner. For different reactions to this rhetoric, which ranged from radical acceptance to ambivalence to outright defiance, see Grace, *Carry A. Nation*, 210, 229, 279–280; Robert G. Barrows, *Albion Fellows Bacon: Indiana's Municipal Housekeeper* (Indianapolis: Indiana University Press, 2000); Kenneth D. Rose, *American Women and the Repeal of Prohibition* (New York: New York University Press, 1996); Tanya Marie Sanchez, "The Feminine Side of Bootlegging," *Louisiana History* 41, no. 4 (2000): 403–433; Mary Murphy, "Bootlegging Mothers and Drinking Daughters: Gender and Prohibition in Butte, Montana," *American Quarterly* 46 (June 1994): 174–194; and Julia Shumaker, interview with author, 1 December 2000.

5. C. Wendell Martin, correspondence with author, 22 March 2003.

6. Shumaker, *Autobiography*, 107; Arthur Shumaker, interview with author, 14 March, 24 March 2000; 1920 Census; Genealogy, Box 2, ESS Papers; Julia Shumaker, correspondence with author, 7 September 2003. Shumaker had been married before, to his college sweetheart, Lena Belle Truax. He remembered her as the quintessential pastor's wife, who enjoyed making visitation trips with him and was an asset in social settings. Their time together, however, was short. In March 1899, after just two years of marriage, she died from a preexisting heart condition. See Shumaker, *Autobiography*, 95–96, 101. Edward and Flora's son Charles went by his middle name of Wayne.

7. *Indianapolis Star*, 15 February 1929; Shumaker, *Autobiography*, 123B, 125–128.

8. McGerr, *A Fierce Discontent*, 51; Julia Shumaker, interview with author, 1 December 2000, correspondence with author, 7 September 2003; Sinclair Lewis, *Main Street* (New York: Signet Classic, 1920); *Journal of the Ninety-Fourth Session Being the Seventh Session Since Unification Northwest Indiana Annual Conference of the Methodist Church, 1945*, 262.

9. Julia Shumaker, interview with author, 8 February 2003; 1920 Census, Indiana Marion, Center Township; S. E. Nicholson to Willie Nicholson, 23 February 1915, S. Edgar Nicholson Papers, EC Archives; 1919 Income Tax Worksheet; 1921 Income Tax Return, 1922 Income Tax Return, 1924 Tax Assessment List, Box 2, ESS Papers; Shumaker, *Autobiography*, 128–129; Keely Family Reunion Speech, 1898, Box 3, ESS Papers; Edward S. Shumaker, *Descendants of Henry Keller of York County, Pennsylvania and Fairfield County, Ohio*

(Indianapolis: Edward S. Shumaker, 1924); Rev. Edward S. Shumaker to Belle Mechling, 6 August 1919, courtesy of Cynthia Hendee Henry, in possession of author.

10. Kirby, "Dearest Ellen," 139–140; Julia Shumaker, correspondence with author, 7 September 2003, emphasis in the original.

11. Arthur Shumaker, interviews with author, 24 March, 19 April 2000; Barbara B. Clay, correspondence with author, 5 February 2003.

12. Anne Firor Scott, "Most Invisible of All: Black Women's Voluntary Associations," *Journal of Southern History* 56 (February 1990): 3, 9; Carl V. Harris, "Reforms in Government Control of Negroes in Birmingham, Alabama, 1890–1920," *Journal of Southern History* 38 (November 1972): 569.

13. Morone, *Hellfire Nation*, 297; James E. Watson to George P. Steward, 28 March 1921, Folder 13, Box 1, George P. Stewart Manuscript Collection, Indiana Historical Society, Indianapolis, Indiana; *Indianapolis Recorder*, 27 October 1928; Myrtle Cook to Herbert Hoover, 30 April 1929, Prohibition Correspondence 1929 April 26–30 file, Box 227, Presidential Series, Herbert Hoover Papers, Herbert Hoover Presidential Library.

14. *Western Christian Advocate*, 14 November 1900; *Indianapolis Recorder*, 22 September 1906, 22 February 1908; *Patriot Phalanx*, 21 November 1907; *Garrett Weekly Clipper*, 8 February 1917.

15. Wayne Flynt, *Alabama Baptists: Southern Baptists in the Heart of Dixie* (Tuscaloosa: University of Alabama Press, 1998), 213–214, 303; Hanes Walton, Jr., and James E. Taylor, "Blacks and the Southern Prohibition Movement," *Phylon* 32 (Third Quarter, 1971), 247–259; Sallie Chapin, "Our Southern Letter," Document 13 in Kerr, "How Did the Reform Agenda of the Minnesota Woman's Christian Temperance Union Change, 1878–1917?"; David M. Fahey, *Temperance and Racism: John Bull, Johnny Reb, and the Good Templars* (Lexington: University Press of Kentucky, 1996); Charles Crowe, "Racial Violence and Social Reform: Origins of the Atlanta Riot of 1906," *Journal of Negro History* 53 (July 1968): 234–256; Harris, "Reforms in Government Control of Negroes in Birmingham, Alabama," 572, 578; Szymanski, *Pathways to Prohibition*, 16; Arthur J. Barton to William H. Anderson, 5 February 1918, Reel 76, Ernest H. Cherrington Papers, Microfilm Edition of the Temperance and Prohibition Papers, Ohio Historical Society. Barton was the superintendent of the Texas ASL; Anderson held the same post with the New York ASL.

16. *Cleveland Gazette*, 6 August 1887; Patrick Rael, *Black Identity and Black Protest in the Antebellum North* (Chapel Hill: University of North Carolina Press, 2002), 68, 194–195; Howard, "Alcohol and Crime," 67–68; Kenneth Christmon, "Historical Overview of Alcohol in the African-American Community," *Journal of Black Studies* 25 (January 1995): 318–330.

17. "An Article in *Outlook*," 14 March 1908, Booker T. Washington Papers, Volume 9, 468–472; Booker T. Washington to Ray Stannard Baker, 13 April 1909; From George H. Bodeker, 18 November 1910; To John L. Staples, 23 November 1910; From Monroe Nathan Work, 20 December 1910; From Monroe Nathan Work, 3 January 1911, Booker T. Washington Papers, Volume 10, 88, 477, 482–483, 509–510, 525–526; "A Statement on Prohibition," 31 October 1911, Booker T. Washington Papers, Volume 11, 351–353; Letter, To Edward Page Gaston, 5 July 1912, Booker T. Washington Papers, Volume 11, 557; "An Article in the Journal of the American Institute of Criminal Law and Criminology," September 1912, Booker T. Washington Papers, Volume 12, 21–30; "An Address on the Negro Race at the First National Conference on Race Betterment at Battle Creek, Michigan," 18 January 1914, Booker T. Washington Papers, Volume 12, 411; "The Story of My Life and Work 1900," Booker T. Washington Papers, Volume 1, 45; Richard W. Thompson to Booker T. Washington, 14 March 1900, Booker T. Washington Papers, Volume 5, 462; Lilliam Marion Norton Ames Stevens to Booker T. Washington, 1 July 1901, Booker T. Washington Papers, Volume 6, 162; "Article in *World's Work*: 'A Town Owned by Negroes: Mound Bayou, Miss. An Example of Thrift and Self-Government," July 1907, Booker T. Washington Papers, Volume 9, 316; "Extracts from an Address in Brooklyn," 8 December 1907, Booker T. Washington Papers, Volume 9, 417–419; Louis R. Harlan, *Booker T. Washington: The Wizard of Tuskegee, 1901–1915* (New York: Oxford University Press, 1983), 230–232; *Hamilton County Ledger*, 9 December 1902; *Indianapolis Star*, 1 January 1909; *Indianapolis Recorder*, 21 March 1908. As for his chief rival for leadership among African Americans, W.E.B. DuBois, historians have detailed little in the way of what DuBois thought about the dry cause. David Levering Lewis's masterful works on him do not even mention Prohibition. See David Levering Lewis, *W.E.B. DuBois: Biography of a Race, 1868–1919* (New York: Henry Holt and Company, 1993); and David Levering Lewis, *W.E.B. DuBois: The Fight for Equality and the American Century, 1919–1963* (New York: Henry Holt and Company, 2000).

18. Flynt, *Alabama Baptists*, 303; *Baptist World*, 16 December 1915, 1 March 1917; Rev. B.F. Riley to Ernest H. Cherrington, 1 June 1909, Reel 2, Ernest H. Cherrington Papers, Temperance and Prohibition Papers; Handbook of Texas Online, "Anti Saloon League of Texas," http://www.tsha.utexas.edu/handbook/online/articles/print/AA/vaa2.html, 9 August 2002. Historians have credited Riley with having enlightened views on race for his time.

19. Dr. L.G. Jordan to F. Scott McBride, 6 November 1925, Reel 4, F. Scott McBride Papers, Temperance and Prohibition Papers.

20. Jordan to A.J. Barton, 27 January 1926; Barton to E.H. Cherrington, 15 January, 30 January 1926; Cherrington to Barton, 26 January 1926, Reel 76, E.H. Cherrington Papers, Temperance and Prohibition Papers.

21. *Noblesville Independent*, 8 February 1878, 19 April, 6 December 1879, 7 February, 30 October 1880; *Hamilton County Ledger*, 8 December 1899, 27 March, 27 July 1900, 18 January, 27 August 1901, 21 November 1902; *Patriot Phalanx*, 11 March, 6 May 1909.

22. *Noblesville Republican Ledger*, 28 November 1884; *Hamilton County Ledger*, 6 December 1907.

23. Christopher Robert Reed, *The Chicago NAACP and the Rise of Black Professional Leadership, 1910–1960* (Indianapolis: Indiana University Press, 1997), 15–16; Emma Lou Thornbrough, "Segregation in Indiana during the Klan Era of the 1920s," *Mississippi Valley Historical Review* 47 (March 1961): 594–597; Emma Lou Thornbrough, *Indiana Blacks in the Twentieth Century* (Indianapolis: Indiana University Press, 2000), 35; James R. Grossman, *Land of Hope: Chicago, Black Southerners, and the Great Migration* (Chicago: University of Chicago Press, 1991), 3, 6; *Indianapolis Recorder*, 20 February 1904, 28 October, 11 November 1916; *Indianapolis Freeman*, 11 March 1916.

24. Thornbrough, *Indiana Blacks in the Twentieth Century*, 7, 24, 31–32, 67; *Indianapolis Minute*, 5 December 1884; *Indianapolis Recorder*, 27 June 1903.

25. American National Baptist Convention 1890; National Baptist Convention 1897; National Baptist Convention 1898; National Baptist Convention 1900; National Baptist Woman's Auxiliary Convention 1902; National Baptist Woman's Auxiliary Convention 1904; National Baptist Convention, 1907; National Baptist Woman's Auxiliary Convention 1907; National Woman's Auxiliary Convention 1908; National Baptist Convention 1909; National Baptist Woman's Auxiliary Convention 1909; National Baptist Convention 1910; National Baptist Convention 1911; National Baptist Convention 1912; National Baptist Woman's Auxiliary Convention 1912; National Baptist Convention 1914; National Baptist Convention 1915; National Baptist Woman's Auxiliary Convention 1916; National Baptist Convention 1918; National Baptist Convention 1920; National Baptist Woman's Auxiliary Convention 1920; National Baptist Woman's Auxiliary Convention 1921; National Baptist Woman's Auxiliary Convention 1922; National Baptist Woman's Auxiliary Convention 1924; National Baptist Woman's Auxiliary Convention 1925, Microfilm edition, SBC Archives.

26. *Indianapolis Recorder*, 17 February, 23 June 1906, 1 June, 20 June 1907; *Evansville Journal*, 14 October 1907; *Muncie Evening Press*, 5 June 1908.

27. Frances Watkins Harper, "Duty to Dependent Races," Document 2 in Kathleen Kerr, "How Did the Reform Agenda of the Minnesota Woman's Christian Temperance Union Change, 1878–1917?" 13 August 2002; Frances Watkins Harper, "Work among Colored People," Document 3 in ibid.; Rev. U. G. Humphrey to Rev. Edward S. Shumaker, 22 March 1907, Box 2, ESS Papers; *Muncie Evening Press*, 10 April, 11 April 1911; *Noblesville Daily Ledger*,

31 July 1915; *Indianapolis Star,* 20 November 1916; *American Issue: Indiana Edition,* 13 October 1928; *Baptist Observer,* 30 March 1911, 24 January, 29 August 1918, 24 April, 3 July 1919.

28. Shumaker, *Autobiography,* 68.

29. *Indianapolis Recorder,* 6 January 1906, 9 March 1907, 1 August, 5 September, 12 September, 26 September 1908; *Lafayette Journal,* 2 November 1908.

30. *Indianapolis Star,* 14 September 1908; *Indianapolis News,* 14 September 1908; *Indianapolis Recorder,* 4 July, 25 July, 1 August, 8 August, 15 August, 29 August, 5 September 1908. There may have also been attempts, in the 1910s, to organize African Americans by the state Leagues in Maryland and Georgia.

31. McGerr, *A Fierce Discontent,* 183–184.

32. Deirdre M. Moloney, *American Catholic Lay Groups and Transatlantic Social Reform in the Progressive Era* (Chapel Hill: University of North Carolina Press, 2002).

33. *Hamilton County Ledger,* July and August 1903; *South Bend Tribune,* 16 September 1907; Mary J. Oates, *The Catholic Philanthropic Tradition in America* (Indianapolis: Indiana University Press, 1995).

34. *Indianapolis News,* 12 November, 28 November 1910; *Indiana Catholic and Record,* 16 May 1919; Francis G. Couvares, "Hollywood, Main Street, and the Church: Trying to Censor the Movies before the Production Code," *American Quarterly* 44 (December 1992): 589; Gregory D. Black, *The Catholic Crusade against the Movies, 1940–1975* (New York: Cambridge University Press, 1998); Stephen Vaughn, "The Devil's Advocate: Will H. Hays and the Campaign to Make Movies Respectable," *Indiana Magazine of History* 101 (June 2005): 125–152. The movie czar was Hoosier Will Hays, a staunch Presbyterian, former state and national chairman of the Republican Party, and past member of Warren Harding's cabinet.

35. *Western Christian Advocate,* 9 January 1850, 23 February 1870, 23 October 1895; *Indianapolis Star,* 4 April, 6 April 1910; *Indiana Catholic,* 4 March, 8 April 1910, 22 September 1911; Jay P. Dolan, *The Immigrant Church: New York's Irish and German Catholics, 1815–1865* (Notre Dame, IN: University of Notre Dame Press, 1987), 161–169; Dolores Liptak, ed., *A Church of Many Cultures: Selected Historical Essays on Ethnic American Catholicism* (New York: Garland Publishing, 1988), 33, 38; Charles Yrigoyen, Jr., "Methodists and Roman Catholics in Nineteenth Century America," *Methodist History* 28 (April 1990): 172–186. Not all immigrants were Catholics and thus did not experience America or its reforms in the same way. Lutherans, for example, were divided over Prohibition with the Missouri Synod standing against it as unneeded "social legislation," while Augustana and Norwegian Lutherans supported it.

Jewish immigrants took a position similar to that of most Catholics on much of American society, including Prohibition. See Jacobson and Trollinger, eds., *Re-Forming the Center*, 248; Judith E. Endelman, *The Jewish Community of Indianapolis, 1849 to the Present* (Bloomington: Indiana University Press, 1984), 122; *Fort Wayne Journal Gazette*, 9 March 1908.

36. *Indiana Catholic*, 3 March, 10 March, 5 May, 10 November 1911, 9 November 1917, 21 November 1919, 27 February, 19 March, 16 April 1920, 9 September 1927, 2 November 1928.

37. *Indiana Catholic and Record*, 29 September 1911, 2 August 1912; *Greencastle Banner*, 27 May 1875; Jay P. Dolan, *The American Catholic Experience: A History from Colonial Times to the Present* (Garden City, NY: Doubleday, 1985), 267–268, 276–277; *Baptist World*, 12 September 1912.

38. Dolan, *The American Catholic Experience*, 294–297, 301–302; Liptak, ed., *A Church of Many Cultures*, 42, 101, 120, 130, 145; Meagher, *Inventing Irish America*, 162, 204, 251, 264; Timothy J. Meagher, "'Why Should We Care for a Little Trouble or a Walk through the Mud': St. Patrick's and Columbus Day Parades in Worcester, Massachusetts, 1845–1915," *New England Quarterly* 58 (March 1985): 5–26.

39. Marvin R. O'Connell, *Edward Sorin* (Notre Dame, IN: University of Notre Dame Press, 2001), 707; John F. Quinn, *Father Mathew's Crusade: Temperance in Nineteenth-Century Ireland and Irish America* (Boston: University of Massachusetts Press, 2002), 172, 182–183, 186; *Baptist Observer*, 2 November 1911, 2 October 1913; Kathleen Flake, *The Politics of American Religious Identity: The Seating of Senator Reed Smoot, Mormon Apostle* (Chapel Hill: University of North Carolina Press, 2004), 153–157. Not all Irish Catholics were Americanists. Bernard John McQuaid, Bishop of Rochester, and Michael Augustine Corrigan, Archbishop of New York, are examples.

40. Colm Kerrigan, *Father Mathew and the Irish Temperance Movement, 1838–1849* (Cork, Ireland: Cork University Press, 1992); Quinn, *Father Mathew's Crusade*.

41. Meagher, *Inventing Irish America*, 91, 163, 166–167; *Western Christian Advocate*, 22 January 1880.

42. Joseph C. Gibbs, *History of the Catholic Total Abstinence Union of America* (Philadelphia: Penn Printing House, 1907); Joan Bland, *Hibernian Crusade: The Story of the Catholic Total Abstinence Union of America* (Washington, DC: The Catholic University of America Press, 1951), 135–136, 245, 274; Dolan, *The Immigrant Church*, 31–32; Kingsdale, "The 'Poor Man's Club,'" 487; John F. Quinn, "'It's Fashionable Here to be a Total Abstainer': Temperance Advocacy at the University of Notre Dame, 1870–1940," *American Catholic Studies* 110 (Spring–Winter 1999): 1–27; *South Bend Tribune*, 14 August 1905; *Greencastle Banner*, 5 September 1878; John Radzilowski, *The Eagle and the Cross:*

A History of the Polish Roman Catholic Union of America, 1873–2000 (New York: Columbia University Press, 2003), 127–131.

43. John Tracy Ellis, *The Life of James Cardinal Gibbons* (popular edition) (Milwaukee: Bruce Publishing Company, 1963), 200; *Valparaiso Daily Vidette,* 29 October 1908; *Marion Chronicle,* 28 October 1908, *South Bend Tribune,* 28 October 1908; *Fort Wayne Journal Gazette,* 1 November 1907, 18 February 1911; 3 March 1908; *Versailles Republican,* 3 March 1909; *Indiana Catholic and Record,* 24 March 1911, 8 January, 30 April, 14 May, 21 May, 23 July, 13 August, 19 November 1915, 17 November 1916, 24 August 1928.

44. Hofstadter, *The Age of Reform,* 181–182; M. Nelson McGeary, *Gifford Pinchot: Forester, Politician* (Princeton, NJ: Princeton University Press, 1960), 243–244; Cannon, *Bishop Cannon's Own Story,* 337.

45. *Indiana Issue,* May 1906; *American Issue: Indiana Edition,* 24 January 1925; *Franklin Evening Star,* 7 November 1916; *Indianapolis News,* 24 February 1915, 1 May 1923; *Indiana Catholic,* 1 July 1910; *South Bend News-Times,* 30 October, 2 November, 14 November 1918, 6 February 1920; "Indiana" in Cherrington, gen. ed., *Standard Encyclopedia of the Alcohol Problem,* Volume 3, 1310. Kubacki's tenure at the parish was ended in 1920, when Bishop Herman Aldering (a German American) of the Diocese of Fort Wayne fired him because he did not send all of St. Adalbert's Christmas offering to the diocese. Instead, in Kubacki's words, he directed some money to the "naked-despoiled-starving-Hun-made-orphans of ruined Poland who of our nation, of our blood, are our orphans to whom no German or Irish will extend charity."

46. *Indiana Catholic and Record,* 2 January 1920; Edward S. Shumaker to F. Scott McBride, 13 March 1925, McBride to Shumaker, 11 April 1925, Reel 8, F. Scott McBride Papers, Temperance and Prohibition Papers. That this incident took place during the height of Indiana's Ku Klux Klan era is instructive. For more on sacramental wine during Prohibition, see Joseph C. Linck and Raymond J. Kupke, eds., *Building the Church in America: Studies in Honor of Monsignor Robert F. Trisco on the Occasion of His Seventieth Birthday* (Washington, DC: The Catholic University of America Press, 1999), 161–195.

47. Quinn, *Father Mathew's Crusade,* 190; Bates, *Senator Thomas J. Walsh of Montana,* 1, 152, 261; John F. Quinn, "Father Mathew's Disciples: American Catholic Support for Temperance, 1840–1920," *Church History* 65 (December 1996): 639–640; *Fort Wayne Journal Gazette,* 1 March 1908; *South Bend Tribune,* 19 February 1904, 19 January 1920; *Lafayette Journal,* 11 November 1907; Patrick Allitt, *Catholic Converts: British and American Intellectuals Turn to Rome* (Ithaca: Cornell University Press, 1997), 165–166.

48. *Indianapolis Times,* 29 January 1917; William E. Ellis, "Patrick Henry Callahan: A Kentucky Democrat in National Politics," Eastern Kentucky University, 9 June 1976, Correspondence Folder, Patrick Henry Callahan Papers,

Archives of the University of Notre Dame, Notre Dame, Indiana, hereafter cited as CLN Papers, ND Archives; Patrick H. Callahan to William H. Anderson, 21 November 1927, Reel 76, E.H. Cherrington Papers, Temperance and Prohibition Papers; William E. Ellis, "Patrick Henry Callahan: A Maverick Catholic and the Prohibition Issue," *Register of the Kentucky Historical Society* 92 (Spring 1994): 175–199.

49. Letter to Reverend Peter C. Gannon, 11 September 1933; Letter to Gilbert O. Nations, 12 September 1933, Correspondence Folder, CLN Papers, ND Archives; *Indiana Catholic and Record*, 11 December 1925, 6 May 1927.

50. Alan Brinkley, *Voices of Protest: Huey Long, Father Coughlin, and the Great Depression* (New York: Vintage Books, 1983), 96; Donald Warren, *Radio Priest: Charles Coughlin, the Father of Hate Radio* (New York: The Free Press, 1996), 17–19; Sermon, "On Prohibition," 25 October 1931, Folder 1/57, Charles Coughlin Papers; Letter to Reverend William M. Houlb, N.D.; *Louisville Times*, 23 September 1936, 14 December 1939 clippings; Letter to Jack J. Spaulding, N.D., Correspondence Folder, CLN Papers, ND Archives.

51. Dumenil, "'The Insatiable Maw of Bureaucracy,'" 500, 516; Kyvig, ed., *Repealing National Prohibition*; Arthur C. Lay to Herbert Hoover, 16 January 1930, Prohibition Correspondence 1930 January 16–20 file, Box 230, Presidential Series, Herbert Hoover Papers, Herbert Hoover Presidential Library; John A. Daily, "The Intemperance of Fanaticism," *Notre Dame Lawyer* 1 (April–May 1926): 185; Clarence Manion, "What Price Prohibition?" *Notre Dame Lawyer* 2 (January 1927): 88; Clarence J. Rudy, "Hypocrisy—A By-product of Paternalism," *Notre Dame Lawyer* 4 (March 1929): 374; Forrest Revere Black, "The 'Right of Castle' and Prohibition Enforcement," *Notre Dame Lawyer* 5 (February 1930): 249–254. To some degree, Catholic drys, as a part of the broader trend of Americanization, had been on shaky ground since 1899 when Pope Leo XIII issued his *Testem Benevolentiae Nostrae*, which condemned "Americanism" and came within the context of the papacy's temporal power within Italy. See Peter R. D'Agostino, *Rome in America: Transnational Catholic Ideology from the Risorgimento to Fascism* (Chapel Hill: University of North Carolina Press, 2004).

6 | *Dangerous Friends*

1. Eric S. Jacobson, "Silent Observer or Silent Partner: Methodism and the Texas Ku Klux Klan, 1921–1925," *Methodist History* 31 (January 1993): 104–112.

2. John Moffatt Mecklin, *The Ku Klux Klan: A Study of the American Mind* (New York: Harcourt, Brace and Company, 1924); John Higham, "The Mind

of a Nativist: Henry F. Bowers and the A.P.A.," *American Quarterly* 4 (Spring 1952): 16; Frank Bohn, "The Ku Klux Klan Interpreted," *American Journal of Sociology* 30 (January 1925): 385, 391; H.L. Mencken, *A Carnival of Buncomb* (Baltimore: The Johns Hopkins University Press, 1956); *The Nation*, 27 July 1927, 81–82, 24 August 1927, 177–178, 5 October 1927, 332–333. Budenz was from Indianapolis and was a Catholic before becoming a Communist (and later an anti-Communist). He was, in other words, hardly the most objective observer of the IASL and Klan. See Louis Francis Budenz, *This Is My Story* (New York: McGraw-Hill Company, 1947), 3–8, 15–16, 27, 38; Moloney, *American Catholic Lay Groups and Transatlantic Social Reform in the Progressive Era*, 137–138; Allitt, *Catholic Converts*, 323–324.

3. Shawn Lay, ed., *The Invisible Empire in the West: Toward a New Historical Appraisal of the Ku Klux Klan of the 1920s* (Chicago: University of Illinois Press, 1992), 7; David A. Horowitz, ed., *Inside the Klavern: The Secret History of a Ku Klux Klan of the 1920s* (Carbondale: Southern Illinois University Press, 1999), 134, 150; Nancy MacLean, *Behind the Mask of Chivalry: The Making of the Second Ku Klux Klan* (New York: Oxford University Press, 1994), 5–12; Shawn Lay, *War, Revolution, and the Ku Klux Klan: A Study of Intolerance in a Border City* (El Paso: Texas Western Press, 1985); William D. Jenkins, *Steel Valley Klan: The Ku Klux Klan in Ohio's Mahoning Valley* (Kent, OH: Kent State University Press, 1990); Shawn Lay, *Hooded Knights on the Niagara: The Ku Klux Klan in Buffalo, New York* (New York: New York University Press, 1995), 20, 25, 68, 146; Glenn Feldman, *Politics, Society, and the Klan in Alabama, 1915–1949* (Tuscaloosa: University of Alabama Press, 1999), 29, 37, 42, 60, 93, 101–105, 133; *Greencastle Banner*, 17 July 1879.

4. Frederick A. Norwood, *History of the North Indiana Conference: North Indiana Methodism in the Twentieth Century, 1917–1956* (Winona Lake, IN: Light and Life Press, 1957), 52; Bulletin, 11 November 1917, Bulletins 1871–1922 book, MSUMC Archives; *Indianapolis News*, 12 December 1917; *Evansville Journal*, 28 March 1915; *Noblesville Daily Ledger*, 23 July, 26 November 1917, 8 January 1918; Harold Feightner, Oral History Project, Indiana Division, Indiana State Library, 1968, 8.

5. Leonard J. Moore, *Citizen Klansmen: The Ku Klux Klan in Indiana, 1921–1928* (Chapel Hill: University of North Carolina Press, 1991); Madison, *Indiana through Tradition and Change*, 3, 14; *Noblesville Daily Ledger*, 5 October, 24 October, 3 November, 4 November 1922.

6. M. William Lutholtz, *Grand Dragon: D. C. Stephenson and the Ku Klux Klan in Indiana* (West Lafayette, IN: Purdue University Press, 1993); Jenkins, *Steel Valley Klan*, 10–15; Wyn Craig Wade, *The Fiery Cross: The Ku Klux Klan in America* (New York: Touchstone Book, 1987), 215–232; Deposition of Hugh F. Emmons, 20 February 1928, *Indiana v. The Knights of the Ku Klux Klan*; *Fiery*

Cross, 16 May, 8 August 1924; John and Joann Randall, Conner Prairie Rural History Project RHP 165, 7 December 2000; MacLean, *Behind the Mask of Chivalry*, 54–63. Hamilton County's chapters, for example, included ministers, store clerks, power and water company employees, printers, merchants, grocers, firemen, mechanics, railroad employees, photographers, barbers, telephone company and post office employees, plumbers, and farmers. See Joe H. Burgess, Hamilton County Historian Transcribed Klan Lists, Hamilton County Historical Society, Noblesville, Indiana.

7. Bulletins, 5 December 1920, 2 January, 9 January, 13 February, 27 March, 10 April, 17 July 1921, 2 April 1922, Bulletins 1871–1922 book, Bulletin, 18 November 1923, Bulletins 1923–1926 book, MSUMC Archives; *Terre Haute Tribune*, 19 February 1908; *Fort Wayne Journal Gazette*, 15 November, 18 November 1907, 7 April 1908; *South Bend Tribune*, 7 March 1908; *Rochester Republican*, 14 April 1904; *Bedford Daily Mail*, 28 January, 29 January, 30 January, 31 January, 1 February, 3 February, 4 February, 7 February, 20 February, 21 February, 28 February 1908; *Noblesville Daily Ledger*, 7 November 1919, 24 December, 27 December, 28 December, 31 December 1920; Meeting, 30 January 1920, Board of Directors Meeting Minutes, Folder 8 (1920), Box 1, Indianapolis Rotary Club Collection, Indiana Historical Society, Indianapolis, Indiana; *Western Christian Advocate*, 14 July 1880; "The Dynamo," 25 June 1920, 25 February 1921, Central Avenue Methodist Episcopal Church file, Archives of the Polis Center, IUPUI; Philip D. Jordan, "Immigrants, Methodists, and a 'Conservative Social Gospel,' 1865–1908," *Methodist History* 17 (October 1978): 16–43.

8. Bulletins, 11 April, 25 April 1920, First Baptist Bulletins, 1920–1922, Archives of First Baptist Church, Indianapolis.

9. "Law Observance and Enforcement," N.D.; "The Constitution and Prohibition," 3–9 August 1925; Rev. Edward S. Shumaker to Wayne Wheeler, 15 May 1925, Box 2, ESS Papers.

10. *Noblesville Daily Ledger*, 8 March 1926.

11. *Baptist Observer*, 22 February, 28 March, 1 August, 5 September, 19 December 1912, 6 August, 17 December 1914.

12. Deposition of Hugh F. Emmons, 20 February 1928, *Indiana v. The Knights of the Ku Klux Klan*; Bertrand M. Tipple, *Alien Rome* (Washington, DC: The Protestant Guards, 1924). Tipple was a Methodist minister who had served in Rome.

13. "The Dynamo," 13 June 1924.

14. *Fiery Cross*, 8 December 1922.

15. Robert E. Burns, *Being Catholic, Being American: The Notre Dame Story, 1842–1934* (Notre Dame, IN: University of Notre Dame Press, 1999), 267–269; *Indiana Catholic and Record*, 21 April 1922; Michael Newton, *The Invisible Em-*

pire: The Ku Klux Klan in Florida (Gainesville: University Press of Florida, 2001), 37–38, 57–68.

16. Burns, *Being Catholic, Being American,* 262, 310–322, 335–336; Todd Tucker, *Notre Dame vs. the Klan: How the Fighting Irish Defeated the Ku Klux Klan* (Chicago: Loyola Press, 2004); Margaret Wolfer, *Commemorating the 75th Anniversary of St. Ann's Church, Indianapolis, Indiana, 1917–1992* (Indianapolis: St. Ann's Catholic Church, 1992), 15; Flynt, *Alabama Baptists,* 358.

17. *Fiery Cross,* 25 May 1923; *Marion Chronicle,* 31 October 1924; *Noblesville Daily Ledger,* 8 February 1927; Emma Lou Thornbrough, "Segregation in Indiana during the Klan Era of the 1920s," 594–618; Thornbrough, *Indiana Blacks in the Twentieth Century,* 48–60; Neil Betten and Raymond A. Mohl, "The Evolution of Racism in an Industrial City, 1906–1940: A Case Study of Gary, Indiana," *Journal of Negro History* 59 (January 1974): 53.

18. *Wabash Daily Plain Dealer,* 2 November 1908; *Anderson Herald,* 10 November 1928; *Noblesville Daily Ledger,* February (daily coverage), 30 September 1922, 8 January, 11 January, 17 January, 3 February, 5 February, 7 February, 8 February, 9 February, 19 February, 26 February, 19 May, 22 June, 14 July 1923, 7 March 1924, 2 February 1927, 19 November 1938; *Fiery Cross,* 2 February, 16 February, 16 March 1923. For an account of a revival lead by Barr, see *Liberty Herald,* 5 January, 12 January, 19 January, 26 January 1917.

19. John F. Cady, *The Origin and Development of the Missionary Baptist Church in Indiana* (Berne, IN: Berne Witness Company, 1942), 294–295; Deborah Ballee Markisohn, "Ministers of the Klan: Indianapolis Clergy Involvement with the 1920s Ku Klux Klan" (M.A. thesis, Indiana University, 1992); Detzler, *The History of the Northwest Indiana Conference of the Methodist Church,* 127–128; Norwood, *History of the North Indiana Conference,* 98, 203; John Baughman, "United Methodism in Indiana: Address to the South Indiana Conference United Methodist Historical Society," 27 April 1996, pamphlet, 18; E. Carver McGriff, *Amazing Grace: A History of Indiana Methodism, 1801–2001* (Franklin, TN: Providence House Publishers, 2001), 76–77; McAllister and Tucker, *Journey in Faith,* 356–358.

20. *Hamilton County Ledger,* 11 September 1906; *Noblesville Daily Ledger,* 24 September 1921; Clawson, *Constructing Brotherhood,* 258.

21. *Noblesville Daily Ledger,* 16 January 1923, 19 March, 31 March 1925.

22. *Goshen Daily Democrat,* 5 January, 8 January 1917; *Bloomfield News,* 15 February 1917; *Liberty Herald,* 2 February 1917; *Crawfordsville Journal,* 24 January 1917; *Anderson Herald,* 1 February 1917; *Lafayette Journal,* 16 January 1917; *Noblesville Daily Ledger,* 20 January 1917, 2 January, 23 January, 24 January, 26 January, 29 January, 9 February 1923, 14 January, 24 April, 2 August, 4 August 1924; *Fiery Cross,* 14 December 1923, 15 January, 14 March 1924. The movie *The Traitor Within* was produced and distributed by Cavalier

Motion Picture Company, and "produced for, owned, and controlled by Protestants."

23. *Noblesville Daily Ledger*, 26 March, 30 June, 2 July 1923; *Fiery Cross*, 9 February, 6 April, 31 August 1923, 25 January, 22 August 1924; Lois Kaiser Costomiris, *Rail Fences, Rolling Pins, and Rainbows: Hamilton County Bygone Days* (Indianapolis: Guild Press of Indiana, 1994), 183; Denzel Hufford, Conner Prairie Rural History Project RHP 112, 19 February 2000; Fannie B. Glover, Conner Prairie Rural History Project RHP 123, 16 May 2000.

24. Stanley Coben, *Rebellion against Victorianism: The Impetus for Cultural Change in 1920s America* (New York: Oxford University Press, 1991), 27, 136, 146–147; MacLean, *Behind the Mask of Chivalry*, 110; Clark, *Deliver Us from Evil*, 83; Grace, *Carry A. Nation*, 165; Timothy J. Gilfoyle, "The Moral Origins of Political Surveillance: The Preventive Society in New York City, 1867–1918," *American Quarterly* 38 (Autumn, 1986): 639–640; *Noblesville Independent*, 8 May 1880, 10 February 1882; *Hamilton County Ledger*, 17 August, 24 August 1900; *South Bend Tribune*, 29 April 1903, 2 June 1904; *Indiana Daily Student*, 10 February 1908; *Rochester Republican*, 1 June 1911.

25. *Goshen Democrat*, 17 December 1907; *Peru Evening Journal*, 5 October 1908; *Columbus Evening Republican*, 5 October 1908; *Rochester Sentinel*, 3 September 1921; *Noblesville Daily Ledger*, 30 July, 20 September 1921; *Fort Wayne Journal Gazette*, 14 November 1925; Kenneth T. Jackson, *The Ku Klux Klan in the City, 1915–1930* (Chicago: Ivan R. Dee, 1992), 146–147; MacLean, *Behind the Mask of Chivalry*, 170–171; "Constitution and Bylaws of Guilford Detective Association (1897)" and D. C. Stephenson to Robert K. Eby, 9 February 1924, Correspondence and Records January 1924–April 1924, Folder 3, Box 1, D.C. Stephenson Papers, Indiana Historical Society, Indianapolis, Indiana.

26. David M. Chalmers, *Hooded Americanism: The History of the Ku Klux Klan* (Durham, NC: Duke University Press, 1987), 166; Deposition of Hugh F. Emmons, 20 February 1928, *Indiana v. The Knights of the Ku Klux Klan*; *Fiery Cross*, 16 March, 30 March 1923. For an account of what could happen when the HTDA and the Klan followed the IASL into a community, see coverage in the *Daily Clintonian* from January 1923 for events in Vermillion County.

27. *Fort Wayne Journal Gazette*, 30 August 1923. In another incident, the HTDA was sued for $50,000 by a Mishawaka couple whose home was raided by the group and which caused the wife to miscarry. See *South Bend Tribune*, 8 November 1925; *Cummins v. State*, 89 Ind. App. 256; 166 N.E. 155 (1929).

28. *Rochester Sentinel*, 26 May 1923; *Indianapolis Star*, 5 July 1923; *Fiery Cross*, 8 December 1922, 5 October 1923; Hiram Wesley Evans to D.C. Stephenson, 2 August 1923, Correspondence and Records, August 1923–December 1923, Folder 2, Box 1, D.C. Stephenson Papers, Indiana Historical Society. Leonard J. Moore's findings put active Klan membership in 1925 at about 166,000 men

and do not include the women's or children's auxiliaries. As Moore points out, whether one accepts his numbers as too low, or the Klan's promotional estimates as too high, the Klan was obviously attracting large numbers of Hoosiers. See Moore, *Citizen Klansmen*, 46–52.

29. *Indianapolis Star*, 17 February, 14 October, 25 October, 4 November 1922; *Fiery Cross*, 7 March 1924.

30. Dean Albertson, *Roosevelt's Farmer: Claude R. Wickard in the New Deal* (New York: Columbia University Press, 1961), 40; Harold Feightner, Oral History Project, Indiana Division, Indiana State Library, 1968, 18; Walsh, *The Sesquicentennial History of the Indiana General Assembly*, 406.

31. *Indiana Catholic and Record*, 8 December 1922; Letter from Thomas R. Marshall, 26 June 1923, Folder 6/34, Governor's File: Thomas R. Marshall, Series 2, John W. Cavanaugh Papers, Archives of the University of Notre Dame, Notre Dame, Indiana; Marshall, *Recollections of Thomas R. Marshall*, 59. Marshall was worried enough about his supposed endorsement to write Notre Dame's former president John W. Cavanaugh, promising that "you are no more opposed to the KKK than I am." Marshall denounced the Klan in his memoirs.

32. *Indianapolis Times*, 31 March 1923; *Indiana Catholic and Record*, 6 April 1923; *Indianapolis Star*, 8 May, 9 May, 10 May, 11 May, 12 May, 13 May, 14 May, 15 May 1924; *Fort Wayne Journal Gazette*, 22 October 1924; Ralph Bradford to James P. Goodrich, 7 October 1926, Indiana Politics Correspondence 1921–1934 file, Box 12; Harry S. New to James P. Goodrich, 10 November 1926, Harry S. New 1911–1928 file, Box 13, James P. Goodrich Papers, Herbert Hoover Presidential Library; Madison, *Indiana through Tradition and Change*, 33; Burns, *Being Catholic, Being American*, 423.

33. *Indianapolis Times*, 1 October, 15 October, 27 October 1923, 25 July, 1 August 1927; *Madison Courier*, 2 October, 10 October, 20 October 1923; *Indianapolis Star*, 24 April, 25 April, 27 April, 30 April, 1 May, 2 May 1924; *Noblesville Daily Ledger*, 25 February, 29 April, 30 April 1924; *Terre Haute Tribune*, 1 May 1924; *Evansville Journal*, 27 April 1924; *South Bend Tribune*, 1 November 1923; *Indiana Catholic and Record*, 16 September 1927; William P. Evans, Oral History Project, Indiana Division, Indiana State Library, 1969, 21–23; Harold Feightner, Oral History Project, Indiana Division, Indiana State Library, 1968, 78; Warren T. McCray to Charles L. Harper, 24 November 1923, November 1923–1925, Folder 1, Warren T. McCray Collection, Indiana Historical Society. There is some precedent for believing that McCray's troubles were caused by the Klan, as is shown in the impeachment of Oklahoma's governor because of his opposition to the organization. Goodrich and Taggart tried to help McCray, but his troubles were too much for the old politicians to handle behind the scenes.

34. Edward S. Shumaker to F. Scott McBride, 9 May 1924, Reel 8, F. Scott McBride Papers, Temperance and Prohibition Papers; *Frankfort Evening News*, 22 October 1924; *Greenfield Daily Reporter*, 30 October 1924; *Goshen Daily Democrat*, 1 November, 4 November 1924; *Oxford Gazette*, 11 April, 12 September 1924; *Indiana Daily Student*, 1 November, 6 November 1924.

35. *Indianapolis Star*, 17 January, 4 May, 6 May, 7 May, 10 May, 12 May 1924; *Indianapolis News*, 3 May, 5 May, 6 May 1924; *Fiery Cross*, 29 June, 24 August, 31 August, 9 November 1923, 25 April, 25 July 1924; *South Bend Tribune*, 16 October 1924; *Fort Wayne Journal Gazette*, 23 October 1924; *Rochester Sentinel*, 29 October 1924; *Indiana Catholic and Record*, 31 October 1924; *Lebanon Pioneer*, 8 May 1924; *The Nation*, 21 November 1923, page 570; D. C. Stephenson to Ed Jackson, 17 January 1925, Correspondence and Records January 1925–March 1925, Folder 7, Box 1, D. C. Stephenson Papers, Indiana Historical Society. McCulloch's father was the Social Gospel minister Oscar Carleton McCulloch of Indianapolis's Plymouth Congregational Church. See Genevieve C. Weeks, *Oscar Carleton McCulloch, 1843–1891: Preacher and Practitioner of Applied Christianity* (Indianapolis: Indiana Historical Society, 1976).

36. *Indianapolis Star*, 22 May 1924; *Indianapolis News*, 2 June 1924; *Noblesville Daily Ledger*, 5 June 1924; *Indiana Catholic and Record*, 27 June, 4 July 1924; D. C. Stephenson to David M. Hoover, 7 March 1925, Hoover to Stephenson, 10 March 1925, Folder 18, Box 181, Harold Feightner papers in the Roger D. Branigin Papers, The B. F. Hamilton Library, Franklin College, Franklin, Indiana.

37. *Lafayette Journal and Courier*, 1 November 1924; *Indianapolis Star*, 5 November 1924; *Anderson Daily Bulletin*, 5 November 1924; *Lake County Times*, 5 November 1924; *Warsaw Daily Union*, 6 November 1924; *Jeffersonville Evening News*, 6 November 1924, 4 November 1925; *Columbus Evening Republican*, 1 November 1924.

38. John Bodnar, *Remaking America: Public Memory, Commemoration, and Patriotism in the Twentieth Century* (Princeton, NJ: Princeton University Press, 1992), 78–88; Endelman, *The Jewish Community of Indianapolis*, 121; Burns, *Being Catholic, Being American*, 295, 298–299; *Indianapolis Times*, 19 March, 27 March, 13 April 1923; *Indianapolis News*, 17 March 1923; *Indianapolis Star*, 11 July 1923; *Columbus Evening Republican*, 27 July 1921, 6 November 1924; *South Bend Tribune*, 25 March 1923; *Evansville Journal*, 28 April 1924. The Johnson-Reed Immigration Act of 1924, which set a 2-percent quota on immigrants from Southern and Eastern Europe based on the 1890 Census, also helped to quiet the fears of native-born Americans that they were going to be overwhelmed by hordes of foreigners.

39. *Indianapolis Star*, 6 July 1923; *Noblesville Daily Ledger*, 18 October, 19 October 1923; *Indiana Catholic and Record*, 12 January 1923; Executive

Committee, 5 February 1923, 1920–1925 Folder 4; 4 October 1927, 1925–1927 Folder 5; 6 March 1928, 1928–1929 Folder 6, Box 1, Indianapolis Church Federation Executive Committee Minutes, Indiana Historical Society. The Church Federation's position on the Klan is interesting because, by October 1927, the Reverend G. L. K. Smith was chairman of the Public Morals Committee. Under his leadership the committee took an aggressive stance in defending the dry status quo, arguing that members should observe the law and fight wet politicians.

40. George S. Turnbull, *An Oregon Crusader* (Portland, OR: Binfords and Mort Publishers, 1955), 63–169; *Indianapolis Times*, 1 November, 5 November 1924; *Fiery Cross*, 31 October, 14 November 1924.

41. Robert Moats Miller, "A Note on the Relationship between the Protestant Churches and the Revived Ku Klux Klan," *Journal of Southern History* 22 (August 1956): 355–368.

42. E. F. Jones to F. Scott McBride, 19 November 1924, Reel 4, F. Scott McBride Papers; William H. Anderson to E. H. Cherrington, 10 September 1925; Anderson to Patrick H. Callahan, 23 November 1927; Anderson to Callahan, 8 November 1927, Reel 76, Ernest H. Cherrington Papers, Temperance and Prohibition Papers.

43. Markisohn, "Ministers of the Klan"; Feightner, Oral History, 7, 133; Walsh, *The Sesquicentennial History of the Indiana General Assembly*, 369; Leibowitz, *My Indiana*, 182, 208–209; Bohn, "The Ku Klux Klan Interpreted," 399.

44. Dwight W. Hoover, "Daisy Douglas Barr: From Quaker to Klan 'Kluckeress,'" *Indiana Magazine of History* 87 (June 1991): 171–195; Wade, *The Fiery Cross*, 171–174; "The Klan in Action 1925: Instructions for Exalted Cyclops: Standard Plan for the Organization and Operation of Klans in Pennsylvania," Ku Klux Klan (Pennsylvania) Folder 2, Ku Klux Klan Papers, Indiana Historical Society, Indianapolis, Indiana; *Fiery Cross*, 5 September 1924; *American Issue: Indiana Edition*, 30 April 1927.

45. Deposition of Hugh F. Emmons, 20 February 1928; Deposition of D. C. Stephenson, 15 October 1928, *Indiana v. The Knights of the Ku Klux Klan*. As we will see, however, this meeting is supposed to have taken place at the same time that the national ASL's F. Scott McBride was observing Shumaker's field day firsthand.

46. Shumaker to McBride, 25 July 1924, Reel 8, F. Scott McBride Papers, Temperance and Prohibition Papers.

47. *Indianapolis Times*, 3 May, 4 May 1928.

48. Kathleen M. Blee, *Women of the Klan: Racism and Gender in the 1920s* (Los Angeles: University of California Press, 1991), 103–104; Pegram, *Battling Demon Rum*, 171.

49. Braeman, *Albert J. Beveridge*, 270–288; Claude G. Bowers, *Beveridge and the Progressive Era* (New York: The Literacy Guild, 1932), 581–582; Shumaker to Albert J. Beveridge, 10 November, 4 December 1919, Folder S, Box 218, Shumaker to Beveridge, 13 January, 13 February, 26 February, 4 May, 12 May 1920, Beveridge to Shumaker, 16 January, 16 February 1920, Folder S, Box 224, Shumaker to Beveridge, 2 March, 8 April, 3 May, 27 May, 19 September, 6 October, 12 October, 24 October 1922, Beveridge to Shumaker, 25 September, 9 October, 22 November 1922, Folder SH, Box 239, Albert J. Beveridge Papers, Library of Congress. For an example of Beveridge's response to a questioning dry letter, see Beveridge to R. D. Goble, 6 April 1922, Folder GO, Box 234, Albert J. Beveridge Papers, Library of Congress.

50. Leibowitz, *My Indiana*, 182; Flynn, ed., *The Indianapolis Area of the Methodist Episcopal Church*, 16.

51. *Indiana Catholic and Record*, 13 March 1925; *Goshen Daily Democrat*, 10 November 1924; *Indianapolis Star*, 19 October 1926, 1 May 1928; *Indianapolis News*, 2 November, 3 November 1928; Burns, *Being Catholic, Being American*, 382.

52. Indictment, 16 April 1925; Autopsy Report, 21 April 1925, Criminal Proceedings (Oberholtzer) April 16 1925–April 23 1925, Folder 13, Box 1, D. C. Stephenson Papers, Indiana Historical Society; Bob Gilkey, Conner Prairie Rural History Project RHP 172, 12 February 2001.

53. *Indianapolis News*, 12 October, 3 November 1925; *Indianapolis Star*, 29 October, 13 November, 14 November 1925; *Madison Courier*, 12 October 1925; *Noblesville Daily Ledger*, May, June, July, August, September, October, November 1925; Feightner, Oral History, 38; *Frankfort Morning Times*, 30 October, 3 November, 6 November, 13 November 1925; *Greenfield Republican*, 5 November 1925; *Tipton Daily Tribune*, 13 November 1925; *Greenfield Daily Reporter*, 7 November 1925; *Vincennes Commercial*, 14 November 1925; *Indianapolis Times*, 16 October, 13 November 1925; *Sheridan News*, 30 March 1928. Stephenson's lawyers included Floyd Christian and Ralph Waltz, both of whom were Klan members. Christian was the nephew of former Hamilton County judge Ira Christian. See Joe H. Burgess, Hamilton County Historian Transcribed Klan Lists, Hamilton County Historical Society. It should be noted that though the Indiana Supreme Court consistently kept Stephenson in jail, not even they believed the state's story in full when it came to the cause of Oberholtzer's death. See *Stephenson v. State*, 205 Ind. 141; 179 N.E. 633 (1932).

54. *Indianapolis News*, 14 November 1925; *Indianapolis Star*, 6 October, 16 November 1925; *Anderson Daily Bulletin*, 14 November, 16 November 1925; *Greenfield Daily Reporter*, 16 November 1925; *Evansville Journal*, 15 November 1925; *Fort Wayne Journal Gazette*, 16 November 1925; *South Bend Tribune*, 16 November 1925; *Indianapolis Times*, 16 November 1925; *Kokomo Daily Tri-*

bune, 16 November 1925. Four years later, the presiding judge of the Stephenson case, Will Sparks, was elevated to the Seventh Circuit Federal Court. See *Madison Courier*, 19 October 1929.

55. *Noblesville Daily Ledger*, 4 June, 17 July, 18 July, 1 August, 7 August, 8 August, 10 August, 19 August, 22 August 1925, 24 March 1926; *South Bend Tribune*, 1 November, 5 November 1925; *Madison Courier*, 16 November 1925; *Marion Chronicle*, 31 October 1925; Feightner, Oral History, 40.

56. Feldman, *Politics, Society and the Klan in Alabama*, 7, 159; *Noblesville Daily Ledger*, 30 July 1921, 21 November, 25 November 1922, 14 May 1924; *Evansville Journal*, 11 November 1923; *South Bend Tribune*, 10 November 1923; *Vincennes Commercial*, 13 August 1927; *Indiana Catholic and Record*, 24 June 1921.

57. D.C. Stephenson to H.W. Evans, 12 October 1923, Correspondence and Records August 1923–December 1923, Folder 2, D.C. Stephenson to Dr. C.L. Clawson, 10 March 1924, Correspondence and Records January 1924–April 1924, Folder 3, D.C. Stephenson to Roy V. West, 9 August and 28 August 1924, Correspondence and Records May 1924–August 1924, Folder 4, Box 1, D.C. Stephenson Papers, Indiana Historical Society; *Indianapolis Times*, 7 March 1924, 2 April 1928, 9 April 1965; Wade, *The Fiery Cross*, 233–235; Chalmers, *Hooded Americanism*, 168–169; *Noblesville Daily Ledger*, 20 December 1928, 22 May 1931; *Stephenson v. Daly*, 200 Ind. 196; 158 N.E. 289 (1927); *Stephenson v. State*, 205 Ind. 141; 186 N.E. 293 (1933).

58. Bob Gilkey, Conner Prairie Rural History Project RHP 180, 6 April 2001; *Madison Courier*, 24 October 1924; Deposition of Hugh F. Emmons, 20 February 1928, *Indiana v. The Knights of the Ku Klux Klan*.

59. *Ninety–Sixth Session of the Indiana Annual Conference of the Methodist Episcopal Church*, 1927; *Lebanon Daily Reporter*, 23 October, 4 November 1925; *Indianapolis Star*, 27 March, 21 October, 26 October 1926; *Evansville Journal*, 15 November 1925; *Noblesville Daily Ledger*, 22 January, 4 March 1926; *Lebanon Daily Reporter*, 14 November 1925; *Lebanon Reporter*, 15 August 1927; Deposition of Hugh F. Emmons, 20 February 1928, *Indiana v. The Knights of the Ku Klux Klan*.

60. *Indianapolis Star*, 23 February 1927; *Indianapolis News*, 4 January 1928; *Indiana Catholic and Record*, 2 September 1927, 6 January 1928; *Noblesville Daily Ledger*, 24 July 1930.

61. Leibowitz, *My Indiana*, 211; Paul L. Murphy, "Sources and Nature of Intolerance in the 1920s," *Journal of American History* 51 (June 1964): 68; Allen Safianow, "The Klan Comes to Tipton," *Indiana Magazine of History* 95 (September 1999): 202–231; Lay, *The Invisible Empire in the West*, 217; Newton, *The Invisible Empire*, 72–73, 86–87; *Marion Chronicle*, 17 August 1927; *Noblesville Daily Ledger*, 27 March, 17 April 1930, 5 October 1933.

62. Denzel Hufford, Conner Prairie Rural History Project RHP 112, 19 February 2000; Robert S. Lynd and Helen Merrell Lynd, *Middletown: A Study in American Culture* (New York: A Harvest Book, 1957), 332–335; Jenkins, *Steel Valley Klan*, 165; *Indiana Catholic and Record*, 4 November 1927; Kerr, *Organized for Prohibition*, 230–231.

7 | Trials and Tribulations

1. Clark, *Deliver Us from Evil*, 140; McNeil, *Valiant for Truth*, xi. Meridian Street Methodist Church in Indianapolis and St. Paul's Memorial Methodist Church in South Bend were representative of Hoosier Methodism's continued support of the IASL and the dry cause. See Board Meeting, 11 January 1927, Archives of St. Paul's Memorial United Methodist Church, South Bend, Indiana; Bulletins 1871–1922 book; Bulletins 1923–1926 book; Bulletins 1927–1929 book; Bulletins 1930–1932 book; Official Board Meeting, 7 February 1924, Minutes and Board Meetings, 1904–1935 book, MSUMC Archives.

2. *Indianapolis News*, 12 September 1925; Edward S. Shumaker to F. Scott McBride, 16 September 1925, Reel 8, F. Scott McBride Papers, Temperance and Prohibition Papers; James J. Flink, *The Automobile Age* (Cambridge, MA: The MIT Press, 1993); Lewis S. Bowman et al., eds., *Indiana 1926* (Indianapolis: William B. Burford, 1926), 42; Behr, *Prohibition*, 162, 167, 241; *Terre Haute Tribune*, 3 February 1923; *Indianapolis Times*, 14 March, 19 March, 24 March, 29 March, 31 March 1923; *Gary Evening Post*, 1 February 1923; *Rochester Sentinel*, 15 March 1923; *Marion Chronicle*, 17 March 1923; *Pike County Democrat*, 27 March 1925; Howard H. Peckham, *Indiana: A History* (Chicago: University of Illinois Press, 2003), 121. As Peckham points out, the mayor was released from jail in 1925 and reelected to his old job in 1929. The majority of Hoosiers, Peckham believes, saw Gary as "atypical, an exotic region somehow not part of the state."

3. *Noblesville Daily Ledger*, 28 October 1927, 18 September 1928; *Meno v. State*, 197 Ind. 16, Supreme Court of Indiana, May 1925; *Lafayette Journal and Courier*, 11 November 1924; Wayne and Helen Musselman, Conner Prairie Rural History Project RHP 129, 1 June 2000.

4. Bulletins, 16 December 1923, 6 April 1924, 25 October 1925, Bulletins 1923–1926 book, Bulletins, 16 January, 23 January, 19 June 1927, Bulletins 1927–1929 book, Bulletins, 23 February, 11 May, 18 May 1930, Bulletins 1930–1932 book, MSUMC Archives; *Indiana Daily Student*, 3 October 1925; *Ninety-Fifth Session of the Indiana Annual Conference of the Methodist Episcopal Church*, 1926; *The Nation*, 24 March 1926, 306; Cleveland State University Library, "Cleveland: Confused City on a Seesaw by Philip W. Porter," http://

web.ulib.csuohio.edu/SpecColl/porter/index.html, 1 August 2002. This is an e-book version of Porter's work; in the original 1976 book, see pages 111–113.

5. D. L. McBride to Herbert Hoover, 6 September 1932, Prohibition Enforcement 1932–1933 and Undated file, Box 237, Presidential Series, Herbert Hoover Papers, Herbert Hoover Presidential Library; Sanchez, "The Feminine Side of Bootlegging," 432; Walsh, *The Sesquicentennial History of the Indiana General Assembly,* 422; Madison, *Indiana through Tradition and Change,* 41.

6. *Indianapolis Times,* 16 September 1926; Rev. Edward S. Shumaker to Gov. Edward Jackson, 14 November 1925, Correspondence Shields-Shunk folder, Box 8, Jackson Papers, Indiana State Archives.

7. *Shacklett v. State,* 197 Ind. 323 (1925).

8. *Indianapolis Times,* 20 April 1923, 28 February 1925; *North Vernon Sun,* 27 August 1925; *Indiana Catholic and Record,* 6 March 1925; *Garrett Weekly Clipper,* 5 January 1925; *Indianapolis News,* 17 January, 27 January, 2 February 1925; *Indianapolis Star,* 3 February, 14 February, 18 February, 24 February, 26 February, 28 February, 3 March, 5 March 1925; *Adams County (Berne) Witness,* 18 February, 9 March 1925; *Journal of the House of Representatives of the State of Indiana During the 74th Session of the General Assembly* (Indianapolis: William B. Burford, 1925), 182–183; 2 October 1925 entry, 1925 Notebook, Reel 1, Frank M. Robinson Papers, W. O. Holman Notes and Records, Indiana Division, Indiana State Library, Indianapolis, Indiana. The later charge that the bill passed only because of the Klan's domination of the Republican Party is incorrect. To the extent that the Klan did support the bill, it did so because the sentiment for it already existed.

9. Edward S. Shumaker to F. Scott McBride, 6 October 1925, Reel 8, F. Scott McBride Papers, Temperance and Prohibition Papers; Engelmann, *Intemperance,* 78–81, 149; Morone, *Hellfire Nation,* 320–323; *Richmond Item,* 10 November 1925; *Adams County (Berne) Witness,* 11 November 1925; Catherine Gilbert Murdock, *Domesticating Drink: Women, Men, and Alcohol in America, 1870–1940* (Baltimore: Johns Hopkins University Press, 1998), 36.

10. Shumaker to McBride, 24 October 1924, 8 January, 18 May, 9 September, 14 December 1925, 8 January 1926, Shumaker to Thomas Nicholson, 6 April 1925, Reel 8, F. Scott McBride Papers, Temperance and Prohibition Papers; "The Spirit of the World League against Alcoholism" pamphlet, Digital collections @ Brown University, 21 February 2005.

11. Shumaker to McBride, 9 May, 2 July, 26 August, 2 September 1924, Reel 8; F. Scott McBride Report to the ASL Executive Committee, 4 June 1925, McBride to Shumaker, 26 January, 27 January 1926, Reel 14, F. Scott McBride Papers, Temperance and Prohibition Papers; *Indianapolis News,* 11 March 1926.

12. *Garrett Weekly Clipper,* 19 January 1925; *South Bend Tribune,* 3 May 1928; *Jeffersonville Evening News,* 4 May 1928; *Vincennes Commercial,* 19 October, 22 October, 23 October, 24 October, 25 October, 26 October, 28 October, 29 October, 30 October, 2 November 1924, 4 May 1928; *Vincennes Sun,* 24 October, 25 October, 27 October, 28 October, 29 October, 30 October, 6 November, 7 November 1924, 6 November 1929. As we will see, Adams was instrumental in routing the Klan from the state. The two Democrats whom Shumaker supported in Knox County were also members of the Klan; see Moore, *Citizen Klansmen,* 178–179.

13. *Kokomo Daily Tribune,* 6 November 1924; *Vincennes Commercial,* 1 November 1924; *Indianapolis News,* 1 November 1924; *Noblesville Daily Ledger,* 4 June 1924; *Goshen Daily Democrat,* 10 November 1924; *Lebanon Reporter,* 27 January 1925; *Richmond Evening Item,* 6 November 1924; *Indianapolis Star,* 18 November 1924; *Pulaski County Democrat,* 20 November 1924; *Rochester Sentinel,* 7 November 1924; *Warsaw Daily Union,* 6 November 1924; *Huntington Herald,* 7 November 1924.

14. *American Issue: Indiana Edition,* 10 January, 31 January, 14 February, 21 March 1925, 9 January 1926; Paul Shumaker, undated statement, in possession of author; *Indianapolis Star,* 10 January, 21 January, 29 January, 4 February, 18 February, 19 February 1925; *Indianapolis News,* 20 December 1924, 10 March 1925; *Huntington Herald,* 7 November, 15 November 1924, 10 March 1925; *Pulaski County Democrat,* 6 November 1924; *Vincennes Commercial,* 7 November, 8 November 1924; *Indianapolis Times,* 14 November 1924; 27 January and 14 February 1925, *Opinions of the Attorney General of Indiana for the Period from January 1 1925 to January 1 1927* (Indianapolis: William B. Burford, 1927). Gilliom's reasoning was later used by the state Supreme Court to bar circuit courts in individual counties from initiating recounts in statewide races in their jurisdiction alone. See *State Ex Rel. Robertson et al. v. Circuit Court of Lake County et al.,* 215 Ind. 18; 17 N.E. 2d 805 (1938).

15. Richard L. Gilliom, interview with author, 21 February 2003; *Indianapolis News,* 1 November 1924, 3 December 1928; *Berne Witness,* 23 July 1912; *Vincennes Commercial,* 14 October 1924; Clyde Walb to Arthur Gilliom, 28 May 1924, Arthur Gilliom Papers, in possession of Richard L. Gilliom, Indianapolis, Indiana; *South Bend News-Times,* 23 May 1924; *Indiana Catholic and Record,* 19 November 1926; *Madison Courier,* 28 October 1924; *South Bend Tribune,* 24 October 1924; *Goshen Daily Democrat,* 5 November 1924; *Jasper County Democrat,* 8 November 1924; *Indianapolis News,* 1 November 1924. His opponent was Harvey Harmon of Princeton, who had served as state senator from Pike and Gibson counties since 1912 and was previously a highly regarded prosecutor for Gibson and Posey counties.

16. *Adams County (Berne) Witness,* 2 November 1925; *American Issue: Indiana Edition,* 5 September 1925; Richard H. Gemmecke, Sesquicentennial

Indiana History Conference, Indiana Division, Indiana State Library, 1966, 28; Richard L. Gilliom, interview with author, 21 February 2003; Arthur L. Gilliom, "Searches and Seizures in the Administration of the Criminal Law of Indiana," *Indiana Law Journal* 1 (February 1926): 65–73.

17. Shumaker to McBride, 25 January 1926, Reel 14, F. Scott McBride Papers, Temperance and Prohibition Papers; *American Issue: Indiana Edition*, 23 January, 6 February 1926; IASL 1926 Annual Report; *Indianapolis Times*, 12 October, 15 October 1925.

18. Shumaker to Boyd P. Doty, 8 April 1925, Reel 8, F. Scott McBride Papers, Temperance and Prohibition Papers.

19. *Gary Evening Post*, 2 March 1926; *Adams County (Berne) Witness*, 24 March 1926; Arthur Gilliom to IASL Board of Trustees, 25 February 1926, Reel 14, F. Scott McBride Papers, Temperance and Prohibition Papers. The Corrupt Practices Act read: "The following persons shall be guilty of corrupt practices and shall be punished in accordance with the provisions of this act. Every person who shall, directly or indirectly, by himself or another, give or offer or promise to any person any money, gift, advantage, preferment, entertainment, aid, emoluments, or any valuable thing whatever, for the purpose of inducing or procuring any person to vote, or refrain from voting, for or against any person, or for or against any measure or proposition at any election or primary election or political convention or session of the General Assembly of the State of Indiana or either house thereof. Every person who shall be guilty of any corrupt practice as aforesaid, shall be fined not less than $300, nor more than $1,000, or be imprisoned for not more than one year, or both, and shall be ineligible to any public office or public employment for the period of four years from and after the time of the commission of such offense." Section 7671, Burns' 1926 (section 11, Acts 1911, c.121, p. 288) as quoted in *Duvall v. State*, 92 Ind. App. 134; 166 N.E. 603, (1929).

20. Gilliom to IASL Board of Trustees, 25 February 1926, Reel 14, F. Scott McBride Papers, Temperance and Prohibition Papers.

21. *Indianapolis Times*, 11 March, 21 October 1926; *Indianapolis News*, 11 March 1926; *Indianapolis Star*, 10 March, 11 March, 12 March, 22 March, 6 October 1926; *South Bend Tribune*, 1 November 1926.

22. *Indianapolis News*, 21 April 1926; *Adams County (Berne) Witness*, 23 April, 12 May, 14 May 1926. For a time, one of Shumaker's attorneys was former Indiana attorney general James Bingham.

23. Shumaker to McBride, 7 May 1926, Reel 14, F. Scott McBride Papers, Temperance and Prohibition Papers.

24. *Indianapolis Times*, 18 September 1926; Allen County Republican Party to Gilliom, 3 March 1926; Floyd J. Mattice to Gilliom, 4 March 1926; State Senator Russell B. Harrison to Gilliom, 5 March 1926; Starke County Republican Party to Gilliom, 30 April 1926; W. H. Chester to Gilliom, 30 April

1926; H.E. Negley to Gilliom, 23 April 1926; Isaac R. Strouse to Gilliom, 10 September 1926; William Daly to Gilliom, 21 September 1926; Charles P. Tighe to Gilliom, 24 September 1926; Frank A Rogers to Gilliom, 27 May 1927, Arthur Gilliom Papers, in possession of Richard L. Gilliom, Indianapolis, Indiana.

25. *Indianapolis Star*, 15 March, 17 March 1926; *American Issue: Indiana Edition*, 3 April 1926, 2 September, 17 September, 1 October 1927; *Adams County (Berne) Witness*, 20 September, 1 October, 22 October 1926; *South Bend Tribune*, 14 October 1926; *Northwest Indiana Conference of the Methodist Episcopal Church*, 1929, 222; John W.V. Smith, *The Quest for Holiness and Unity: A Centennial History of the Church of God (Anderson, Indiana)* (Anderson, IN: Warner Press, 1980), 200, 260; *Richmond Item*, 9 August 1927; *Noblesville Daily Ledger*, 16 February 1929; Shumaker to McBride, 23 September 1926, Reel 14, F. Scott McBride Papers, Temperance and Prohibition Papers; *Indianapolis Times*, 13 September 1926, 27 January, 28 January 1928.

26. *Adams County (Berne) Witness*, 9 June, 23 June, 16 July 1926; Shumaker to McBride, 16 June 1926, Reel 14, F. Scott McBride Papers, Temperance and Prohibition Papers.

27. *Indianapolis News*, 12 October 1920; *Indianapolis Star*, 13 November 1915, 4 June 1926, 10 April 1927, 29 April 1928, 13 March 1931, 1 August 1937, 16 February 1944, 13 November 1968. The members were Cassius C. Shirley, Dan Simms, Evan B. Stotesenburg, George Dix, Moses B. Lairy, and Fred C. Gause. Shirley served as special judge on the Willoughby-Denton, Shumaker, and Duvall cases.

28. *Indianapolis Star*, 26 July 1926; Shumaker to McBride, 3 July 1926, Reel 14, F. Scott McBride Papers, Temperance and Prohibition Papers.

29. Shumaker to McBride, 20 July 1926, Reel 14, F. Scott McBride Papers, Temperance and Prohibition Papers; *Indianapolis Star*, 16 July 1926; *Adams County (Berne) Witness*, 16 July 1926.

30. Shumaker to McBride, 3 July 1926, Reel 14, F. Scott McBride Papers, Temperance and Prohibition Papers; *Indianapolis Star*, 17 September, 22 November 1927; *Indianapolis Times*, 23 April, 25 April 1930; *Madison Courier*, 5 October 1927; *Indiana v. Shumaker*, Oral Evidence on Motion to Increase Penalty, 21 November 1927, pages 1–8, Box 2, ESS Papers.

31. *Marion Chronicle*, 23 October 1924; *Evansville Journal*, 6 August 1927; *Lafayette Journal and Courier*, 6 August 1927; *Indianapolis Times*, 25 July, 30 July 1927; *Dale v. State*, 198 Ind. 110; 150 N.E. 647 (1926). Dale was actually charged with two counts of contempt in the above-cited case. The first, for which he was convicted, involved the actual publishing of the article; and the second, for which he was acquitted, came about when he entered the article into evidence.

32. *American Issue: Indiana Edition*, 22 January 1927; *Indianapolis Star*, 31 July 1927; Frank C. Ball to H. W. Baldridge, 19 July 1927; Frank M. Hedges to John B. Campbell, 9 July 1927; Rev. Claude H. King to Baldridge, 26 July 1927; W. C. Belman to Campbell, 8 July 1927; H. M. Ferguson to Campbell, 18 July 1927; Gustav Schlosser to Campbell, 25 July 1927; McBride to Baldridge, 22 July 1927, Box 2, ESS Papers.

33. *Indianapolis News*, 25 May 1935, 6 January 1960, 11 March 1961; *Indianapolis Star*, 6 July 1920, 11 July 1933, 8 March 1953, 4 May 1972. Justice Myers served as the chairman of the Indiana Alcoholic Beverage Commission from 1935 to 1937. Louis B. Ewbank was on the state Supreme Court when the action against Shumaker started, but he retired before the decision was handed down.

34. *Goshen Daily Democrat*, 6 August 1927; *Bedford Daily Mail*, 6 August 1927; *Lake County Times*, 6 August 1927; *Evansville Journal*, 6 August 1927; *Indianapolis Star*, 6 August 1927; *Indianapolis Times*, 5 August, 6 August 1927; *Chicago Daily Tribune*, 17 August 1927; *Lafayette Journal and Courier*, 6 August 1927; *Muncie Evening Press*, 6 August 1927; *Vincennes Commercial*, 19 August 1927.

35. *State v. Shumaker*, 200 Ind. 623; 157 N.E. 769, (1927).

36. Ibid.

37. Recent Cases, *Harvard Law Review* 41 (1927–1928): 254–255; Recent Case Notes, *Yale Law Journal* 38 (1928–1929): 819–820; Recent Case Notes, *Indiana Law Journal* 3 (1927–1928): 149; Recent Case Notes, *Indiana Law Journal* 4 (1928–1929): 550–551; Recent Important Decisions, *Michigan Law Review* 26 (1927–1928): 440–441; Notes and Comment, *Cornell Law Quarterly* 14 (1928–1929): 484–489; Recent Cases, *Texas Law Review* 6 (1927–1928): 388–389.

38. Recent Cases, *University of Pennsylvania Law Review* 76 (1927–1928): 210–211; Recent Cases, *Illinois Law Review* 22 (1928): 768–770; Recent Decisions, *St. John's Law Review* 2 (1927): 88–89; Paul Butler, "Contempt and Executive Power to Pardon," *Notre Dame Lawyer* 4 (April 1929): 443–447.

39. *Evansville Journal*, 6 August 1927; *Jasper Herald*, 12 August 1927.

40. *Kokomo Daily Tribune*, 6 August 1927; *Lafayette Journal and Courier*, 6 August 1927; *Delphi Citizen*, 11 August 1927.

41. *Indianapolis Times*, 18 September 1926, 6 August 1927; *Evansville Journal*, 16 August, 17 August 1927; *Kokomo Daily Tribune*, 6 August 1927; *Marion Chronicle*, 5 October 1927; *Columbus Evening Republican*, 8 August 1927; *Lebanon Reporter*, 12 April 1928; *Fort Wayne Journal Gazette*, 26 January, 28 January 1929; *Richmond Item*, 27 October 1929.

42. *Indianapolis Times*, 25 July 1927.

43. *Indianapolis Star*, 19 August 1927; 1927 World League against Alcoholism Congress at Winona Lake Program, Reel 1, World League Papers,

Temperance and Prohibition Papers; *South Bend Tribune*, 17 August 1927; *Goshen Daily Democrat*, 19 August 1927; *Lafayette Journal and Courier*, 19 August 1927; *Marion Chronicle*, 19 August 1927; *Lebanon Reporter*, 19 August 1927; *Noblesville Daily Ledger*, 22 August, 25 August, 29 August 1927.

44. *Indianapolis News*, 23 May, 9 June 1927; Richard L. Gilliom, interview with author, 21 February 2003; *Indianapolis Times*, 23 May 1927; *New York Telegraph*, 24 May 1927; *New York Evening World*, 24 May, 25 May 1927; *Chicago Journal*, 25 May 1927.

45. Richard L. Gilliom, interview with author, 21 February 2003; *Indianapolis Star*, 11 June, 6 October 1927; *Oxford Gazette*, 3 June, 2 December 1927; *Madison Courier*, 23 May, 6 October, 11 October 1927; *Noblesville Daily Ledger*, 11 June 1927; *Milwaukee Journal Sentinel*, 15 January 1998.

46. *Indianapolis Times*, 22 July 1927; *American Issue: Indiana Edition*, 19 February, 5 March, 28 May, 11 June, 25 June 1927; *Indianapolis News*, 4 October 1927; Richard L. Gilliom, interview with author, 21 February 2003.

47. Edward B. Dunford to Shumaker, 9 November 1928; Shumaker to Dunford, 12 November 1928, 6 February 1929, Reel 1, Legislative and Legal Papers, Temperance and Prohibition Papers; *Fort Wayne Journal Gazette*, 28 January 1929.

48. Ernest H. Cherrington to Shumaker, 6 August 1927, Reel 92, E. H. Cherrington Papers, Temperance and Prohibition Papers; Alpheus Thomas Mason, *Harlan Fiske Stone: Pillar of the Law* (New York: Viking Press, 1956), 163, 358, 582; *Bridges v. State of California*, 62 S.Ct. 190 (1941). Chief Justice Stone had served as Attorney General during the Coolidge administration and, though he fought to uphold Prohibition, privately considered the Volstead Act and the Eighteenth Amendment mistakes. Shumaker had backers in the Federal District Court in Indianapolis, which was noted for its staunch support of Prohibition. See George W. Geib and Donald B. Kite, Sr., *Federal Justice in Indiana: The History of the United States District Court for the Southern District of Indiana* (Indianapolis: Indiana Historical Society, 2007).

49. *New York Times*, 18 September, 2 October, 22 November 1927, 21 July, 26 July 1928; *Indianapolis Star*, 22 November, 15 December 1927; *Indiana v. Shumaker*, Oral Evidence on Motion to Increase Penalty, 21 November 1927, pages 8–38, Box 2, ESS Papers.

50. *Terre Haute Tribune*, 24 May 1924; *South Bend Tribune*, 20 October, 21 October, 22 October, 28 October, 29 October 1926; *Indianapolis Times*, 22 October, 29 October 1926; "Watson Writes Shumaker: From the *South Bend Mirror*, Reprinted by the Reverend William Brandon," pamphlet, Box 2, ESS Papers.

51. Flynt, *Alabama Baptists*, 269; Clipping from *Jacksonville Journal* in McBride Papers, 2 June 1925, Reel 2, Shumaker to McBride, 7 May 1926; McBride to Shumaker, 17 July 1926, Reel 14, F. Scott McBride Papers, Tem-

perance and Prohibition Papers; *Fort Wayne Journal Gazette,* 21 July 1923; *New York Times,* 28 February 1922, 31 January, 8 April, 25 July, 9 September 1923, 21 January, 30 January, 10 February, 22 February, 30 March, 6 April 1924, 8 April, 20 October 1926.

52. *Adams County (Berne) Witness,* 28 June, 1 November 1926; *Marion Chronicle,* 6 October 1927; *Indianapolis Star,* 13 October 1927; *Cincinnati Enquirer,* 27 July 1927, 6 January 1928; *Indiana Catholic and Record,* 16 September, 30 September, 14 October 1927; South Bend Press Release, 27 March 1928, Arthur Gilliom Papers, in possession of Richard L. Gilliom, Indianapolis.

53. James P. Goodrich to Arthur R. Robinson, Arthur R. Robinson 1919–1934 file, Box 15, James P. Goodrich Papers, Herbert Hoover Presidential Library; *Indianapolis Star,* 15 October, 18 October, 19 October, 20 October 1925, 17 September 1927; *American Issue: Indiana Edition,* 31 October 1925; *Indianapolis Times,* 15 October, 24 October 1925, 22 October 1926; *Muncie Evening Press,* 15 October 1925; *Lake County Times,* 21 October 1925; *Richmond Item,* 21 October 1925; *Noblesville Daily Ledger,* 7 April 1927; *Fort Wayne Journal Gazette,* 1 May 1928; *Berne Witness,* 16 October, 21 October 1925. On the other hand, Beveridge would be dead within two years. *Indianapolis News,* 27 April 1927; *Indianapolis Star,* 30 April 1927.

54. *Kokomo Daily Tribune,* 19 April 1928; *Richmond Item,* 25 April 1928; *Vincennes Commercial,* 3 May 1928; *Lafayette Journal and Courier,* 5 May 1928; *Muncie Evening Press,* 7 May 1928; *South Bend Tribune,* 7 May 1928.

55. *Noblesville Daily Ledger,* 28 September 1926, 11 July, 12 July, 13 July, 14 July 1927.

56. *Madison Courier,* 3 October 1927; *Marion Chronicle,* 3 October 1927; *South Bend Tribune,* 17 October, 19 October 1926, 6 May 1928; *Indiana Catholic and Record,* 23 April 1926; *Indianapolis Recorder,* 27 October 1928; *New York Times,* 21 February 1928; Shumaker to McBride, 12 January 1926 and 25 January 1926, Reel 14, F. Scott McBride Papers, Temperance and Prohibition Papers. R. Earl Peters, chair of the state Democratic Party, became angry that the attorney general was linking the party to the Klan by his accusation that the Klan had helped elect Ralston and refused to jump on the Gilliom bandwagon.

57. *Indianapolis Star,* 21 July 1928; *Indiana Catholic and Record,* 7 January, 4 March, 23 September 1927.

58. *Indianapolis Times,* 30 April 1928; *Indianapolis Star,* 1 March, 4 May, 6 May, 7 May 1928, 3 December 1945; *Indianapolis News,* 27 August 1919, 26 December 1925; *American Issue: Indiana Edition,* 4 September 1926, 15 October 1927, 17 March, 31 March, 12 May, 23 June 1928.

59. *South Bend Tribune,* 1 May, 2 May 1928; *Indianapolis News,* 30 April 1928; *Indianapolis Times,* 6 April, 30 April 1928; *Indianapolis Star,* 3 April,

30 April 1928; *Kokomo Daily Tribune*, 27 April 1928; *Lake County Times*, 1 May 1928; *Terre Haute Tribune*, 2 May 1928; *Columbus Evening Republican*, 30 April 1928; *Richmond Item*, 1 May 1928; *Madison Courier*, 27 April, 30 April 1928; *Lafayette Journal and Courier*, 3 May 1928.

60. *Indianapolis News*, 1 May 1928; *Indianapolis Star*, 7 May 1928; *Indianapolis Times*, 1 May 1928.

61. *Madison Courier*, 1 May, 3 May, 4 May 1928; *Lafayette Journal and Courier*, 1 May 1928; *South Bend Tribune*, 1 May 1928; *Lebanon Reporter*, 1 May 1928; *Indianapolis Star*, 1 May, 6 May 1928.

62. *New York Times*, 2 October 1927.

63. *Indianapolis Star*, 9 May 1928; *South Bend Tribune*, 1 May, 3 May, 12 May 1928; *Terre Haute Tribune*, 17 April 1928; *Columbus Evening Republican*, 7 May, 9 May 1928; *Oxford Gazette*, 11 May 1928; *Lake County Times*, 10 May 1928; *Vincennes Commercial*, 10 May 1928; *Lafayette Journal and Courier*, 9 May 1928.

64. *State v. Shumaker*, 200 Ind. 623; 162 N.E. 441 (1928); *State v. Shumaker*, 200 Ind. 623; 163 N.E. 272, (1928); *Marion Chronicle*, 8 August 1927; *Indianapolis Star*, 21 July, 10 October, 19 October, 20 October 1928; *Noblesville Daily Ledger*, 19 October 1928; *State v. Shumaker*, 200 Ind. 623; 164 N.E. 408 (1928); Recent Case Notes, *Yale Law Journal* 38 (1928–1929): 819–820.

65. "Statement of the Headquarters Committee of IASL," pamphlet; W.H. Hickman to Shumaker, 27 November 1927; "Legal Aspects of the Shumaker Contempt of Court Case by E.A. Miles, Attorney," pamphlet; Report to the Executive Committee Anti-Saloon League of America Meeting held in Washington D.C., Tuesday 5 March 1929, Box 2, ESS Papers; Arthur Shumaker, interview with author, 24 March 2000.

66. Ernest H. Cherrington, ed., *Anti-Saloon League Yearbook 1928* (Westerville, OH: The American Issue Press, 1928), 6; *American Issue: Indiana Edition*, 15 September, 13 October, 24 November, 8 December, 22 December 1928; *Oxford Gazette*, 22 April 1927; S.E. Nicholson to Clayton C. Morrison, Letter, 8 May 1928; "Personal Statement to the Friends of Peace" by S.E. Nicholson, 15 October 1928, S. Edgar Nicholson Papers, EC Archives; Rev. Ralph J. Haughton to Rev. J. Frank Norris, 23 October 1928, Folder 1800, Box 40, SBC Archives; Burns, *Being Catholic, Being American*, 465–469; Herbert Hoover, *The Memoirs of Herbert Hoover: The Cabinet and the Presidency, 1920–1933* (New York: The Macmillan Company, 1952), 200–201; Hohner, *Prohibition and Politics*, 230–231; Bulletin, 14 April 1929, Bulletins 1927–1929 book, MSUMC Archives; Norwood, *History of the North Indiana Conference*, 173; Robert A. Slayton, *Empire Statesman: The Rise and Redemption of Al Smith* (New York: The Free Press, 2001).

67. *Fort Wayne Journal Gazette*, 26 January, 13 February 1929; *Evansville Journal*, 30 January, 31 January 1929; *Goshen Daily Democrat*, 14 January 1929;

South Bend Tribune, 7 January 1929; *Lebanon Reporter,* 16 January, 11 February 1929; *Madison Courier,* 15 December 1928; John O. Motto to James P. Goodrich, 28 January 1928, Indiana Politics Correspondence 1921–1934 file, Box 12, James P. Goodrich Papers, Herbert Hoover Presidential Library.

68. *Greencastle Herald,* 6 February 1929; *Indianapolis News,* 11 February 1929; *Connersville News Examiner,* 12 February 1929; *Madison Courier,* 12 February 1929.

69. Arthur Shumaker, interview with author, 24 March 2000; *South Bend Tribune,* 1 January 1929; *Fort Wayne Journal Gazette,* 4 January 1929; *Evansville Journal,* 20 January 1929; *Lafayette Journal and Courier,* 2 January 1929; *Muncie Evening Press,* 4 January 1929; Robert H. Ferrell, *The Presidency of Calvin Coolidge* (Lawrence: University of Kansas Press, 1998), 104–107.

70. *Indianapolis Star,* 15 February 1929; *Indianapolis Times,* 12 February 1929; *Lake County Times,* 12 February 1933; *Columbus Evening Republican,* 12 February 1929. For more on the state farm, see *Indiana Daily Student,* 12 April 1915.

71. *Indianapolis Times,* 12 February 1929; *Fort Wayne Journal Gazette,* 1 January 1929; *Evansville Journal,* 8 January 1929; *Martinsville Democrat,* 15 February 1929; *Terre Haute Tribune,* 25 January, 26 January 1929; *Lafayette Journal and Courier,* 12 January, 25 January 1929; *Indiana Catholic and Record,* 15 February 1929.

8 | *The Death of a Man and His Dream*

1. Bowman et al., eds., *Indiana 1926,* 24; Arthur Shumaker, interview with author, 24 March, 19 April 2000; *Muncie Evening Press,* 12 February 1929; *Lebanon Reporter,* 12 February, 13 February 1929.

2. *Indianapolis Star,* 5 April, 6 April 1929; *Vincennes Commercial,* 26 October 1929.

3. *Indianapolis Star,* 5 April 1929; *Indianapolis Times,* 4 April 1929.

4. *Indianapolis News,* 4 April 1929; *Indianapolis Star,* 6 April 1929.

5. *Indianapolis Times,* 3 April, 4 April, 5 April, 6 April 1929; *Indianapolis Star,* 5 April, 6 April 1929; *Indianapolis News,* 1 April, 2 April, 4 April 1929; *Noblesville Daily Ledger,* 4 April 1929; Executive Committee, 2 April 1929, 1928–1929 Folder 6, Box 1, Indianapolis Church Federation Executive Committee Minutes, Indiana Historical Society.

6. *Indianapolis Star,* 13 February, 8 March 1929.

7. *Indianapolis Times,* 5 April 1929; Shumaker, *Autobiography,* First and Second Forewords; *Indianapolis News,* 26 October 1929; *Muncie Evening Press,* 26 October 1929.

8. *Indianapolis Star,* 5 April 1929; *Goshen Daily Democrat,* 26 October 1929; *Columbia City Post,* 26 October 1929; Arthur Shumaker, interviews with author, 24 March, 19 April 2000. The *Lake County Times* has a good picture of Shumaker taken before his death. See *Lake County Times,* 26 October 1929.

9. John Harvey Kellogg to Bishop Thomas Nicholson, 3 June 1929; Howard Hyde Russell to Rev. Edward S. Shumaker, 4 June 1929; Russell to Kellogg, 4 June 1929; Kellogg to Shumaker, 4 June 1929; Russell to Shumaker, 7 June 1929; Sanitarium Credit Manager to Shumaker, 14 July 1929; J. W. Harrison to Shumaker, 27 July 1929; Case N. 212699 Book; Shumaker to IASL Headquarters Committee, 6 July 1929, Box 2, ESS Papers.

10. Shumaker to IASL Headquarters Committee, 6 July 1929, Box 2, ESS Papers.

11. *Martinsville Democrat,* 27 September 1929; *Indianapolis News,* 26 October 1929.

12. *Rushville Daily Republican,* 26 October 1929; *Jeffersonville Evening News,* 26 October 1929; *Bloomington Evening World,* 26 October 1929; *Richmond Item,* 26 October 1929; *Lafayette Journal and Courier,* 26 October 1929; *Greencastle Herald,* 26 October 1929. Son Wayne, a student at DePauw, was not at his father's bedside that day with the rest of the family.

13. *Indianapolis News,* 26 October, 28 October 1929; "Edward Seitz Shumaker In Memoriam," pamphlet, Box 2, ESS Papers; Arthur Shumaker, interview with author, 19 April 2000; Crown Hill Cemetery Records, Indiana State Library, Indianapolis, Indiana. State Leagues that contributed to the memorial were New Jersey, Maryland, Michigan, Nebraska, Wisconsin, Ohio, Nevada, Texas, Virginia, West Virginia, Alabama, Oklahoma, North Dakota, New Hampshire, and Illinois.

14. *Indianapolis Star,* 26 October 1929; *Minutes of the Seventy-Ninth Session of the Northwest Indiana Annual Conference of the Methodist Episcopal Church, 1930,* 447.

15. Mr. and Mrs. Christgau to Mrs. E. S. Shumaker and Family, 26 October 1929, Reel 2, Anti-Saloon League of America Papers, Temperance and Prohibition Papers.

16. *Evansville Journal,* 26 October 1929; *Oxford Gazette,* 1 November 1929; *Lake County Times,* 26 October 1929; *Connersville News Examiner,* 26 October 1929; *Anderson Herald,* 26 October 1929; *Shelbyville Republican,* 26 October 1929; *Kokomo Daily Tribune,* 26 October 1929.

17. *Indianapolis Star,* 26 October 1929.

18. Arthur Shumaker, interview with author, 24 March 2000; Julia Shumaker, interview with author, 1 December 2000, 13 March 2001.

19. Julia Shumaker, interview with author, 13 March 2001; 1930 Census; Shumaker, *Autobiography,* 128, Second Foreword.

20. *Lebanon Reporter*, 26 October 1929; *Indianapolis News*, 1 November 1919; *Indianapolis Star*, 12 March, 14 March 1930, 21 January 1931, 29 March 1946, 10 February 1955; A. H. Beardsley to James P. Goodrich, 18 July 1930, Indiana Politics Correspondence 1921–1934 file, Box 12, James P. Goodrich Papers, Herbert Hoover Presidential Library; Kerr, *Organized for Prohibition*, 207–213.

21. *Indianapolis Star*, 3 May 1930; *Jeffersonville Evening News*, 11 February 1931.

22. *Goshen Daily Democrat*, 12 February 1931; *Lake County Times*, 31 January 1931; *Jeffersonville Evening News*, 9 February, 17 February 1931; *Vincennes Sun Commercial*, 11 February, 12 February 1931; *Indianapolis Times*, 7 January, 11 February, 12 February 1931; *Indianapolis Star*, 12 February 1931; *Noblesville Daily Ledger*, 12 February 1931; *Columbus Evening Republican*, 11 February, 12 February 1931; *Madison Courier*, 12 February 1931; *Fort Wayne Journal Gazette*, 12 February 1931; *Richmond Item*, 12 February 1931; *Lafayette Journal and Courier*, 31 January 1931; *Indiana Catholic and Record*, 16 January 1931; *New York Times*, 24 April, 12 June 1932; Harold Feightner, Oral History Project, Indiana Division, Indiana State Library, 1968, 33–34, 149.

23. *Noblesville Daily Ledger*, 8 January, 9 January 1925; *Lebanon Reporter*, 6 August 1927; *Goshen Daily Democrat*, 8 October 1926; *Vincennes Commercial*, 3 October, 5 October, 6 October, 7 October, 8 October, 9 October, 10 October, 13 October, 15 October, 16 October, 17 October, 23 October, 24 October, 27 October, 30 October, 2 November 1926; *Indianapolis Star*, 8 October, 9 October, 10 October, 11 October, 13 October, 23 October 1926.

24. *Indianapolis Times*, 5 October, 11 October, 13 October, 18 October, 21 October, 22 October 1926, 11 July 1927, 13 February, 15 February, 21 April, 27 April, 8 May 1928; *Noblesville Daily Ledger*, 14 February, 15 February, 16 February, 17 February 1928. Much of the revelations about James E. Watson came out during the Reed Committee hearings on political corruption. See *Vincennes Commercial*, 20 October, 21 October, 23 October, 26 October, 29 October, 31 October 1926; *Warsaw Daily Union*, 20 October, 21 October, 28 October, 30 October 1926; *Oxford Gazette*, 10 February 1928; *Lake County Times*, 27 April 1928; *Columbus Evening Republican*, 26 April 1928.

25. Rev. A. Ward Applegate to Gov. H.G. Leslie, 9 July 1932; A.W. Clark to Leslie, 11 July 1932; Rev. Frank K. Dougherty to Leslie, 16 July 1932, General Assembly-Prohibition file, Leslie Papers, Indiana State Archives, Indianapolis, Indiana; *Indianapolis Times*, 22 January, 31 January 1931; *Indianapolis News*, 12 February 1931; *Indianapolis Star*, 7 April, 16 April, 18 April 1932.

26. Mark M. Dodge, ed., *Herbert Hoover and the Historians* (West Branch, IA: Herbert Hoover Presidential Library Association, 1989), 60; Lewis L.

Strauss, interviewed by Raymond Henle, 13 February 1967, Hoover Presidential Library Oral History Project, Herbert Hoover Presidential Library; Goshen District of the North Indiana Conference of the Methodist Church to Herbert Hoover, 21 March 1929, Prohibition Correspondence 1929 March 16–30 file; New Albany District of the Indiana Methodist Conference to Hoover, May 1929, Prohibition Correspondence 1929 May 1–5 file, Box 227; Evansville District of the Indiana Methodist Conference to Hoover, 12 June 1929, Prohibition Correspondence 1929 June 11–15 file; I. Bruce Book to Hoover, 24 June 1929, Prohibition Correspondence 1929 June 21–25 file, Box 228; Indiana Conference of the Wesleyan Methodist Church to Hoover, 19 August 1929; Oakwood Park Assembly of the Indiana Conference of the Evangelical Church to Hoover, 19 August 1929, Prohibition correspondence 1929 August 16–30 file; Indianapolis Area Council of the Methodist Church, 14 December 1929, Prohibition Correspondence 1929 December, Box 229, Presidential Series, Herbert Hoover Papers, Herbert Hoover Presidential Library. The following contain only Indiana letters as a sampling: D. C. Murray to Hoover, 4 May 1929, Prohibition Correspondence 1929 May 1–5 file, Box 227; Charles Bief and C. R. McBride to Herbert Hoover, 8 May 1929, Prohibition Correspondence 1929 May 6–10 file; Oliver W. Stewart to Hoover, 21 May 1929, Prohibition Correspondence 1929 May 21–25 file; Sumner W. Haynes to Hoover, 21 June 1929, Prohibition Correspondence, 1929 June 21–25 file, Box 228; Mrs. E. E. Mittman to Hoover, 14 January 1930, Prohibition Correspondence 1930 January 11–15 file, Box 229; Arthur C. Lay to Hoover, 16 January 1929, Prohibition Correspondence 1930 January 16–20 file; Omer S. Whiteman to Hoover, 28 January 1930, Prohibition Correspondence 1930 January 26–31, Box 230; Charles Tinkham to Hoover, 20 January 1931, Prohibition Correspondence 1931 January 16–31, Box 232; Flying Squadron Foundation to Herbert Hoover, 16 June, 17 June, 18 June 1929, Prohibition Correspondence 1929 June 16–20 file; Flying Squadron Foundation to Hoover, 21 June, 23 June, 25 June 1929, Prohibition Correspondence 1929 June 21–25 file; Flying Squadron Foundation to Hoover, 30 June 1929, Prohibition Correspondence 1929 June 26–30 file, Box 228; Thomas Smart to Herbert Hoover, 17 July 1929, Prohibition Correspondence 1929 July 16–31 file; Flying Squadron Foundation to Hoover, 13 September 1929, Prohibition Correspondence 1929 September 1–15 file, Box 229, Herbert Hoover Papers, Herbert Hoover Presidential Library. The Flying Squadron Foundation's efforts stretched west into Wisconsin, Illinois, and Iowa, north into Michigan, and east into Ohio, Pennsylvania, New York, and Connecticut.

27. W. O. Olsen to Herbert Hoover, 16 June 1932, Prohibition Correspondence 1932 June 16–30 file, Box 235; Mrs. Luther Albert to Hoover, 23 January 1933, Prohibition WCTU Correspondence 1932–1933, Box 239;

P. R. Wadsworth to Walter H. Newton, 23 April 1932, Prohibition Correspondence 1932 April 21–25 file, Box 233; L. H. Higley to Hoover, 22 November 1932, Prohibition Correspondence 1932 November 16–30 file, Box 236, Presidential Series, Herbert Hoover Papers, Herbert Hoover Presidential Library.

28. Mrs. George R. B. Taylor to Hoover, 28 April 1932, Prohibition Correspondence 1932 April 26–30 file, Box 233, Presidential Series, Herbert Hoover Papers, Herbert Hoover Presidential Library.

29. S. E. Nicholson to Hoover, 9 June 1932, Prohibition Modification and Repeal 1932–1933 file, Box 238; Omer S. Whiteman to Hoover, 30 July 1932, Prohibition Correspondence 1932 July 26–30 file, Box 235; Evangeline Booth to Hoover, 19 September 1932, Prohibition Correspondence 1932 September 16–20 file, Box 236, Presidential Series, Herbert Hoover Papers, Herbert Hoover Presidential Library.

30. Paula S. Fass, *The Damned and the Beautiful: American Youth in the 1920s* (New York: Oxford University Press, 1979); Engelmann, *Intemperance*, 171–177; *The Franklin*, 9 November 1932. For these and many more letters from colleges and universities across the country, see "College Opinions Folder," Reel 1, Intercollegiate Prohibition Association Papers, Microfilm Edition of the Temperance and Prohibition Papers, Ohio Historical Society, Columbus, Ohio. Fass did not utilize the ASL papers for her book.

31. Rev. Atticus Webb to Rev. J. Frank Norris, 2 January 1932, Folder 1557, Box 35, J. Frank Norris Papers, SBC Archives; *Ninety-Ninth Session of the Indiana Annual Conference of the Methodist Episcopal Church*, 1930; *Noblesville Daily Ledger*, 13 January, 9 June, 15 September 1930, 15 September 1931.

32. Bulletins, 24 April, 15 May, 24 July 1927, Bulletins 1927–1929 book, 12 January 1930, Bulletins 1930–1932 book, MSUMC Archives; Irving Fisher, *The Noble Experiment*. (New York: Alcohol Information Committee, 1930); Behr, *Prohibition*, 233; Clark, *Deliver Us from Evil*, 167; Burnham, *Bad Habits*, 31; Engelmann, *Intemperance*, 201; Adam Frick to Harry Leslie, included in Frick to Franklin D. Roosevelt, 14 March 1933, Arthur Viat to Franklin D. Roosevelt, 3 June 1933, courtesy of Franklin D. Roosevelt Presidential Library, Hyde Park, New York. Frick was a member of the state legislature of Ohio and Viat represented the Fort Wayne Building Trades Council.

33. James P. Goodrich to James E. Watson, 10 June 1932, James E. Watson 1931–1933 file, Box 28, James P. Goodrich Papers, Herbert Hoover Presidential Library; Madison, *Indiana through Tradition and Change*, 43–44; *Indianapolis Star*, 22 June 1932; H. O. Miles to Hoover, 30 January 1932, Prohibition Correspondence 1932 January file, Box 233; Anna M. Poyntz to Herbert Hoover, 19 May 1932, Prohibition Correspondence 1932 May 16–20 file, Box 234, Presidential Series, Herbert Hoover Papers, Herbert Hoover Presidential

Library; Walter E. Leuchtenburg, *Franklin D. Roosevelt and the New Deal, 1932–1940* (New York: Harper Torchbooks, 1963), 9.

34. *Rensselaer Evening Republican*, 26 July, 11 August 1932; *Noblesville Daily Ledger*, 3 October 1932.

35. Kyvig, *Repealing National Prohibition*, 3, 178; Clark, *Deliver Us from Evil*, 210; Leuchtenburg, *Franklin D. Roosevelt and the New Deal*, 46; *Goshen Daily Democrat*, 4 November 1932; *Indianapolis News*, 6 February 1932; *Jeffersonville Evening News*, 10 November 1932; *Terre Haute Tribune*, 1 November 1932; L. E. York to H. B. Sowers, 10 November 1932, Reel 1, American Issue Publishing Company Papers, Temperance and Prohibition Papers; *The Nation*, 2 November 1932, 428–429; Joseph J. Elias to Herbert Hoover, 22 April 1932, Prohibition Correspondence 1932 April 21–25 file, Box 233, Presidential Series, Herbert Hoover Papers, Herbert Hoover Presidential Library.

36. *Indianapolis Times*, 25 February 1933; *Jeffersonville Evening News*, 15 March 1933; *South Bend Tribune*, 1 March 1933; *Goshen Daily Democrat*, 8 March 1933; *Noblesville Daily Ledger*, 14 February, 25 February 1933; *Indianapolis News*, 25 February 1933; *Terre Haute Tribune*, 27 February, 28 February, 1 March, 2 March 1933; *Evansville Journal*, 24 February, 25 February, 1 March, 2 March 1933; *Warsaw Daily Union*, 8 April 1933; *Fort Wayne Journal Gazette*, 4 April 1933.

37. *Goshen Daily Democrat*, 23 March 1933; *Versailles Republican*, 5 April 1933; Letter from Wayne Coy, 4 December 1933, Letter from Paul V. McNutt, 13 December 1933, Letter from Paul Fry, 13 December 1933, Folder 16/60; Letter to Wayne Coy, 27 January 1934, Folder 16/61; Letter from Paul Fry, 1 February 1934, Folder 16/62; Letter from Paul Fry, 6 February 1933, Folder 16/62; Letter from Bishop Joseph Ritter, 13 April 1934, Folder 16/64, Governor's File: Paul V. McNutt, Series 2, John W. Cavanaugh Papers, Archives of the University of Notre Dame; *Indianapolis Star*, 27 January 1975. McHale was also the author of the Public Service Communication Act, the Gross Income Tax Act, and the Utility Tax Act.

38. Walsh, *The Sesquicentennial History of the Indiana General Assembly*, 455–457; "Legislative Message of Governor Paul V. McNutt to the 79th Session of the Indiana General Assembly, 10 January 1935," Paul V. McNutt and Family Biography Clippings File, Indiana State Library, Indianapolis, Indiana; *Indianapolis Star*, 18 March 1933; *Indianapolis Times*, 31 March, 7 April 1933; *Indianapolis News*, 3 April, 7 April, 13 April, 14 April, 17 April 1933; *Franklin Democrat*, 1 June 1933; *Noblesville Daily Ledger*, 11 January, 21 March 1933; *Lake County Times*, 5 June 1933; *Jeffersonville Evening News*, 15 April 1933; *Madison Courier*, 2 June 1933; *Daily Clintonian*, 29 May 1933; *Evansville Journal*, 12 April, 6 June 1933; *Lafayette Journal and Courier*, 28 March 1933; *Kokomo Daily Tribune*, 23 March 1933; *Logansport Pharos Tribune*, 29 May 1933; *The Franklin*, 29 March 1933.

39. *Goshen Daily Democrat*, 7 April 1933; *Warsaw Daily Union*, 13 May 1933.

40. *Indianapolis Times*, 20 February, 21 February, 22 February, 24 February, 27 February 1933.

41. *New York Times*, 26 February 1933; *Indianapolis News*, 23 May, 3 June, 6 June 1933; *Indianapolis Times*, 27 February 1933; *Columbia City Post*, 5 June, 6 June 1933; *Valparaiso Daily Vidette*, 2 June 1933; *Knightstown Banner*, 26 May 1933; *Richmond Item*, 6 June 1933; *Vincennes Sun Commercial*, 3 June 1933; *Rushville Daily Republican*, 3 June 1933; *Jasper Herald*, 2 June 1933; *Pike County Democrat*, 2 June 1933; *Goshen Daily Democrat*, 6 June 1933. The nine states in question were Illinois, New York, Michigan, New Jersey, Rhode Island, Wisconsin, Wyoming, Delaware, and Nevada.

42. *Indianapolis Times*, 1 June 1933; *Kokomo Daily Tribune*, 23 March 1933; *Daily Clintonian*, 26 May 1933; *Valparaiso Daily Vidette*, 2 June 1933.

43. Meeting, 23 May 1932, 13 March, 10 April, 21 April 1933, Minutes and Correspondence, 1932–1936, Folder 1, Box 1, Series 1, Church Women United Collection, Indiana Historical Society, Indianapolis, Indiana; Executive Committee, 1 November 1932, 4 April, 6 June 1933, 1931–1933 Folder 8, Box 1, Indianapolis Church Federation Executive Committee Minutes, Indiana Historical Society; *Northwest Indiana Conference of the Methodist Episcopal Church*, 1933, 184; *Franklin Evening Star*, 20 May, 22 May, 29 May 1933; *Anderson Herald*, 6 May, 10 May 1933; *Angola Herald*, 5 May 1933; *Wabash Daily Plain Dealer*, 31 May 1933; *Owen Leader*, 6 April, 13 April, 18 May 1933; *Kokomo Daily Tribune*, 15 May 1933; *Fort Wayne Journal Gazette*, 8 April 1933; *Garrett Clipper*, 17 April 1933; *Pike County Democrat*, 28 April 1933; *Huntington Herald*, 29 May 1933; *Muncie Evening Press*, 11 May 1933; *Cannelton Telephone*, 26 May 1933; *Tipton Daily Tribune*, 16 May 1933; *Shoals News*, 2 June 1933; Meeting Minutes, 8 May, 15 May 1932, 2 April, 23 April 1933, Records of Tabernacle Presbyterian Church (Formerly Third Presbyterian Church), Indianapolis, Indiana State Library, Indianapolis, Indiana..

44. *Garrett Clipper*, 17 April 1933; *Garrett Weekly Clipper*, 20 April, 27 April 1933; *Columbia City Post*, 24 May 1933; *Versailles Republican*, 25 May 1933; *Greensburg Daily News*, 22 May 1933; *Terre Haute Star*, 1 May, 4 May 1933; *Peru Republican*, 5 May 1933; *Delphi Journal*, 11 May 1933; *Noble County Democrat*, 18 May 1933; *Noblesville Daily Ledger*, 25 May 1933; *Lebanon Reporter*, 1 June 1929; *Plymouth Daily News*, 13 May 1933; *New Albany Weekly Ledger*, 26 May 1933; *Vincennes Sun Commercial*, 3 June 1933.

45. *Seymour Tribune*, 27 May 1933; *Attica Ledger Tribune*, 12 May 1933; *Anderson Herald*, 16 May, 27 May 1933; *Tipton Daily Tribune*, 17 May 1933; *Greencastle Herald*, 22 May 1933; *Monticello Herald*, 18 May 1933; *Indianapolis News*, 18 May 1933.

46. *Terre Haute Star*, 25 May 1933.

262 | Notes to Pages 171–173

47. Walsh, *The Sesquicentennial History of the Indiana General Assembly*, 440;
Indianapolis Star, 16 December 1932; *Tipton Daily Tribune*, 20 May, 23 May, 24
May 1933; *Anderson Herald*, 20 May, 30 May 1933; *Jeffersonville Evening News*,
5 June 1933.

48. *Marion Chronicle*, 28 March 1933; *Franklin Evening Star*, 7 June 1933;
Crawfordsville Journal, 12 May 1933.

49. *Peru Republican*, 24 March 1933; "The Address of Moderator Ortho
Winger," Faculty/Staff Collection: Ortho Winger, MC2002/104u, Archives
and Brethren Historical Collection, Funderburg Library, Manchester College,
North Manchester, Indiana; Ortho Winger, *History and Doctrines of the Church
of the Brethren* (Elgin, IL: Brethren Publishing House, 1919), 216–217; Richard
V. Pierard, "The Church of the Brethren and the Temperance Movement,"
Brethren Life and Thought 26 (1981): 36–44.

50. *Indiana Daily Student*, 31 March, 1 April 1933; *Bloomington Evening
World*, 3 February, 5 February 1917; *Albion New Era*, 17 May 1933; Bulletins,
11 March, 10 June 1928, Bulletins 1927–1929 book, MSUMC Archives; William Lowe Bryan Biography Clippings File, Indiana State Library, Indianapolis, Indiana; William Lowe Bryan to G. Arthur Holloway, 21 April 1914,
Alcohol folder; H. S. Bonsib to William Lowe Bryan, 5 December 1928, Oliver
W. Stewart to Bryan, 28 February 1929, Earl Godwin to Bryan 23 June 1932,
Prohibition 1928–1936 folder, William Lowe Bryan Papers, Archives of Indiana University, Bloomington, Indiana.

51. "Out of the Jungle—Straight On," included in S. W. Haynes to
Hoover, 21 June 1929, Prohibition Correspondence 1929 June 21–25 file, Box
228, Presidential Series, Herbert Hoover Papers, Herbert Hoover Presidential
Library.

52. William E. Ellis, *"A Man of Books and a Man of the People": E. Y. Mullins
and the Crisis of Moderate Southern Baptist Leadership* (Macon, GA: Mercer University Press, 1988), 213; *Baptist Observer*, 1 June 1933; *Oxford Gazette*, 12 May
1933; *Fort Wayne Journal Gazette*, 3 June 1933; *Brown County Democrat*, 21 April,
2 June 1933; *Garrett Weekly Clipper*, 27 April, 1 May 1933; *Crawfordsville Journal*, 3 May 1933; *Liberty Herald*, 4 May 1933; *Wakarusa Tribune*, 1 June 1933;
Warren Review Republican, 1 June 1933; *Corydon Democrat*, 17 May 1933.

53. *French Lick Springs Valley Herald*, 27 April, 18 May 1933; *Martinsville
Democrat*, 12 May, 26 May 1933.

54. *Terre Haute Tribune*, 25 April 1933; *Plymouth Daily News*, 5 June 1933;
Huntington Herald, 24 May 1933; *Tipton Daily Tribune*, 24 May 1933; *Crawfordsville Journal*, 20 May, 2 June, 3 June 1933; *Wabash Daily Plain Dealer*, 3 June
1933; *Terre Haute Star*, 25 May 1933; *Anderson Herald*, 1 June 1933; *Jeffersonville
Evening News*, 1 June 1933; *Evansville Journal*, 15 March, 23 March 1933. FDR
put Farley in charge of the repeal effort. Farley's mother had run a saloon

when he was younger, but as a good Catholic, she made sure that her son took the church temperance pledge, which he said he kept until he was an adult. See James A. Farley, *Behind the Ballots: The Personal History of a Politician* (New York: Harcourt, Brace and Company, 1938), 13–14, 222.

55. *Valparaiso Daily Vidette*, 25 May 1933; *Bedford Daily Mail*, 5 June 1933; *Tipton Daily Tribune*, 3 June 1933; *Martinsville Democrat*, 2 June 1933; *Jasper Herald*, 2 June 1933; *Kentland Democrat*, 1 June 1933; *Seymour Tribune*, 3 June 1933; *Aurora Bulletin*, 1 June 1933; *Sullivan Times Democrat*, 1 June 1933; *Lafayette Journal Courier*, 25 May, 5 June 1933.

56. *Indianapolis News*, 3 June 1933; *Indianapolis Times*, 2 June 1933; *New York Times*, 9 April 1933; *Logansport Pharos Tribune*, 5 June 1933; *Booneville Weekly Enquirer*, 2 June 1933; *Poseyville News*, 2 June 1933; *Jasper Herald*, 2 June 1933; *Bluffton Evening News*, 3 June 1933, emphasis in the original.

57. *Logansport Pharos Tribune*, 29 May 1933; *Bloomfield News*, 25 May 1933; *Bluffton Evening News*, 3 June, 5 June 1933; *Crawfordsville Journal*, 5 June 1933.

58. *Anderson Herald*, 6 June 1933; *Terre Haute Star*, 3 June 1933; *Indianapolis News*, 3 June 1933; *Jeffersonville Evening News*, 3 June 1933.

59. *Indianapolis Times*, 7 June 1933; *Seymour Tribune*, 6 May, 10 May, 7 June 1933; *Vevay Reveille*, 10 May, 7 June 1933; *Pulaski County Democrat*, 25 May 1933; *Goshen Daily Democrat*, 7 June 1933.

60. *Warren Review Republican*, 8 June 1933; *Oxford Gazette*, 2 June, 9 June 1933.

61. *Garrett Weekly Clipper*, 12 June 1933; *Bedford Daily Mail*, 8 June 1933; *Bluffton Evening News*, 8 June 1933; *Lake County Times*, 8 June 1933; *Anderson Herald*, 7 June 1933.

62. Hendrickson, *Hoosier Heritage*, 9; *Lebanon Reporter*, 7 June 1933.

63. Kyvig, *Repealing National Prohibition*, 173–175; *Bloomfield News*, 6 April 1933; *Owen Leader*, 25 May 1933; *Scott County Journal*, 31 May 1933; *Peru Republican*, 24 March 1933; *New York Times*, 19 March 1933; *Fort Wayne Journal Gazette*, 4 April 1933; *Gary Evening Post*, 6 June 1933; *Warsaw Daily Union*, 6 June 1933; *Crawfordsville Journal*, 6 June 1933; *Muncie Evening Press*, 6 June 1933; *Winchester Democrat*, 8 June 1933; *French Lick Springs Valley Herald*, 1 June 1933; *Richmond Item*, 6 June 1933; *Terre Haute Tribune*, 9 April 1933.

64. *Jasper Herald*, 9 June 1933; *Peru Republican*, 9 June 1933; *Fort Wayne Journal Gazette*, 7 June 1933; *Connersville Evening News*, 7 June 1933; *Shelbyville Republican*, 7 June 1933; *Martinsville Democrat*, 9 June 1933; *Columbia City Post*, 7 June 1933; *Evansville Journal*, 7 June 1933; *Gary Evening Post*, 7 June 1933; *North Vernon Sun*, 8 June 1933; *Brown County Democrat*, 9 June 1933; *Noble County Democrat*, 8 June 1933; *Brookville American*, 8 June 1933; *Rising Sun Recorder*, 7 June 1933; *Sullivan Daily Times*, 7 June 1933; *Booneville Weekly Enquirer*, 9 June 1933; *Monticello Herald*, 8 June 1933; *White County Democrat*,

9 June 1933; *Rockville Tribune*, 7 June 1933; *Versailles Republican*, 8 June 1933; *Kokomo Daily Tribune*, 7 June 1933; *Columbus Evening Republican*, 7 June 1933; *Richmond Item*, 7 June 1933; *Vincennes Sun Commercial*, 7 June 1933; *Shoals News*, 9 June 1933; *Lafayette Journal and Courier*, 7 June 1933; *New Albany Weekly Ledger*, 9 June 1933; *Cannelton Telephone*, 9 June 1933; *Garrett Weekly Clipper*, 8 June 1933; *Logansport Pharos Tribune*, 7 June 1933; *Pulaski County Democrat*, 8 June 1933; 1930 Census. The foreign-born population may have been something of a tipping factor, but the presence of large numbers of immigrants tended to reinforce other factors, such as total population and more concentrated urbanization, that contributed to counties voting wet. Though the counties that recorded the highest numbers of Germans, Irish, Italian, Polish, and Hungarian-born citizens all voted wet, wets also did well in counties with few foreign-born residents.

65. *Middlebury Independent*, 8 June 1933; *Warsaw Daily Union*, 7 June 1933; *Winchester Democrat*, 8 June 1933; *Pike County Democrat*, 9 June 1933; *Delphi Journal*, 8 June 1933; *Owen Leader*, 8 June 1933; *Corydon Democrat*, 7 June 1933; *Attica Ledger Tribune*, 7 June 1933; *Scott County Journal*, 14 June 1933; *Knightstown Banner*, 9 June 1933; *Frankfort Morning Times*, 7 June 1933; *Wabash Daily Plain Dealer*, 7 June 1933; *Warren Review Republican*, 8 June 1933; *Bluffton Evening News*, 7 June 1933; *Greensburg Daily News*, 7 June 1933; *Liberty Herald*, 8 June 1933; *Princeton Clarion News*, 7 June 1933; *Crawfordsville Journal*, 7 June 1933; *French Lick Springs Valley Herald*, 8 June 1933; *Plymouth Daily News*, 7 June 1933; *Franklin Democrat*, 8 June 1933; *Starke County Republican*, 7 June 1933; *Valparaiso Daily Vidette*, 7 June 1933; *Lebanon Reporter*, 7 June 1933.

66. *Indianapolis Times*, 26 June, 27 June 1933; *Indianapolis News*, 26 June 1933.

67. Norwood, *History of the North Indiana Conference*, 174–175; *New York Times*, 26 June 1933; *Kokomo Daily Tribune*, 5 April, 7 June 1933; *Indianapolis News*, 7 June 1933; *Madison Courier*, 27 June 1933.

68. Donald Meyer, *The Protestant Search for Political Realism, 1919–1941* (Middletown, CT: Wesleyan University Press, 1988), 11–12.

9 | *Everything Old Is New Again*

1. *Noblesville Daily Ledger*, 6 December 1933; *Indianapolis News*, 26 June 1933.

2. Engelmann, *Intemperance*, 194; David J. McCullough, "Bone Dry? Prohibition New Mexico Style, 1918–1933," *New Mexico Historical Review* 63 (January 1988): 25–42; Morone, *Hellfire Nation*, 282; Boyer, *Urban Masses and Moral Order in America*, 285–287; Gary Gerstle, *American Crucible: Race and Na-*

tion in the Twentieth Century (Princeton, NJ: Princeton University Press, 2001), 93–95, 114; Lewis A. Erenberg, "From New York to Middletown: Repeal and the Legitimization of Nightlife in the Great Depression," *American Quarterly* 38 (Winter 1986): 761–778; Jonathan Zimmerman, *Distilling Democracy: Alcohol Education in America's Public Schools, 1880–1925* (Lawrence: University of Kansas Press, 1999).

3. Bulletin, 15 January 1928, Bulletins 1927–1929 book, MSUMC Archives; Wardin, *Tennessee Baptists*, 415, 425; Howard Hyde Russell to Lincoln-Lee Chain supporters, 29 June 1933, Reel 12, American Issue Publishing Papers, Temperance and Prohibition Papers; Hendrickson, *Hoosier Heritage*, 91–92; *One Hundred and First Session of the Indiana Annual Conference of the Methodist Episcopal Church*, 1932; Cady, *The Origin and Development of the Missionary Baptist Church in Indiana*, 314; Heller, *Indiana Conference of the Methodist Church, 1832–1956*, 175; Resolution on Temperance and Prohibition, June 1935; Untitled Resolution, June 1936; Resolution on the Liquor Situation, June 1938, Southern Baptist Convention Resolutions, http://www.sbc.net/resolutions, 3 February 2004; "Destructive Forces" pamphlet and "The Way to Win A War" pamphlet, Digital Collections @ Brown University.

4. Alcoholics Anonymous, "Alcoholics Anonymous Historical Data: The Birth of A.A. and its growth in U.S./Canada," http://www.alcoholics-anonymous.org/english/E_FactFile/M–24_d14.html, 30 November 2001; Hamilton B., *Getting Started in AA* (Center City, MN: Hazelden Press, 1995), xiv; Jean-Charles Sournia, *A History of Alcoholism* (Cambridge, MA: Basil Blackwell, 1990), 101–102, 199; Matthew J. Raphael, *Bill W. and Mr. Wilson: The Legend and Life of AA's Cofounder* (Amherst: University of Massachusetts Press, 2000), 54, 60–73; Alfred McClung Lee, "Techniques of Social Reform: An Analysis of the New Prohibition Drive," *American Sociological Review* 9 (February 1944): 69, 71; Charlie Bishop, Jr., and Bill Pittman, *To Be Continued: The AA World Bibliography, 1935–1994* (Wheeling WV: The Bishop of Books, 1994), viii.

5. *Indianapolis Star*, 3 November 1937, 10 February 1955, 18 February 2001; *Indianapolis News*, 12 September 1934; *Indiana Issue*, September–October 1948; *American Issue (Indiana Edition)* clipping, May 1939; Register of Visitors and Record of Flowers, Folder 2, WCTU (1939), WCTU Papers, Indiana Historical Society; Ellis B. Hargrave to H.B. Sowers, 27 October 1950, Reel 1, American Issue Publishing Company Papers, Temperance and Prohibition Papers; *Cincinnati Enquirer*, 4 November 2000, 2 January 2003; *Advocate Messenger*, 14 August 2002; *Louisville Courier Journal*, 1 January 2003; *Oregonian*, 26 May 2002; Georgia Council for Moral and Civic Concerns, "History," http://www.gcmcc.org/history.htm, 19 December 2002.

6. Kerr, *Organized for Prohibition*, 9–10, 243, 246, 276–277; The Callahan Correspondence, 2 August 1928, Microfiche 122, 1438/2044, E.Y.

Mullins Papers, SBC Archives; Social Service Commission Recommendation, June 1929, Southern Baptist Convention Resolutions, http://www.sbc.net/resolutions, 3 February 2004.

7. Albertson, *Roosevelt's Farmer*, 52–55; McGerr, *A Fierce Discontent*, 317; Olive Beldon Lewis, Oral History Project, Indiana Division, Indiana State Library, Indianapolis, Indiana, 1969, 14; Ellsworth Barnard, *Wendell Willkie: Fighter for Freedom* (Marquette: Northern Michigan University Press, 1966), 12–13, 62; *Indianapolis Times*, 15 September 1957; *Delphi Citizen*, 11 February 1932, 1 June, 8 June 1933.

8. Elkhart County Prohibition Committee Letter, 22 October 1960; Mrs. Galen Bowman to Joe Ludd, 17 August 1962; Indiana Prohibition Committee Letter, 14 January 1967, Folder 1, Box 1; Letter, J. Ralston Miller to the Rev. Lee Cory, 19 April 1962; W. E. Yeater to Robert L. Gildea, 11 June 1966, Folder 28, Box 1, Prohibition Party of Indiana Papers, Manuscripts Division, Indiana State Library, Indianapolis, Indiana; Prohibition Party, Convention Sites, http://www.prohibitionists.org/History/convention_sites/body_convention_sites.html, 13 July 2001; Prohibition Party, "Local Chapters," http://www.prohibitionists.org/Chapters/body_chapters.html, 1 August 2003; *Indianapolis Star*, 20 March 2004.

9. Rev. John B. Wantz, interview with author, 13 February 2003.

10. McGeary, *Gifford Pinchot*, 382–383.

11. Hays, *The Memoirs of Will H. Hays*, 28–29, 323–324; McGerr, *A Fierce Discontent*, 274.

12. *Franklin Evening Star*, 15 January, 23 January, 3 February, 7 February 1917; *Lebanon Reporter*, 2 January 1934; Russell B. Pulliam, Correspondence with author, 21 November 2002; Pulliam, *Publisher: Gene Pulliam*, 109–110. According to his grandson, Pulliam was busy expanding his newspaper empire in the 1920s and did not participate much in Indiana politics during the decade.

13. *Jasper County Democrat*, 8 November 1924; *Rensselaer Evening Republican*, 15 January, 26 January, 30 January 1935; Henry Z. Scheele, *Charlie Halleck: A Political Biography* (New York: Exposition Press, 1966), 35, 38–41, 53; James F. Dewey to Charles A. Halleck, 7 June 1948, June 1–10 1948 file, Box 16, Charles A. Halleck Papers, Lilly Library, Indiana University, Bloomington, Indiana. Halleck was like other formerly dry politicians, such as Hugo Black. See Roger K. Newman, *Hugo Black: A Biography* (New York: Pantheon Books, 1994), 39–45, 63–65, 89–129, 148, 239–263.

14. Leibowitz, *My Indiana*, 213; *Indianapolis Times*, 23 July 1927; *New York Times*, 22 September 1935; Glenn Jeansonne, *Gerald L. K. Smith: Minister of Hate* (Baton Rouge: Louisiana State University Press, 1997), 22–23; William Ivy Hair, *The Kingfish and His Realm: The Life and Times of Huey P. Long* (Baton

Rouge: Louisiana State University Press, 1991), 110, 128–129, 143, 273; T. Harry Williams, *Huey Long* (New York: Alfred A. Knopf, 1969), 699–700; Harnett T. Kane, *Louisiana Hayride: The American Rehearsal for Dictatorship, 1928–1940* (New York: William Morrow and Company, 1941), 150–154. Smith always denied any association with the Klan.

15. Hohner, *Prohibition and Politics*, 289.

16. Letter to Reverend Peter Gannon, N.D. [1933], Letter to *Louisville Courier-Journal*, 13 October 1936, Correspondence Folder, CLN; "The Church and Temperance" pamphlet, 4/8, POSV, Archives of the University of Notre Dame.

17. Robert Moats Miller, *Harry Emerson Fosdick: Preacher, Pastor, Prophet* (New York: Oxford University Press, 1985), 432–433; Rev. E.Y. Mullins to W.O. Carver, 23 October 1907, Folder 41, Box 4, William O. Carver Papers, SBC Archives. In the letter, Mullins worried that if the drys "go to extremes," the temperance cause would be lost.

18. McNeil, *Valiant for Truth*, 75–76, 124; Rev. Victor E. Stoner to Gov. H.G. Leslie, 12 July 1932; Rev. J. Newton Jessup to Leslie, 14 July 1932, General Assembly-Prohibition file, Leslie Papers, Indiana State Archives, Indianapolis, Indiana.

19. Link and Link, *American Epoch: A History of the United States since 1900*, volume 1, 212–213; Gregory A. Mark and Christopher L. Eisgruber, "Introduction: Law and Political Culture," *University of Chicago Law Review* 55 (Spring 1988): 422.

20. Sinclair Lewis, *Elmer Gantry* (New York: Signet Classic, 1927).

21. Walter Myers, *The "Guv": A Tale of Midwest Law and Politics* (New York: Frederick Fell, 1947), 264–265, 269–271, 277.

22. Detzler, *The History of the Northwest Indiana Conference of the Methodist Church*, 129; "Maple Avenue Methodist Church: Terre Haute: Golden Anniversary, October 5–October 12, 1941," Box 2, ESS Papers.

23. Julia Shumaker, interview with author, 13 March 2001. On a side note, see John Wooden with Jack Tobin, *They Call Me Coach* (Chicago: Contemporary Books, 1988), in which Wooden, born in Hall, Indiana, ascribes much of his success on and off the basketball court to his dry evangelical Protestant upbringing.

24. Kyvig, *Repealing National Prohibition*, xxv; "The Spirit of Story" Postcard, in possession of author; *Indiana Daily Student*, 14 February 2001.

25. David M. Fahey 2000 Presidential Address, "The Politics of Drink in Britain: Anglo-American Perspectives," http://www.athg.org/fahey presidential.html, 23 October 2002; "National WCTU's First Nation-Wide Survey of Legalized Liquor's Effects," 13 March 1937, Folder 11, Box 20, Samuel F. Lowe Papers, SBC Archives.

26. Gilbert Seldes, *The Future of Drinking* (Boston: Little, Brown and Company, 1930); Bob Gilkey, Conner Prairie Rural History Project RHP 172, 12 February 2001; Banham, *Coors: A Rocky Mountain Legend*, 47; *Switzer et al. v. State*, 211 Ind. 690; 8 N.E. 2d 80 (1937); Vincent T. Lyon, "The Repeal of Prohibition: The End of Oklahoma's Noble Experiment," *Chronicle of Oklahoma* 76, no. 4 (1998–1999): 416–435.

27. Virginia Somes Jenckes, Oral History Project, Indiana Division, Indiana State Library, Indianapolis, Indiana, 1967, 6–7; *Indianapolis Star*, 7 November 1971; *Nuvo*, June 11–18, 2003.

28. Burnham, *Bad Habits*, 73–85, 271–296; Ron Roizen, "The American Discovery of Alcoholism, 1933–1939" (Ph.D. diss., University of California, Berkeley, 1991); Mark and Eisgruber, "Introduction: Law and Political Culture," 426; O.N. Cranor to Herbert Hoover, 23 September 1932, Prohibition Correspondence 1932 September 21–25 file, Box 236, Presidential Series, Herbert Hoover Papers, Herbert Hoover Presidential Library; Kyvig, *Repealing National Prohibition*, 202; *New York Times*, 19 September 2003; *Indianapolis Star*, 5 May 2004. Alaska had the highest excise tax ($1.07) while Wyoming had the lowest ($.02).

29. Joseph R. Gusfield, *Contested Meanings: The Construction of Alcohol Problems* (Madison: University of Wisconsin Press, 1996), 40–41; Danny M. Wilcox, *Alcoholic Thinking: Language, Culture, and Belief in Alcoholics Anonymous* (Westport, CT: Praeger, 1998), 7; Anheuser Busch, "Our Commitment: Community Programs to Promote Alcohol Awareness," pamphlet, 2000; "Busted Bars Suing Underage Drinkers," 29 July 2003, Foxnews.com; *Indianapolis Star*, 5 January 2002, 31 August 2003, 25 April, 4 June 2004, 21 August 2005; *Los Angeles Times*, 15 December 2001.

30. *Little Beverage Co., Inc. and Miami Beverage, Inc., v. Indiana Alcohol and Tobacco commission, and Anheuser-Busch, Inc.*, 777 N.E. 2d 74 (2002).

31. *New York Times*, 24 August 2003; *Ganholm v. Heald*, 125 S.Ct. 1885 (2005).

32. Don Vaccaro, ed., *Corpus Juris Secundum: A Contemporary Statement of American Law*, Volume 17 (St. Paul, MN: West Group, 1999), 70, 74–75; *Indianapolis Star*, 1 August, 5 November 2002. For some contempt cases heard in the years after the Shumaker case, see *State Ex Rel. Stanton v. Murray, Judge, Stanton v. State of Indiana*, 231 Ind. 223; 108 N.E. 2d 251 (1951); *Grimm, Jr. v. State of Indiana*, 240 Ind. 125; 162 N.E. 2d 454 (1959).

33. Morone, *Hellfire Nation*, 26, 282, 329; Kyvig, *Repealing National Prohibition*, xviii.

34. Murdock, *Domesticating Drink*, 3–8.

35. George Chauncey, *Gay New York: Gender, Urban Culture, and the Making of the Gay Male World, 1890–1940* (New York: Basic Books, 1994), 301, 305–310, 327, 334–339.

36. Meeting at the Fairbanks Center, Indianapolis, Indiana, observed by author, 11 May 2004.

37. Indeed, as the *Indianapolis Star* has reported, Hoosiers remain a very religious people who largely expect their politicians to be religious as well. See *Indianapolis Star*, 27 June, 28 June 2004.

Bibliography

Archives and Repositories

Archives and Brethren Historical Collection, Funderburg Library, Manchester College, North Manchester, Indiana.

Archives of the Congregational Church, Boston, Massachusetts.

Archives of Earlham College, Library, Richmond, Indiana.

Archives of First Baptist Church, Indianapolis, Indiana.

Archives of Franklin College, Franklin, Indiana.

Archives of Indiana University, Bloomington, Indiana.

Archives of Indiana University-Purdue University Indianapolis, Indianapolis, Indiana.

Archives of Meridian Street United Methodist Church, Indianapolis, Indiana.

Archives of the Polis Center, Indiana University-Purdue University Indianapolis, Indianapolis, Indiana.

Archives of Roberts Park United Methodist Church, Indianapolis, Indiana.

Archives of St. Paul's Memorial United Methodist Church, South Bend, Indiana.

Archives of Second Presbyterian Church, Indianapolis, Indiana.

Archives and Special Collections, Roy O. West Library, DePauw University, Greencastle, Indiana.

Archives of the University of Notre Dame, Notre Dame, Indiana.

Conner Prairie Archives, Conner Prairie Living History Museum, Fishers, Indiana.

Franklin D. Roosevelt Presidential Library, Hyde Park, New York.

Hamilton County Historical Society, Noblesville, Indiana.

Herbert Hoover Presidential Library and Museum, West Branch, Iowa.

Indiana Historical Society, Indianapolis, Indiana.

Indiana State Archives, Indianapolis, Indiana.

Indiana State Library, Indianapolis, Indiana.

Library of Congress, Washington, DC.

Lilly Library, Indiana University, Bloomington, Indiana.

Ohio Historical Society, Columbus, Ohio.

Seitz Family Materials, courtesy of Cynthia Hendee Henry, in possession of author.

Southern Baptist Historical Library and Archives, Nashville, Tennessee.

Westerville Public Library, Westerville, Ohio.

Articles: Primary

Black, Forrest Revere. "The 'Right of Castle' and Prohibition Enforcement." *Notre Dame Lawyer* 5 (February 1930): 249–254.

Butler, Paul. "Contempt and Executive Power to Pardon." *Notre Dame Lawyer* 4 (April 1929): 443–447.

Crooker, Joseph Henry. "The Psychology of Drink." *American Journal of Sociology* 18 (July 1912): 21–32.

Daily, John A. "The Intemperance of Fanaticism." *Notre Dame Lawyer* 1 (April–May 1926): 182–185.

Gilliom, Arthur L. "Searches and Seizures in the Administration of the Criminal Law of Indiana." *Indiana Law Journal* 1 (February 1926): 65–73.

Howard, George Elliot. "Alcohol and Crime: A Study in Social Causation." *American Journal of Sociology* 24 (July 1918): 61–80.

Manion, Clarence. "What Price Prohibition?" *Notre Dame Lawyer* 2 (January 1927): 73–94.

Notes and Comment. *Cornell Law Quarterly* 14 (1928–1929): 484–489.

Recent Case Notes. *Indiana Law Journal* 3 (1927–1928): 149.

Recent Case Notes. *Indiana Law Journal* 4 (1928–1929): 550–551.

Recent Case Notes. *Yale Law Journal* 38 (1928–1929): 819–820.

Recent Cases. *Harvard Law Review* 41 (1927–1928): 254–255.

Recent Cases. *Illinois Law Review* 22 (1928): 768–770.

Recent Cases. *Texas Law Review* 6 (1927–1928): 388–389.

Recent Cases. *University of Pennsylvania Law Review* 76 (1927–1928): 210–211.

Recent Decisions. *St. John's Law Review* 2 (1927): 88–89.

Recent Important Decisions. *Michigan Law Review* 26 (1927–1928): 440–441.

Rudy, Clarence J. "Hypocrisy—A By-product of Paternalism." *Notre Dame Lawyer* 4 (March 1929): 374–381.

Articles: Secondary

Bederman, Gail. "'The Women Have Had Charge of the Church Work Long Enough': The Men and Religion Forward Movement of 1911–1912 and the Masculinization of Middle-Class Protestantism." *American Quarterly* 41 (September 1989): 432–465.

Betten, Neil and Raymond A. Mohl. "The Evolution of Racism in an Industrial City, 1906–1940: A Case Study of Gary, Indiana." *Journal of Negro History* 59 (January 1974): 51–64.

Blocker, Jack S., Jr. "Did Prohibition Really Work? Alcohol Prohibition as a Public Health Innovation." *American Journal of Public Health* (February 2006): 233–343.

Bohn, Frank. "The Ku Klux Klan Interpreted." *American Journal of Sociology* 30 (January 1925): 385–407.

Butler, Jon. "Jack-in-the-Box Faith: The Religion Problem in Modern American History." *Journal of American History* 90 (March 2004): 1357–1378.

Campbell, Ballard C. "Did Democracy Work? Prohibition in Late Nineteenth-Century Iowa: A Test Case." *Journal of Interdisciplinary History* 8 (Summer 1977): 87–116.

Canup, Charles E. "Temperance Movements and Legislation in Indiana." *Indiana Magazine of History* 16 (March 1920): 3–37.

———. "The Temperance Movement in Indiana." *Indiana Magazine of History* 16 (June 1920): 112–151.

Christmon, Kenneth. "Historical Overview of Alcohol in the African-American Community." *Journal of Black Studies* 25 (January 1995): 318–330.

Couvares, Francis G. "Hollywood, Main Street, and the Church: Trying to Censor the Movies before the Production Code." *American Quarterly* 44 (December 1992): 584–616.

Crowe, Charles. "Racial Violence and Social Reform: Origins of the Atlanta Riot of 1906." *Journal of Negro History* 53 (July 1968): 234–256.

Davies, Andrew. "The Police and the People: Gambling in Salford, 1900–1939." *Historical Journal* 34 (March 1991): 87–115.

Dumenil, Lynn. "'The Insatiable Maw of Bureaucracy': Antistatism and Education Reform in the 1920s." *Journal of American History* 77 (September 1990): 499–524.

Eagles, Charles W. "Congressional Voting in the 1920s: A Test of Urban-Rural Conflict." *Journal of American History* 76 (September 1989): 528–534.

Ellis, William E. "Patrick Henry Callahan: A Maverick Catholic and the Prohibition Issue." *The Register of the Kentucky Historical Society* 92 (Spring 1994): 175–199.

Erenberg, Lewis A. "From New York to Middletown: Repeal and the Legitimization of Nightlife in the Great Depression." *American Quarterly* 38 (Winter 1986): 761–778.

Evans, C. Wyatt. "Of Mummies and Methodism: Reverend Clarence True Wilson and the Legend of John Wilkes Booth." *Journal of Southern Religion* (2002).

Feldman, Egal. "Prostitution, the Alien Woman and the Progressive Imagination, 1910–1915." *American Quarterly* 19 (Summer 1967): 192–206.

Filene, Peter G. "An Obituary for the 'Progressive Movement.'" *American Quarterly* 22 (Spring 1970): 20–34.

Gilfoyle, Timothy J. "The Moral Origins of Political Surveillance: The Preventive Society in New York City, 1867–1918." *American Quarterly* 38 (Autumn, 1986): 637–652.

Griffin, Clifford S. "Religious Benevolence as Social Control, 1815–1860." *Mississippi Valley Historical Review* 44 (December 1957): 423–444.

Handy, Robert T. "The Protestant Quest for a Christian America, 1830–1930." *Church History* 22 (March 1953): 8–20.

———. "The American Religious Depression, 1925–1935." *Church History* 29 (March 1960): 3–16.

Hanes, Walton, Jr., and James E. Taylor. "Blacks and the Southern Prohibition Movement." *Phylon* 32 (Third Quarter, 1971): 247–259.

Harris, Carl V. "Reforms in Government Control of Negroes in Birmingham, Alabama, 1890–1920." *Journal of Southern History* 38 (November 1972): 567–600.

Hatch, Nathan O. "The Puzzle of American Methodism." *Church History* 63 (June 1994): 175–189.

Higham, John. "The Mind of a Nativist: Henry F. Bowers and the A.P.A." *American Quarterly* 4 (Spring 1952): 16–24.

Hoover, Dwight W. "Daisy Douglas Barr: From Quaker to Klan 'Kluckeress.'" *Indiana Magazine of History* 87 (June 1991): 171–195.

Hutchison, William R. "Cultural Strain and Protestant Liberalism." *American Historical Review* 76 (April 1971): 386–411.

Jacobson, Eric S. "Silent Observer or Silent Partner: Methodism and the Texas Ku Klux Klan, 1921–1925." *Methodist History* 31 (January 1993): 104–112.

Jordan, Philip D. "Immigrants, Methodists, and a 'Conservative Social Gospel,' 1865–1908." *Methodist History* 17 (October 1978): 16–43.

Kingsdale, Jon M. "The 'Poor Man's Club': Social Functions of the Urban Working-Class Saloon." *American Quarterly* 25 (October 1973): 472–489.

Kirby, James E. "Dearest Ellen: Correspondence between Bishop Matthew Simpson and His Wife." *Methodist History* 42 (April 2004): 135–147.

Kramer, Paul. "Empires, Exceptions, and Anglo-Saxons: Race and Rule between the British and United States Empires, 1880–1910." *Journal of American History* 88 (March 2002): 1315–1353.

Lee, Alfred McClung. "Techniques of Social Reform: An Analysis of the New Prohibition Drive." *American Sociological Review* 9 (February 1944): 65–77.

Lyon, Vincent T. "The Repeal of Prohibition: The End of Oklahoma's Noble Experiment." *Chronicle of Oklahoma* 76, no. 4 (1998–1999): 416–435.

Mark, Gregory A., and Christopher L. Eisgruber. "Introduction: Law and Political Culture." *University of Chicago Law Review* 55 (Spring 1988): 413–427.

McCullough, David J. "Bone Dry? Prohibition New Mexico Style, 1918–1933." *New Mexico Historical Review* 63 (January 1988): 25–42.

Meagher, Timothy J. "'Why Should We Care for a Little Trouble or a Walk through the Mud': St. Patrick's and Columbus Day Parades in Worcester, Massachusetts, 1845–1915." *New England Quarterly* 58 (March 1985): 5–26.

Miller, Robert Moats. "A Note on the Relationship between the Protestant Churches and the Revived Ku Klux Klan." *Journal of Southern History* 22 (August 1956): 355–368.

Moats, Francis I. "The Rise of Methodism in the Middle West." *Mississippi Valley Historical Review* 15 (June 1928): 69–88.

Monkkonen, Eric H. "A Disorderly People? Urban Order in the Nineteenth and Twentieth Centuries." *Journal of American History* 68 (December 1981): 539–559.

Morrow, Ralph E. "Northern Methodism in the South during Reconstruction." *Mississippi Valley Historical Review* 41 (September 1954): 197–218.

Murphy, Mary. "Bootlegging Mothers and Drinking Daughters: Gender and Prohibition in Butte, Montana." *American Quarterly* 46 (June 1994): 174–194.

Murphy, Paul L. "Sources and Nature of Intolerance in the 1920s." *Journal of American History* 51 (June 1964): 60–76.

Norrell, Robert J. "Labor at the Ballot Box: Alabama Politics from the New Deal to the Dixiecrat Movement." *Journal of Southern History* 57 (May 1991): 201–234.

Pegram, Thomas R. "The Dry Machine: The Formation of the Anti-Saloon League of Illinois," *Illinois Historical Journal* 83 (Autumn 1990): 173–186.

―――. "Temperance Politics and Regional Political Culture: The Anti-Saloon League in Maryland and the South, 1907–1915." *Journal of Southern History* 63 (February 1997): 57–90.

Pierard, Richard V. "The Church of the Brethren and the Temperance Movement." *Brethren Life and Thought* 26 (1981): 36–44.

Quinn, John F. "Father Mathew's Disciples: American Catholic Support for Temperance, 1840–1920." *Church History* 65 (December 1996): 624–640.

―――. "It's Fashionable Here to be a Total Abstainer": Temperance Advocacy at the University of Notre Dame, 1870–1940." *American Catholic Studies* 110 (Spring–Winter 1999): 1–27.

Riegel, Robert E. "Changing American Attitudes toward Prostitution (1800–1920)." *Journal of the History of Ideas* 29 (July–September 1968): 437–452.

Robins, Roger. "Vernacular American Landscape: Methodists, Camp Meetings, and Social Respectability." *Religion and American Culture* 4 (Summer 1994): 165–191.

Safianow, Allen. "The Klan Comes to Tipton." *Indiana Magazine of History* 95 (September 1999): 202–231.

―――. "'You Can't Burn History': Getting Right with the Klan in Noblesville, Indiana." *Indiana Magazine of History* 100 (June 2004): 109–154.

Sanchez, Tanya Marie. "The Feminine Side of Bootlegging." *Louisiana History* 41, no 4 (2000): 403–433.

Scott, Anne Firor. "Most Invisible of All: Black Women's Voluntary Associations." *Journal of Southern History* 56 (February 1990): 3–22.

Shryock, Richard H. "Sylvester Graham and the Popular Health Movement, 1830–1870." *Mississippi Valley Historical Review* 18 (September 1931): 172–183.

Spann, Glenn. "Theological Transition within Methodism: The Rise of Liberalism and the Conservative Response." *Methodist History* 43 (April 2005): 198–212.

Stearns, Peter N. "The Effort at Continuity in Working-Class Culture." *Journal of Modern History* 52 (December 1980): 626–655.

Szymanski, Ann-Marie E. "Dry Compulsions: Prohibition and the Creation of State-Level Enforcement Agencies." *Journal of Policy History* 11 (1999): 115–146.

Thelen, David P. "LaFollette and the Temperance Crusade." *Wisconsin Magazine of History* 47 (Summer 1964): 291–300.

Thornbrough, Emma Lou. "Segregation in Indiana during the Klan Era of the 1920s." *Mississippi Valley Historical Review* 47 (March 1961): 594–618.

Vaughn, Stephen. "The Devil's Advocate: Will H. Hays and the Campaign to Make Movies Respectable." *Indiana Magazine of History* 101 (June 2005): 125–152.

Yankelovich, Daniel. "Poll Positions: What Americans Really Think about U.S. Foreign Policy." *Foreign Affairs* 84 (September/October 2005): 2–16.
Yrigoyen, Charles Jr. "Methodists and Roman Catholics in Nineteenth Century America." *Methodist History* 28 (April 1990): 172–186.

Books: Primary

Aptheker, Herbert. Editor. *Writings by WEB DuBois in Periodicals Edited by Others*, Volume 2, *1910–1934*. Milwood, NY: Kraus-Thomgon Organization, 1982.
Artman, Samuel R. *The Legalized Outlaw*. Indianapolis: Levey Brothers and Company, 1908.
B., Hamilton. *Getting Started in AA*. Center City, MN: Hazelden Press, 1995.
Bagnell, Robert. *Economic and Moral Aspects of the Liquor Business*. New York: Funk and Wagnalls Company, 1912.
Ball, Frank Clayton. *Memoirs of Frank Clayton Ball*. Muncie, IN: Scott Printing Company, 1937.
Barker, John Marshall. *The Saloon Problem and Social Reform*. Boston: The Everett Press, 1905.
Beadle, J. H. *The Women's War on Whisky*. Cincinnati: Wilstach, Baldwin and Company, 1874.
Beecher, Lyman. *Six Sermons on the Nature, Occasions, Signs, Evils, and Remedy of Intemperance*. New York: American Tract Society, 1827.
Bishop, Charlie, Jr., and Bill Pittman. *To Be Continued: The AA World Bibliography, 1935–1994*. Wheeling, WV: The Bishop of Books, 1994.
Bowman, Lewis S., Charles Kettleborough, Christopher B. Coleman, Edward F. Warfel, and J. Otto Lee. Editors. *Indiana 1926*. Indianapolis: William B. Burford, 1926.
Budenz, Louis Francis. *This Is My Story*. New York: McGraw-Hill Company, 1947.
Cannon, James, Jr. *Bishop Cannon's Own Story: Life as I have seen it*. Durham, NC: Duke University Press, 1955.
Catton, Bruce. *Waiting for the Morning Train: An American Boyhood*. Detroit: Wayne State University Press, 1987.
Cherrington, Ernest Hurst. General Editor. *Standard Encyclopedia of the Alcohol Problem*. Volume 3 and Volume 5. Westerville, OH: American Issue Publishing Company, 1926, 1929.
———. Editor. *Anti-Saloon League Yearbook 1928*. Westerville, OH: The American Issue Press, 1928.
Costomiris, Lois Kaiser. *Rail Fences, Rolling Pins, and Rainbows: Hamilton County Bygone Days*. Indianapolis: Guild Press of Indiana, 1994.

Davis, Jerome. Editor. *Christianity and Social Adventuring*. New York: The Century Company, 1927.

Downey, David G., E. W. Halford, and Ralph Welles Keeler. Editors. *Militant Methodism: The Story of the First National Convention of Methodist Men*. Cincinnati: The Methodist Book Concern, 1913.

Eliot, T. S. *Christianity and Culture: The Idea of a Christian Society and Notes towards the Definition of Culture*. New York: A Harvest Book, 1976.

Farley, James A. *Behind the Ballots: The Personal History of a Politician*. New York: Harcourt, Brace and Company, 1938.

Fernald, James C. *The Economics of Prohibition*. New York: Funk and Wagnalls, 1890.

Fisher, Irving. *The Noble Experiment*. New York: Alcohol Information Committee, 1930.

Gladden, Washington. *Applied Christianity: Moral Aspects of Social Questions*. New York: Houghton Mifflin, 1914.

Gorn, Elliot J. Editor. *The McGuffey Readers: Selections from the 1879 Edition*. New York: Bedford/St. Martin's, 1998.

Graham, Thomas E. Editor. *The Agricultural Social Gospel in America: The Gospel of the Farm by Jenkin Lloyd Jones*. Lewiston, NY: The Edwin Mellen Press, 1986.

Hanly, J. Frank, and Oliver Wayne Stewart. Editors. *Speeches of the Flying Squadron*. Indianapolis: Hanly and Stewart, 1915.

Hays, Will H. *The Memoirs of Will H. Hays*. Garden City, NY: Doubleday and Company, 1955.

Homan, J. A. *Prohibition: The Enemy of Temperance*. Cincinnati, OH: The Christian Liberty Bureau, 1910.

Hoover, Herbert. *The Memoirs of Herbert Hoover: The Cabinet and the Presidency, 1920–1933*. New York: The Macmillan Company, 1952.

Hudson, Winthrop S. Editor. *Walter Rauschenbusch: Selected Writings*. New York: Paulist Press, 1984.

Journal of the House of Representatives of the State of Indiana.

Journal of the Indiana State Senate.

Journal of the Indiana Annual Conference of the Methodist Episcopal Church.

Journal of the Northwest Indiana Annual Conference of the Methodist Episcopal Church.

Leibowitz, Irving. *My Indiana*. Englewood Cliffs, NJ: Prentice-Hall, 1964.

MacFarland, Charles S. Editor. *Christian Unity at Work: The Federal Council of the Churches of Christ in America in Quadrennial Session at Chicago, Illinois, 1912*. New York: Federal Council of Churches, 1913.

Marshall, Thomas R. *Recollections of Thomas R. Marshall, Vice President and Hoosier Philosopher: A Hoosier Salad*. Indianapolis: Bobbs-Merrill Company, 1925.

Mathews, Shailer. *The Individual and the Social Gospel.* New York: Missionary Education Movement of the U.S. and Canada, 1914.

Monahan, M. *A Text-book of True Temperance.* New York: U.S. Brewers Association, 1911.

Opinions of the Attorney General of Indiana for the Period from January 1 1925 to January 1 1927. Indianapolis: William B. Burford, 1927.

Rauschenbusch, Walter. *Christianity and the Social Crisis.* New York: MacMillan Company, 1908.

———. *Christianizing the Social Order.* New York: MacMillan Company, 1913.

———. *A Gospel for the Social Awakening.* New York: Association Press, 1950.

Rohrer, Fred. *Saloon Fight at Berne, Indiana: Not a Novel, But Real History: Truth Stranger than Fiction.* Berne, IN: The Berne Witness Company, 1913.

Sanford, Elias B. Editor. *Federal Council of the Churches of Christ in America: Report of the First Meeting of the Federal Council, Philadelphia, 1908.* New York: The Revell Press, 1909.

———. *Origin and History of the Federal Council of the Churches of Christ in America.* Hartford, CT: S.S. Scranton Company, 1916.

Seldes, Gilbert. *The Future of Drinking.* Boston: Little, Brown and Company, 1930.

Shumaker, Edward S. *Descendants of Henry Keller of York County, Pennsylvania and Fairfield County, Ohio.* Indianapolis: Edward S. Shumaker, 1924.

———. *The Autobiography of Edward Seitz Shumaker.* Unpublished, 1929.

Tipple, Bertrand M. *Alien Rome.* Washington, DC: The Protestant Guards, 1924.

Tumulty, Joseph P. *Woodrow Wilson As I Know Him.* New York: Doubleday, Page and Company, 1921.

Washington, Booker T. *Up from Slavery: An Autobiography.* Garden City, NY: Doubleday and Company, 1901.

Watson, James E. *As I Knew Them: Memoirs of James E. Watson, Former United States Senator from Indiana.* Indianapolis: Bobbs-Merrill Company, 1936.

Weeden, William B. *The Morality of Liquor Laws.* Boston: Roberts Brothers, 1875.

Wilson, Clarence True. *The Case for Prohibition: Its Past, Present Accomplishments, and Future in America.* New York: Funk and Wagnalls Company, 1924.

Winger, Ortho. *History and Doctrines of the Church of the Brethren.* Elgin, IL: Brethren Publishing House, 1919.

Wooden, John, with Jack Tobin. *They Call Me Coach.* Chicago: Contemporary Books, 1988.

The World League against Alcoholism November 24–29, 1922 Meeting in Toronto. Westerville, OH: American Issue Press, 1922.

Books: Secondary

Albertson, Dean. *Roosevelt's Farmer: Claude R. Wickard in the New Deal*. New York: Columbia University Press, 1961.

Allitt, Patrick. *Catholic Converts: British and American Intellectuals Turn to Rome*. Ithaca: Cornell University Press, 1997.

Ambrose, Stephen E. *Crazy Horse and Custer: The Parallel Lives of Two American Warriors*. New York: Anchor Books, 1996.

Ashby, Leroy. *The Spearless Leader: Senator Borah and the Progressive Movement in the 1920s*. Chicago: University of Illinois Press, 1972.

Atherton, Lewis. *Main Street on the Middle Border*. Bloomington: Indiana University Press, 1984.

Banham, Russ. *Coors: A Rocky Mountain Legend*. Lyme, CT: Greenwich Publishing Group, 1998.

Barnard, Ellsworth. *Wendell Willkie: Fighter for Freedom*. Marquette: Northern Michigan University Press, 1966.

Barrows, Robert G. *Albion Fellows Bacon: Indiana's Municipal Housekeeper*. Indianapolis: Indiana University Press, 2000.

Barrows, Susanna, and Robin Room. Editors. *Drinking: Behavior and Belief in Modern History*. Los Angeles: University of California Press, 1991.

Barton, Bruce. *The Man Nobody Knows: A Discovery of the Real Jesus*. Indianapolis: Bobbs-Merrill Company, 1925.

Bateman, Newton. Editor. *Effingham County*. Chicago: Munsell Publishers, 1910.

Bates, J. Leonard. *Senator Thomas J. Walsh of Montana: Law and Public Affairs from TR to FDR*. Chicago: University of Illinois Press, 1999.

Becker, Edwin L. *From Sovereign to Servant: The Church Federation of Greater Indianapolis, 1912–1987*. Indianapolis: The Church Federation of Greater Indianapolis, 1987.

Behr, Edward. *Prohibition: Thirteen Years that Changed America*. New York: Arcade Publishing, 1996.

Bell, Marion L. *Crusade in the City: Revivalism in Nineteenth-Century Philadelphia*. Lewisburg, PA: Bucknell University Press, 1977.

Bennett, David J. *He Almost Changed the World: The Life and Times of Thomas Riley Marshall*. Bloomington, IN: Author House Press, 2007.

Black, Edwin. *War against the Weak: Eugenics and America's Campaign to Create a Master Race*. New York: Four Walls Eight Windows, 2003.

Black, Gregory D. *The Catholic Crusade Against the Movies, 1940–1975*. New York: Cambridge University Press, 1998.

Blake, I. George. *Paul V. McNutt: Portrait of a Hoosier Statesman*. Indianapolis: Central Publishing Company, 1966.

Bland, Joan. *Hibernian Crusade: The Story of the Catholic Total Abstinence Union of America.* Washington, DC: The Catholic University of America Press, 1951.

Blee, Kathleen M. *Women of the Klan: Racism and Gender in the 1920s.* Los Angeles: University of California Press, 1991.

Blocker, Jack S., Jr. *Retreat from Reform: The Prohibition Movement in the United States, 1890–1913.* Westport, CT: Greenwood Press, 1976.

———. *American Temperance Movements: Cycles of Reform.* Boston: Twayne Publishers, 1989.

Blumhofer, Edith L. *Aimee Semple McPherson: Everybody's Sister.* Grand Rapids, MI: William B. Eerdmans Publishing Company, 1993.

Bodnar, John. *Remaking America: Public Memory, Commemoration, and Patriotism in the Twentieth Century.* Princeton, NJ: Princeton University Press, 1992.

Bogue, Allan G. *From Prairie to Corn Belt: Farming on the Illinois and Iowa Prairies in the Nineteenth Century.* Chicago: University of Chicago Press, 1963.

Bordin, Ruth. *Frances Willard: A Biography.* Chapel Hill: University of North Carolina Press, 1986.

Bowers, Claude G. *Beveridge and the Progressive Era.* New York: The Literacy Guild, 1932.

Boyer, Paul. *Urban Masses and Moral Order in America, 1820–1920.* Cambridge, MA: Harvard University Press, 1997.

Braeman, John. *Albert J. Beveridge: American Nationalist.* Chicago: University of Chicago Press, 1971.

Brinkley, Alan. *Voices of Protest: Huey Long, Father Coughlin, and the Great Depression.* New York: Vintage Books, 1983.

———. *Liberalism and Its Discontents.* Cambridge, MA: Harvard University Press, 1998.

Bruce, Dickson D. *And They All Sang Hallelujah: Plain-Folk Camp-Meeting Religion, 1800–1845.* Knoxville: University of Tennessee Press, 1974.

Bucke, Emory Stevens. General Editor. *The History of American Methodism,* Volume 3. New York: Abingdon Press, 1964.

Buenker, John D. *Urban Liberalism and Progressive Reform.* New York: Charles Scribner's Sons, 1973.

Burnham, John C. *Bad Habits: Drinking, Smoking, Taking Drugs, Gambling, Sexual Misbehavior, and Swearing in American History.* New York: New York University Press, 1993.

Burns, Eric. *The Spirits of America: A Social History of Alcohol.* Philadelphia: Temple University Press, 2003.

Burns, James MacGregor. *Roosevelt: The Lion and the Fox.* New York: Harcourt, Brace, and World, 1956.

Burns, Robert E. *Being Catholic, Being American: The Notre Dame Story, 1842–1934.* Notre Dame, IN: University of Notre Dame Press, 1999.

Butler, Brian. *An Undergrowth of Folly: Public Order, Race, Anxiety, and the 1903 Evansville, Indiana Riot*. New York: Garland Publishing, 2000.

Cady, John F. *The Origin and Development of the Missionary Baptist Church in Indiana*. Berne, IN: Berne Witness Company, 1942.

Carter, Paul A. *The Decline and Revival of the Social Gospel: Social and Political Liberalism in American Protestant Churches, 1920–1940*. Ithaca, NY: Cornell University Press, 1956.

Carter, Stephen L. *God's Name in Vain: The Wrongs and Rights of Religion in Politics*. New York: Basic Books, 2000.

Cayton, Andrew R. L., and Peter S. Onuf. *The Midwest and the Nation: Rethinking the History of an American Region*. Indianapolis: Indiana University Press, 1990.

Chadwick, Owen. *The Secularization of the European Mind in the Nineteenth Century*. New York: Cambridge University Press, 1995.

Chalmers, David M. *Hooded Americanism: The History of the Ku Klux Klan*. Durham, NC: Duke University Press, 1987.

Chambers, John Whiteclay, II. *The Tyranny of Change: America in the Progressive Era, 1890–1920*. New Brunswick, NJ: Rutgers University Press, 2000.

Chauncey, George. *Gay New York: Gender, Urban Culture, and the Making of the Gay Male World, 1890–1940*. New York: Basic Books, 1994.

Clark, Norman H. *Deliver Us from Evil: An Interpretation of American Prohibition*. New York: W. W. Norton and Company, 1976.

Clark, Thomas D. *Indiana University, Mid-Western Pioneer: In Middle Passage*. Bloomington: Indiana University Press, 1973.

Clawson, Mary Ann. *Constructing Brotherhood: Class, Gender, and Fraternalism*. Princeton, NJ: Princeton University Press, 1989.

Coben, Stanley. *Rebellion against Victorianism: The Impetus for Cultural Change in 1920s America*. New York: Oxford University Press, 1991.

Coffey, Thomas M. *The Long Thirst: Prohibition in America, 1920–1933*. New York: Dell Publishing Company, 1976.

Creech, Joe. *Righteous Indignation: Religion and the Populist Revolution*. Chicago: University of Illinois Press, 2006.

Crunden, Robert M. *Ministers of Reform: The Progressives' Achievement in American Civilization, 1889–1920*. Chicago: University of Illinois Press, 1984.

Cummins, Cedric C. *Indiana Public Opinion and the World War, 1914–1917*. Indianapolis: Indiana Historical Bureau, 1945.

D'Agostino, Peter R. *Rome in America: Transnational Catholic Ideology from the Risorgimento to Fascism*. Chapel Hill: University of North Carolina Press, 2004.

Detzler, Jack J. *The History of the Northwest Indiana Conference of the Methodist Church, 1852–1951*. Nashville, TN: The Parthenon Press, 1953.

Develling, C. T. *History of the 17th Regiment, 1st Brigade, 3rd Division, 14th Corps, Army of the Cumberland, War of the Rebellion*. Zanesville, OH: E. R. Sullivan, 1889.

Dingle, A. E. *The Campaign for Prohibition in Victorian England: The United Kingdom Alliance, 1872–1895.* New Brunswick, NJ: Rutgers University Press, 1980.

Dodge, Mark M. Editor. *Herbert Hoover and the Historians.* West Branch, IA: Herbert Hoover Presidential Library Association, 1989.

Dolan, Jay P. *The American Catholic Experience: A History from Colonial Times to the Present.* Garden City, NY: Doubleday, 1985.

———. *The Immigrant Church: New York's Irish and German Catholics, 1815–1865.* Notre Dame, IN: University of Notre Dame Press, 1987.

Dorsett, Lyle W. *Billy Sunday and the Redemption of Urban America.* Grand Rapids, MI: William B. Eerdmans Publishing Company, 1991.

Douglas, Ann. *The Feminization of American Culture.* New York: Alfred A. Knopf, 1979.

Duis, Perry R. *The Saloon: Public Drinking in Chicago and Boston, 1880–1920.* Chicago: University of Illinois Press, 1983.

Dumenil, Lynn. *In the Modern Temper: American Culture and Society in the 1920s.* New York: Hill and Wang, 1995.

Dunbar, Willis F., and George S. May. *Michigan: A History of the Wolverine State.* Grand Rapids, MI: William B. Eerdmans Publishing Company, 1995.

Eisenach, Eldon J. Editor. *The Social and Political Thought of American Progressivism.* Indianapolis: Hackett Publishing Company, 2006.

Ellis, John Tracy. *The Life of James Cardinal Gibbons* (popular edition). Milwaukee: Bruce Publishing Company, 1963.

Ellis, William E. *"A Man of Books and a Man of the People": E. Y. Mullins and the Crisis of Moderate Southern Baptist Leadership.* Macon, GA: Mercer University Press, 1988.

Endelman, Judith E. *The Jewish Community of Indianapolis, 1849 to the Present.* Bloomington: Indiana University Press, 1984.

Engelmann, Larry. *Intemperance: The Lost War against Liquor.* New York: The Free Press, 1979.

Fadely, James Philip. *Thomas Taggart: Public Servant, Political Boss, 1856–1929.* Indianapolis: Indiana Historical Society, 1997.

Fahey, David M. *Temperance and Racism: John Bull, Johnny Reb, and the Good Templars.* Lexington: University Press of Kentucky, 1996.

Fass, Paula S. *The Damned and the Beautiful: American Youth in the 1920s.* New York: Oxford University Press, 1979.

Fausold, Martin L. *The Presidency of Herbert C. Hoover.* Lawrence: University of Kansas Press, 1985.

Feldman, Glenn. *Politics, Society, and the Klan in Alabama, 1915–1949.* Tuscaloosa: University of Alabama Press, 1999.

Ferrell, Robert H. *The Presidency of Calvin Coolidge.* Lawrence: University of Kansas Press, 1998.

Flake, Kathleen. *The Politics of American Religious Identity: The Seating of Senator Reed Smoot, Mormon Apostle*. Chapel Hill: University of North Carolina Press, 2004.

Flink, James J. *The Automobile Age*. Cambridge, MA: The MIT Press, 1993.

Flynn, Clarence E. Editor. *The Indianapolis Area of the Methodist Episcopal Church, 1924–1928: A Record and History*. Anderson, IN: Herald Publishing Company, 1928.

Flynt, Wayne. *Cracker Messiah: Governor Sidney V. Catts of Florida*. Baton Rouge: Louisiana State University Press, 1977.

———. *Alabama Baptists: Southern Baptists in the Heart of Dixie*. Tuscaloosa: University of Alabama Press, 1998.

Foster, Charles I. *An Errand of Mercy: The Evangelical United Front, 1790–1837*. Chapel Hill: University of North Carolina Press, 1960.

Foster, Gaines M. *Moral Reconstruction: Christian Lobbyists and the Federal Legislation of Morality, 1865–1920*. Chapel Hill: University of North Carolina Press, 2002.

Geib, George W., and Donald B. Kite, Sr. *Federal Justice in Indiana: The History of the United States District Court for the Southern District of Indiana*. Indianapolis: Indiana Historical Society, 2007.

Gerber, Philip L. *Theodore Dreiser*. New York: Twayne Publishing, 1964.

Gerstle, Gary. *American Crucible: Race and Nation in the Twentieth Century*. Princeton, NJ: Princeton University Press, 2001.

Gibbs, Joseph C. *History of the Catholic Total Abstinence Union of America*. Philadelphia: Penn Printing House, 1907.

Glad, Paul W. *The Trumpet Soundeth: William Jennings Bryan and His Democracy, 1896–1912*. Lincoln: University of Nebraska Press, 1960.

Goodwyn, Lawrence. *Democratic Promise: The Populist Moment in America*. New York: Oxford University Press, 1976.

Gorrell, Donald K. *The Age of Social Responsibility: The Social Gospel in the Progressive Era, 1900–1920*. Macon, GA: Mercer University Press, 1988.

Grace, Fran. *Carry A. Nation: Retelling the Life*. Indianapolis: Indiana University Press, 2001.

Graham, Otis L., Jr. *An Encore for Reform: The Old Progressives and the New Deal*. New York: Oxford University Press, 1967.

Gray, Ralph D. Editor. *Gentlemen from Indiana: National Party Candidates, 1836–1940*. Indianapolis: Indiana Historical Bureau, 1977.

Grossman, James R. *Land of Hope: Chicago, Black Southerners, and the Great Migration*. Chicago: University of Chicago Press, 1991.

Gugin, Linda C., and James E. St. Clair. *Sherman Minton: New Deal Senator, Cold War Justice*. Indianapolis: Indiana Historical Society, 1997.

Gusfield, Joseph R. *Symbolic Crusade: Status Politics and the American Temperance Movement*. Chicago: University of Illinois Press, 1986.

————. *Contested Meanings: The Construction of Alcohol Problems.* Madison: University of Wisconsin Press, 1996.

Hair, William Ivy. *The Kingfish and His Realm: The Life and Times of Huey P. Long.* Baton Rouge: Louisiana State University Press, 1991.

Hamm, Richard F. *Shaping the Eighteenth Amendment: Temperance Reform, Legal Culture, and the Polity, 1880–1920.* Chapel Hill: University of North Carolina Press, 1995.

Hamm, Thomas D. *The Transformation of American Quakerism: Orthodox Friends, 1800–1907.* Indianapolis: Indiana University Press, 1992.

Hangen, Tona J. *Redeeming the Dial: Radio, Religion, and Popular Culture in America.* Chapel Hill: University of North Carolina Press, 2002.

Harlan, Louis R. *Booker T. Washington: The Wizard of Tuskegee, 1901–1915.* New York: Oxford University Press, 1983.

Harrison, Harry P., and Karl Detzer. *Culture under Canvas: The Story of Tent Chautauqua.* New York: Hastings House, 1958.

Hatch, Nathan O. *The Democratization of American Christianity.* New Haven, CT: Yale University Press, 1989.

Hattersley, Roy. *Blood and Fire: William and Catherine Booth and Their Salvation Army.* New York: Doubleday, 2000.

Heller, Herbert L. *Indiana Conference of the Methodist Church, 1832–1956.* Indianapolis: History Conference of the Indiana Conference, 1957.

Hendrickson, Frances. *Hoosier Heritage, 1874–1974: Woman's Christian Temperance Union.* Indianapolis: WCTU of Indiana, 1974.

Herlihy, Patricia. *The Alcoholic Empire: Vodka and Politics in Late Imperial Russia.* New York: Oxford University Press, 2002.

Hinson, E. Glenn. *A History of Baptists in Arkansas, 1818–1978.* Little Rock: Arkansas Baptist State Convention, 1979.

Hofstadter, Richard. *The Age of Reform: From Bryan to FDR.* New York: Vintage Books, 1955.

Hohner, Robert A. *Prohibition and Politics: The Life of Bishop James Cannon, Jr.* Columbia: University of South Carolina Press, 1999.

Hopkins, Charles Howard. *The Rise of the Social Gospel in American Protestantism, 1865–1915.* New Haven, CT: Yale University Press, 1967.

Horowitz, David A. Editor. *Inside the Klavern: The Secret History of a Ku Klux Klan of the 1920s.* Carbondale: Southern Illinois University Press, 1999.

Howe, Daniel Walker. *The Political Culture of the American Whigs.* Chicago: University of Chicago Press, 1979.

Huntington, Samuel P. *The Clash of Civilizations and the Remaking of World Order.* New York: Simon and Schuster, 2003.

Jackson, Kenneth T. *The Ku Klux Klan in the City, 1915–1930.* Chicago: Ivan R. Dee, 1992.

Jacobson, Douglas, and William Vance Trollinger, Jr. Editors. *Re-Forming the Center: American Protestantism, 1900 to the Present.* Grand Rapids, MI: William B. Eerdmans Publishing Company, 1998.

Jacobson, Matthew Frye. *Whiteness of a Different Color: European Immigrants and the Alchemy of Race.* Cambridge, MA: Harvard University Press, 1999.

James, William. *The Varieties of Religious Experience: A Study in Human Nature.* New York: A Mentor Book, 1958.

Jeansonne, Glenn. *Gerald L. K. Smith: Minister of Hate.* Baton Rouge: Louisiana State University Press, 1997.

Jenkins, William D. *Steel Valley Klan: The Ku Klux Klan in Ohio's Mahoning Valley.* Kent, OH: Kent State University Press, 1990.

Jensen, Richard. *The Winning of the Midwest: Social and Political Conflict, 1888–1896.* Chicago: University of Chicago Press, 1971.

Johnson, Paul E. *A Shopkeeper's Millennium: Society and Revivals in Rochester, New York, 1815–1837.* New York: Hill and Wang, 1978.

Johnston, Robert D. *The Radical Middle Class: Populist Democracy and the Question of Capitalism in Progressive-Era Portland, Oregon.* Princeton, NJ: Princeton University Press, 2003.

Jones, Donald G. *The Sectional Crisis and Northern Methodism: A Study in Piety, Political Ethics, and Civil Religion.* Metuchen, NJ: The Scarecrow Press, 1979.

Kane, Harnett T. *Louisiana Hayride: The American Rehearsal for Dictatorship, 1928–1940.* New York: William Morrow and Company, 1941.

Kantrowitz, Stephen. *Ben Tillman and the Reconstruction of White Supremacy.* Chapel Hill: University of North Carolina Press, 2000.

Kerr, K. Austin. *Organized for Prohibition: A New History of the Anti-Saloon League.* New Haven, CT: Yale University Press, 1985.

Kerrigan, Colm. *Father Mathew and the Irish Temperance Movement, 1838–1849.* Cork, Ireland: Cork University Press, 1992.

Kleppner, Paul. *The Cross of Culture: A Social Analysis of Midwestern Politics, 1850–1900.* New York: The Free Press, 1970.

———. *Who Voted? The Dynamics of Electoral Turnout, 1870–1980.* New York: Praeger Publishers, 1982.

Kobler, John. *Ardent Spirits: The Rise and Fall of Prohibition.* New York: G. P. Putnam's Sons, 1973.

Kyvig, David E. Editor. *Law, Alcohol, and Order: Perspectives on National Prohibition.* Westport, CT: Greenwood Press, 1985.

———. *Repealing National Prohibition.* Kent, OH: Kent State University Press, 2000.

Lane, Belden C. *Landscapes of the Sacred: Geography and Narrative in American Spirituality.* New York: Paulist Press, 1988.

Lawson, Melinda. *Patriot Fires: Forging a New American Nationalism in the Civil War North.* Lawrence: University of Kansas Press, 2002.

Lay, Shawn. *War, Revolution, and the Ku Klux Klan: A Study of Intolerance in a Border City.* El Paso: Texas Western Press, 1985.

———. Editor. *The Invisible Empire in the West: Toward a New Historical Appraisal of the Ku Klux Klan of the 1920s.* Chicago: University of Illinois Press, 1992.

———. *Hooded Knights on the Niagara: The Ku Klux Klan in Buffalo, New York.* New York: New York University Press, 1995.

Lears, T.J. Jackson. *No Place of Grace: Antimodernism and the Transformation of American Culture, 1880–1920.* Chicago: University of Chicago Press, 1994.

Leopold, Richard W. *Elihu Root and the Conservative Tradition.* Boston: Little, Brown and Company, 1954.

Leuchtenburg, Walter E. *Franklin D. Roosevelt and the New Deal, 1932–1940.* New York: Harper Torchbooks, 1963.

Levine, Lawrence W. *Defender of the Faith: William Jennings Bryan: The Last Decade, 1915–1925.* New York: Oxford University Press, 1965.

Lewis, David Levering. *WEB DuBois: Biography of a Race, 1868–1919.* New York: Henry Holt and Company, 1993.

———. *W.E.B. DuBois: The Fight for Equality and the American Century, 1919–1963.* New York: Henry Holt and Company, 2000.

Lewis, Sinclair. *Main Street.* New York: Signet Classic, 1920.

———. *Elmer Gantry.* New York: Signet Classic, 1927.

Linck, Joseph C., and Raymond J. Kupke. Editors. *Building the Church in America: Studies in Honor of Monsignor Robert F. Trisco on the Occasion of His Seventieth Birthday.* Washington, DC: The Catholic University of America Press, 1999.

Link, William A., and Arthur S. Link. *American Epoch: A History of the United States since 1900,* Volume 1, *War, Reform, and Society, 1900–1945.* New York: McGraw-Hill, 1993.

Liptak, Dolores. Editor. *A Church of Many Cultures: Selected Historical Essays on Ethnic American Catholicism.* New York: Garland Publishing, 1988.

Longfield, Bradley J. *The Presbyterian Controversy: Fundamentalists, Modernists, and Moderates.* New York: Oxford University Press, 1991.

Lower, Richard Coke. *A Bloc of One: The Political Career of Hiram W. Johnson.* Stanford, CA: Stanford University Press, 1993.

Lutholtz, M. William. *Grand Dragon: D.C. Stephenson and the Ku Klux Klan in Indiana.* West Lafayette, IN: Purdue University Press, 1993.

Lynd, Robert S., and Helen Merrell Lynd. *Middletown: A Study in American Culture.* New York: A Harvest Book, 1957.

MacLean, Nancy. *Behind the Mask of Chivalry: The Making of the Second Ku Klux Klan.* New York: Oxford University Press, 1994.

Madison, James H. *Indiana through Tradition and Change: A History of the Hoosier State and Its People, 1920–1945.* Indianapolis: Indiana Historical Society, 1982.

————. *The Indiana Way: A State History*. Indianapolis: Indiana University Press, 1990.

Maffly-Kipp, Laurie F. *Religion and Society in Frontier California*. New Haven, CT: Yale University Press, 1994.

Magnuson, Norris. *Salvation in the Slums: Evangelical Social Work, 1865–1920*. Metuchen, NJ: The Scarecrow Press, 1977.

Manhart, George B. *DePauw through the Years*, Volume 1, *1837–1919*. Greencastle, IN: DePauw University, 1962.

Marsden, George M. *Fundamentalism and American Culture: The Shaping of Twentieth Century Evangelicalism, 1870–1925*. New York: Oxford University Press, 1982.

————. *Jonathan Edwards: A Life*. New Haven, CT: Yale University Press, 2003.

Martin, Robert F. *Hero of the Heartland: Billy Sunday and the Transformation of American Society, 1862–1935*. Indianapolis: Indiana University Press, 2002.

Marty, Martin E. *Pilgrims in Their Own Land: 500 Years of Religion in America*. Boston: Little, Brown, and Company, 1984.

Mason, Alpheus Thomas. *Harlan Fiske Stone: Pillar of the Law*. New York: Viking Press, 1956.

Mattson, Donald E. *One Hundred Fifty Years in Broad Ripple: Celebrating Methodism's Outpost for Preaching the Gospel in Broad Ripple, 1852–2002*. Indianapolis: Broad Ripple United Methodist Church, 2002.

May, Henry. *Protestant Churches and Industrial America*. New York: Harper and Brothers, 1949.

McAllister, Lester G., and William E. Tucker. *Journey in Faith: A History of the Christian Church (Disciples of Christ)*. St. Louis: CBD Press, 1989.

McGeary, M. Nelson. *Gifford Pinchot: Forester, Politician*. Princeton, NJ: Princeton University Press, 1960.

McGerr, Michael E. *The Decline of Popular Politics: The American North, 1865–1928*. New York: Oxford University Press, 1986.

————. *A Fierce Discontent: The Rise and Fall of the Progressive Movement in America, 1870–1920*. New York: The Free Press, 2003.

McGriff, E. Carver. *Amazing Grace: A History of Indiana Methodism, 1801–2001*. Franklin, TN: Providence House Publishers, 2001.

McKenna, Marian C. *Borah*. Ann Arbor: University of Michigan Press, 1961.

McLoughlin, William G., Jr. *Modern Revivalism: Charles Gradison Finney to Billy Graham*. New York: The Ronald Press, 1959.

McMath, Robert C., Jr. *American Populism: A Social History, 1877–1898*. New York: Hill and Wang, 1993.

McNeil, Robert Dean. *Valiant for Truth: Clarence True Wilson and Prohibition*. Portland, OR: Oregonians Concerned about Addiction Problems, 1992.

Meagher, Timothy J. *Inventing Irish America: Generation, Class, and Ethnic Identity in a New England City, 1880–1928.* Notre Dame, IN: University of Notre Dame Press, 2001.

Mecklin, John Moffatt. *The Ku Klux Klan: A Study of the American Mind.* New York: Harcourt, Brace and Company, 1924.

Mencken, H. L. *A Carnival of Buncomb.* Baltimore: The Johns Hopkins University Press, 1956.

Meyer, Donald. *The Protestant Search for Political Realism, 1919–1941.* Middletown, CT: Wesleyan University Press, 1988.

Miller, Robert Moats. *Harry Emerson Fosdick: Preacher, Pastor, Prophet.* New York: Oxford University Press, 1985.

Miller, Timothy. *Following In His Steps: A Biography of Charles M. Sheldon.* Knoxville: University of Tennessee Press, 1987.

Moloney, Deirdre M. *American Catholic Lay Groups and Transatlantic Social Reform in the Progressive Era.* Chapel Hill: University of North Carolina Press, 2002.

Moore, Leonard J. *Citizen Klansmen: The Ku Klux Klan in Indiana, 1921–1928.* Chapel Hill: University of North Carolina Press, 1991.

Morone, James A. *Hellfire Nation: The Politics of Sin in American History.* New Haven, CT: Yale University Press, 2003.

Morris, Edmund. *Theodore Rex.* New York: Random House, 2001.

Morrison, Jeffrey H. *John Witherspoon and the Founding of the American Republic.* Notre Dame, IN: University of Notre Dame Press, 2005.

Moseley, James G. *A Cultural History of Religion in America.* Westport, CT: Greenwood Press, 1981.

Murdock, Catherine Gilbert. *Domesticating Drink: Women, Men, and Alcohol in America, 1870–1940.* Baltimore: Johns Hopkins University Press, 1998.

Murray, Robert K. *The Harding Era: Warren G. Harding and His Administration.* Minneapolis: University of Minnesota Press, 1969.

Myers, Walter. *The "Guv": A Tale of Midwest Law and Politics.* New York: Frederick Fell, 1947.

Newman, Roger K. *Hugo Black: A Biography.* New York: Pantheon Books, 1994.

Newsome, David. *The Victorian World Picture: Perceptions and Introspections in an Age of Change.* New Brunswick, NJ: Rutgers University Press, 1997.

Newton, Michael. *The Invisible Empire: The Ku Klux Klan in Florida.* Gainesville: University Press of Florida, 2001.

Niebuhr, H. Richard. *The Kingdom of God in America.* Hamden, CT: The Shoe String Press, 1956.

———. *Christ and Culture.* New York: HarperSanFrancisco, 2001.

Ninkovich, Frank. *The Wilsonian Century: U.S. Foreign Policy since 1900.* Chicago: University of Chicago Press, 1999.

Norwood, Frederick A. *History of the North Indiana Conference: North Indiana Methodism in the Twentieth Century, 1917–1956*. Winona Lake, IN: Light and Life Press, 1957.

Nugent, Walter T.K. *The Tolerant Populists: Kansas Populism and Nativism*. Chicago: University of Chicago Press, 1963.

O'Connell, Marvin R. *Edward Sorin*. Notre Dame, IN: University of Notre Dame Press, 2001.

O'Leary, Cecilia Elizabeth. *To Die For: The Paradox of American Patriotism*. Princeton, NJ: Princeton University Press, 1999.

Oates, Mary J. *The Catholic Philanthropic Tradition in America*. Indianapolis: Indiana University Press, 1995.

Orsi, Robert A. Editor. *Gods of the City: Religion and the American Urban Landscape*. Indianapolis: Indiana University Press, 1999.

Parsons, Elaine Frantz. *Manhood Lost: Fallen Drunkards and Redeeming Women in the Nineteenth-Century United States*. Baltimore: Johns Hopkins University Press, 2003.

Peckham, Howard H. *Indiana: A History*. Chicago: University of Illinois Press, 2003.

Pegram, Thomas R. *Battling Demon Rum: The Struggle for a Dry America, 1800–1933*. Chicago: Ivan R. Dee, 1998.

Philips, Clifton J. *Indiana in Transition: The Emergence of an Industrial Commonwealth, 1880–1920*. Indianapolis: Indiana Historical Bureau and Indiana Historical Society, 1968.

Pollack, Norman. Editor. *The Populist Mind*. Indianapolis: The Bobbs-Merrill Company, 1967.

Powers, Madelon. *Faces along the Bar: Lore and Ore* in *the Workingman's Saloon, 1870–1920*. Chicago: University of Chicago Press, 1998.

Pulliam, Russell. *Publisher: Gene Pulliam, Last of the Newspaper Titans*. Ottawa, IL: Jameson Books, 1984.

Putney, Clifford. *Muscular Christianity: Manhood and Sports in Protestant America, 1880–1920*. Cambridge, MA: Harvard University Press, 2003.

Quinn, John F. *Father Mathew's Crusade: Temperance in Nineteenth-Century Ireland and Irish America*. Boston: University of Massachusetts Press, 2002.

Radcliff, William Franklin. *Sherman Minton: Indiana's Supreme Court Justice*. Indianapolis: Guild Press of Indiana, 1996.

Radzilowski, John. *The Eagle and the Cross: A History of the Polish Roman Catholic Union of America, 1873–2000*. New York: Columbia University Press, 2003.

Rael, Patrick. *Black Identity and Black Protest in the Antebellum North*. Chapel Hill: University of North Carolina Press, 2002.

Raphael, Matthew J. *Bill W. and Mr. Wilson: The Legend and Life of AA's Cofounder*. Amherst: University of Massachusetts Press, 2000.

Rauchway, Eric. *Murdering McKinley: The Making of Theodore Roosevelt's America.* New York: Hill and Wang, 2003.

Read, James H. *Power versus Liberty: Madison, Hamilton, Wilson, and Jefferson.* Charlottesville: University Press of Virginia, 2000.

Reed, Christopher Robert. *The Chicago NAACP and the Rise of Black Professional Leadership, 1910–1960.* Indianapolis: Indiana University Press, 1997.

Rhodes, Benjamin D. *James P. Goodrich, Indiana's "Governor Strangelove": A Republican's Infatuation with Soviet Russia.* Selinsgrove, PA: Susquehanna University Press, 1996.

Robinson, Edgar Eugene. *The Roosevelt Leadership, 1933–1945.* New York: J. B. Lippincott Company 1955.

Rodgers, Daniel T. *Atlantic Crossings: Social Politics in a Progressive Age.* Cambridge, MA: The Belknap Press of Harvard University Press, 1998.

Rorabaugh, W. J. *The Alcoholic Republic: An American Tradition.* New York: Oxford University Press, 1981.

Rose, Kenneth D. *American Women and the Repeal of Prohibition.* New York: New York University Press, 1996.

Rosenzweig, Roy. *Eight Hours for What We Will: Workers and Leisure in an Industrial City, 1870–1920.* New York: Cambridge University Press, 1986.

Rumbarger, John J. *Profits, Power, and Prohibition: American Alcohol Reform and the Industrializing of America, 1800–1930.* New York: State University of New York Press, 1989.

Salvatore, Nick. *Eugene V. Debs: Citizen and Socialist.* Chicago: University of Illinois Press, 1982.

Scheele, Henry Z. *Charlie Halleck: A Political Biography.* New York: Exposition Press, 1966.

Schmidt, Leigh Eric. *Hearing Things: Religion, Illusion, and the American Enlightenment.* Cambridge, MA: Harvard University Press, 2000.

Shain, Barry Alan. *The Myth of American Individualism: The Protestant Origins of American Political Thought.* Princeton, NJ: Princeton University Press, 1994.

Shaw, Henry K. *Hoosier Disciples: A Comprehensive History of the Christian Churches (Disciples of Christ) in Indiana.* Indianapolis: Bethany Press, 1966.

Simpson, Jeffrey. *Chautauqua: An American Utopia.* New York: Harry N. Abrams Publishers, 1999.

Slayton, Robert A. *Empire Statesman: The Rise and Redemption of Al Smith.* New York: The Free Press, 2001.

Smith, John W. V. *The Quest for Holiness and Unity: A Centennial History of the Church of God (Anderson, Indiana).* Anderson, IN: Warner Press, 1980.

Smith, Lacey Baldwin. *Fools, Martyrs, Traitors: The Story of Martyrdom in the Western World.* New York: Alfred A. Knopf, 1997.

Smith, Timothy L. *Revivalism and Social Reform: American Protestantism on the Eve of the Civil War.* Baltimore: Johns Hopkins University Press, 1980.

Smucker, Donovan E. *The Origins of Walter Rauschenbusch's Social Ethics.* Montreal: McGill-Queen's University Press, 1994.

Sournia, Jean-Charles. *A History of Alcoholism.* Cambridge, MA: Basil Blackwell, 1990.

Starbuck, Dane. *The Goodriches: An American Family.* Indianapolis: Liberty Fund, 2001.

Storey, John W. *Texas Baptist Leadership and Social Christianity, 1900–1980.* College Station: Texas A&M University Press, 1986.

Sweet, William Warren. *The Methodist Episcopal Church and the Civil War.* Cincinnati: Methodist Book Concern Press, 1912.

Szymanski, Ann-Marie E. *Pathways to Prohibition: Radicals, Moderates, and Social Movement Outcomes.* Durham, NC: Duke University Press, 2003.

Tate, Cassandra. *Cigarette Wars: The Triumph of "the Little White Slaver."* New York: Oxford University Press, 1999.

Taves, Ann. *Fits, Trances, and Visions: Experiencing Religion and Explaining Experience from Wesley to James.* Princeton, NJ: Princeton University Press, 1999.

Thelen, David P. *Robert M. LaFollette and the Insurgent Spirit.* Boston: Little, Brown and Company, 1976.

Thornbrough, Emma Lou. *Indiana Blacks in the Twentieth Century.* Indianapolis: Indiana University Press, 2000.

Thornton, Mark. *The Economics of Prohibition.* Salt Lake City: University of Utah Press, 1991.

Timberlake, James H. *Prohibition and the Progressive Movement, 1900–1920.* Cambridge, MA: Harvard University Press, 1963.

Traxel, David. *Crusader Nation: The United States in Peace and the Great War, 1898–1920.* New York: Alfred A. Knopf, 2006.

Trollinger, William Vance, Jr. *God's Empire: William Bell Riley and Midwestern Fundamentalism.* Madison: University of Wisconsin Press, 1990.

Tucker, Todd. *Notre Dame vs. the Klan: How the Fighting Irish Defeated the Ku Klux Klan.* Chicago: Loyola Press, 2004.

Turnbull, George S. *An Oregon Crusader.* Portland, OR: Binfords and Mort Publishers, 1955.

Tyrrell, Ian. *Woman's World, Woman's Empire: The Woman's Christian Temperance Union in International Perspective, 1880–1930.* Chapel Hill: University of North Carolina Press, 1991.

Vaccaro, Don. Editor. *Corpus Juris Secundum: A Contemporary Statement of American Law,* Volume 17. St. Paul, MN: West Group, 1999.

Wade, Wyn Craig. *The Fiery Cross: The Ku Klux Klan in America.* New York: Touchstone Book, 1987.

Walsh, Justin E. *The Sesquicentennial History of the Indiana General Assembly, 1816–1978.* Indianapolis: Indiana Historical Bureau, 1987.

Wardin, Albert W., Jr. *Tennessee Baptists: A Comprehensive History, 1779–1999.* Brentwood, TN: Executive Board of the Tennessee Baptist Convention, 1999.

Warren, Donald. *Radio Priest: Charles Coughlin, the Father of Hate Radio.* New York: The Free Press, 1996.

Weeks, Genevieve C. *Oscar Carleton McCulloch, 1843–1891: Preacher and Practitioner of Applied Christianity.* Indianapolis: Indiana Historical Society, 1976.

Wheeler, Marcia Lee. *A Journey of Faith in the Heartland: A History of the First Christian Church, 1834–1999.* Noblesville, IN: First Christian Church, 1999.

White, Ronald C., Jr. and C. Howard Hopkins. *The Social Gospel: Religion and Reform in Changing America.* Philadelphia: Temple University Press, 1976.

Wiebe, Robert H. *Businessmen and Reform: A Study of the Progressive Movement.* Cambridge, MA: Harvard University Press, 1962.

———. *The Search for Order, 1877–1920.* New York: Hill and Wang, 1999.

Wilcox, Danny M. *Alcoholic Thinking: Language, Culture, and Belief in Alcoholics Anonymous.* Westport, CT: Praeger, 1998.

Williams, Philip. *Walls that Human Hands Have Raised: A History of Central Avenue United Methodist Church.* Indianapolis: Central Avenue United Methodist Church, 2000.

Williams, T. Harry. *Huey Long.* New York: Alfred A. Knopf, 1969.

Wolfer, Margaret. *Commemorating the 75th Anniversary of St. Ann's Church, Indianapolis, Indiana, 1917–1992.* Indianapolis: St. Ann's Catholic Church, 1992.

Wood, Gordon S. *The Creation of the American Republic, 1776–1787.* Chapel Hill: University of North Carolina Press, 1998.

Zimmerman, Jonathan. *Distilling Democracy: Alcohol Education in America's Public Schools, 1880–1925.* Lawrence: University of Kansas Press, 1999.

Censuses

1860 U.S. Census
1870 U.S. Census
1880 U.S. Census
1890 U.S. Census
1900 U.S. Census
1910 U.S. Census
1920 U.S. Census
1930 U.S. Census

Court Cases

Barnes v. Wagener. 169 Ind. 511; 82 N.E. 1037. (1907).

Bridges v. State of California. 62 S.Ct. 190. (1941).

Cummins v. State. 89 Ind. App. 256; 166 N.E. 155. (1929).

Dale v. State. 198 Ind. 110; 150 N.E. 647. (1926).

Duvall v. State. 92 Ind. App. 134; 166 N.E. 603. (1929).

Ganholm v. Heald. 125 S.Ct. 1885. (2005).

Grimm, Jr. v. State of Indiana. 240 Ind. 125; 162 N.E. 2d 454. (1959).

Hawke v. Smith. 253 U.S. 221. (1920).

Little Beverage Co., Inc., and Miami Beverage, Inc., v. Indiana Alcohol and Tobacco Commission, and Anheuser-Busch, Inc. 777 N.E. 2d 74. (2002).

Meno v. State. 197 Ind. 16. (1925).

Peter Mugler v. State of Kansas. 123 US 663. (1887).

Nichols v. Lehman et al. 42 Ind. App. 384; 85 N.E. 786. (1908).

Schmitt, Superintendent of Police v. F. W. Cook Brewing Company. 187 Ind. 623; 120 N.E. 19. (1918).

Shacklett v. State. 197 Ind. 323. (1925).

Sopher v. State. 169 Ind. 177, 81 N.E. 913. (1907).

State v. Dudley. 33 Ind. App. 640, 71 N.E. 975. (1904).

State v. Shumaker. 200 Ind. 623; 157 N.E. 769. (1927).

State v. Shumaker. 200 Ind. 623; 162 N.E. 441. (1928).

State v. Shumaker. 200 Ind. 623; 163 N.E. 272. (1928).

State v. Shumaker. 200 Ind. 623; 164 N.E. 408. (1928).

State Ex Rel. Robertson et al. v. Circuit Court of Lake County et al. 215 Ind. 18; 17 N.E. 2d 805. (1938).

State Ex Rel. Stanton v. Murray, Judge, Stanton v. State of Indiana. 231 Ind. 223; 108 N.E. 2d 251. (1951).

Stephenson v. Daly. 200 Ind. 196; 158 N.E. 289. (1927).

Stephenson v. State. 205 Ind. 141; 179 N.E. 633. (1932).

Stephenson v. State. 205 Ind. 141; 186 N.E. 293. (1933).

Switzer et al. v. State. 211 Ind. 690; 8 N.E. 2d 80. (1937).

Ver Wilst v. State. 200 Ind. 30; 161 N.E. 249. (1928).

Dissertations and Theses

Corn, Kevin J. "'Forward Be Our Watchword': Indiana Methodism and the Modern Middle Class." M.A. Thesis, Indiana University, 1996.

Hoy, Suellen M. "Samuel M. Ralston: Progressive Governor, 1913–1917." Ph.D. Dissertation, Indiana University, 1975.

Markisohn, Deborah Ballee. "Ministers of the Klan: Indianapolis Clergy In-volvement with the 1920s Ku Klux Klan." M.A. Thesis, Indiana Univer-sity, 1992.

Milkman, Howard Louis, Jr. "Thomas DeWitt Talmage: An Evangelical Nineteenth Century Voice on Technology, Urbanization, and Labor-Management Conflicts." Ph.D. Dissertation, New York University, 1979.

Rissler, Herbert J. "Charles Warren Fairbanks: Conservative Hoosier." Ph.D. Dissertation, Indiana University, 1962.

Roizen, Ron. "The American Discovery of Alcoholism, 1933–1939." Ph.D. Dis-sertation, University of California, Berkeley, 1991.

Interviews and Oral Histories

Clay, Barbara B. Correspondence with author. 5 February 2003.

Evans, William P. Oral History Project. Indiana Division. Indiana State Library. Indianapolis, Indiana, 1969.

Feightner, Harold. Oral History Project. Indiana Division. Indiana State Library. Indianapolis, Indiana, 1968.

Gemmecke, Richard H. Sesquicentennial Indiana History Conference. Indi-ana Division. Indiana State Library. Indianapolis, Indiana, 1966.

Gilkey, Bob. Conner Prairie Rural History Project RHP 172 and RHP 180. 12 February 2001 and 6 April 2001.

Gilliom, Richard L. Interview with author. 21 February 2003.

Glover, Fannie B. Conner Prairie Rural History Project RHP 123. 16 May 2000.

Hufford, Denzel. Conner Prairie Rural History Project RHP 112. 19 February 2000.

Jenckes, Virginia Somes. Oral History Project. Indiana Division. Indiana State Library. Indianapolis, Indiana, 1967.

Lewis, Olive Beldon. Oral History Project. Indiana Division. Indiana State Library. Indianapolis, Indiana, 1969.

Martin, C. Wendell. Correspondence with author. 22 March 2003.

Musselman, Wayne and Helen. Conner Prairie Rural History Project RHP 129. 1 June 2000.

Pulliam, Russell B. Correspondence with author. 21 November 2002.

Randall, John and Joan. Conner Prairie Rural History Project RHP 165. 7 De-cember 2000.

Seitz, Karl. Correspondence with author. 22 February 2004.

Shumaker, Arthur. Interviews with author. 14 March, 24 March, and 19 April 2000.

Shumaker, Julia. Interviews with author. 1 December 2000, 13 March 2001,
8 February, 7 September 2003.
Strauss, Lewis L. Interviewed by Raymond Henle. Hoover Presidential Library
Oral History Project. Herbert Hoover Presidential Library. West Branch,
Iowa. 13 February 1967.
Wantz, John B. Senior Pastor of Meridian Street United Methodist Church.
Indianapolis, Indiana. Interview with author. 13 February 2003.

Manuscript Collections

American Turners Records. Archives of Indiana University-Purdue Univer-
sity Indianapolis. Indianapolis, Indiana.
Albert J. Beveridge Papers. Library of Congress. Washington, DC.
Roger D. Branigin Papers. The B.F. Hamilton Library. Franklin College.
Franklin, Indiana.
Patrick Henry Callahan Papers. Archives of the University of Notre Dame.
Notre Dame, Indiana.
John W. Cavanaugh Papers. Archives of the University of Notre Dame. Notre
Dame, Indiana.
Church Women United Collection. Indiana Historical Society. Indianapolis,
Indiana.
Charles Warren Fairbanks Papers. Lilly Library. Indiana University. Bloom-
ington, Indiana.
Arthur Gilliom Papers. In possession of Richard L. Gilliom. Indianapolis,
Indiana.
James P. Goodrich Papers. Herbert Hoover Presidential Library. West Branch,
Iowa.
Charles A. Halleck Papers. Lilly Library. Indiana University. Bloomington,
Indiana.
Herbert Hoover Papers. Herbert Hoover Presidential Library. West Branch,
Iowa.
Indianapolis Church Federation Executive Committee Minutes. Indiana His-
torical Society. Indianapolis, Indiana.
Ku Klux Klan Papers. Indiana Historical Society. Indianapolis, Indiana.
Warren T. McCray Collection. Indiana Historical Society. Indianapolis, Indiana.
F.T. McWhirter Manuscript Collection. Lilly Library. Indiana University.
Bloomington, Indiana.
S.E. Nicholson Papers. Archives of Earlham College Library. Richmond,
Indiana.
Prohibition Party of Indiana Papers. Manuscripts Division. Indiana State
Library. Indianapolis, Indiana.

Frank M. Robinson Papers. W.O. Holman Notes and Records. Indiana Division. Indiana State Library. Indianapolis, Indiana.

Edward S. Shumaker Papers. *Shumaker's papers were kept by the family from the time of his death until the spring of 2000, when they were given to the author for his use in preparing this work. The papers have since been deposited in the De-Pauw University Archives at Greencastle, Indiana. Citations in this work indicate the box in which items were given to the author, which may not correspond with the subsequent cataloging of the papers at DePauw.*

D.C. Stephenson Papers. Indiana Historical Society. Indianapolis, Indiana.

George P. Stewart Manuscript Collection. Indiana Historical Society. Indianapolis, Indiana.

Temperance and Prohibition Papers. Microfilm Edition. Ohio Historical Society. Columbus, Ohio.

Booker T. Washington Papers. Louis R. Harlan, editor. Chicago: University of Illinois Press, 2000.

Woodrow Wilson Papers. Arthur S. Link, editor. Princeton, New Jersey: Princeton University Press, 1986.

Woman's Christian Temperance Union Papers. Indiana Historical Society, Indianapolis. Indiana.

Newspapers

There is at least one newspaper from each of Indiana's ninety-two counties in the list below. Out-of-state papers are in italics.

Adams County (Berne) Witness
Advocate (Newark, Ohio)
Advocate Messenger (Danville, Kentucky)
Albion New Era
American Issue (National ASL paper, sometimes with an Indiana edition)
Anderson Daily Bulletin
Anderson Herald
Anderson Morning Herald
Angola Herald
Attica Ledger
Attica Ledger Tribune
Aurora Bulletin
Baptist Observer
Baptist World (Kentucky Southern Baptist newspaper)
Bedford Daily Mail
Berne Witness
Bloomfield News
Bloomington Evening World
Bluffton Evening News
Booneville Weekly Enquirer
Brookville American
Brown County Democrat
Cannelton Telephone
Chicago Journal
Cincinnati Enquirer
Clay County Enterprise
Cleveland Gazette
Columbia City Commercial Mail

Columbia City Post
Columbus Evening Republican
Connersville Evening News
Connersville News Examiner
Corydon Democrat
Crawford County Democrat
Crawfordsville Journal
Daily Clintonian
Daviess County Democrat
Delphi Citizen
Delphi Journal
Elkhart Truth
Evansville Courier
Evansville Journal
Fiery Cross
Fort Wayne Journal Gazette
Frankfort Daily Crescent
Frankfort Evening News
Frankfort Morning Times
The Franklin
Franklin Democrat
Franklin Evening Star
French Lick Springs Valley Herald
Garrett Clipper
Garrett Weekly Clipper
Gary Evening Post
Goshen Daily Democrat
Goshen Democrat
Greencastle Banner
Greencastle Herald
Greenfield Daily Reporter
Greenfield Republican
Greensburg Daily News
Greensburg New Era
Hamilton County Ledger
Hartford City News
Huntington Herald
Indiana Catholic
Indiana Catholic and Record
Indiana Daily Student
Indiana Phalanx
Indianapolis Freeman

Indianapolis Minute
Indianapolis News
Indianapolis Recorder
Indianapolis Star
Indianapolis Sun
Indianapolis Times
Jasper County Democrat
Jasper Herald
Jasper Weekly Courier
Jeffersonville Evening News
Kentland Democrat
Knightstown Banner
Kokomo Daily Tribune
Lafayette Journal
Lafayette Journal and Courier
Lake County News
Lake County Times
Lebanon Pioneer
Lebanon Reporter
Liberty Herald
Logansport Pharos
Logansport Pharos Tribune
Logansport Reporter
Los Angeles Times
Louisville Courier Journal
Madison Courier
Marion Chronicle
Marion County Mail
Martinsville Democrat
Michigan City Evening News
Michigan City News
Middlebury Independent
Milwaukee Journal Sentinel
Monticello Evening Journal
Monticello Herald
Muncie Evening Press
New Albany Daily Ledger
New Albany Evening Tribune
New Albany Weekly Ledger
New York Evening World
New York Telegraph
New York Times

Noble County Democrat
Noblesville Daily Ledger
Noblesville Independent
Noblesville Ledger
Noblesville Republican Ledger
North Vernon Plain Dealer
North Vernon Sun
Oregonian (Portland)
Owen Leader
Oxford Gazette
Patriot Phalanx
Pekin Advance
Peru Evening Journal
Peru Republican
Pike County Democrat
Plainfield Friday Caller
Plainfield Messenger
Plymouth Daily News
Plymouth Tribune
Portland Commercial Review
Poseyville News
Princeton Clarion News
Pulaski County Democrat
Remington Press
Rensselaer Evening Republican
Richmond Evening Item
Richmond Item
Rising Sun Recorder
Rochester Republican
Rochester Sentinel
Rockport Democrat
Rockville Tribune
Rushville Daily Republican
Scott County Journal
Scottsburg Chronicle

Seymour Daily Republican
Seymour Tribune
Shelbyville Democrat
Shelbyville Republican
Sheridan News
Shoals News
South Bend News-Times
South Bend Tribune
Starke County Republican
Stars and Stripes
Sullivan Daily Times
Sullivan Democrat
Sullivan Times Democrat
Terre Haute Express
Terre Haute Star
Terre Haute Tribune
Tipton Daily Tribune
Topeka Journal
Valparaiso Daily Vidette
Vanceburg Sun (Kentucky)
Versailles Republican
Vevay Reveille
Vincennes Commercial
Vincennes Sun
Vincennes Sun Commercial
Wabash Daily Plain Dealer
Wakarusa Tribune
Warren Review
Warren Review Republican
Warsaw Daily Union
Weekly Clintonian
Western Christian Advocate
White County Democrat
Winchester Democrat
Winchester Journal

Pamphlets

Anheuser Busch. "Anheuser Busch Companies at a Glance," 2001.
———. "Our Commitment: Community Programs to Promote Alcohol Awareness," 2000.

Baughman, John. "United Methodism in Indiana: Address to the South Indiana Conference United Methodist Historical Society," 27 April 1996.

Brethren Publishing House. "The Address of Moderator Ortho Winger," 1928.

Indiana Yearly Meeting of Friends. "An Appeal to Christians and Especially Friends for More Diligent, Consecrated, and Consistent Effort to Overthrow the Modern 'bomination of Desolations,' the Liquor Traffic," 1891. Indiana Historical Society, Indianapolis, Indiana.

Postcard. "The Spirit of Story." In possession of author.

Watson, James E. "Policies of Republicanism in State and Nation: Keynote Speech of the Honorable James E. Watson Republican Candidate for Governor of Indiana, Delivered at Ft. Wayne, August 26 1908." Indianapolis: William B. Burford, 1908.

Periodicals

The Nation
Newsweek
Notre Dame Magazine
Nuvo (Indianapolis)
Time Magazine

Websites

Alcoholics Anonymous. "Alcoholics Anonymous Historical Data: The Birth of A.A. and its growth in U.S./Canada." http://www.alcoholics-anonymous .org/english/E_FactFile/M–24_d14.html. 30 November 2001.

American Breweriana. "Brewing in Fort Wayne, Indiana." http://www .americanbreweriana.org/history/ftwayne.htm. 16 October 2002.

Anti-Saloon League. "Related Organizations: World League against Alcoholism." http://www.wpl.lib.oh.us:80/AntiSaloon/related/World.html. 4 May 2000.

Austin Genealogy Society. "Calculate Consumer Price Index." http://www .austintxgensoc.org/calculatecpi.html. 13 June 2003.

Christian Endeavor. "The History of Christian Endeavor." http://www .christianendeavor.org/history.htm. 22 August 2002.

Cleveland State University Library. "Cleveland: Confused City on a Seasaw by Philip W. Porter." http://web.ulib.csuohio.edu/SpecColl/porter/index .html. 1 August 2002.

Digital Collections @ Brown University.

Donald W. Dayton. "The Holiness Churches: A Significant Ethical Tradition." http://www.religion-online.org/showarticle.asp?title=1862. 6 March 2005.

Effingham County. "Early Effingham County." http://www.effingham.com/kperkins/early.htm. 18 February 2002.

———. "History of Effingham County Townships." http://www.effingham .com/kperkins/Townships.htm. 22 August 2002.

Ehistory.com. *The War of the Rebellion: A Compilation of the Official Records of the Union and Confederate Armies.* http://www.ehistory.com. 15 February 2003.*

David M. Fahey 2000 Presidential Address. "The Politics of Drink in Britain: Anglo-American Perspectives." http://www.athg.org/faheypresidential .html. 23 October 2002.

Fairfield County Chapter OGS. "Fairfield County in the Civil War." http:// www.fairfieldgenealogy.org/research/faircivil.html. 10 February 2003.

Fisher Library, University of Virginia. "United States Census." http://fisher .lib.virginia.edu/cgi-local/censusbin/census/cen.pl. 15 October 2002.

Fox News. http://www.foxnews.com.

General Board of Church and Society. "The United Methodist Building." http://www.umc-gbcs.org/75th-book.htm. 20 September 2002.

Georgia Council for Moral and Civic Concerns. "History." http://www.gcmcc .org/history.htm. 19 December 2002.

Handbook of Texas Online. "Anti Saloon League of Texas." http://www .tsha.utexas.edu/handbook/online/articles/print/AA/vaa2.html. 9 August 2002.

Kathleen Kerr. "How Did the Reform Agenda of the Minnesota Woman's Christian Temperance Union Change, 1878–1917?" http://womhist .binghamton.edu/wctu/intro.htm. 13 August 2002.

McKendree College. "Then and Now." http://www.mckendree.edu/A_03/ Welcome/then_now.htm. 28 August 2003.

Oregon State Archives. "Prohibition in Oregon: The Vision and the Reality." http://arcweb.sos.state.or.us/50th/prohibition1/prohibintro.html. 20 August 2002.

Prohibition Party. "Convention Sites." http://www.prohibitionists.org/History/ convention_sites/body_convention_sites.html. 13 July 2001.

———. "Local Chapters." http://www.prohibitionists.org/Chapters/body_ chapters.html. 1 August 2003.

---

* I am indebted to the staff at http://www.ehistory.com for putting the *Official Records* online, complete with a search feature that is second to none.

Sons of Union Veterans of the Civil War. "Department of Indiana Commanders and Encampments." http://suvcw.org/in/indeptcmd.html. 5 February 2003.

Southern Baptist Convention Resolutions. http://www.sbc.net/resolutions. 3 February 2004.

University of North Carolina at Chapel Hill Libraries Documenting the American South. "Anti-Saloon League of Charlotte, N.C.: It Helps Business and Is a Blessing. What Leading Business Men, Bankers, Farmers, Laborers and Others Say about Prohibition in Charlotte, N.C." http://docsouth.unc.edu/nc/antisallon/antisaloon.html. 19 July 2002.

Utah History Encyclopedia. "Prohibition." http://www.media.utah.edu/UHE/p/PROHIBITION.html. 20 August 2002.

Index

JASON S. LANTZER

is an adjunct history faculty member of Indiana University-Purdue University, Indianapolis, and Butler University.